D1523098

URBAN LIFE AND
URBAN LANDSCAPE
SERIES

Contributors

Ronald J. Busch, Professor of Political Science, Cleveland State University, Cleveland, Ohio

Robert J. Kolesar, Associate Professor of History, John Carroll University, Cleveland, Ohio

Leon Weaver (deceased), Professor Emeritus of Political Science, Michigan State University, East Lansing, Michigan

James L. Blount, Local Historian and Journalist, Hamilton, Ohio

Dennis M. Anderson, Professor of Political Science, Bowling Green State University, Bowling Green, Ohio.

Proportional Representation and Election Reform in Ohio

■ ■ ■

Kathleen L. Barber
With a Foreword by John B. Anderson

OHIO STATE UNIVERSITY PRESS
Columbus

324.9771
B234p

Publication of this book has been aided by a grant from the
Murray and Agnes
Seasongood Good Government Foundation.

Library of Congress Cataloging-in-Publication Data

Barber, Kathleen L., 1924–
   Proportional representation and election reform in Ohio / Kathleen
L. Barber; with a foreword by John B. Anderson.
     p.   cm.—(Urban life and urban landscape series)
   Includes bibliographical references (p.   ) and index.
   ISBN 0-8142-0660-3 (cloth : alk. paper). —ISBN 0-8142-066101
(pbk. : alk. paper)
   1. Municipal government—Ohio—Case studies. 2. Local elections—
Ohio—Case studies. 3. Proportional representation—Ohio—Case
studies. 4. Proportional representation. I. Title. II. Series.
JS451.035B37 1995
324.9771—dc20   95-12273
                                             CIP

Text and jacket design by Gore Design.
Type set in Melior by Carlisle Communications, Ltd., Dubuque, Iowa.
Printed by Thomson-Shore, Inc., Dexter, Michigan.

The paper in this book meets the guidelines for permanence and durability of the
Committee on Production Guidelines for Book Longevity of the Council on Library
Resources. ∞

9 8 7 6 5 4 3 2 1

To
D. R. B.

Contents

Foreword

AS WE PREPARE at mid-decade not only for a new century but for crossing the threshold of a new millennium, the politics of America are in considerable ferment. The partisan loyalties of the past show signs of shifting and in some cases even disappearing entirely. The most recent general election altered a pattern of control of the U.S. Congress that had lasted for four decades. The presidential election of 1992 saw virtually one out of five voters who participated casting a ballot for an Independent candidate for president, something that had not occurred to that extent since shortly after the dawning of the present century. However unusual these particular indicators of unrest may be, they are unfortunately not necessarily portents or precursors of genuine political reform. A cynic might even argue that these reflections of changes in voter attitudes are only "rearranging the deck chairs on the Titanic," when so few Americans participate in the process. Indeed, only about 37% of eligible registered voters cast ballots in the 1994 Congressional election, which was hailed, at least by the victors, as a historic turning of the tide—a realignment of American politics the likes of which we had not seen for more than 60 years. That statistic does not confirm my faith in the notion that our electoral system speaks for a majority of the voters, let alone for a majority of the population.

Perhaps another sign of fundamental discontent with our representative democracy is the rapid rise of direct democracy in the form of plebiscitary lawmaking. Although it has been widely criticized as an antidemocratic form of governance capable of playing havoc with minority rights (one need only think of California's adoption in November 1994 of Proposition 187, which denies public education and nonemergency health services to illegal immigrants), it is symptomatic of the deeper disaffection that underlies our electoral process. When people do not succeed—even when they dutifully go to the polls and cast their vote—in electing representatives whom they really wanted to

represent them, there are most often two results, both of which are bad
for democracy. First, voters who are left feeling that they are not
represented are very likely to feel alienated and detached, and as
nonparticipants they are unwilling to shoulder the sacrifices that may
be required to promote the common good. Second, their elected
representatives, conscious of that wall of separation and indifference,
proceed to fashion policies that ignore the needs and desires of the
very people who already feel unrepresented as soon as the vote tallies
are announced.

By considering alternative forms of determining our representation
in the councils of government, Kathleen Barber's book makes a strong
case for the basic reform of our electoral process. She demonstrates,
from a broad perspective of eighteenth- and nineteenth-century historical experience in Europe, that political reform was associated with
such alternative systems as proportional representation (PR) and the
single transferable vote (STV). She carries this story forward into the
American experience and the Progressive Era of the early twentieth
century, when PR/STV was tried in five Ohio cities as a substitute for
the old winner-take-all method.

The recounting of how PR/STV electoral systems worked between
their initial introduction and their disappearance a little over a
generation ago is commendably frank and objective. PR/STV did not
"demonstrably shape" voter turnout. However, equally important perhaps is the finding that the introduction of new alternatives did not
add to political conflict among council members in cities that adopted
these alternative voting systems. They were not polarizing and divisive, even though they were essentially antiparty in an age when the
two major parties were both relatively strong. In short, PR and STV
were ideas that were really ahead of their time, given the very
powerful pull of a party ethos.

In a concluding chapter in which the author traces the evolution
both through legislation and through court decisions of the right to fair
representation and the development of the concept of minority vote
dilution, the book makes an impressive contribution to fresh thinking
in this area. She points out that the validity of proportionality as a
standard for the measurement of fair representation is now accepted by
the U.S. Supreme Court. The future of alternative voting systems such
as PR/STV may be far different from their past, during the part of our
history involved in the Tale of the Five Cities in Ohio. The courts and
perhaps ultimately state and federal legislative bodies will, one hopes,
expand the legal concept of the right of representation now that the

right of simply casting a vote has been secured by the Voting Rights Act. This will in turn increase the attractiveness of new ideas such as those advanced by Kathleen Barber.

When we broaden our horizons to see that our first-past-the-post plurality system based on single-member districts lies at the root of our current problems, it is only another step to begin a survey of possible alternatives. I share the author's conviction that proportional representation could help us build a strong and more muscular democracy. It could help avoid political gerrymandering and other methods that work at cross-purposes to the broader goal of national unity, constructed on the base of a participatory democracy. It would be predicated on what voters really think and believe and less on political geography and where they happen to live. This, I firmly believe, is the kind of true political reform that America needs as we face forward to the challenges of the twenty-first century.

JOHN B. ANDERSON
Chair, Center for Voting and Democracy
Washington, D.C.

Acknowledgments

THE AGNES and Murray Seasongood Good Government Foundation of Cincinnati has demonstrated its interest in the electoral system debate by supporting the research for this five-city study. The participants in this project express their gratitude to the foundation and especially to its president, Bruce I. Petrie Sr. Additional support from John Carroll University is also much appreciated.

Special mention must also be made of the key role played by the late Leon Weaver of Michigan State University. An expert on local electoral systems, Leon initiated this project, undertook the Hamilton research, and was unfailingly generous with collegial advice until his death in 1991. Gratitude is owed to Zane Miller, Marian J. Morton, Philip A. Macklin, and Robert Richie for reading all or parts of the manuscript and commenting helpfully. Deepest appreciation is owed to Henry Shapiro, whose critical mind and probing questions contributed invaluable insights to this endeavor.

■ ■ ■

Introduction

QUESTIONS OF REPRESENTATION lie at the heart of democratic theory and practice. Because democracy is both so difficult to achieve and so complex to maintain in a rapidly changing world, it is not surprising that the approach of the twenty-first century brings with it both new and old issues about how elections should be conducted. Electoral systems allocate representation, and the power that is represented shapes public policy and the distribution of benefits.

Debates about the nature of representation are taking place today not only in the transition from closed to open systems in Eastern Europe but also in well-established democracies such as Great Britain and France, and in American cities in their legislative, judicial, and school districts. Groups defined by ideology, ethnicity, race, and gender strive to be heard in the cacophony of democratic policy making along with political parties and economic interests.

From Cincinnati, Ohio, to New Zealand, electoral system change is ardently sought through popular initiatives, even government-initiated reforms, and in the courts. In the United States, the right to vote has evolved into the right to representation, but it is a right whose dimensions are fluid and controversial.

Electoral systems have political consequences, often unnoticed or dimly understood by voters. The ways in which candidate choices are structured and votes are counted influence the outcomes of elections and the kind of representation that ensues. Most Americans are accustomed to having their votes counted on the plurality principle: whoever gets the most votes wins. This is so simple and obvious to Americans who have grown up in a winner-take-all system that its impact on representation is seldom questioned.

1

It is generally believed that the United States is a majority-rule system, but a majority is "the number greater than half." Apart from the problem of the large number of nonvoters, who in many elections are in fact a majority in the United States, "majority rule" among participants even in a single district is the result of a race in which only two candidates contend. In a three-candidate race the majority may have voted for someone other than the winner who captures the prize. The prize is all of the representation.

The United States is joined by only a few other democracies in the use of plurality voting. Most democracies prefer some form of proportional representation that permits seat shares in a governing body to be determined by vote shares. In nineteenth-century Europe, the transition from minority tyranny or oligarchy to political democracy created fear of tyranny by the uneducated majority. This fear led in turn to the invention of electoral systems which would ensure some continued representation by the educated minority. Various forms of proportional representation (PR) were introduced as democracy developed in theory and practice.

In the late nineteenth century, some American reformers were drawn to proportional representation as a means of freeing legislatures from the grip of powerful interests and corrupt political parties. These urban Progressives advocated electoral reform to break the power of city bosses, to improve city government, and to provide representation to independents and to minorities excluded by ward-based, winner-take-all contests. PR was only one of the numerous strategies for municipal reform promoted by progressive and populist forces in early twentieth-century America. Cumulative voting (CV) and limited voting (LV), which were alternative electoral systems (often called semi-proportional), were also tried out.

Between 1915 and 1950, the "Hare" system of proportional representation by single transferable vote (PR/STV), named for Thomas Hare and promoted by John Stuart Mill as "among the very greatest improvements yet made in the theory and practice of government" (Mill [1861] 1962, p. 151), was adopted in almost two dozen American cities. Because party machines were viewed as the principal enemy of good government, nonpartisanship ranked high on the agenda of municipal reformers, and PR/STV was adaptable to a nonpartisan ballot. Councils were elected by PR/STV in these cities for varying lengths of time, in some for several decades.

PR was subsequently abandoned in most of the cities that had adopted it. Ashtabula, Ohio, in 1915 the first to adopt, was also the first to abandon its PR electoral system; others followed. In one state, PR was outlawed by the legislature and in two others it was invalidated by the courts. The rest—all but one—were repealed by popular referendum. Today, Cambridge, Massachusetts, is the only American city that has persisted in using a PR system of elections, although school boards in New York City are elected on PR ballots, and a number of private associations find the system to be a viable strategy for fair representation in governance.

This book is an attempt to examine the circumstances under which PR/STV was advocated and adopted, the problems it was intended to solve, the manner of its implementation and operation, its relationship to other proposals for structural reform of American municipal government, its effectiveness, and the circumstances surrounding its abandonment. Its immediate focus, however, is on PR in Ohio.

Between the Civil War and the New Deal, Ohio was an important state politically, sharing the dominant Republican identity of the country, voting consistently for the winner of presidential elections, and indeed sending seven presidents to the White House. Ohio was considered representative of the nation not only in politics but in demographics and economic development. While retaining a strong agricultural component, the state became a significant locus of rapid industrialization, drawing immigrants from Europe and the old South to work in its factories and to crowd its cities (Knepper, 1989, pp. 264–75).

Ohio was fertile ground for municipal reform. Heavy industry had drawn hundreds of thousands of immigrants to its cities, creating unprecedented needs for public services. Modernization was transforming an agrarian society into a chaos characterized by conflicting land uses, unchecked urban growth, and an emergent mass society in which groups supplanted individuals, and small town lawyers and farmer-legislators were replaced in positions of power by corrupt politicians. The rapidly expanding corporate sector allied itself with Mark Hanna's powerful state Republican organization, which in turn worked closely with the dominant urban Republican machines of such legendary bosses as George B. Cox of Cincinnati.

In 1912 Ohio's Progressives, a diverse coalition of Democrats, Independent Republicans, Independents, and labor leaders, won their first major reform battle with the adoption of a "home rule" amendment to the Ohio Constitution. Home rule was meant to enable the boss-ridden cities to initiate local charters and choose their own form of government.

Whereas thirty-eight Ohio cities adopted the better-known features of Progressive reform—the city manager form of government with a small council elected at-large by plurality—five other cities, among them the three largest, added elections by proportional representation to this reform model. Following Ashtabula's adoption in 1915 were Cleveland (1924), Cincinnati (1925), Hamilton (1926), and Toledo (1935). Ohio and its cities seemed to be in the forefront of Progressive reform.

If Ohio and its cities could achieve reform, might not the burdens of modernization be tempered by some redistribution of its benefits, even by social justice? PR was one of the strategies that a substantial body of reformers thought might accomplish this end, and Ohio was the place where it was actually happening. But did it happen? Did PR change anything? These are the questions this book attempts to answer, through case studies of the five PR cities in Ohio.

Most accounts of Progressive activity fail even to mention PR as an item on the reform agenda, an omission this work seeks to remedy. The traditional view of reformers cast them in the role of virtuous, civic-minded stalwarts battling evil monopolists and corrupt politicians. The prize to be won was good government (Godkin, 1894; Steffens, 1906). Mid-twentieth-century revisionists turned this group portrait on its head, presenting the Progressive movement as a reactionary effort of declining elites to reimpose order and upper-class control on an unruly industrial society, whereas the bosses were heroic protectors of helpless immigrants and the poor (Hofstadter, 1955; Link, 1959; Huthmacher, 1962; Kolko, 1963; Hays, 1964). Some of these accounts complained, however, of the paucity of research at the state and local level, and they suggest puzzlement on the part of the authors about what was actually going on (Link, 1959; Buenker, 1973).

Recent historians have identified more complex motivations for reform and have found both reformers and bosses at work in shifting coalitions to address the real problems of their time (Filene, 1970; Rodgers, 1982). The simple dichotomy of boss versus reformer, ethno-cultural party politics versus individualistic modernizers, began to disappear as the conflicts within alternative paradigms surfaced. The politics of fluid, issue-oriented groups, organized by activists committed to particular policy outcomes, are revealed as key to understanding the larger transition that was occurring from a simpler, agrarian America to a far more complex industrial order (Buenker, 1988; McCormick, 1986, chap. 7; Teaford, 1982). In this context, the forgotten proportionalists make extraordinary sense.

Chapter 1, then, examines the origins of proportional representation in the context of eighteenth- and nineteenth-century debates in the United States, Great Britain, and France about the danger of majority tyranny in a democracy. Chapter 2 shows how PR entered into a stream of Progressive thought in the United States and was integrated into the strategy for municipal reform. In chapter 3, the theory and mechanics of PR elections are explored. Many versions of proportional and semi-proportional systems have been used, both at the local level and nationally in other countries. The most widely practiced is the party list system, which produces proportional results for the participating political parties. PR/STV is also adaptable to a partisan system, as Ireland's 70 years of successful practice in both national and local elections demonstrates. In contrast, most proportional representation elections in American cities have combined the nonpartisan ballot with the single transferable vote. The PR/STV ballot allows voters to rank order their choices in either at-large or multi-member district elections. With each ballot ultimately counting toward the election of one candidate, voters' preferences can be transferred to second or subsequent choices if their most preferred candidate is already elected or has no chance of election, thus maximizing the proportion of effective votes and permitting minorities to win their share of seats.

Case studies of PR elections in Ashtabula, Cleveland, Cincinnati, Hamilton, and Toledo follow. A common framework for the empirical analysis of each city's experience with PR elections provides opportunities for comparison and evaluation. Contemporary accounts of these PR elections are for the most part polemical, depicting vividly the expectations of both advocates and opponents of electoral change. Over time, high hopes were tempered by outcomes shaped by what participants in the struggle saw as human frailty. A judicious reading of this record provides the basis for the history of PR in America.

Daily newspapers in the five cities, biographies of a few reform leaders, and occasional surviving campaign pamphlets were available for research. The American advocates of PR organized the Proportional Representation League in 1893 and reported their progress in its official journal, the *Proportional Representation Review (PRR),* and in other Progressive magazines such as *Equity,* from 1893 to 1932. In 1932 the Proportional Representation League, unable to fund its separate existence, merged with the National Municipal League (NML), America's leading urban reform group, which since 1914 had endorsed

PR/STV for city elections in its *Model City Charter*. The *PRR* was folded into the *National Municipal Review (NMR)*, in which reports of campaigns to adopt and repeal PR continued to appear. Local reform organizations, such as the Citizens League of Cleveland, published newsletters in which the electoral reform debate raged, as well as lists of endorsed candidates and their backgrounds. From 1890 to 1961 the *Readers' Guide to Periodical Literature* listed articles under the category "Proportional Representation."[1]

Encyclopedias of the period identified the hopeless position of minorities in plurality voting systems as the defect of the then existing electoral schemes that proportional representation would remedy. In the 1897 edition of *The Encyclopedia of Social Reform*, W. D. McCrackan wrote of "the inevitable consequence of the manner in which the votes are now taken, to the complete disfranchisement of minorities," a condition aggravated by "the habit of manipulating the boundaries of electoral districts for party purposes . . . nicknamed the *gerrymander*" (McCrackan, 1897, p. 1123). In the 1908 edition, *The New Encyclopedia of Social Reform*, Robert Tyson revised McCrackan's earlier entry, adding examples of proportional systems that had by then been enacted around the world. These new voting systems, Tyson wrote, provided representation to minorities previously excluded by "defective electoral machinery" (Tyson, 1908, pp. 975–78). In the still later *Encyclopaedia of the Social Sciences* (1934, 1948), political scientist Harold F. Gosnell described and evaluated proportional representation as the single most useful governmental device to protect minorities from exploitation by the majority (Gosnell, 1934, p. 541).

Official records of PR elections in Ohio vary among local jurisdictions, ranging from complete vote counts, including transfer data, in Lucas County (Toledo), to records limited to first counts and final counts in Cuyahoga County (Cleveland). Because of a courthouse fire, no official records exist for Ashtabula elections in the period of the study, leaving unofficial newspaper reports as virtually the only source of electoral statistics.

With these sources, enriched by a few interviews with former participants, the PR experience has been reconstructed here for each of these five Ohio cities. The findings of the case studies are summarized in chapter 9, where representational outcomes are compared and contrasted. Because opponents of PR argued (and still do) that diverse representation on councils would lead to fragmentation and political conflict, the impact of electoral systems on consensus in governing these growing cities has been measured by the percentage of nonunanimous votes cast on ordinances and resolutions by councils elected in periods before, during, and after PR was used. Bases for comparison of policy outcomes from councils produced by different electoral systems proved to be elusive, although outcomes were recognized as a compelling result of any reform.

Great claims were made for electoral reform in the Progressive period. When reforms were adopted, the "problem of corruption" was "solved" in some cities but not others. An analytical problem the authors of the case studies faced was the common adoption of a reform package composed of several structural changes, such as the city manager plan and at-large (or large-district) elections whose impacts were difficult to disentangle from effects of the new way of voting.

In the 1950s reformist belief that political structure made a significant difference in the quality of governance was challenged by behavioralists introducing new modes of inquiry. Political outcomes were attributed to individual and group behavior flowing through institutions and rules rather than being shaped by them (Easton, 1953). More recently, however, scholarly attention has turned again to institutions, building on a more complex and empirical understanding of the interaction between human behavior and constraining forces such as political structures. "Political democracy," write March and Olsen, "depends not only on economic and social conditions but also on the design of political institutions. . . . They are political actors in their own right" (1984, p. 738).

This academic evolution of ideas both reflects and fuels the current revival of attention to mechanisms that produce representation. Today new electoral systems, both proportional and semi-proportional, are promoted for a different kind of expansion of democracy: to bring underrepresented minorities of race, ethnicity, and gender to the table of public policy making. In an ironic twist, the fear of democracy is expressed now by opponents of PR, who are reluctant to allow too many voices, or perhaps the wrong voices, to be heard.

For many years the struggle by minorities—particularly by African Americans—for the right to vote eclipsed the question of what kind of representation would be achieved by the act of voting. When the right to vote was finally enforced by the federal government through the Voting Rights Act of 1965 (nearly a century after adoption of the Fifteenth Amendment's "guarantee" of the right to vote), it became clear that votes can be not only denied but diluted. Whereas the U.S. Supreme Court's "one person, one vote" ruling established an individual right to equal representation, the implementation of the ruling over time has seldom produced governing bodies representative of groups in the electorate. The right to vote is diluted when voters have formal access to the polls but electoral rules obstruct their opportunity to elect representatives of their choice. The rules that translate votes into seats of power are vital to realization of the promise of democracy.

In 1982 Congress responded to this new understanding by amending the already much-amended Voting Rights Act to ensure that both racial and language minorities have the chance to choose their own representatives. This mandate has brought electoral reform into the federal courts, where minorities are battling winner-take-all systems to achieve fair representation.

Federal judges now recognize that plurality/at-large elections provide an opportunity for a voting majority (whether ethnic, racial, or partisan) to win most or all available seats on a city council. Because of the exclusionary effect of at-large winner-take-all elections, judges have mandated single-member-district plurality elections in most cities where minorities have brought cases under the Voting Rights Act to court.

However, single-member-district elections present two hurdles to the achievement of fair minority representation. First, only minorities that are residentially segregated can use such districts to achieve representation. Second, manipulation of district lines (gerrymandering) may structure representation artificially in favor of some groups and not others. Deference is usually paid to incumbents when lines are drawn.

Frustrated by the difficulty of shaping or even defining fair representation in single-member urban districts, some judges have responded to suggestions that where proportional representation of groups is the goal, the proportional electoral systems should be considered. This judicial debate reached the U.S. Supreme Court, where Justices Stevens and O'Connor have engaged in juridical sallies about what's fair, whereas Justices Thomas and Scalia have attacked the Court's majority for adopting proportionality as a "driving principle" (*Holder v. Hall,* 1994, 62 LW at 4748). A "right to representation" has emerged but its boundaries are unclear and its meaning is hotly debated in the context of racially defined congressional districts of the 1990s.

Finally, chapter 10, oriented to present-day issues, presents my conclusion that PR/STV would respond even more powerfully to the representational needs of contemporary American democracy than it did in the Progressive Era.

Currently, lively debates about electoral systems and their consequences are occurring in Britain and France. In Italy and Japan, new and less proportional electoral systems have been adopted as "cures" for corruption, whereas in New Zealand a more proportional plan for voting has been put into effect. New Zealand's adoption (by referendum) of electoral reform was driven by "overwhelming disillusionment with politicians and the political system" (Nagel, 1994, p. 526).

In the United States, interest across the country in proportional and semi-proportional voting systems has led to the organization of vibrant new grassroots groups that advocate electoral reform.[2] Although the voices of American electoral system activists are often drowned out by the din of rancorous political debate, the decade of the 1990s seems propitious for them to address constructively the widespread alienation from politics and the popular anger directed at its practitioners in this country.

ONE

■ ■ ■

The Roots of Proportional Representation

> It was soon after the publication of *Thoughts on Parliamentary Reform* that I became acquainted with Mr. Hare's admirable system of personal representation. . . . I saw in this great practical and philosophical idea the greatest improvement of which the system of representative government is susceptible; an improvement which, in the most felicitous manner, exactly meets and cures the grand, and what before seemed the inherent, defect of the representative system; that of giving to a numerical majority all power, instead of only a power proportional to its numbers, and enabling the strongest party to exclude all weaker parties from making their opinions heard in the assembly of the nation, except through such opportunity as may be given to them by the accidentally unequal distribution of opinions in different localities.
>
> John Stuart Mill, *Autobiography*, 1873

THE PROXIMATE ROOTS of proportional representation for local elections in the United States are to be found in the Progressive Era, but the ideas that underlie the workings of PR were actively discussed by political theorists and statesmen as long ago as the American and French Revolutions. In the late eighteenth century, war and revolution furnished the seedbed of democracy, which came to be understood as representative government. This concept of "democracy" was then debated on both sides of the Atlantic, not as a principle but as a problem of implementation: *who* should participate in public decisions (the suffrage question) and *how* should that participation be transformed into representation (the electoral system question).

11

As participation broadened on both sides of the Atlantic, concerns grew that systems approaching majority rule could quickly tumble into majority tyranny or rule by the mob. In the face of such fears, systems of proportional representation were advocated as devices to secure the continuing presence of the educated minority in government. In the Progressive Era the argument shifted, as proponents of democratization sought to use proportional electoral systems to restore power to ordinary people from whom they believed it had been seized by corrupt party bosses and corporate monopolists. Today, proportional representation is promoted to facilitate more accurate representation of racial, ethnic, and gender groups in policy-making bodies.

Thus the history of PR demonstrates both its persistence as a technical solution to the electoral problems of republican governance and its ability to bear the freight of diverse and even conflicting political ideas under differing circumstances.

Origins of PR in the Debate over Minority Rights

From the revolutionary period onward, in both the United States and France, the problem of majority tyranny in a democratic society was debated. In the American debate over the organization of government under the Articles of Confederation and then under the Constitution, *proportional representation* was used to mean representation of the states in proportion to their population (instead of, one state, one vote). Neither of the founding documents of American nationhood, however, addressed the question of which of the persons enumerated for proportional representation in their states were to vote for the representatives, or the question of how those votes should be cast. Both questions were left for the states, and ultimately the courts, to decide.

In the battle over ratification of the Constitution, James Madison later justified its institutional checks and balances as democracy's strongest protection against the tyranny of the majority. Moreover, he argued that a "social check" would also serve this end through the system of representation. Representation by mere numbers was not enough. The Constitution was designed to insure the representation of diverse interests, groups defined primarily in economic terms, which would check each other, preventing the dominance of any one interest. With respect to sectional interests, the argument was unassailable. The slaveholding interest would be represented through southern delegates; commerce and shipping by men from New England and the mid-Atlantic states. But the adoption by the states of electoral systems based on plurality voting in small districts—the English model they knew best—forced the representation of diverse interests to depend on the accurate territorial distribution of those interests. Furthermore, minority interests within each district, such as small family farmers in the South, for example, could not represent themselves. Although Madison did not identify this difficulty, he recognized the danger that a "majority faction" might be elected that could carry "schemes of oppression" into effect to support its "ruling passion or interest" (A. Hamilton et al., [1788] 1945, pp. 56–60).

Later political theorists would point to this potential outcome as an inherent flaw in a small-district plurality voting system: if a majority faction prevailed in all or most districts (with one person to be elected, the winner "takes all"), minorities would have little or no voice and the "schemes of oppression" Madison feared could indeed be executed. The use of plurality voting in geographically based districts, borrowed from England, was rooted in the medieval practice of representing communities in decision making. The homogeneity of community life sustained territorial representation. With the growth of political parties based on cleavages in society, the familiar old electoral system persisted in both Britain and the United States, in spite of its tendency to overrepresent the majority party and systematically underrepresent small parties (Commons, 1907, pp. 25–28; Bogdanor, 1991, p. 195).

In 1792 Madison's ideas about representation became accessible in Paris when the first French translation of *The Federalist* was published (A. Hamilton et al., [1788] 1945, p. vii). French theorists such as Mirabeau, Condorcet, and Saint Just explored the significance of the American Revolution and the democratic ideas taking shape across the Atlantic with Benjamin Franklin, Thomas Jefferson, Thomas Paine, and John Adams, both in Paris and through transatlantic correspondence (Palmer, 1959, vol. 1, pp. 270–75, 469–70). Unlike the Americans, however, these French philosopher-politicians were not content with a representative assembly that reflected merely the location of population. They wished instead a representative assembly that would reflect all elements of society, not of the majority alone. A representative body, Mirabeau declared, should "present a reduced picture of the people—their opinions, aspirations and wishes. . . . the value of each element is dependent for its importance to the whole and for the whole" (quoted in Sterne, [1871] 1970, pp. 50–51; Hoag and Hallett, 1926, pp. 162–63; DeGrazia, 1951, pp. 83, 186).

The question of how to achieve this goal was never even fully debated in France. Instead, disagreement over questions of the suffrage, direct or indirect election of representatives, and the role of the assembly itself provided the occasion for factional division and the eventual abandonment of representative government altogether in the Age of Napoleon.

During the 1830s, in the context of France's attempt at parliamentary government under a restored monarchy, the issue of the representativeness of the national assembly was again discussed. Now, however, the new "parties" were assumed to be numerous enough, and themselves representative enough, to reflect the "opinions, aspirations and wishes . . . of the people." The problem was to make certain that each *party* was represented. In 1834 Victor Considerant, a French socialist, proposed a party list system of proportional representation for election of a national assembly. His plan was based on the increasing organization of political life into acknowledged parties and on his belief that all significant parties were entitled to representation. Proportional representation by party list (PR/PL) enabled voters to cast a single vote for their party's list of candidates for a national parliament, either in the nation as a whole or in large multimember districts. After votes were counted, the percentage of votes won by each party would be translated into a percentage of seats in the representative body, with the party determining which of its candidates would fill the allotted seats (Kent, 1937, pp. 133–50, 214; Cole and Campbell, 1989, pp. 43–45; Newman, 1987, pp. 386–90).

During this period Alexis de Tocqueville emerged as Europe's most vigorous proponent of PR/PL (O'Leary, 1979, p. 3; MacKenzie, 1958, pp. 78–79; Hogan, 1945, chap. 9). Tocqueville's political views were shaped by his family history: his grandparents and other relatives had been guillotined. He himself was passionately committed to democracy and to the extension of political representation to the working class, a tendency he saw in any case as inevitable in modern political affairs. During his decade of service as a deputy in the French Assembly (1839–48), he attributed the political instability of his own time to the narrow base of French suffrage. Exclusion of the working class from power and responsibility inevitably created irresponsible and extremist views among its leaders, he argued. It was to avoid both a socialist revolution from the left and the tyranny of the middle class on the right that Tocqueville urged universal male suffrage and other electoral reforms (quoted in Lively, 1965, p. 120; Tocqueville, [1850] 1959, part 2, pp. 186–206).

The efforts of nineteenth-century European proportionalists were to bear fruit not in France but in other European nations. PR/PL was first used in Swiss cantonal elections in the 1860s, where its adoption was hastened by the swings between extremes experienced under plurality voting in a closely divided society. Its first use for national elections, in 1899, was in Belgium, where differences between the Liberal and Catholic Parties, reinforced by the linguistic division between Walloon and Flemish speakers, caused "violent and danger-ous oscillations" in the parliament. After 1899, when both major groupings were proportionally represented, tensions were reduced (MacKenzie, 1958, pp. 75–76).

PR/PL was not widely adopted until after the turn of the century. Adoptions accelerated after the breakup of empires in 1917–21, when the issue of choosing a voting system had to be decided in many European nations at once. France finally adopted proportional repre-sentation by party list in the Fourth Republic (1945–58), long after PR/PL had been implemented in other European nations, returning to it again briefly in 1985–86 at the instigation of Socialist president Mitterand. Today, PR/PL is used in a majority of the world's democra-cies and indeed in all European countries except Britain and France (O'Leary, 1979, p. 3; Cole and Campbell, 1989, pp. 6, 72–88, 135–41; Bogdanor, 1991, p. 195).[1]

Party list voting, suggested by Considerant and put into practice much later, did not, in its original form, allow for individual candidate choice. In the eighteenth century, however, recognition of the flaws of plurality voting had led Condorcet and his compatriot Jean-Charles de Borda, a mathematician and astronomer, to propose procedures that would allow voters to both choose individual candidates and express more than one preference. If their preferred candidate could not win, who would be next best? Borda had invented a system in which voters could rank candidates in order of choice by assigning decreasing numbers of points to them. The candidate with the largest total number of points would win. Condorcet, seeking a majority winner if possible, advocated successive pairwise comparisons of candidates for an office, with the winning candidate emerging as the one preferred to all others. This led, as Condorcet himself recognized, to the possibility of the paradox that no candidate is preferred to all others (Reeve and Ware, 1992, pp. 148–49; Fishburn, 1990, pp. 397–99).[2]

Considerant's party list system with multimember districts avoided this problem. With more than one candidate to be elected and parties responsible for their candidates, multiple choices could be accommo-dated. In France itself, however, the single-member district was re-tained, and the problem of a plurality winner was addressed by the use of a two-stage election, with a second ballot (similar to a run-off election) to force majority support for one of the leading candidates on the first ballot. The second ballot, however, was susceptibile to manipulation by coalitions based on deals struck by parties in the interval between the two ballots. Often, as well, centrist candidates are eliminated in the first round, and voters may be faced on the second ballot by a choice between extremes (Cole and Campbell, 1989, pp. 3–6, 26–27, and passim).

It is curious that even though PR/PL voting manifestly cures the defects of plurality voting, it failed to take hold in the English-speaking world. Of the nineteenth-century American proponents of proportional voting systems, only Thomas Gilpin of Philadelphia, a manufacturer and a Quaker with a deep concern about the prospect of majority tyranny, advocated Considerant's party-oriented plan for minority representation. In 1844 Gilpin proposed the use of PR/PL voting for city elections to provide representation on the Philadelphia city council of all significant interests in the community (Gilpin, 1844; Hoag and Hallett, 1926, pp. 457–64). Mechanics in Philadelphia had been demanding representation by mechanics themselves since the revolutionary period (Williamson, 1960, p. 86), but even Pennsylvania's relatively broad electorate had not elected working men by the plurality voting system. Gilpin's proposal, however, was not adopted.

Indeed, although the use of PR/PL elections spread rapidly through European parliamentary systems, the system has not to this day been tried in the United States. The antiparty sentiments of the framers of the Constitution shaped the American political culture such that future American reformers shied from an electoral system that would so enhance the power of political parties. Called "factions" by the nation's early leaders, parties were viewed as divisive elements in political life. In spite of the critical role played by nineteenth-century parties in the development of American democracy, in conducting militant campaigns, legitimizing the opposition, and articulating the interests of a diverse nation, the parties continued to be subject to distrust. After the Civil War, as the parties' political machines became entrenched, liberal reformers capitalized on the underlying popular suspicion that parties were self-interested factions (McGerr, 1986, pp. 43–54). Debate over electoral systems would turn on how to diminish, not how to strengthen, the role of parties in American political life.

Among nineteenth-century theorists of electoral systems, however, other proportional methods to achieve both majority and minority representation were being developed. The single transferable vote form of PR, which could be used with or without the participation of political parties, was proposed as early as 1821 by Thomas Wright Hill, an English schoolmaster sometimes called the first inventor of PR/STV.

As in the case of PR/PL, in the case of PR/STV more than one representative would be elected in a political unit in order to provide for representation of both the majority and the minority or minorities of voters. Instead of voting for a party that in turn would name the winning candidates (PR/PL), however, the voter would choose a list of candidates, numbering them in order of preference. Each ballot would count toward the election of one candidate only. If the voter's first choice already had enough votes to be elected, or was trailing so far behind as to be a hopeless loser, the ballot would be transferred to his second choice or, if necessary, to the third or later choice. The number of votes needed for election would be calculated by simply dividing the total number of votes by the number of seats to be filled.[3] The counting of ballots and transfer of preferences would continue until all seats were filled. Hill's early formulation of proportional representation by single transferable vote (PR/STV) would be subjected to technical improvements with experience, but the principle would not change.

Thomas Hill's son, Sir Rowland Hill, introduced the practice of PR/STV balloting into elections for the governing committee of a private society in order to achieve "as nearly as possible an accurate representation of the whole body." As secretary of the Colonization Commission of South Australia, Rowland Hill also introduced PR/STV in Australia, where it was used in a public election in Adelaide in 1840. It was on this occasion that Catherine Helen Spence noted that PR/STV gave workingmen a chance to elect their foreman to the city council. It changed her life: she would spend the next 50 years writing and lecturing on behalf of PR, not only in her native Australia but also in Canada, Great Britain, and the United States (Hoag and Hallett, 1926, pp. 165–70).

Meanwhile, in the 1840s Carl George Andrae, a Danish mathematician and minister of finance, independently devised a plan for a single transferable vote as a means to integrate the German minority of Schleswig into Danish political life by giving it parliamentary representation (Bogdanor, 1991, p. 195). A political conservative, Andrae developed comprehensive rules for counting STV ballots, and he insisted that the ballot be secret, then a controversial notion in England. His plan was used in 1856 to elect the Danish national parliament, following which Andrae became prime minister (Hoag and Hallett, 1926, pp. 172–75). What was widely viewed as a successful experience with PR/STV in Denmark encouraged its English advocates to renew their efforts (Mill, [1865, 1910] 1947, pp. 275–76).

English Electoral Reform and John Stuart Mill

The interplay of suffrage issues and electoral system reform is nowhere more evident than in the work of John Stuart Mill. Raised by his father, James Mill, in the Utilitarian tradition, and as an adult a leader among Philosophic Radicals, John Stuart Mill was continuously engaged in analysis of the benefits of liberty and the costs of democracy. His life (1806–73) spanned most of the century in which English men fought for the right to vote. As a precocious child Mill probably knew of the working-class agitation for the vote from 1815 until 1819, when the Peterloo Massacre in Manchester ended in death for peaceful demonstrators at the hands of the police. At that time, less than three percent of the population was eligible to vote for parliamentary representatives, since eligibility was based primarily on landownership (Kingdom, 1991, pp. 162, 542).

Popular reaction against the government's violent repression of citizens seeking to participate in political life ultimately led to the Whig victory of 1830, which in turn made possible the passage in 1832 of the Representation of the People Act. This reform favored the middle class by continuing property ownership as a qualification for voting but expanding the definition of property to include income and assets, the forms of property of the rising urban industrial elite. As a result, an estimated 20% of English and Welsh men became eligible to vote. Continuing agitation through the middle decades of the nineteenth century resulted in the Representation of the People Act of 1867, which extended the vote to "all male urban householders." The addition of "male rural householders" in the Franchise Act of 1884 almost doubled the electorate to what was called universal suffrage, although under its definition less than two-thirds of the men in England and Wales qualified to vote. Women over 30 years of age won the vote in 1918, after two decades of increasingly violent agitation and imprisonment; 10 years later the Equal Franchise Act lowered the age for women to qualify to that for men (Kingdom, 1991, pp. 165–67).

During parliamentary debates about the British Reform Acts of 1832 and 1867, the American "experiment" with what was called universal suffrage was cited by both advocates and opponents of a wider suffrage in Britain. Advocates saw the United States as an ideal society inhabited by "happy and contented" people, while opponents cited poverty and corruption in American cities as evidence of the dangers of popular voting (Williamson, 1960, pp. 296–98).

The struggle that generated the gradual expansion of the suffrage in England and Wales over the course of the nineteenth and early twentieth centuries was primarily about class. The assumption that the upper class was best qualified to rule was deeply rooted in feudal society. Furthermore, upper-class control was legitimized by the theory of "virtual representation," which held that the lower classes were represented by their betters who knew what was good for them, just as, in later debates, it was argued that men represented "their" women (DeGrazia, 1951, pp. 241–51).

The rise of individualism in the eighteenth century and the development of the ideas of liberty and equality in the nineteenth led to demands for direct representation that made even the most passionate advocates of these liberating ideas uncomfortable. John Stuart Mill was one of these. Like Tocqueville he believed profoundly in democracy, which he equated with representative government. To be representative (i.e., democratic) in a system in which the people are sovereign, citizens had to exercise their sovereignty by participation. Mill rejected virtual representation out of hand. Even if rulers were wise, they could not experience the lives of ordinary people and hence could not know their interests, let alone represent them. People must represent themselves, he said, an assertion in which Mill included both the working class and women (Mill, [1861] 1962, chap. 3).

Mill saw democracy not only as the best form of government but as inevitable, because of demands by the excluded to participate. However, Mill was not an optimist like the Enlightenment thinkers who preceded him. He was not sure that democracy could succeed. The lessons of the French Revolution and its Terror were vivid still. Mill feared that democracy, like oligarchy, would degenerate into tyranny when those who ruled (in the case of democracy the majority) failed to act in the general interest. Later, in his *Autobiography,* Mill would credit his study of Tocqueville's *Democracy in America* for enlightening him on both "the excellences of democracy" and "the specific dangers which beset democracy, considered as the government of the numerical majority" (Mill, [1873] 1964, pp. 142–44).[4] Drawing on both American and British experience, he recognized that racial, religious, or sectional minorities could be subject to oppression by a tyrannical majority. He wrote: "Suppose the majority to be whites, the minority negroes, or *vice versa:* is it likely that the majority would allow equal justice to the minority? Suppose the majority Catholics, the minority Protestants, or the reverse; will there not be the same danger? Or let the majority be English, the minority Irish, or the contrary: is there not a great probability of similar evil?" ([1861] 1962, p. 128).

What Mill most feared in England, however, was the tyranny of class. He considered the laboring class intelligent enough not to attack "the security of property" directly; nevertheless, such a majority might in the long run destroy initiative by unfair taxation of the rich and might lower productivity by imposing equal wages or enacting protective trade legislation ([1861] 1962, pp. 128–29).

This fear of working-class control—as distinct from its representation—shaped Mill's opposition to the secret ballot, one of the demands of the mid-century Chartist movement of workers seeking greater political rights. Believing as he did that voting is not a personal right but a public trust, Mill wanted ballots to be cast in a public polling place (proposals in parliament included mailed ballots that could be marked in the privacy of the home), with signatures affixed, and open to examination. An elector, he argued, like a representative, exercises power over others and therefore is under "an absolute moral obligation to consider the interest of the public, not his private advantage." Although Mill conceded the hazard of "coercion by landlords, employers and customers," he concluded that the greater danger lay in the "selfishness . . . of the voter himself," who would be tempted by secrecy to vote according to his private inclination, not the public interest ([1861] 1962, pp. 204–7, 209).

Mill's public policy orientation is illustrated by his example of the potential power of public ballots. Supposing the suffrage were extended to all men, he suggests,

> the voters would still have a class interest, as distinguished from women. Suppose that there were a question before the legislature specially affecting women; as whether women should be allowed to graduate at Universities; whether the mild penalties inflicted on ruffians who beat their wives daily almost to death's door, should be exchanged for something more effectual; or suppose that anyone should propose in the British Parliament, what one State after another in America is enacting not by a mere law, but by a provision of their revised Constitutions—that married women should have a right to their own property. Are not a man's wife and daughters entitled to know whether he votes for or against a candidate who will support these propositions? ([1861] 1962, p. 212).

Still, in spite of his differences with the Chartists' agenda, Mill participated in mass meetings and, at least once in 1866, addressed a crowd of "tens of thousands of workers" about the need for working-class suffrage (D. F. Thompson, 1976, p. 52). The Chartists, disappointed by the meager results of the 1832 Reform Act, sought not only "universal" male suffrage but also an end to property qualifications for parliamentary candidates, salaries for members of Parliament to enable working-class people to serve, annual elections, and constituencies of equal population, as well as the secret ballot to protect workers from intimidation by employers (Kingdom, 1991, p. 164).

The successful opposition to this "People's Charter" was grounded in fears for security of property such as those expressed by Thomas B. (Lord) Macauley in a speech delivered in the House of Commons in 1842. Conceding that the Chartists' petition for universal suffrage and other reforms had been signed by "hundreds of thousands of males of twenty-one [years of age]," he warned that if they were entrusted with power, "the first use which they will make of it will be to plunder every man in the kingdom who has a good coat on his back and a good roof over his head" (1877, vol. 1, p. 317). The Whig government, alarmed by what it viewed as the Chartists' dangerous agenda, suppressed the movement, largely by imprisonment of its leaders (Kingdom, 1991, p. 164).

Clearly, in spite of his doubts, Mill did not share the government's extreme fear of democracy. In his view, broader political participation would alleviate the threat of "class legislation," a term he used to mean legislation in the interest of the working class. Voting was an act that would educate and uplift the majority, justifying the widest possible suffrage. At a time when property ownership and male gender were the two leading qualifications for voting in England, Mill argued that the only exclusions from the suffrage should be based on illiteracy, failure to pay any taxes, and receipt of parish relief. Like Condorcet in the previous century, he saw even these limitations as temporary, placing on the government the responsibility to educate all children and to levy a modest head tax on all adults enabling them to qualify for voting ([1861] 1962, pp. 170–74).

To balance the high value that he placed on political participation, and to alleviate such hazards as both he and its opponents foresaw, Mill proposed two major ways to protect the principle of competence in governing. One proposal was that since wise persons merited extraordinary influence in governing, they should be able to cast two votes instead of one. University graduates in England already cast two votes, as did business owners.[5] The problem was how to do it. In developing his weighted voting plan, Mill had difficulty determining the criteria to use for measuring "individual mental superiority," which he considered "the only thing which can justify reckoning one person's opinion as equivalent to more than one." To choose property as a criterion would be "supremely odious," he wrote, since "accident has so much more to do than merit with enabling men to rise in the world." He considered occupation as a proxy for merit, since he found employers, skilled laborers, managers, and professionals generally more able than unskilled laborers and tradesmen. Occupation, however, suffered the flaws of property as a measure of merit. Education would be the only correct standard, he concluded. Yet in the absence of a national system of education equally open to all, education as a standard too was imperfect. In the end, Mill concluded that only university graduates could clearly qualify for weighted votes, and even such a franchise should never give any class enough weight to outvote the majority ([1861] 1962, pp. 176–84).

Mill's other major proposal to prevent majority tyranny and to ensure competence in democratic governance was to change the electoral system by adopting proportional representation by single transferable vote (PR/STV). Mill had discovered PR/STV by reading English barrister Thomas Hare's 1859 pamphlet, "On the Election of Representatives, Parliamentary and Municipal."[6] In 1861 Mill called Thomas Hare's "scheme" for proportional representation by single transferable vote, which was patterned on Thomas Hill's earlier work, "among the very greatest improvements yet made in the theory and practice of government" ([1861] 1962, p. 151).[7]

Mill knew of other electoral "expediencies," voting systems that would allow for some minority representation. Both limited voting[8] and cumulative voting[9] were electoral reforms that had been unsuccessfully introduced in Parliament to allow for three-member constituencies in which a minority as large as a third of the electorate could return one of the three members. Although Mill felt that both of these "makeshift" plans "recognised the right principle," neither reached the "degree of perfection" of Hare's proposal ([1861] 1962, pp. 146–47).

Mill found Hare's explanation of his purpose persuasive. PR/STV would increase both the liberty of the individual voter and the accountability of the representative. The voter would gain freedom, Hare had argued, by being liberated from a small district and by being empowered to vote either for candidates anywhere in the country or for candidates in a large multimember district. Since candidates would be nominated by petition, the voter would not be limited to the candidates presented by the major parties. These features led some to call the system "free nomination" and "free voting." The representative would become more accountable because his tie to his constituents would be direct, each voter being a member of a unanimous and voluntary constituency. In contrast, the representative in a single-member district, once elected, "represents" those who voted against him as well as those who voted for him, an unlikely if not impossible task. The direct tie between constituent and representative created by PR/STV led Hare to call his system "Personal Representation." Like Mill, Hare advocated that each voter sign his ballot. Hare's goal was to ensure accountability by the representative. The voter would be able to trace his ballot through transfers to the candidate for whom it was counted. The voter would then know whom, in a multimember delegation, to hold responsible for representing him (Hare, 1859, chap. 7; Mill, [1861] 1962, chap. 10). Under this electoral system, Hare argued, a "natural community of interest" would gain representation untrammeled by district boundaries (Lakeman and Lambert, 1959, p. 245; Hoag and Hallett, 1926, p. 176).

Mill, like those electoral theorists on whose work he built, viewed plurality voting as an electoral procedure opening the way for majority tyranny. Since the candidate first-past-the-post wins, not only could a majority of voters win all, or a disproportionately large share, of the seats in a governing body, but a majority of the majority that might itself be a minority of the whole could prevail (Mill, [1861] 1962, pp. 142–43). The drawing of district boundaries, the clustering or dispersal of voters of a particular persuasion, and the actual turnout of eligible voters shaped the outcomes of plurality voting systems in ways voters seldom understood.

These were matters that, in Mill's view, were controlled by the political parties for the furtherance of their own interests. In dealing with the absence of minority representation in a single-member district plurality vote system, Mill cited as his foremost example distortions imposed by the party system. "The electors who are on a different side in party politics from the local majority, are unrepresented," he wrote. The majority itself is "misrepresented," he argued, because the majority party is capable of imposing on its followers a candidate whose opinions may differ from the party's loyal voters in all but one respect. Even candidates with no significant opinions may be nominated by the parties, since a candidate to whom no one can object may be the most electable.[10] Mill found "nothing ... more certain than that the virtual blotting-out of the minority is no necessary or natural consequence of freedom." Minorities should not rule, but they should be present and be heard in policy deliberations in a democratic state ([1861] 1962, pp. 144–46).

The minority whose potential powerlessness Mill found most disturbing was the intellectual elite. Under the existing system, "able men of independent thought" were unlikely to be elected by the average voter, who would be swayed by "local influence," "lavish expenditure," or party direction ([1861] 1962, p. 153). Even so, in imagining the "ideally best polity," Mill "support[ed] the claim of all to participate in the sovereign power," including the working class:

> Does Parliament, or almost any of the members composing it, ever for an instant look at any question with the eyes of a working man? When a subject arises in which the labourers as such have an interest, is it regarded from any point of view but that of the employers of labour? I do not say that the working men's view of these questions is in general nearer to truth than the other: but it is sometimes quite as near; and in any case it ought to be respectfully listened to, instead of being, as it is, not merely turned away from, but ignored. ([1861] 1962, pp. 59–61)

Not only would workingmen have an appropriate voice in Parliament, but "the instructed minority" could influence the entire decision-making process:

> In the actual voting, [these educated representatives would] count only for their numbers, but as a moral power they would count for much more, in virtue of their knowledge, and of the influence it would give them over the rest. An arrangement better adapted to keep popular opinion within reason and justice, and to guard it from the various deteriorating influences which assail the weak side of democracy, could scarcely by human ingenuity be devised. ([1861] 1962, p. 161)

Since Hare's voting system would result in the fair representation of both the independent intellectual minority and the working class, Mill would abandon his plan for weighted voting if PR/STV could be instituted ([1861] 1962, p. 184).

In the second and third editions of his *Considerations on Representative Government,* Mill added an analysis of the objections to PR/STV that he had heard since publication of the first edition, and he answered them as "either unreal or easily surmountable." The two principal objections were, first, that small groups ("knots or cliques ... or bodies united by class interests or community of religious persuasion") would gain disproportionate power; and, second, that political parties could manipulate the system by promoting "tickets," or slates of candidates (Mill, [1865, 1910] 1947, pp. 271–76).

In response to these dire warnings, Mill conceded only that organization is an advantage under any electoral system, PR/STV as well as others. Nevertheless, "able independents" would have a greater chance of election under PR/STV than under any other method, because of nomination by petition and voting in larger constituencies. A "personal merit" ticket could be effective. And "the minor groups would have precisely the amount of power which they ought to have"—no more and no less; they would be unable to control an assembly but able to be heard ([1865, 1910] 1947, pp. 271–74).

As a member of Parliament from 1865 to 1868, Mill participated in debates on the Reform Bill of 1867, offering amendments to accomplish what he called "the two greatest improvements which remain to be made in representative government." The first of these was "Mr. Hare's plan" for election of parliamentary representatives; the other was a motion to strike out the limitation of the franchise to males. Neither of these moves succeeded, but Mill would later consider their introduction to be his most important contribution to public life ([1873] 1964, pp. 210–11).

In 1868 a few three-member districts were established, in which voters were limited to casting two votes, an LV plan that permitted some minority party representation. The Liberal Party in Birmingham, for example, gained representation through this system (Reeve and Ware, 1992, pp. 61–62). Mill's followers, however, continued to press for "the best" means of achieving fair representation. Mill's PR/STV bill was introduced anew in 1872, when it was debated inconclusively, and again in 1884 as part of a major reform initiative. By then the House of Commons was elected by plurality vote from multimember districts that encompassed whole towns or boroughs. The 1884 parliamentary debate tied together the extension of the franchise (to male rural voters), the reallocation of seats from rural areas to the growing cities, and the voting system itself. Consideration was given to various devices for achieving "proportionate" representation within the existing multimember districts, including an extension of LV, CV, or PR/STV.

Despite evidence that Prime Minister Gladstone himself preferred multimember constituencies with some form of proportional representation, the Liberal government struck a deal with the Tories in which it accepted small, single-member districts in exchange for the extension of the franchise. Gladstone defended his capitulation on the small-

district system by claiming that minorities or "separate interests and
pursuits" could secure representation in the new one-member constituencies (Bogdanor, 1985, pp. 271–77). The 1884 Representation of
the People Act incorporated single-member district plurality voting for
parliamentary elections, ending Britain's 16-year small-scale experiment with limited voting. The continued exclusion of minority parties
within single-member districts has led to periodic reexamination of
the British electoral system ever since (Lakeman, 1970, app. 10).

Mill's advocacy and the efforts of the British Electoral Reform
Society were to bear a little fruit for a time in the twentieth century. In
1917, although PR/STV for all parliamentary elections was defeated
again by a narrow margin in the Commons, the 1917 Representation of
the People Act established election by PR/STV for the university seats.
From 1918 through 1945, most university seats were contested, and
whereas Conservatives won the majority of these PR/STV elections, as
they had traditionally won the university seats when they were
elected by plurality, Independents were occasionally chosen (Lakeman, 1970, pp. 217–20).

The American Debate

Mill corresponded about electoral systems with interested Americans
and his writings were widely read in the United States.[11] Disciples of
his theories of liberty and representation included Philadelphian J.
Francis Fisher, who published *The Degradation of Our Representative
System and Its Reform* in 1863, in which he advocated the use of
PR/STV. Like Mill, Fisher believed that the electoral system could
affect policy outcomes. He argued that the Civil War could have been
averted if minority political views had been represented in both
northern and southern delegations to Congress. Antislavery Southern-
ers and pro–states' rights Northerners, incapable of winning election in
a winner-take-all election, could have been elected in PR/STV contests,
in Fisher's view, and, once in Congress, would have introduced
moderate perspectives that might in turn have led to more serious
consideration of alternatives to war (Fisher, 1863).

Instead, from colonial days on, plurality voting in geographically
based districts was the universally accepted practice in the United
States. Most districts elected one member only, but more than three-
quarters of the states used some multimember districts with plurality
voting for state legislative elections in the nineteenth century (Niemi,
Jackman, and Winsky, 1991, p. 91). From 1842 to 1852 (and again from

1862 to 1929), Congress required the states to elect members of the U.S. House of Representatives from single-member districts, a measure passed to protect minority *party* representation from the effects of winner-take-all elections statewide or in multimember districts. In the critical years leading up to the Civil War, however, even this modest protection for congressional representation of minority interests within states was dropped (Hacker, 1964, pp. 48–50).

Simon Sterne, another Philadelphian, went to England in 1865, met with Hare, Mill, and other British advocates of PR, and returned with their encouragement to lead a PR movement in the United States (Sterne, [1871] 1970; Hoag and Hallett, 1926, p. 183). Like Mill, Sterne was eager to secure the representation of the educated minority in order to protect democracy from the demos. He did find it "odd," however, that Mill, and Hare as well, should advocate women's suffrage at a time when women were so obviously ignorant and manipulable (Sterne, [1871] 1970, pp. 176–78; Mill, 1972–88, vol. 19, p. 370).

The political context of the nineteenth-century electoral system debate in the United States showed striking similarities to the British framework. The issue was primarily class. As in England, the steady expansion of the suffrage to include men with less property or different kinds of property exacerbated elite concerns about majority tyranny. In the late eighteenth century, weighted voting had been practiced in some U.S. jurisdictions. In New York State, for example, property owners were allowed to vote in local elections in each jurisdiction in which they owned land. In 1804 the Jeffersonian-Republican majority in the state assembly abolished this practice, giving "tradesmen, mechanics and carters" occasion to celebrate a "second Declaration of Independence" (Williamson, 1960, p. 164).

The absence of a feudal tradition in the new United States and the patriotic passion for equality stirred by the American Revolution combined to accelerate the acceptance of democracy, but state control of qualifications for voting led to great diversity in suffrage practice. The basic notion that only property holders should vote derived from belief, as in England, that if the poor voted, they would either destroy the security of property or sell their votes to the rich, thus distorting the power of wealth (Williamson, 1960, pp. 11–12). Although the status of "freeholder"was the basic property qualification for voting in most states, the term was defined differently in different states. The amount of land owned, the value of the land, income from rents, and taxpayer status were among the criteria for granting suffrage to men of property. Property qualifications, however, were steadily undermined in practice. In several states depreciation of paper money after the Revolution broadened the franchise by making specified monetary requirements, such as "being worth 50 pounds," both easy to achieve and worthless. Men without property and youths less than 21 years of age who had fought in the Revolution were admitted to the franchise by some grateful state legislatures (Williamson, 1960, pp. 83, 113, 121).

In addition, party competition contributed to broadening the franchise. Jeffersonian Republicans (later Democrats) strove to expand their support through efforts in state legislatures and constitutional conventions to achieve universal male suffrage. Although Federalists (and later Whigs) opposed extension of the suffrage, they were known to manufacture votes by giving temporary deeds for small lots to potential supporters who would return the deeds after the election (Williamson, 1960, pp. 168–69).

Although property qualifications for voting were eroding by the 1840s, racial restrictions on voting were not uncommon outside of New England. Five states admitted to the Union between 1796 and 1821 confined voting to white males with various property qualifications (Williamson, 1960, p. 219). In 1802 Ohio's first constitution, for example, which was hailed as symbolic of democracy on the new frontier because the only property restriction was payment of a tax, limited the suffrage to "white male inhabitants" (Ohio Const., 1802, art. 4, sec. 1; K. H. Porter, 1918, pp. 36–37). While this tax appeared to be a tax on real property, the difficulties of surveying land and granting titles on the frontier made literal application of the requirement impractical. Otherwise eligible men were permitted to meet the qualification by "work[ing] out a tax on the public highway." K. H. Porter calls this alternative "a last weak, expiring tribute to the property interests" (1918, p. 37).

Issues of race and gender as well as class were raised. Ohio's new constitution of 1851 dropped the taxpaying requirement for voting, added citizenship, and retained the racial qualification ("every white male citizen," Ohio Const., 1851, art. 5, sec. 1). Whigs had advocated a literacy test instead of either property or racial qualifications, but Democrats controlled the 1851 convention and prevented debate on the issue (Williamson, 1960, p. 267). Strenuous efforts by advocates of "negro" suffrage to get their petitions accepted for consideration were futile. "Even petitions advocating the expulsion of all free negroes from the state had a better reception," reported an early twentieth-century historian (K. H. Porter, 1918, p. 108). In 1867, three years before the Fifteenth Amendment to the U.S. Constitution was adopted to prohibit the states from denying the vote on account of race, Ohio voters rejected a proposed state constitutional amendment that would have enfranchised blacks and disfranchised all who bore arms in support of insurrection or rebellion against the United States (Patterson, 1912, p. 170).

The period of Jacksonian democracy was actually restrictive for black voters in America, as race came to replace class as a qualification to vote in states that had not discriminated earlier. Agitation against slavery in the North and slave rebellions in the South led to racist fears of a democracy that would include blacks as participants in political life. Southern states that had once permitted free blacks to vote disfranchised them between 1835 (North Carolina) and 1851 (Virginia). White supremacy, binding poor whites to the interests of slave-owners, was promulgated to prevent the development of unified interests among propertyless whites and blacks (Williamson, 1960, pp. 232–40). In the North as well, states such as New York, Pennsylvania, and New Jersey, which had permitted black freeholders to vote, withdrew the privilege by confining the suffrage to white adult males. By 1858 free blacks still voted only in a few New England states (Williamson, 1960, pp. 278–79; Litwack, 1961, p. 75).

Women had voted only in New Jersey, which withdrew that right in 1810 (Litwack, 1961, pp. 180–81). Male corruption has been cited as the reason for this setback: incidents were reported of men voting early in the day and returning to the polls a second time in women's dress to vote again (Stanton et al., [1881] 1969, vol. 1, p. 453). Women were apparently powerless to prevent their own disfranchisement in New Jersey. With the initiation of the women's rights movement in 1848, inclusion in the suffrage became an issue that would grow in importance for the rest of the century (Stetson, 1991, p. 45). American woman suffrage activists were familiar with Mill's work. The leading intellectual of the suffrage movement, Elizabeth Cady Stanton, shared his philosophy of individualism and natural rights. In 1868 she wrote that the ballot alone was not what women needed, but "a revolution in society, politics, and religion" (quoted in Banner, 1980, p. 88).

Not all the American advocates of PR/STV, however, were friendly to women's claims. Simon Sterne, for example, although captivated by Mill's electoral system analysis, rejected his feminist theories on the ground that "to one . . . Mrs. Stanton, there are half a million of women whose political education is nil; and though the ballot-box has an educational influence, that much-be-praised and overrated education machine is as yet very far from having fully impregnated [*sic*] every suffragan with sound politico-economical ideas" ([1871] 1970, p. 178).

Mill's vision of PR as a mechanism to allow representation of the educated minority should not, in Sterne's view, include the educated female minority. Ironically, the fear of too much democracy was shared by suffragists themselves. Concerned about the illiteracy of both freedwomen and immigrant women, many suffrage leaders supported an "educated franchise" (Flexner, 1975, pp. 225, 309). Furthermore, many nineteenth-century feminists deemed immigrant women to be controlled by their husbands who were mere pawns of the machine bosses, powerful politicians who instructed male legislators to vote down any public policy steps toward women's equality.

While suffrage would remain at the top of the feminist agenda until 1920 (when the vote was at last won), the grounds for women's claim to the vote shifted significantly in the late nineteenth century. Since 1848 arguments for political rights had rested on the theory, articulated as well by Mill, that women were persons equal to men, entitled to the franchise on that ground alone. As the decades slipped by and women won few battles for self-representation, they began to assert entitlement based on their higher moral capacity. By the 1890s woman suffrage leaders were contending that if only women had the vote, they could clean up corruption in the cities; improve education, sanitation and health; and help to alleviate the harsh burdens that industrial life had imposed on society, particularly on women and children (Stetson, 1991, p. 48). These claims activated new enemies—the liquor interests, antiregulatory forces in business, and above all, the bosses—but they also placed the women's movement in the mainstream of developing Progressive thought.

Between the Civil War and the end of the nineteenth century, the fear of majority tyranny or an "excess of democracy" was reignited in both the North and South by several major social and political forces. Demographic and political trends led such minorities as white men in the South, Protestant elites in the urban North, Republicans in Democratic-dominant states, and Democrats in Republican-dominant ones to try experiments with electoral systems that would preserve their influence or control in the governance of cities, states, political parties, and even Congress. The limited vote (LV) and the cumulative vote (CV) were most often considered, but PR/STV was also debated.

In the South, racial issues were dominant. In 1867, by military rule, Congress enfranchised the newly freed male slaves and disfranchised former Confederate leaders. Black majorities existed in the new electorates of five states. State constitutional conventions were convened, and new state constitutions were proposed and adopted, confirming the black male franchise under state authority. Although the new black voters did not win control of any state government, many black officeholders were elected, and in South Carolina blacks won a majority of one house of the state assembly (Morison, 1965, pp. 716–17).

White reaction was intense and violent across the South. Northern friends of Negro suffrage, many of them from states that had disfranchised free blacks before the Civil War, were alarmed by reports from Southern states of white retaliation against black voters that ranged from intimidation to murder. The Radical Republicans in Congress determined that only a federal constitutional amendment to prohibit state denial of the vote on account of race could resolve both the issue of hypocrisy in the North (outside of New England) and the threat of betrayal of the promise of black freedom in the South.

While the Fifteenth Amendment was being debated, alternative electoral systems were also proposed in Congress as means of protecting black voters against exclusion from representation in the new South. The focus of this debate over electoral systems was a bill introduced in 1867 by Senator Charles R. Buckalew of Pennsylvania that would have required the use of cumulative voting (CV) for members of Congress from the "reconstructed" states of the former Confederacy. Identifying "plurality rule" as the "evil which exists," Buckalew argued that CV ("the free vote") would alleviate growing racial antagonisms in the South by allowing Negro representation from that region in Congress. Buckalew's proposal was defeated by opponents who contended that such a major change in congressional election procedures should not be sectional in nature. In 1869 Buckalew expanded his proposal to apply to all the states, only to have it defeated again (Buckalew, 1872, pp. 82–86; DeGrazia, 1951, pp. 187–89).

In the Southern states, the debate about alternative electoral systems focused instead on protection of the white minority. Not surprisingly, South Carolina was the locus of action. The ratification in 1870 of the Fifteenth Amendment, a federal guarantee of black voting rights, precipitated consideration in the South Carolina state legislature of PR/STV, LV, or CV for legislative elections, as a safeguard against further consolidation of power by the black majority, which, voting by plurality, might continue to win all or most of the assembly seats. In 1871 the cumulative vote was adopted and used for state legislative elections, until the withdrawal of northern military power in 1877, when the end of Reconstruction opened the way for the white minority to exclude the black majority from the electorate altogether (Commons, 1907, pp. 247–51, 352). After 1877 the white minority used literacy tests, the poll tax, intimidation, and violence to prevent blacks from voting and, safely in control again, restored plurality elections.

Political leaders in the Northern states were becoming preoccupied with their own problems of democracy. The massive immigration of European workers, often illiterate and inexperienced in the ways of democracy, made universal male suffrage controversial in the North as well. Between 1870 and 1900, more than 11 million immigrants poured into the United States, most of them building their new lives in the cities of the Northeast and the Middle West (Boyer, 1978, p. 123). Moreover, political party organizations became adept at recruiting these new residents into their ranks, developing their loyalties by serving their basic needs, and collecting their reward at the polls on election day.

Educated reformers who deplored the ability of party organizations to gain and hold power through the ballot box promoted electoral system experiments that might maintain at least some representation for independents and for antimachine partisans. Semi-proportional electoral systems were used in a variety of settings. Limited voting was adopted for the election of delegates to the New York Constitutional Convention of 1867. The success of the LV strategy in producing what was believed to be fair representation of New York's Democratic minority in a Republican-majority convention led to further consideration of electoral system change. In the course of the convention, Horace Greeley proposed the use of cumulative voting (CV) for election of New York's U.S. senators and representatives in order to end the "tyranny" of election results in which plurality or majority winners could take all of the representation. This proposal was defeated, but partisans learned that electoral system experiments might serve their own purposes (DeGrazia, 1951, pp. 187–89).

In 1872 the Republican majority in the New York legislature attempted to impose the cumulative vote on New York City, then firmly in the hands of the Tammany (Democratic) machine, which routinely elected all council members by the winner-take-all plurality system. The measure was vetoed by the Democratic governor of New

York, but the following year the legislature tried again to introduce some proportionality into New York City elections, this time success-fully with a limited vote plan. For council elections the city was divided into nine districts with three members each; no voter could cast more than two votes. This plan, which remained in effect for almost a decade, enabled the Republican minority in the city's elec-torate to elect at least one member in several of the new districts (Commons, 1907, pp. 251, 261). Still, this reform did not last, and the city returned to one-party rule.

Edwin L. Godkin, editor of the *Nation,* and one of Mill's American intellectual heirs, worried about the abuse of universal suffrage by "the boss" in governing a large city such as New York. He saw control of the city shifting into the hands of poor, illiterate immigrants, "the danger-ous classes," who voted as told by the demagogue who helped them. The "respectable classes," on the other hand, he complained, split their votes between parties and thereby allowed crime and ignorance to prevail in municipal affairs (Godkin, 1894, pp. 879–81).

In 1870 Illinois adopted the cumulative vote for its lower house as a means of surmounting the polarization of politics in the wake of the Civil War. The war had left allegiances in the state deeply divided between the North and the South. Plurality voting allowed Republi-cans to monopolize representation in the northern districts of the state, whereas in southern Illinois only Democrats could win district elec-tions. To overcome both this sectional cleavage and the failure of the smaller party to win representation in any district, three-member districts were drawn to replace the assembly's single-member districts, and cumulative voting was implemented. Voters had several options. They could cast 3 votes for one candidate, 1½ votes for each of 2 candidates, or 1 vote for each of 3 candidates. By limiting nominations and concentrating votes, the minority party in each district could secure representation. Third parties were usually excluded in spite of significant support statewide, because they were unlikely to win over one-fourth of the vote in a district. Still, between 1872 and 1898 partisan representation improved markedly as the division of seats in the Illinois House approximated the division of the two-party vote. The system was retained for over a century, its persistence making it an exception to the usual pattern of fleeting electoral reform (Blair, 1960; Argersinger, 1989, pp. 83–86; DeGrazia, 1951, pp. 187–89).[12]

By the end of the nineteenth century, although in a few state and local legislative bodies the use of cumulative and limited voting continued as a means of achieving minority representation, agitation for opening up the system of representation to minority parties or interests failed. The existing electoral system contained an insuperable barrier to change. The two dominant parties, which benefited from the exaggeration of their strength implicit in small-district plurality voting, controlled Congress and most state legislative chambers, the very bodies that held the power to change—or preserve—the winner-take-all electoral system (Argersinger, 1989, p. 65). Electoral reformers clearly understood this power structure, and they began to unite in support of nonpartisanship as a critical step on the road to achieving their other goals.

Electoral System Reform Efforts in Ohio

Ohio was hardly immune to the agitation arising over electoral systems and representation in the late nineteenth century. Congressional debates about minority representation were fueled by electoral results distorted by winner-take-all voting. Ohio offered a particularly egregious example because of the close division of popular sentiment and intense competition between the two major parties. In the last quarter of the nineteenth century, the percentage of votes won for a party's congressional candidates had little relationship to the share of seats won by the party.[13] The switch of a small margin of votes from one party to the other would swing a significant number of districts into the other party's camp. From election to election, party control of the Ohio delegation swung from Republican to Democratic and back again. These swings in turn drove repeated redistricting, as each majority party of the moment in the Ohio legislature sought to retain its temporary advantage.

Whereas Ohio's assembly districts were based on county lines (from 1852 until 1966) and were therefore immune to manipulation by districting authorities, congressional district lines were (and still are) drawn by state legislative enactment. The party that controlled the legislature drew the lines. When party control changed in mid-decade, the new legislature upon convening would quickly draw new congressional districts. Between 1876 and 1886, a new districting plan was enacted in Ohio for each of six successive elections (Argersinger, 1989, p. 71).

Even some members of Congress whose seats were secure worried that the legitimacy of the political system as a whole was being undermined by what they called "practical disfranchisement." James A. Garfield, Republican congressman from Ohio and later president, criticized the electoral system because "a large portion of the voting people [are] permanently disfranchised. . . . There are about ten thousand Democratic voters in my district, and they have been voting there for the last forty years, without any more hope of having a Representative on this floor than of having one in the Commons of Great Britain" (*Cong. Globe*, 41 Cong., 2nd sess., 23 June 1870, pp. 4737–38, quoted in Argersinger, 1989, p. 63).

In 1874, under the rubric of "virtual disfranchisement," representation became a leading issue in debates over Ohio constitutional revision, and the Illinois experiment with cumulative voting attracted intense interest. Because Ohio's elective judiciary was also perceived as captive of the majority party, both the legislature and the bench were targets of reform. In a proposed new constitution, CV was introduced for state legislative elections in the multimember urban counties of Ohio, then only Cuyahoga and Hamilton counties. The declared purpose of CV was to enable minority party voters in those counties to gain some representation in the assembly (proposed art. 14, sec. 12, 1874, in Patterson, 1912, p. 176).

In the same election, a separate constitutional amendment, called the "Minority Representation Amendment," was submitted to Ohio's voters, providing for limited voting (LV) for state judges in the counties in which more than one judge was elected at a time (Proposition 1, 1874). Voters would be permitted to vote for only as many judicial candidates as constituted a majority of judges in their county, but not for all seats on the bench. For example, if three judges were to be elected countywide, voters could vote for two judicial candidates; if five judges, three votes. Both of these provisions attempted to break the monopoly that the majority party could achieve with countywide multimember plurality voting, and both were defeated by the voters in 1874 (Patterson, 1912, pp. 176, 223).

A different path proposed in Ohio to secure minority party representation was the division of multimember counties into single-member districts for the election of state legislators. Three times in the nineteenth century—in 1857, 1889, and 1893—constitutional amendments were initiated to "subdistrict" the populous urban counties of Ohio for state legislative elections. All three proposals were defeated by the voters. The prevailing argument against single-member districts was the horror of the gerrymander, which had been practiced so effectively by the dominant party in the legislature from 1802 until 1852, when Ohio's new constitution established counties as the basic unit of legislative representation (Patterson, 1912, pp. 166–67, 259, 274).

Since power in competitive party states depended on the geographical distribution of partisan voters, the small-district plurality voting system enhanced the stakes in districting and apportionment decisions. The gerrymander has historically been a key tool in the hands of the party that controlled the state legislatures for shaping in turn the party composition of Congress, and thus its policy output. Ohio congressional districts were frequently used as examples of partisan misrepresentation by means of the electoral system. It should not be surprising that it was Representative Tom Johnson of Ohio (later mayor of Cleveland) who introduced into Congress in 1892 the first bill to elect its members by proportional representation (Commons, 1907, pp. 114–15).

Conclusion

By the end of the century the major parties had secured a firm lock on access to power in the United States. While the parties were intensely competitive nationally and in states like Ohio, and participation of those eligible remained high, the political system seemed undemocratic and the economic system unjust to growing numbers of citizens. The drive for more democracy would coalesce outside the party organizations, and the parties would become leading targets of attack in the name of democracy instead of its instruments.

Electoral system reform came to the fore because representation was at the fulcrum of controversy. Who would be allowed to vote was still a key issue to the excluded—primarily to women and African Americans. There was, however, a growing awareness that how votes were translated into power, the reality of representation, profoundly affected the ability of voters to influence public decisions.

In structuring the American government, the framers of the Constitution had relied on institutional checks and balances—the separation of powers and the federal system—to prevent the tyranny of the majority so feared in that revolutionary period of Western political development. The need for Madison's "social check" on the potential tyranny of the majority was believed to arise out of the inequalities deeply embedded in human nature, and therefore built into the politics of the system. As the citizenry became more diverse, however, through both the end of slavery and new waves of immigration, nineteenth-century Americans confronted different problems.

Unable to break into the multifaceted structure of political practices and institutions, a significant number of antiparty reformers gradually narrowed their focus to local elections and to alternative electoral systems. Both LV and CV had been tried in a variety of settings. As these turn-of-the-century Progressives took up the challenge of expanding grassroots democracy while at the same time attempting to preserve competence in governance, they were drawn to PR/STV by its technical elegance, its reliably proportional results, and its unqualified endorsement by John Stuart Mill.

TWO

■ ■ ■

Proportional Representation as a Progressive Cause

> The underlying rationale of proportional representation is the desire to prevent the exclusion of minorities from the benefits of the state—a rationale based on the democratic premise that in the absence of some means of protection minorities may be exploited by the majority.
>
> Gosnell, "Proportional Representation," 1948

B ETWEEN 1890 AND 1920, American political life was charged with optimism about the potential for improving the human condition and with anger about social, economic, and political inequities, particularly in the rapidly expanding cities. At the same time, insecurity spread among native working-class and upper-middle-class professionals about their ability to maintain their way of life in the face of industrialization and the massive new immigration of Europeans to the United States.

During this period, individuals and groups calling themselves "Progressives" generated a flow of reform activities to solve the problems they identified as critical to the health of the nation. At federal, state, and local levels they actively sought to secure protective labor legislation, antimonopoly laws, and tax reform to mitigate the impact of unregulated capitalism on workers and small businesses. They also sought to change the very structures of government through which such meliorative laws were to be passed and by which they were to be administered: from popular election of U.S. senators, direct primaries, and women's suffrage to charter reform in the cities.

Among the urban reformers, diverse goals were evident. Some were concerned primarily with political participation, working for direct democracy in the form of initiative, referendum and recall, women's suffrage for school board and municipal elections, and nonpartisan elections to remove control of city government from political machines. Others, eager to attack economic inequality directly, worked for public ownership of utilities, tax equity, minimum wage–maximum hour legislation for municipal workers, and local measures to protect women and children in the workplace. Economy in public affairs ranked high in importance for some, as they viewed with alarm the rising cost of government at all levels. Still others placed a high priority on structural changes in municipal government. This complex agenda was held together, if only in an amorphous way, by an underlying yearning for morality in public life and by confidence that political change could make a difference.

The first barrier the reformers found to promoting change was the traditional and widespread state control of municipal affairs. State control, entrenched in state constitutions and reinforced by Dillon's Rule in the courts, was felt to be particularly oppressive. Reformers contended that rural-dominated state legislatures oppressed the cities. Under common law as applied in 46 states, Dillon's Rule required a narrow construction of municipal power as opposed to state power. Cities could do only what states permitted them to do, either expressly or by necessary implication of expressly granted powers.[1] In the period of rapid urbanization following the Civil War and accelerating at the turn of the century, cities were totally dependent on their state legislatures to permit accommodations to new conditions created by concentrated growth of population. Thus structural reforms were blocked by the inability of cities to choose or to change their form of government, or even to legislate locally on critical new concerns such as child labor or the electoral system. "Home Rule" therefore became a Progressive rallying cry and a precursor of further reform (Cassella, 1975, p. 442).

Constitutional home rule, allowing cities to choose their own form of government, was first adopted by Missouri in 1875, where early reformers in St. Louis pressed their case; but not until twentieth-century Progressives organized and fought for reform was home rule widely adopted. Ohio Progressives were national leaders in this effort. Reform Republicans such as Mayor Brand Whitlock of Toledo, city council member Frederic Howe of Cleveland, and city council member

Washington Gladden of Columbus—who also led the Social Gospel movement of American Protestantism—campaigned nationally for home rule, as did such Democrats as Mayor Tom Johnson of Cleveland and his friend Newton D. Baker. Baker would write Ohio's home rule amendment, as well as Cleveland's first charter, and under the latter would become mayor (Howe [1925] 1988; Warner 1964, pp. 488–89).[2]

In the heated competitive politics of the late nineteenth century, urban party organizations consolidated their power in Ohio as elsewhere, providing services not otherwise available to dependent immigrant populations in exchange for their votes. The expanding African-American populations of these cities were also more welcomed by "the bosses" than by other urban elites; African-American community leaders became precinct captains and occasionally elected officials as well as voters. Services provided by the urban machines were financed by the growing corporate sector, which was willing to pay the required graft to obtain the utility franchises and tax favors that facilitated their consolidation of private economic power (Warner, 1964, chap. 1; DuBois, 1899, pp. 383–84).

Ohio's ruling party organizations were largely Republican. Dayton's Joseph E. Lowes, Cleveland's Robert S. McKisson and Maurice Maschke, Cincinnati's George B. Cox, and Toledo's Walter F. Brown were prototypical bosses, all Republicans who operated in these now legendary ways. Reacting against such party organizations, forces loosely called "Progressive"—often united only by their opposition to the existing paradigm of power—sought reform.

The leadership of the Ohio Progressive movement was primarily urban and emerged from the large cities where Republican machines had kept a tight grip on the perquisites of power and policy. The local Democratic Party organization in these cities was often a subservient satellite of the dominant Republican Party, accepting a modest share of patronage in exchange for quiescence on reform (Warner, 1964, pp. 5–6). This failure of the "opposition" to oppose created the opportunity eagerly seized by a shifting Progressive coalition to promote multiple reform agendas.

Although these reformers were primarily native-born Protestants, in other ways they were a diverse lot. A study of the lives and careers of 91 Ohio Progressive leaders included a small number of foreign-born and several Catholics and Jews. Fewer than half were college educated; about a third were lawyers; 11 were businessmen; 8 were labor leaders; while others were journalists, ministers, and educators. Two-thirds were Democrats; the rest were Independent

Republicans and Theodore Roosevelt Progressives.[3] In the first decade of the twentieth century it was clear that a strong moral impulse inspired their activities—they sought not just political reform but "spiritual regeneration" (Warner, 1964, pp. 22–24).

The Republican-dominated Ohio legislature had prevented structural changes in government that might undermine the rule of Republican bosses in Cincinnati, Cleveland, Toledo, and Dayton. The 1900 census, which showed the state's population approaching an urban majority, frightened the legislature and then the state's voters into adopting a constitutional amendment in 1903 to guarantee rural control of the lower house. Called the Hanna Amendment, in honor of U.S. Senator Marcus A. Hanna, the Republican state leader who conceived and promoted it, this provision allotted at least one representative to each of the state's 88 counties, no matter how small its population (Barber, 1981, p. 257). Previously, apportionment of both houses had been based primarily on population, with the county as an integral unit of representation. In rural areas, whole counties could be combined to form districts; in urban areas, counties became multimember districts with members added to accommodate population growth after each decennial census (Ohio Const., 1851, art. 11).[4] While the Hanna Amendment's impact was relatively limited at first, it contained the seed of resistance to the changes sought by the Progressives. As in other states, this deliberate, turn-of-the-century malapportionment preserved a structural barrier to reform initiatives at the state level (Buenker, 1973, p. 14).

In reaction to this and other regressive measures, the state's Progressives pursued a reform agenda characterized by the slogan "antibossism." Virtually written by then-mayor Tom Johnson of Cleveland and adopted in 1905 by the Ohio Democratic Party as its platform, this urban revolt called for the initiative, referendum, and recall; home rule for cities; popular election of senators; women's suffrage; railroad rate regulation; municipal ownership of utilities or taxation of utilities at full value; protective labor legislation; and tax equity. Seeking "economic, not personal reform," Ohio's reform leaders tried to avoid the issue of prohibition, which they saw as a diversion from the "real" issue—"the struggle of the people against Privilege."[5] Their waffling on the issue of prohibition opened Ohio reformers to the charge of selling out to the bosses, but they kept prohibition off the state Democratic platform and added to their arguments for home rule the option for cities to remain wet when their surrounding counties went dry (Warner, 1964, pp. 70, 185–91).[6]

The popular appeal of the battle against privilege was demonstrated by the electorate in 1905. Ohio was a state in which being Republican was, according to Independent Republican Brand Whitlock of Toledo, "elemental . . . a synonym for patriotism, another name for the nation. . . . One became a Republican just as the Eskimo dons fur clothes" (1914, p. 27). Yet in this year of Progressive revolt, a Democratic governor was swept into office; Cleveland, Columbus, Dayton, and Cincinnati elected Democratic mayors; and Toledo elected Whitlock as mayor on an antimachine platform (Warner, 1964, pp. 160–65). The reform momentum continued to build for the rest of the decade, assisted by revelations of graft and fraud in the offices of the Republican state treasurer and auditor. Moreover, six legislators were convicted and four imprisoned for soliciting bribes in exchange for their votes against labor legislation and for a bill sought by the insurance industry. Although these six official miscreants were both Democratic and Republican, urban and rural, they nevertheless shared a common antipathy to the reform agenda (Warner, 1964, pp. 276–77).

Major reform victories followed. In 1910 not only was a Democratic governor elected, but also a Democratic majority of both houses of the legislature and 16 of Ohio's 21 members of Congress (Warner, 1964, pp. 258–60). This paved the way for the legislature to call for the election in 1911 of a constitutional convention to meet in 1912 for the purpose of removing state constitutional barriers that stood in the way of the Progressive agenda.[7] The delegates, equal to the number of representatives in the lower house of the assembly, were to be nominated by petition and elected by county on a nonpartisan ballot (102 O.L. 298, 1911, in Ohio, 1912, *Proceedings,* pp. 21–22). Progressives—Independents as well as reform Democrats and Republicans—proceeded to win a 75% majority of delegate seats at that convention.[8] Although they were unable to reach consensus on repeal of the Hanna Amendment, the delegates proposed a total of 42 amendments to the Ohio Constitution that furthered their goals. Among the 34 amendments subsequently adopted by the voters were those providing for initiative and referendum, which enabled the voters to circumvent the legislature by taking proposed laws and constitutional amendments to the voters for approval or rejection, nonpartisan election of state judges, the direct primary for nomination of state elected officials, permissive authority for minimum wage and maximum hour legislation, and home rule for cities (Warner, 1964, chap. 12).[9]

Under the home rule amendment, Ohio municipalities (defined to include both cities and villages) were at last permitted, if their voters so chose, to write their own governing charters and to exercise all powers of local self-government, including municipal ownership of public utilities (Ohio Const., 1851, art. 18, secs. 1, 3, 7, 1912). In 1913 Cleveland became the first Ohio city to adopt its own charter. Three other cities—Columbus, East Cleveland, and Lakewood—followed soon after with charters that, among other reforms rejected at the state level, permitted women to vote in municipal elections. The potential for local action under home rule charters was exhilarating.[10]

Between 1875 and 1974, 41 states would adopt home rule provisions in their constitutions. Peaks of home rule adoptions occurred in response to intense Progressive activity around 1912 and 1923–24 (Glendening and Reeves, 1984, pp. 138–39). In Ohio, as in many other states, the urban reformers now had the opening they had been seeking. Home rule not only made possible a broad array of structural reforms in the cities; its adoption signaled the growth of a civic culture that fostered change.

As home rule charters were written and adopted in the cities of Ohio and across the country, electoral systems were prime ingredients of reform. The large, ward-based councils of major cities still provided the building blocks of the bosses' power (Miller, 1968). That power— financed by contributions from legitimate businessmen who received franchises and other favors and by kickbacks from gamblers and vice-ring operators whose illegal activities were in turn protected—was used to govern cities through patronage practices. It was opposition to this structure of power that united the diverse forces of reform. The key structural proposals to undermine or destroy that power were the city manager plan and small councils to be elected at-large by proportional representation (PR/STV).

Citywide office, many reformers believed, would draw "better men" as council candidates, instead of the parochial ward politicians then holding sway in the large, single-member-district councils of the machine-dominated city. PR/STV elections would be conducted at-large, creating representative councils that could legitimately debate and determine policy. The city manager, responsible to this representative council, would bring expertise to bear on the problems of the city, with impartial administration replacing favoritism and graft. The application of scientific techniques to government operations would increase economy and efficiency in the public sphere (Haber, 1964; Svara, 1990).

Yet PR/STV was the one element of this institutional agenda that was omitted from the reform charters of most cities. The adoption of citywide plurality elections for either small, at-large councils or commissions resulted in homogeneous representation that lent credence to the notion that the reforms were elitist in purpose and character. However, contrary to some historians' stereotype of the structural reformers as men with mere ambition to shore up their declining power (e.g., Hofstadter, 1955; Mowry, 1951), many of these reformers were deeply interested in technical aspects of electoral systems, and especially in their consequences for the reality of representation.

Accounts of the period often stress the Progressive ideal that city government should be run like a business corporation, to be managed as economically and efficiently as possible. The city manager was said to be in effect the president of the corporation, the city council its board of directors, the voters its shareholders. The separation of politics from administration was seen by many Progressives as the key to scientific management, which would in turn insulate government from "both class prejudice and the ballot box" (Haber, 1964, p. 103).

By 1905, however, distinct paths of reform activity could be identified. While some reformers were concerned exclusively with issues of budgeting, the professionalization of administration, and social control, others stressed "economic justice, human opportunities, and rehabilitated democracy" (Wiebe, 1967, p. 176; see also Link, 1959; Huthmacher, 1962; Filene, 1970; Buenker, 1973). Among this latter group were historian Charles A. Beard of Columbia University and labor economist John R. Commons, a professor at the University of Wisconsin. In 1907 Commons flatly rejected the analogy between the city and a business corporation. The business corporation's sole purpose was to increase dividends, he said. By contrast, "the city is a compulsory corporation into which men are born."

> In a political corporation different classes of citizens have often different interests. Therefore all interests and classes should be represented in its administration. In what direction its sovereign powers shall be employed is a *political* question, involving justice and expediency as well as business. Shall taxes be levied to protect health, to extend free schools, to cleanse the slums, to buy water-works or street-car lines?— these are a few of the political questions which cities must consider. (Commons, 1907, pp. 200–201)

It is not surprising, therefore, that Commons, like Beard, became a leader of the proportional representation movement. With all interests represented on the local legislative body, he argued, differences would be negotiated and social cooperation would prevail in the making of policy. The executive's job would be to carry out that policy. In fact, the legislative supremacy implicit in the city manager plan magnified the importance of a representative council (Hoag and Hallett, 1926, pp. 193, 230).

Commons's vision of group representation illustrates a changing cluster of ideas supporting the use of PR/STV. He contrasted the "worry" of Mill's day—protecting representation of the educated minority—with new concerns: "PR is no longer needed to defend the rich against the poor. Its problem now is to defend the masses against the monopolists." Commons identified campaign contributions from corporate elites to unelected party leaders as the mechanism for monopoly control of the political process (Commons, 1907, p. 352).

He noted that the urban political machines won working-class votes, but then ignored their needs for schools, decent housing, parks, and playgrounds. He called for "social invention," promoted by the science of sociology, to advance human progress. But "science alone is inadequate," Commons argued. Only by having all interests represented in a city's council could human feelings and needs be taken into account in the making of municipal policy. Social invention could then "proceed, not by the coercive arm of the state, but by mutual concession" (Commons, 1907, pp. 224–30).

Commons was careful to distinguish this kind of representation from the rigid rule by special interests that he saw as the vice of machine control. Free nomination, by which he meant nomination by petition, and free voting, or choosing individual representatives unfettered by small-unit boundaries, acknowledged the fluidity of people's real interests (Commons, 1907, pp. 361–62). As the appeal of PR was expounded in journals and newspapers, broader representational goals for PR were expressed, expanding from class to "political, racial, religious, ethnic, and vocational groups and classes" the need for self-representation (Hatton, 1915; R. A. Burnham, 1992, pp. 205–6).

Prevailing accounts of Progressive-inspired electoral reform present a polarity between the bosses' practical dependence on plurality/single-member district (ward) elections, on the one hand, and the reformers' advocacy of plurality/at-large elections, on the other. The PR debate, however, shows that PR advocates among the reformers rejected both of these polar alternatives. In fact, PR was seen as drawing together representational qualities from each type of system. PR elections would be held citywide, freeing voters from geographical limitations on choice. If large, multimember districts were preferred, candidates could run in districts other than their place of residence and appeal to voters in districts of their choosing. At the same time, because constituencies within this larger framework would be voluntary, voters could select their personal representative by whatever characteristics were important to them. In this way, the mechanics of PR were seen by these Progressives to meld the advantages of citywide election promoted by advocates of the plurality/at-large system and the personal relationship believed inherent in the plurality/single-member district (ward) system.

Clarence Hoag, secretary of the P.R. League, found it a "strange belief" among many Progressives that lines of division among voters would vanish if elections were held by plurality/at-large voting. Of course all should work for the "good of the city," he wrote, but "*what is* for the good of the city" could not be imposed by one group. "All shades of opinion" should be represented in council, he argued, to "foster mutual understanding and cooperation" (Hoag, 1913, pp. 80–81).

The accuracy with which the PR/STV system could translate votes from the electorate into seats in a legislative body was a key attraction, not only to Commons and Augustus R. Hatton but also to those Progressives who placed a higher value on scientific method. The quantitative details of the count, the complexity of which would become the focus of later attacks on PR systems, were clear enough to its advocates. Proportional representation thus provided a significant conceptual linkage between the ideas of the technical and professional elites of the Progressive movement and those of their more participatory and populist allies. In the first instance, PR/STV elections were believed to provide a scientifically demonstrable, nonpartisan method of selecting the best council; at the same time social and cultural pluralism could be accommodated in governmental decision making, because minorities (identified by whatever characteristics were important to them) would be represented in proportion to their actual strength in the voting population.

The Organized Campaign for PR

Although by 1910 PR was only one of the tools Progressive reformers sought to use in addressing the ills of the American city, it had its own history as well, deriving from the nineteenth-century debate over electoral reform, discussed above. It was in this context that the Proportional Representation League of the United States was founded in 1893, when Progressivism had not yet coalesced as a movement. The league was modeled on the British Proportional Representation Society, which had been founded in 1884 to conduct an educational campaign on behalf of PR/STV elections for the British Parliament. British reformers believed that John Stuart Mill's bill for PR/STV elections had failed to pass because of inadequate understanding of the problem of minority representation in a plurality election system.

Although British proportionalists had not yet succeeded in winning the minds of British lawmakers, American advocates adopted their educational approach. The Proportional Representation Congress was called in conjunction with the Chicago World's Fair in August 1893. Participants included Catherine Helen Spence of Australia, John Commons, W. D. McCrackan, William H. Gove, a Massachusetts legislator who had devised a form of transferable vote known as the "Schedule System," and Alfred Cridge—a friend of Senator Charles R. Buckalew of Pennsylvania—who moved to California and spent the rest of his life working for electoral reform (Hoag and Hallett, 1926, pp. 55, 186). Out of this congress grew the organization that would provide leadership to the electoral reform movement in the United States for almost four decades. With William Dudley Foulke of Indiana as president and Stoughton Cooley of California as secretary, the league attempted to reach consensus on the one best form of PR.

The term "proportional representation" was used loosely in the United States as well as in Britain to apply to limited voting (LV), cumulative voting (CV), and PR/STV; experiments with all three voting systems were encouraged. In 1892, Ohio Democratic Representative Tom Johnson, later reform mayor of Cleveland, had introduced a bill in the U.S. House of Representatives to provide for election of its members by the "free list system," a modified PR/STV. The league agreed to back Johnson's bill but welcomed other proportional proposals as well. Unity in support of a single system of voting was difficult to achieve (Commons, 1907, pp. 114–15; Hoag and Hallett, 1926, p. 187).

Consensus on a general purpose was achieved:

> to promote reform of legislative assemblies, by abandoning the present system of electing single representatives on a majority or plurality vote in limited territorial districts, and by substituting the following provisions:
>
> (1) That all representatives be elected 'at-large,' on a general ticket either without district divisions or in districts as large as practicable.
>
> (2) That the election be in such form that the several parties or political groups shall secure representation in proportion to the respective number of votes cast by each. (Tyson, 1908a, p. 38)

Following the British model, American "proportionalists," as they called themselves, determined the need for staff and a publication. The *Proportional Representation Review (PRR)*, edited by Cooley, was launched in 1893 to reach the public about the need for some form of proportional representation. After three years of publication, funds ran out and the quarterly ceased to appear. However, interest persisted, and meetings of the league followed in Buffalo (1899) and Detroit (1901). The presence at these meetings of Robert Tyson of Toronto, who conducted sample PR/STV elections for participants, resulted in a growing consensus in favor of this "perfect" strategy for representation. One of many Canadians involved in the activities of the P.R. League, Tyson edited and published the *PRR*, from 1901 until 1913, as a department of various other publications, and he served as secretary of the league until 1909. He was succeeded as secretary for two years by William Hoag of Boston, a former member of the Massachusetts legislature, and then by Hoag's brother Clarence, a professor at the University of Pennsylvania. ("It was pretty academic then," remarked Richard S. Childs, a fellow activist and chronicler of the movement). The gathering steam of twentieth-century municipal reform enabled Clarence Hoag to reposition *PRR* as an independent publication, which it remained from 1913 until 1932 (Hoag and Hallett, 1926, pp. 187–88; Childs, 1952, p. 242).

Foulke, also president of the National Municipal League, organized a governing council that included such eminent Americans as historian Charles A. Beard; Jane Addams, founder of Hull House; the scientist Charles P. Steinmetz; Charles Frederick Adams, great grandson of a U.S. president; Margaret Dreier Robins of the Women's Trade Union League; Richard S. Childs, founder and secretary of the National Short Ballot Organization; Charles W. Eliot, president emeritus of Harvard University; and Professors Felix Adler of Columbia University and Jeremiah W. Jenks of New York University.

From the beginning, the P.R. League was committed to enlarging participation in political life for "those considerable classes of voters, like farmers, mechanics and laboring men" who were underrepresented in Congress and the state legislatures (*PRR*, 1894, 1:105). In the early years its focus was on state and national elections. Foulke advocated the use of the party list system for state legislative and congressional elections (Foulke, 1915, pp. 76–77). The P.R. League also advocated proportional division of the electoral vote for president, although the league conceded that retention of senatorial electors in its plan would somewhat diminish the proportionality of the outcome (proposed amendment, art. 18; *Equity,* 1914, 16.1:43−47; 1917, 19.1:42−43).

With the formation of the League of Nations after World War I, the P.R. League would expand its advocacy to the international level. Not only should the members of the League of Nations guarantee "fair and true representation of all elements" in their own parliaments, but the delegates themselves should be chosen by proportional election (by member parliaments), so that minorities within nations could combine with each other at League of Nations meetings. The purpose of PR elections was to create capacity in the new international body to "think internationally" about the issues confronting it (Hoag, 1919, p. 74).

The impetus for reform was frequently recharged by examples of distorted representation resulting from plurality elections. One such outcome occurred in the 1906 contest for the 60-seat Oregon state House of Representatives: 59 Republicans and one Democrat were elected. Voters, however, had divided their choices among candidates of four parties as follows: 57% Republican, 32% Democratic, 7% Socialist and 5% Prohibitionist (Tyson, 1908b). With a Republican majority in all but one district, the 44% non-Republican minorities had won less than 2% of the representation. Proportionalists conducted a statewide campaign for PR to correct the "defective electoral machinery," namely plurality voting, that could produce such a result. This drive culminated in the 1908 passage of an initiative permitting PR/STV elections in Oregon's multimember legislative districts where elections were conducted at large. However, in subsequent years this permissive authority was not used; four efforts to adopt the reform, one in the legislature and three by initiative, were defeated (Hoag and Hallett, 1926, pp. 188−89).

A contemporary economist and statistician, N. I. Stone, urged the state-by-state adoption of proportional representation elections for congressional delegations, to be chosen "within the broad boundaries of the State, or large natural divisions of the State," in order to allow both majority and minority parties their fair share of seats in Congress. Although he would start with New York ("Let the Empire State blaze the way for a reform which will be certain to sweep the country"), he argued that PR's greatest impact would be felt in the South where it could break up the "solid South." Political and economic issues would replace sectionalism in a "more wholesome division of the electorate." Stone showed how control of Congress had swung back and forth between Republicans and Democrats from 1888 to 1912, owing to marginal changes in the total vote, creating instability on such issues as tariff policy, his special area of expertise. PR, he argued, would in contrast allow for more continuity in policy development (Stone, 1915, pp. 136–37, 141–43).

Still, no adoptions occurred in the deeply majoritarian American system for almost two decades after the founding of the league, and efforts shifted to local elections. In 1912 C. G. Hoag persuaded the organization to target city council elections as a more realistic goal than elections for state and national legislative bodies. Hoag believed that small-scale demonstrations of PR's merits were necessary if broader acceptance were to be achieved (Hoag and Hallett, 1926, p. 188). Chester C. Maxey, a Western Reserve University political science professor and P.R. League activist, identified a secondary but tactical purpose in shifting the PR campaign to the municipal level. The city manager plan, he argued, was a more popular structural reform; to link the PR electoral system to this new mode of administration would facilitate its acceptance in the United States (Maxey, 1924, p. 5; Hermens, 1941, p. 360).

Dayton, Ohio, where business leaders were promoting a new charter to "clean up" their city, was a promising venue for reform. In 1913 a charter commission had been elected that was committed to consideration of the city manager plan. Progressives were joined by the local Socialist Party in petitioning the commission to propose PR/STV city council elections as a critical institutional partner to complement professional administration. Only PR elections, they argued, would ensure the fully representative council needed to make policy that the city manager would be obliged to carry out. This rationale was not persuasive in Dayton, but it was widely discussed in reform circles. Dayton subsequently became the first city in Ohio and the first large city in the country to adopt the city manager plan, but the policy-making body that was adopted was a commission, elected by plurality/at-large (Warner, 1964, pp. 450–51). J. L. Conger, a friend of PR, lamented a few years later: "To those of us who try to see in the city manager the ideal form of city administration none can fail to see that the fundamental weakness in the Dayton scheme as at present constituted is the non-representative character of the commission, which must stand between the city manager and public opinion" (1920, p. 59).

This linkage between PR elections and the city manager plan was persuasive to the P.R. League's strong partner in reform efforts, the National Municipal League (NML), as well. Founded in 1894 by Progressives to advance a broad "good government" agenda at the state and local levels, the NML's principal concern was cities. State control of municipal affairs, however, forced it to address both state and local issues. Inefficiency and corruption were seen as the overwhelming ills of American cities; the party bosses were the villains. The NML's agenda to attack these ills, from its founding to 1914, featured nonpartisan elections and the short ballot. In 1914 the NML endorsed both the election of city councils at-large by PR/STV and the city manager plan, and it stressed the linkage between them. The NML promoted the P.R. League's theory that enhancing efficiency in municipal government by assigning the executive function to a trained expert called for a more representative council to make municipal policy. In its deliberations all important elements of the city should be heard.[11]

By 1921 the NML's commitment to PR/STV had also grown to encompass the state level. The *Model State Constitution* published by the NML in that year recommended a single-house legislature, to be elected by PR/STV from districts electing from three to seven members (Hoag and Hallett, 1926, p. 123).[12] The unicameral principle was considered derivative of the kind of representation produced under PR/STV. "When one legislative body is made really representative, why try to check it with another?" asked Hallett (1940, p. 167). By 1930 the NML sought to encourage these structural reforms at the county level and endorsed adoption of a state law that would explicitly permit counties to adopt a county manager plan with a county council to be elected at-large by PR/STV (Cassella, 1990, p. 322). For the next two decades the NML circulated its recommended county charter, finally published in 1956, incorporating these features (NML, 1956, *Model County Charter*).[13]

During the years in which the NML was developing its broader reform agenda, the P.R. League pursued its own campaign for electoral system reform. For two decades, from 1913 to 1932, its staff traveled the country to testify, exhort, write PR charter provisions, provide expert advice on the conduct of PR elections, and defend existing PR systems under attack in repeal referenda. The addition of a field secretary in 1917, Walter J. Millard, and an assistant secretary in 1919, George H. Hallett Jr., to the P.R. League staff expanded the capacity of the organization. Hallett became the executive secretary in 1926 (Hoag and Hallett, 1926, p. 194). By this time other renowned reformers had joined its council, including historian Arthur N. Holcombe of Harvard and economist Paul H. Douglas of the University of Chicago, journalist Walter Lippmann, suffragists Carrie Chapman Catt and Belle Sherwin, the first and second presidents of the National League of Women

"For gentlemen must live!" By Hal Donahey. *Cleveland Plain Dealer*, 8 August 1925, p. 1

Voters, and U.S. Senators George W. Norris of Nebraska, Robert L. Owen of Oklahoma, and George Wharton Pepper of Pennsylvania.

The P.R. League and the NML cooperated in electoral reform efforts, leading Ferdinand Hermens, an opponent of PR who taught at Notre Dame University, to complain that "the great authority of the official reform movement in this country has been behind PR" (1941, p. 360).

"Trying to put one over on us!" By Hal Donahey. *Cleveland Plain Dealer,* 10 August 1925, p. 1

The Progressive Party, organized in 1912 to capture national power from the old parties, adopted in its platform a section entitled "The Rule of the People," endorsing women's suffrage, the short ballot, and the initiative, referendum, and recall. Proportional representation was not listed, although proportionalists were well represented among the organizers. Jane Addams, for example, social feminist, founder of Hull

House in Chicago, and early member of the P.R. League's advisory council, played a leading role in the organization of the party and seconded the nomination of Theodore Roosevelt at the party's national convention (Flexner, 1975, pp. 266, 271).

The Progressive attack on the ills of industrial capitalism drew allies on particular issues from the ranks of old Populists and new Socialists. The high tide of Socialist electoral success in the United States was reached in 1912, by which time over a thousand Socialists had been elected to public office in the United States. Most held local office, but in 1910 Socialist Victor Berger was elected to Congress from a Wisconsin district, and in 1912 Eugene V. Debs won six percent of the vote for president on the Socialist ticket (Draper, 1957, pp. 41–42). The Socialist Party endorsed both direct legislation (the initiative, referendum, and recall) and "proportional representation nationally as well as locally" (K. H. Porter, 1924, pp. 336, 367).

In 1913 Carl D. Thompson, head of the information bureau of the national Socialist Party in Chicago, published an article in the *National Municipal Review* explaining the party's position on charter reform. Guided by the "vital and necessary principles" of good city government, "democracy and efficiency," he wrote, certain basic elements were needed: home rule, direct legislation, proportional representation elections, and the city manager plan. The professional administrator was endorsed as a means of effectively carrying out the "steadily increasing extension of the functions of municipal government" advocated by Socialists (C. D. Thompson, 1913, p. 426). Two important caveats, however, limited these forthright endorsements of the Progressive municipal reform agenda. The recall, an important feature of direct legislation, would have to "operate against the whole group and not against a single councilman," in order to protect the minorities elected by PR from arbitrary recall by the majority. Furthermore, the PR ballot should identify the candidates' parties in order to enable voters to relate their choices to the policies they wanted adopted (C. D. Thompson, 1913, pp. 419, 421–23).

This attack on nonpartisanship led C. G. Hoag and Robert Tyson to concede that "it may be necessary where the Socialists are strong for those who would prefer the Hare system to accept instead . . . a party-list system." Ultimately, however, Hoag and Tyson hoped that "the Socialists would come to realize that the Hare system without party names is not only fair to all parties, but also fair to all factions of any one party" (*Equity,* Oct. 1913, 15.4:231–32).

Although many Socialists and later Communists rejected the reformist Progressive agenda as backward and irrelevant, such "fusion" attempts at cooperation were frequent. During World War I, when Socialist members of city councils and school boards, as in Cleveland, were paying the price of expulsion for their opposition to the war, pro-war Socialists established a separate organization, the Social Democratic League of America. In 1917, drawing together activists from the ranks of Progressives, prohibitionists, and woman suffragists, the group anticipated developing a new political party. Its platform featured proportional representation for state and federal legislative elections, along with women's suffrage, prohibition, direct legislation, the short ballot, public ownership of railroads and public utilities, old age pensions, and the abolition of child labor. Charles A. Beard and Frederic Howe were among the PR advocates on the platform-writing committee. To be called the National Party, this coalition did not survive beyond its organizational stage (*Equity,* July 1917, 19.3:206; Shannon, 1955, p. 103).

More tenacious was the post–World War I Conference for Progressive Political Action (CPPA), pulled together by leaders of the railroad brotherhoods and including the Socialist Party (Communists were rigorously excluded), the Farmer-Labor Party, the Non-Partisan League, and church groups such as the Methodist Federation of Social Service, the Church League for Industrial Democracy, and the National Catholic Welfare Council. The Socialist Party was committed to formation of a third party like the British Labour Party, but labor leaders resisted formation of a new party. Conferences, aimed toward building an electoral coalition if not a party, were held in Chicago (Feb. 1922), Cleveland (Dec. 1922), and St. Louis (Feb. 1924). A CPPA convention, held in Cleveland on 4 July 1924, nominated Robert M. La Follette as an Independent candidate for President. The CPPA served as an alliance of his supporters, who could not form a party but called themselves "Progressives" throughout the campaign. Their platform demanded such electoral reform as the direct nomination and election of the president and national direct legislation, but not proportional representation. Municipal PR campaigns, however, such as the successful one in Cincinnati that year, were conducted out of local CPPA offices. The Socialist Party accepted La Follette as its presidential candidate and did not publish a separate platform (K. H. Porter, 1924, pp. 516–22). LaFollette's loss in the November election brought to an end, at least for the time being, the "Socialist experiment in cooperating with nonsocialist progressives" (Shannon, 1955, p. 181).

After 1920, with their suffrage battle won, the more political of the women among the suffragists joined the effort to adopt the PR/STV electoral system. Like the broad coalition of Progressives of which they were a part, feminists themselves had diverse goals. Some had pursued political rights, especially the right to vote, while others battled for social and economic goals, such as child labor laws, mothers' pensions, and social justice. In the late stages of the battle for suffrage, women had used traditional stereotypes to justify the vote, such as women's special role in protecting the home and defending the welfare of children. In part, this revealed the conservative character of the women themselves; but it was also a strategic move, designed to reassure conservative men that women's suffrage posed no threat (Cooley, 1913). In this spirit Jane Addams explained women's support of the city manager plan and PR/STV: "City housekeeping has failed partly because women, the traditional housekeepers, have not been consulted as to its multiform activities" (Addams, 1960, p. 115).

PR/STV was promising to reform-oriented women because of their independence of parties. Nomination by petition, the nonpartisan ballot, and the single transferable vote were all features that would facilitate the election of Independents. Because of the influential role that political machines had played in delaying women's suffrage, feminists decried the influence of parties in political life and supported reforms to undermine the bosses' power. They also understood that with PR/STV, women could form "voluntary constituencies" in multimember districts or at-large to elect women to municipal office.

Moreover, electoral reform was seen as instrumental in that the "better" councils elected by PR could implement substantive reforms in the fields of housing, public health and welfare, cleaner air, and city planning. The National League of Women Voters and local leagues across the country were in the forefront of municipal reform battles, along with club women who in many cities had been organized since the late nineteenth century to improve their communities (Lemons, 1973, chap. 4; Chafe, 1972, pp. 12–18).

Women in the settlement house movement also entered the fray on behalf of PR. From the 1890s, settlement house activities had attracted well-educated women who, like many of their male counterparts in the Progressive movement, understood the economic roots of the evil conditions of life in cities and saw the immigrant as "the victim of bad conditions" (Higham, 1955, p. 117). Their central commitment was to live in the settlement houses among the immigrants, not apart from the people they hoped to help. These women were guided by an appreciation of the diverse ethnic cultures they came to know in crowded urban neighborhoods. Rejecting the prevailing "melting pot" theory of

Americanization, they promoted the validity of cultural "contributions," which the immigrants brought from their previous lives, as enrichments of the American culture (Addams, in Warner, 1971, pp. 23–25; Higham, 1955, pp. 120–22; Grabowski, 1986, pp. 32–33). These ideas were congruent with the theory of proportional representation in the political sphere.

Jane Addams of Hull House and Lillian Wald, founder of the Henry Street Settlement in New York City, tried to bridge the cultural and political gap between suffrage advocates and working women, especially immigrant workers living in the slums, where the urban machines were most strongly rooted. In 1903 these social workers joined women trade union organizers to create the National Women's Trade Union League (NWTUL) "to help industrial women help themselves through the trade union movement." Its primary efforts were directed toward organizing women into trade unions; once organized, these new unions were "turned over" to the American Federation of Labor. To protect unorganized women, the NWTUL worked for passage of protective labor legislation to improve conditions of work, to establish maximum hours and minimum wages for women, and to prohibit child labor (Lemons, 1973, p. 142). Yet this work was constantly rendered ineffectual by women's political powerlessness. Thus suffrage became an important tactical goal for these women who at an earlier stage had seen the vote and "equal rights" as a middle-class frill. Endorsing women's suffrage in 1907, NWTUL leaders concluded not only that working women should vote but also, explicitly, that working women should *represent* themselves. It was only a small step from this belief to the endorsement of PR. Through direct political representation, these women could improve their conditions of life and become integrated into the community (Dreier, 1950; Flexner, 1975, chap. 18; Dye, 1980, pp. 122–24).

Little such collaborative activity was attempted to bring African-American women into the struggle for municipal reform. The vast majority of African Americans were at the bottom of the economic heap and had more pressing concerns. In both the North and South, however, there were Colored Women's Clubs, organized in the late nineteenth century to improve life conditions of their race and "of *all* humanity," whose members shared many of the reformers' values. In 1896 two national federations of local and state clubs with an estimated 300,000 members joined to form the National Association of Colored Women (NACW) with Mary Church Terrell as president. Women's suffrage was one of its goals, and its suffrage department conducted "training classes" on the Constitution to prepare its members for civic responsibilities (Lerner, 1992, pp. 440–46).

These women might have been recruited for the causes of municipal reform, but their social and organizational segregation was pervasive. White suffragists rejected alliances with these "colored" women's groups for the "greater" goal of winning the support of southern senators for a federal suffrage amendment. The constitutional requirement of a two-thirds vote to propose an amendment, impossible without southern backing, shaped their strategy and submerged virtually every other consideration (Flexner, 1975, p. 190).

In spite of this exclusionary policy of the suffragists, important African-American leaders endorsed women's suffrage—not only Mary Church Terrell, but also Dr. W. E. B. DuBois and Ida Wells-Barnett—with a view to the long-range importance of expansion of the suffrage for African Americans as well (Flexner, 1975, pp. 318, 374 n. 22). Still, few interracial collaborations were established in the trenches of municipal reform. Not least important in explaining the racial cleavage afflicting electoral reform efforts was the role of the urban boss in meeting the daily needs of African-American constituents. DuBois had noted this before the turn of the century:

> The growth of a higher political morality among Negroes is to-day hindered by their paradoxical position. Suppose the Municipal League or the Woman's Schoolboard movement, or some other reform is brought before the better class of Negroes today; they will nearly all agree that city politics are notoriously corrupt, that honest women should replace ward heelers on school boards, and the like. But can they vote for such movements? Most of them will say No; for to do so will throw many worthy Negroes out of employment: these very reformers who want votes for specific reforms, will not themselves work beside Negroes, or admit them to positions in their stores or offices, or lend them friendly aid in trouble. Moreover Negroes are proud of their councilmen and policemen. What if some of these positions of honor and respectability have been gained by shady 'politics'—shall they be nicer in these matters than the mass of the whites? Shall they surrender these tangible evidences of the rise of their race to forward the good-hearted but hardly imperative demands of a crowd of women? Especially, too, of women who did not apparently know there were any Negroes on earth until they wanted their votes? Such logic may be faulty, but it is convincing to the mass of Negro voters. And cause after cause may gain their respectful attention and even applause, but when election-day comes, the "machine" gets their votes. ([1899] 1967, pp. 383–84)

The reform movement's very reason for being was to destroy the power of those political organizations that effectively served the most downtrodden of the African-American communities of Progressive Era cities. Instead of addressing their needs themselves, civic association reformers, both women and men, criticized African-American voters for their "blind" partisan loyalty.

American Adoptions of PR/STV

PR/STV elections ranked high on the agenda of Ohio's Progressives, sharing such local priorities as the city manager plan, the municipal initiative, referendum and recall, the eight-hour day for city workers, and municipal ownership of utilities. As in the earlier battle for home rule in Ohio, Independent Democrats and Republicans affiliated with the state's Progressive Party were leaders in the campaign for electoral reform. Whitlock and Gladden continued to travel and exhort on behalf of the Progressive agenda. They were joined in the fray by Democratic attorneys Florence Allen and Susan Rebhan of Cleveland, and by populist minister Herbert Bigelow and Democratic attorney Edward Alexander of Cincinnati, who held out successfully for PR elections in exchange for supporting a small at-large council for their city. Antimachine Republican leaders, such as attorney Murray Seasongood, later mayor of Cincinnati, Agnes Hilton, and Marietta Tawney of Cincinnati, campaigned both in their respective cities and in national forums for the adoption of PR/STV.

Ohio is cited as "a particular arena of struggle [where] the League of Women Voters was in the center of nearly every effort and continued when others surrendered" (Abbott, 1949, pp. 107–19; Lemons, 1973, p. 125). Among women's clubs nationally, the Women's City Club of Cleveland and the Woman's City Club of Cincinnati were known for their skill in organizing workers to canvass for votes on behalf of new charters embodying the city manager plan and PR/STV (Beard, 1915, p. 320; Kornbluh, 1986, p. 27). With these local activists as known resources, it is not surprising that the national P.R. League would pour its resources into winning over voters in Ohio.

Ashtabula was just one of many Ohio cities visited by Clarence Hoag in the wake of the adoption of home rule, but there he met a sympathetic local labor leader, William E. Boynton, a railroad engineer and former city council president who invited him to return for further conversations with other leaders and eventually an appearance before the city charter commission. The seed planted by Hoag would grow by 1914 into the adoption of a new charter with the city manager plan, and by 1915 into the first American adoption of PR/STV (Hoag and Hallett, 1926, p. 193).

Adoptions followed in Boulder (1917), Kalamazoo (1918), and Sacramento and West Hartford (1921). Because these were relatively small cities, there was jubilation in the movement when Cleveland adopted PR/STV elections with its new charter in 1921. Not only was Cleveland the largest city yet to try this electoral system, it was ethnically and religiously the most diverse—"polyglot," in the reformers' terms. With favorable press emanating from Cleveland and intense intercity campaigning by reformers in Ohio, Cincinnati (1925), Hamilton (1926), and Toledo (1935) also adopted PR/STV charters, as did nearby Wheeling, West Virginia (1935).

In 1936, over the strenuous opposition of the Tammany organization, which had a virtual monopoly on council, the nation's largest city adopted PR/STV. New York City was alone in adopting this electoral system without the usual corollary feature of a city manager plan. The new charter and a separate issue providing for PR/STV council elections carried all boroughs except Staten Island. Here in the 1930s the reform spirit, with its interest in changing political arrangements, persisted at the local level and blended into the national revival of the spirit of Progressivism in the New Deal.

It must have been more than coincidence that PR and a new city charter were adopted by the voters of New York City on the same ballot with their overwhelming reelection of Franklin D. Roosevelt for his second term as president. In the 1936 campaign, the Democratic city organization warmly supported Roosevelt and stridently opposed both PR/STV and the new charter. Proportional representation had been presented to the voters as a separate issue, lest it drag the charter down to defeat, but the voters swept both local innovations to success along with their presidential preference (Hallett, 1940, p. 147).

Efforts to implement proportional voting were organized in other large cities, but these efforts were obstructed by powerful party organizations, operating in the legislature or the courts, where the judges were usually elected or appointed through partisan channels. As a center of PR activism on the West Coast, Los Angeles had been the first major city to vote on a PR charter amendment. On 24 March 1913 the amendment lost by a narrow margin (*Equity,* 1913, 15.2:137). The issue of fair representation was kept alive for at least a decade in Los Angeles. It was during renewed debate over adoption of PR in 1922 that the state supreme court upheld lower court rulings that PR (adopted in Sacramento) violated the state constitution (*PRR,* 1931, 3rd ser., p. 30; *People ex rel. Devine v. Elkus,* 1922).

Twice during the 1930s, the Pennsylvania legislature refused to grant the city of Philadelphia a PR/city manager charter, sought by its citizens and even recommended in the second instance by a charter commission appointed by the governor. In Massachusetts, where the legislature passed an act in 1937 to permit PR/STV elections for both city and local school board officials, legislators from Boston forced the exclusion of their city from coverage as the price of passage (*NMR,* Oct. 1938, p. 513; Hallett, 1940, p. 165). Between 1938 and 1948, 11 more small cities joined the PR/STV roster, seven of these in Massachusetts. These cities were Yonkers and Long Beach, New York; Coos Bay, Oregon; Hopkins, Minnesota; and Cambridge, Lowell, Worcester, Medford, Quincy, Revere, and Saugus, Massachusetts (Childs, 1952, p. 250).

Like the National Municipal League, the P.R. League kept its collective eye on future opportunities for PR/STV at the state and national levels. In this spirit, committed advocates within the P.R. League and the NML continued to campaign for election by PR/STV of county councils, state legislatures, the U.S. House of Representatives and even presidential electors (Hallett, 1940, pp. 166–76).

During the period of American adoptions, PR/STV was spreading in the English-speaking world as well. The system was adopted not only for the university representatives to the British House of Commons, but also for some municipal (council) or provincial (legislative) elections in Canada, Australia, New Zealand, South Africa, India, and Malta (Hoag and Hallett, 1926, pp. 223–34, 253–54; Hallett, 1940, pp. 158–60; O'Leary, 1979, p. 5).

Ireland, however, became the seat of the most thorough and long-lasting use of PR/STV. The PR Society of Ireland, founded in 1911, was well-organized and militant, urging PR/STV elections in the south to facilitate the representation of Unionists, a Protestant minority, and in the north to promote eventual unity through representation of Ulster's Catholic minority. The Government of Ireland Act of 1920 incorporated these provisions. The subsequent 1923 Irish Free State Constitution for the southern 26 counties retained the PR/STV system, which has been used for election of the Dail ever since. Municipal, school board, county, and special district elections have also been conducted by PR/STV throughout the Irish Free State (now Ireland). The six northern counties, however, reverted to plurality elections after a mere four years of PR/STV. The resulting exclusion of the

Catholic minority from power in Ulster is believed to have contributed to the increasingly violent polarization of that society (O'Leary, 1979, chap. 3).

The Precarious Existence of PR Elections

In the United States, the P.R. League was struck by declining financial support during the Great Depression. Lack of funds forced the P.R. League to merge into the NML in 1932, and its continuing efforts were conducted by volunteers.[14] Still, the innovation continued to spread. By 1964 about 160 PR/STV elections had been held in the United States, including 37 school board elections in Massachusetts cities.

In a few cities, however, where PR had been in use for a decade or more, attempts to repeal the electoral system overlapped with continuing adoptions elsewhere. In 1929 Ashtabula, the first city to adopt PR/STV, became the first to repeal it. Forty-nine repeal issues were placed on the ballots of American PR/STV cities between 1920 and 1961, with some cities, such as those in Ohio, experiencing repeated referenda. Repeal attempts were ultimately successful in 21 cities, leaving Cambridge, Massachusetts, the only American city continuing its adherence to the practice (Childs, 1965, p. 67).

The attack on PR voting was not always launched by popular vote. State legislatures and state courts were also battlefields, where political party leaders who felt threatened could act without the risk or expense of a referendum. Childs would write: "Other reforms have a way of staying put—cities hardly ever go back on nonpartisan elections or council-manager charters or the merit system in the civil service or shortened ballots. But P.R. greatly irritates the politicians and they come back at it unceasingly" (1952, p. 244). The Republican-controlled Connecticut legislature was hostile to PR because of the 1921 results of the first and, as it turned out, only PR election conducted in West Hartford, a strongly Republican suburb. The Republican organization lost its majority on the city council to Independent Republicans. At that time Bridgeport and other Connecticut cities were considering adoption of PR as well. In 1923 the legislature acted quickly to outlaw "preferential or so-called 'proportional' ballot[s] . . . in any election, any charter provision or municipal ordinance of any town, city or borough" in the state (Hoag and Hallett, 1926, p. 208). Later the Massachusetts legislature attempted a similar move. In 1947 alone, five Massachusetts cities adopted PR/STV in addition to the earlier adoptions in Cambridge and Lowell, and several other cities in the state were considering joining what seemed to be a trend. The established political parties grew alarmed and instituted legislative action to outlaw PR. Officials in the seven Massachusetts PR cities and many of their constituents apparently rose up in protest, forcing the legislature into a partial retreat. In 1950 any *further* adoptions of PR in the state were prohibited by law (Childs, 1952, p. 249).

The state courts became an arena for challenges to PR. In Kalamazoo, where PR was adopted in 1918, Michigan party leaders who had been displaced in PR elections joined business leaders who had been adversely affected by tax reforms enacted by the first PR council to challenge the PR system in state court. In 1920 the Michigan Supreme Court overturned the electoral system, finding it a violation of the state constitution's guarantee that voters had a right to vote "at any election." Each candidate's race in an at-large election was interpreted to be a separate election. Therefore, in a multicandidate election, a PR/STV ballot that was ultimately counted for one candidate only was held to prevent the exercise of full voting rights.[15]

This interpretation was repeated two years later in the California courts. The PR/STV section of the Sacramento charter, adopted in 1920, was invalidated on the same grounds, based on a provision in the California Constitution, similar to Michigan's, that guaranteed the right to vote "at all elections."[16] In both states, the judges had ties to their respective Republican party organizations.

In 1923, however, in cases brought to challenge Cleveland's adoption of PR/STV, the Ohio Supreme Court upheld its validity under both the state and federal constitutions.[17] Judge Florence Allen, author of the opinions in the Ohio cases, was an Independent Democrat who, before election to the court, had been active in organizations that favored proportional representation and other Progressive reforms (Tuve, 1984, pp. 92–93). In the first Ohio case, the plaintiff claimed that his state right to vote "at all elections" was violated by a system that allowed a ballot in a multimember district to count for only one council member. Rejecting this claim, Judge Allen wrote: "The Hare System of Proportional Representation does not violate the Ohio constitution, for the elector is not prevented from voting *at any election*. He is entitled to vote at every municipal election, even though his vote may be effective in the election of fewer than the full number of candidates, and he has exactly the same voting power and right as every other elector" (*Reutener v. Cleveland,* 1923, at 137).

The second Ohio case (*Hile v. Cleveland,* 1923) raised federal constitutional issues. George D. Hile, a taxpayer, attempted to equate

Judge Florence E. Allen, 1926.
Courtesy of *The Cleveland Press*
Collection of the Cleveland State
University Archives

plurality voting with the republican form of government guaranteed in Article 4 of the U.S. Constitution. PR/STV, he argued, was not a "republican" mode of election. He also claimed that his equal protection of the laws under the Fourteenth Amendment was violated by his subjection to a form of voting not imposed on citizens of other communities in Ohio. Both arguments were rejected. Judge Allen wrote for the court that the "republican form" was a political, not a judicial, question. If, however, republican form were to be defined as by Lincoln, "of the people, for the people and by the people," Cleveland's charter could not be attacked on this ground, since it "establishes a form of government by express vote of the people, in which the people are by vote to control the government for their own purposes" (*Hile*, at 151). Furthermore, the charter provision could not violate the federal equal protection of the laws, since it applied equally to every citizen of Cleveland. The Fourteenth Amendment did not require every municipality of the state to have the same electoral provisions (*Hile*, at 152–53). In 1924 the U.S. Supreme Court declined to review the Cleveland case (*Hile,* writ of error dismissed, 266 U.S. 582).

A final state constitutional challenge to PR/STV was brought in New York City, where the plaintiff's argument was similar to that of the first Ohio case. There, as in Ohio, the court found no violation of the state right to vote.[18]

The municipal referendum, however, itself a Progressive reform tool to expand popular participation in government, became a formidable weapon in the hands of PR's opponents. No single factor adequately explains the wave of repeals by popular vote. Opponents' contemporary accounts attributed the losses to the complexity of the PR/STV count and its time-consuming character; proponents blamed the continuing opposition of machine politicians who had lost power in reformed cities and sought to recover it. Since the electoral system had been voted in as a corollary of the city manager plan, it was occasionally voted out in the same way. The former city manager of Cleveland, William R. Hopkins, explaining the repeal of PR/STV in Cleveland to a New York City audience, said, "as to PR . . . the manager plan was the dog and P.R. was only the tail" (Hopkins, 1935, p. 29). Hopkins's wry evaluation might have been the advice that led New York City to become the only municipality in the United States to adopt PR/STV without the city manager plan. Other cities in Ohio, however, separated the two reforms and retained their city managers when they discarded PR/STV.

The abandonment of PR/STV in 21 of the 22 cities where it was used in the United States has been attributed to a changing political climate less friendly to experimentation and reform. However, the innovation of PR/STV was still spreading during the period of repeals. The last two successful repeal votes did not occur until 1960 (Hamilton, Ohio, and Worcester, Massachusetts). Cambridge, Massachusetts, voters defeated four repeal referenda, the latest in 1961, and the city continues to practice PR in the 1990s, over 50 years after its adoption. These are instances of the Progressive influence still at work at state and local levels among the forces of organized labor, urban Democrats and Independents, Independent Republicans, social workers, and champions of public power, all of whom were among the persistent advocates of PR/STV.

It would seem that the search for explanations of repeal must be conducted in the context of particular cities and their social and economic development. Yet an underlying explanation for repeal seldom recognized in the literature is the fact that PR/STV did what it was supposed to do, that is, facilitate the representation of minorities of various sorts. Independent professionals often replaced small businessmen, such as tavern owners and undertakers who were ward leaders in their party organizations, thus realizing John Stuart Mill's fondest hopes as well as the expectations of many reform leaders.

Ethnic, religious, and racial minorities, the partisan minority in single-party-dominant cities, and, in many cases, women were elected to council seats for the first time. These results may not have been well understood; in many cases they were not welcome in the 1930s, 1940s, and 1950s. The election of two Communist Party members in New York City in 1945, and of African Americans in Toledo and Cincinnati, figured prominently in repeal campaigns. The history of the repeal campaigns shows that voters generally were not as open to diversity as PR's sponsors had been.

Conclusion

Structural reforms in urban government such as PR/STV may have only occasionally achieved the goals of their early twentieth-century advocates, who sought to expand democracy by undermining party bosses and by restoring control of urban policy to "ordinary people." By "ordinary people" they often meant people like themselves, but the working class was included too. If the workers on whom the burdens of industrial growth fell most heavily could represent themselves, they might ameliorate the harsh conditions of their lives.

In the Progressive Era, conflicting views among reformers sometimes hobbled efforts to achieve wider use of PR/STV in urban areas or in state and federal decision-making bodies. Major barriers to consideration of alternative electoral systems were the hostility of the major parties toward change and widespread popular faith in winner-take-all elections. Electoral reform efforts were lively in the 1920s, however, as municipal reformers built bridges to the New Deal and beyond.

THREE

■ ■ ■

What Is PR/STV?

Rowland Hill records that, when he was teaching in his father's school, his pupils were asked to elect a committee by standing beside the boy they liked best. This first produced a number of unequal groups, but soon the boys in the largest groups came to the conclusion that not all of them were actually necessary for the election of their favourite and some moved on to help another candidate, while . . . the few supporters of an unpopular boy gave him up as hopeless and transferred themselves to the candidate they considered the next best. The final result was that a number of candidates equal to the number required for the committee were each surrounded by the same number of supporters, with only two or three boys left over who were dissatisfied with all those elected. This is an admirable example of the use of the S.T.V.

Lakeman and Lambert, *Voting in Democracies,* 1959

Proportional representation is a simple principle, derived from democratic theory, whereby in a representative body the share of seats won should correspond to the share of votes won. The electoral system is thus the link between the preferences of the voters and the making of policy. The term *proportional representation* is often used loosely to encompass all electoral systems that break up the winner-take-all effect of plurality voting. Strictly speaking, however, proportional representation applies to a much more limited universe of electoral rules. There are two major variants of such electoral systems: party list (PR/PL) and the single transferable vote (PR/STV). Both can

67

be used, and are currently in effect, in various partisan systems; in non-partisan systems only the STV form of PR is appropriate (Gallagher, 1992).

Over time, the definition of minorities that the PR theorists worried about has shifted in emphasis from the propertied or educated elite and minority political parties to the blue-collar worker and, more recently, to groups identified by religious, ethnic, racial, or gender traits. The core of PR thinking has remained constant, however. In a democratic system, individuals and groups with differing views and identities are entitled to their share of representation in the policy-making process. Minorities are not entitled to rule, but they should be heard, and they should have influence in proportion to their numbers.

The mechanics of the misrepresentation inherent in plurality systems are analyzed here in order to clarify why change in electoral systems has been sought and what differences can be anticipated if a new method of casting ballots and counting votes is adopted. Alternative electoral systems in use today are then explored, with the principal emphasis on the single transferable vote form of proportional representation (PR/STV), the particular system that has been used for city council and school board elections in the United States.

Plurality Voting

Plurality voting describes a decision rule. The candidate with the most votes wins, a common British and American practice that has led European observers to call such elections "horse races" because the first horse past the post wins, no matter by an inch or a mile (Rae, 1967, p. 26). In city elections, plurality voting may be used for candidates running either at-large for seats on a small council (plurality/at-large, or PL/AL), or in small wards (plurality/single-member district, or PL/SMD), in which the winner-take-all feature applies in each of many locales.

A popular variant has been the "mixed system," in which some seats are elected by plurality/at-large and some by plurality in wards. In these mixed systems both at-large and district winners are victorious because they have received the most votes (a plurality) in their respective jurisdictions. Ashtabula, Cincinnati, and Hamilton all used such mixed systems before they adopted PR/STV, each city choosing a different combination of district and at-large seats. The mixture was considered a partial reform of PL/SMD systems, preserving the localism of neighborhood representation while balancing this localism with the whole-city perspective of the at-large members. Victory for all seats, however, was still determined by plurality.

The most obvious political effect of these winner-take-all electoral rules is the exaggeration of majority or plurality representation and the shrinkage or elimination of minority representation. Winning an election in which representation is not shared in proportion to voter preferences means winning a bonus for one's party, race, ethnic group, or whatever identity is politically relevant.[1] This consequence is sometimes called the "Matthew effect" after the biblical injunction: "For whosoever hath, to him shall be given, and he shall have abundance: but whosoever hath not, from him shall be taken away even that which he hath" (Matthew, 13:12). This inevitable effect of plurality voting shapes the resulting representation, no matter the magnitude of the district, whether a multimember (at-large) or single-member district.

Plurality/At-Large Voting Systems

In a plurality/at-large election, the voter places an X beside the names of as many preferred candidates as there are seats to be filled (hence, after PR/STV was repealed, "7X" in Hamilton and Ashtabula, or "9X" in Cincinnati and Toledo). The seven or nine candidates with the most votes are elected. No candidate is required to win a majority of the vote (that is, 50% plus one). However, a plurality or majority of the voters that casts bloc votes for all candidates of plurality or majority identity (say by party, race, gender, religion, or ideology) can win all of the seats. Thus, for example, 51% of the voters with characteristic C may elect up to 100% of representatives who also are Cs. When both Cincinnati and Toledo repealed PR/STV in favor of a plurality/at-large system, their first post–PR elections produced all-white councils, although one or two black members had been elected with some regularity under PR/STV.

Minorities can win one or a few seats in a plurality/at-large election in one of two ways, but both ways require majority-group cooperation. First, the plurality or majority may voluntarily choose one or several minority candidates when they vote for all seats, in which case those elected are still majority preferences for minority representation. This is a political strategy not uncommonly used by knowledgeable majorities when plurality/at-large systems are under attack for their exclusionary effects, as white voters did in Houston, Texas, in the 1970s (Davidson and Korbel, 1981, p. 1004).

Second, majority voters may voluntarily limit the number of majority candidates they select, for example voting for six or seven instead of nine in a 9X election, thus permitting a minority (by limiting its votes to two or three) to elect its own representatives. This method depends for its success on sophisticated strategic voting by a substantial share of the electorate.[2]

Plurality/Single-Member-District Voting Systems

Plurality voting in single-member districts (or wards) is the other common form of plurality voting. If minorities are residentially segregated, as Catholic immigrants tended to be in the Progressive Era and as urban blacks in the north became after World War I, they can achieve representation in a plurality single-member district (PL/SMD) system. With wards as basic political units of party organization and districts determined by ward lines, the parties have historically valued this electoral system as a structure that maximizes their control of city councils. If the wards are small enough, and lines are drawn to create wards with majorities or pluralities of minority voters, representation of minorities ensues. For example, Cleveland adopted a 33-district (ward) council when PR/STV was repealed. Three black council members had been elected by PR/STV before its repeal. Because of the combination in Cleveland of housing segregation and majority-minority wards, black representation on council continued through the 1930s.

The characteristics of a PL/SMD electoral system are clear. The election is still by plurality vote. With one seat at stake, the candidate with the most votes is elected ("first past the post" or "winner takes all"). If there are only two candidates, the district majority can elect its candidate, thus winning 100% of the representation. If there are three or more candidates, a plurality winner is possible. If 45% of the voters (a plurality) support the winner, then 55% of the voters, having divided their votes between two other candidates, go unrepresented. In this way, a majority in a council or in a legislative body may be "manufactured" by the electoral system (Rae, 1967, pp. 74–77).

Prior to the adoption of PR/STV in New York City, the Tammany organization traditionally controlled the board of aldermen, elected by PL/SMD. Machine-organized majorities ranging from a bare 50% to two-thirds of the votes would elect all or almost all of its members. The last pre-PR/STV board of aldermen was composed of 62 organization Democrats out of 65 members elected in SMDs (Hallett, 1940, p. 149), a dramatic example of the "Matthew effect."

In the PL/SMD case, representation in the city or the state as a whole depends on the way the population is geographically distributed. Partisan loyalists, racial, or ethnic groups may be clustered or dispersed. The drawing of district (or ward) lines becomes a critical element in the representational outcome. Traditional techniques of gerrymandering have often determined the composition of a council or a state legislative house, either by bunching (often called "packing") partisan, ethnic, or racial groups so that votes contributing to unnecessarily large majorities are wasted, or by spreading minority populations thinly in several districts so that they do not constitute a majority in any district ("cracking"). More recently the affirmative gerrymander has been used to advance representation of minorities historically subjected to discrimination in districting.

The goal of minority representation is more easily accomplished for groups that suffer from housing segregation, such as African Americans, than for minorities such as Hispanics and Asians, whose housing choices are less confined by discrimination. The size and therefore the number of single-member districts in a given political system will affect the number and variety of minorities represented in a council or a legislative body. New York City, which no longer has an ethnic or racial majority, recently expanded its council from 35 to 51 members to allow for greater diversity of representation. The task of creating distinct minority districts fell to computer experts, who could draw convoluted shapes within the city to produce the desired demographic results (Roberts, 1991).

PL/SMD electoral systems have seldom been attacked for their winner-take-all character, or for their tendency to provide structural support for residential segregation. Instead, reformers traditionally alleged that the systems strengthened party bosses, fragmented communities, and encouraged parochial concerns in the governing process. What neighborhood residents viewed as a transcendent advantage—having their own representative be usually of similar class, ethnic, or racial identity—was for many reformers at the root of the problem of corruption.

The Special Case of Majority Formulae

Up to this point, plurality and majority wins have been treated together. A cohesive majority can use a plurality electoral system effectively, but it should be clear that the decision rule is victory by plurality (the most votes); a majority (50% of the total plus one) is not necessary. There are, however, two single-member district systems that require a majority victory at some stage of the process. These are the second ballot system, used in France and in some American primary elections, where the second election is called a "runoff"; and the alternative vote, also known as the majority preferential vote (MPV), used for election of the Australian lower house.

As practiced in France, the second ballot system provides that if any candidate in the single-member district receives a majority of the votes on the first ballot, he or she is elected. Because there is no primary election, few candidates receive a majority vote. A second election is held, usually a week later, at which a plurality winner is elected. This system is used to elect the French president (with the nation as a single district) as well as the parliament. Deals struck in the interval between ballots may include withdrawal of individual candidates in exchange for some post-election benefit. In parliamentary elections the interval between ballots is also used by small parties to trade districts by withdrawing candidates on a reciprocal plan to maximize opportunities for electoral success on the second ballot (Cole and Campbell, 1989, pp. 60–63, 67–70, 93–94, 158–60, 167–72; Rae, 1967, pp. 23–25, 107–10).

The Australian alternative vote, which is accomplished on a single ballot, not only requires a majority winner, but also expands the voter's choices in a single-member district by providing for preferential voting. The voter marks the ballot by placing numbers beside each candidate's name in order of his or her choice.[3] If any candidate wins a majority of first-choice votes, he or she is elected. If not, the lowest ranked candidate is eliminated and his or her second preference votes are added to the first choices of the other candidates. This process continues until a majority winner is produced (Rae, 1967, pp. 23–25, 107–10; Bogdanor, 1984, chap. 3).

The alternative vote could be used instead of plurality voting for the election of one candidate nationwide or statewide, such as the U.S. president, governors, or U.S. senators, giving voters expanded choices and strengthening the claim to power of officials who won with majority support. For legislative elections, however, both the two ballot system and the alternative vote suffer from the same flaws as PL/SMD. Not only are minorities excluded from representation when a single candidate is elected, but outcomes do not depend on the total votes parties receive. Instead, outcomes are biased by the geographical distribution of party supporters and by the configuration of district lines (Bogdanor, 1984, p. 44).

Semi-Proportional Voting Systems

Limited voting (LV) and cumulative voting (CV) are alternative electoral systems that enable a jurisdiction to maintain at-large voting in a multimember district, city, or county, but that at the same time assure some minority representation. The term *semi-proportional* is applied because the decision rules are not precise enough to guarantee a close relationship between the share of votes won by a group and the share of seats allocated to that group in the governing body.

Limited Voting

In the case of limited voting (LV), the voter is restricted to voting for fewer candidates than the number of seats available in an at-large election. For example, the voter may be allowed to cast votes for up to five candidates for a seven-seat council. The minority party or minority groups will quickly learn to maximize their strength by voting for only two or three candidates. This method is used in nonpartisan elections in some Connecticut cities and towns and in Pennsylvania county elections. A variation of this system, which can be used in partisan elections, provides for limited nominations (LN), restricting the number of candidates each party may nominate but allowing voters to vote for all seats. A combination of LN and LV restricts both the number of candidates nominated by each party and the number of votes each voter may cast. At-large members of the Philadelphia city council have been elected by this combined LN/LV (Weaver, 1984).

Cumulative Voting

Cumulative voting (CV), in contrast, gives voters the same number of votes as seats to be filled in a multimember district but permits voters to concentrate their support on one or more candidates instead of voting to fill all seats. The most persistent exercise of this option was the 110-year-old practice in Illinois (1870–1980) for electing the lower house of its legislature. The house was composed of three-member districts. Each voter could cast three votes in one of the following ways: one vote for each of three candidates; two votes for one candidate and one vote for another; one and a half for each of two; or three votes aggregated or "cumulated" for the same candidate. By this system in Illinois, one Republican was generally elected to serve in a Democratic-dominant legislative district, and one Democrat in a Republican-dominant district. A minority making up one-third of the voters was capable of capturing one of the three seats. The decision rule was still plurality voting; the candidates with the most votes won, but the intensity or depth of voter preference was accommodated (Blair, 1960; Everson and Parker, 1983).

Semi-proportional systems are handicapped, however, in an important respect. The opportunity to achieve minority representation is likely to attract more minority candidates to a contest, inevitably inviting dispersal of minority votes over too many candidates. As a result, minority candidates may defeat each other. To produce reliable results from limited or cumulative election systems, strategic voting is called for. Minorities that may or may not be residentially segregated but that learn to vote cohesively can gain some representation in at-large LV or CV voting systems.

Proportional Voting Systems

Proportional Representation/Party List

The party list system is the most common application of PR, found in presidential as well as parliamentary systems around the world in national, state, or provincial elections for legislative assemblies. By aggregating voters' interests, preferences, and ideologies into meaningful collective action, the political party system provides a base for democratic representation in governance. On the PR/PL ballot, candidates are listed by party or, in a few places, such as Israel, only the parties are listed.

Voters choose their preferred party or party list of candidates. The percentage of total votes won by each party is then translated into the share of seats earned, determining the representation of that party in the legislature. The parties decide which candidates will be on their lists (therefore no primary is necessary), and if the entire list is not elected (a likely event, since the winner does *not* take all), the parties decide which of the listed candidates will actually serve to make up the party's voter-determined share of seats. A popular variation of the PR/PL ballot is to allow the voters to rank their choices of candidates within a party list, as in Norway, or even to choose a few candidates from different lists, as in Switzerland, but the emphasis is on fair translation of voters' party preferences into power in the parliament (Rae, 1967, pp. 39–45). A party that wins 55% of the votes will have about 55% of the seats; a party that wins 10% of the votes will have about 10% of the seats, and so on.

Most PR/PL systems today have a threshold percentage that a party must win in order to get any seats at all, 5% being a common minimum requirement (Bogdanor, 1984, p. 10). This threshold corrects what was viewed as a defect of the system of the Weimar Republic of Germany, under which extreme fragmentation made difficult the coalescence of a majority in the parliament. Israel is an example of a contemporary PR/PL system that has had a very low minimum required percentage of votes—1%—to achieve representation. In the 1988 Israeli election, a 5% threshold would have excluded from the Knesset 13 parties that won between 1.2% and 4.7% of the total vote. Only the two major parties, Labor and Likud, received more than 5% of the vote. In 1992 the threshold was raised to 1.5%, a minimal increase but one that reduced the number of parties winning representation from 15 to 10. Facing a higher threshold (3.5% has been considered), the very small parties could accept exclusion as the price of purity, or build a coalition among themselves to surmount the threshold as a few parties did in 1992. Their third option would be to join with one of the two major parties to share in power. Raising the threshold is a leading change sought by Israeli reformers (Bogdanor, 1993, pp. 68, 73).

Different formulae for allocation of seats and different district magnitudes (ranging from 2 in Iceland to 150 in the Netherlands, a district of the whole) add variety to the practice of PR/PL but do not change the basic principle (Rae, 1967, pp. 18–36). Constituencies are territorial, but they tend to be whole political communities such as cities, counties, or provinces. The principle of equality of representation is maintained by raising or lowering the number of members from a district instead of redrawing district lines or further subdividing a political community (Steed, 1985, pp. 194–97).

In Germany, a hybrid variety of PR/PL called a "mixed-member proportional" system (MMP) is practiced, as it was formerly in West Germany. Half of the Bundestag's seats are filled by PL/SMD, and the other half by PR/PL, with the overall composition of the body determined by the party shares won on the PR/PL ballot (Rae, 1967, pp. 11–13). In November 1993, by popular referendum New Zealand became the first English-speaking democracy to adopt this system for its parliamentary elections. Variants of this mixed-member system have also been adopted recently in Japan, Russia, Italy, Hungary, Bulgaria, and Mexico (Nagel, 1994, p. 525).

Because proportional representation was originally promoted in the United States as an antiparty measure, and because PR has been adopted only at the local level where most governments use nonpartisan ballots, PR/PL has not yet been practiced in the United States.

Proportional Representation/Single Transferable Vote

In the PR/STV paradigm, it is not the parties alone that deserve representation, but all interested persons, including independents.

The single transferable ballot makes this possible by giving the voter the opportunity to rank-order his or her preferences. The ballot ultimately counts for one candidate, as it does in a single-member-district system, but it is used where it is needed to best reflect the voter's choices. If the voter's first choice is a very popular candidate who needs no further votes to be elected, or if the first choice was cast for a hopeless loser, the ballot is not wasted. Instead, it is transferred to the voter's second, third, or subsequent choice and added to that candidate's total.

In this way, the PR ballot integrates the advantages of an at-large system and a single-member-district system without their attendant costs. The voter is not constricted by district boundaries in choosing a representative but may join with other like-minded voters throughout the city (or multimember district), creating a voluntary constituency for their council member. If geographical representation is important to the voters, they are free to give neighborhood candidates preference in marking their ballots. If party, race, ethnicity, gender, or ideology is important, voters can join with others of similar interests to elect a candidate.

For the voter, the task is simple. Given a ballot with a list of candidates either running at-large in a city (as at one time in Ashtabula, Cincinnati, Hamilton, and Toledo, and at present in Cambridge, Massachusetts) or in large multimember districts (as formerly in Cleveland and New York City, and now in Ireland), the voter marks the ballot with numerals, giving his or her first preference a "1," the second a "2," and as many successive preferences as desired up to the total number of candidates. As a practical matter most voters will not rank candidates whom they do not prefer at all.

As with PR/PL, the voter is relieved of the double duty of voting twice, first in a primary and then in the general election, since candidates are nominated for the PR ballot by petition and the electorate's rank-ordering of choices serves to both narrow the field and pick the winners.

Although PR/STV has frequently been criticized as too complex for the average voter to understand, it is only the count, which the voter is not responsible for, that is complicated. Advocates of PR/STV often point out that voting becomes, like telling time, driving a car, or buying insurance, something that ordinary people do all the time without any need to understand the underlying technology. They need only have confidence in the counters, a condition relevant to all types of elections. Here, however, an overview of the count will help to explain how proportionality is achieved.[4]

First count. The first step is to sort all ballots by first choices, eliminating invalid ballots (for example, those marked with X's instead of numerals).[5] First-choice votes are counted and the total number of valid ballots is determined. This makes it possible to establish the minimum required number of votes that candidates must earn in order to be elected. This number becomes the threshold for election. In order to minimize wasted votes, the threshold is set at the smallest number that can elect no more members than there are seats. If, for example, there are nine seats to be filled, then one-tenth of the total vote plus just one more vote will prevent 10 candidates from being elected. No votes are wasted in an unnecessarily large majority, as they would be if the threshold were set at (what might seem to be the obvious) one-ninth of the total vote.

At the time that PR/STV was adopted in cities in the United States, the threshold was calculated by a formula developed by British barrister H. R. Droop (then called the "Droop Quota"). The total number of valid votes cast is divided by one more than the number of seats to be filled, and one digit is added to the quotient. If V = the total number of valid ballots and N = the number of seats to be filled, the threshold (T) is found as follows: $T = V/(N + 1) + 1$.

If 1,000 valid ballots are cast to fill nine seats, the threshold is $(1000/10) + 1 = 101$. This is the smallest proportion of the total vote that can elect each of nine candidates (Lakeman and Lambert, 1959, pp. 105, 251–52).[6] At the end of the first count, all candidates receiving the established threshold or more of votes are declared elected. Any excess votes—that is, more than the number necessary to be elected—are declared "surplus."

Second count. The surplus ballots are redistributed to the second preferences marked on these ballots. The method for this transfer varied in the cities using PR/STV. In Cincinnati, all ballots were numbered consecutively on the first count so that the appropriate proportion could be drawn from all wards and precincts. If candidate A's total first-choice votes exceeded the threshold by 25%, then every fourth ballot of A's total vote was withdrawn and allocated to the second choice on that ballot. If the second choice was already elected, the ballot was allocated to the third or, if necessary, subsequent choice.

In Toledo, however, the surplus ballots were those counted last, so that the sequence of counting determined which ballots were redistributed to second or later choices. In the first count, when Candidate A reached the threshold, he was declared elected, "his" ballots were set aside, and all subsequent ballots on which he was given first preference were allocated to second or later preferences (Zimmerman, 1972, p. 75). This practice gave rise to the criticism that the PR count was a lottery.

A third system, used originally in Boulder, Colorado, and statistically refined today, distributes the surplus by a simple mathematical formula, as follows: the elected candidate's surplus (s) is divided by the total vote for the elected candidate (v); the quotient is then multiplied by the number of second preferences (sp) for each un-elected candidate, and these fractional votes (fv) are then allocated to the designated unelected candidates. The formula is then: $(s/v) \times (sp) = fv$ (Rae, 1967, p. 37).

For example, if the threshold is 15,000 and candidate A receives 20,000 votes, the surplus is 5,000. On A's 20,000 first-choice ballots, second choices are divided among five candidates, say 4,000 each for candidates B, C, D, E, and F, or 20% each. Then 20% of 5,000 (or 1,000) surplus fractions of votes are transferred to each of these five candidates. Thus a fractional vote or vote value is actually transferred, representing the proportional share of second or subsequent choices for unelected candidates among the total first-choice votes of an elected candidate. This method is accepted today as the fairest and most accurate distribution of the surplus. After the transfer of all surplus votes from the first count, any candidates reaching the threshold are declared elected.

Third count. At this stage, the lowest-placed candidate on the list is declared eliminated, and his or her ballots are transferred to other unelected candidates in order of second, third, or subsequent viable choices. Any candidates reaching the threshold will then be declared elected; the next lowest candidate will be eliminated, and so on, until the required number of seats has been filled. Unlike the transfer of the surplus, these votes transfer at full value, since they are the universe of votes for eliminated candidates.[7]

Although some ballots may be "exhausted" before they are allocated to a winning candidate, the number is far smaller than those "wasted" in a single-member-district plurality election in which only one choice is counted.[8] As noted earlier, in a three-or-more-candidate PL/SMD race, a majority of ballots may be wasted. In a PR/STV election a ballot is wasted only if the voter opted not to make enough choices to keep the ballot in play, or if each of the voter's choices represented too small a minority to make up one ratio of representation (for example, one-tenth of the total vote plus one for a nine-member council). Typically, 80%–90% of the ballots are effectively counted to elect a member of council, as opposed to 45%–55% in a plurality election.

Final count. On the final count, it is possible for candidates to be elected without reaching the threshold. If the next-to-last remaining candidate has been eliminated, her ballots transferred, and one or more seats remains unfilled, the surviving candidate(s) will be declared elected. In Cleveland council elections—which took place in four large multimember districts, two of which elected seven members, one elected six members, and one, five members—it was not uncommon for several members in each district to be elected without reaching the threshold. With a small number of seats and therefore a relatively large required number of votes, it is not unusual for leaders on the first count to be the winners on the final count (Lakeman and Lambert, 1959, p. 109; Hermens, [1941] 1972, p. 413).

If most of the council members who were finally elected after the transfer process were also among the leaders on the first count (90% was the average in these Ohio cities), does it really make much difference whether an at-large election is held by plurality or by PR/STV? The answer to this important question is a resounding "yes." Not only would 10% minority representation itself make a difference, but a different array of candidates is likely to enter a PR race because of the different structure for opportunity. When a citywide minority of 10%–15% of the electorate has a chance of electing a candidate, as in a seven- or nine-member PR/STV election, there is a distinct incentive for a minority candidate to run. This incentive is absent in a winner-take-all situation, such as 7X or 9X voting, since such a candidate would probably lose out in the plurality contest at either the primary or the election stage.

It will be seen in the individual city accounts that follow that in each Ohio community that adopted PR, there were ardent followers of the count. The count was conducted publicly, with succeeding totals marked up on large chalkboards. Frequently it would take a week to complete the transfers and reach the final results. Some observers have portrayed this process as a civic celebration, as it is apparently experienced today in Cambridge, Massachusetts. Others complained of the delay in knowledge of the outcome.

Computer tally. If PR were to be reintroduced today, computer programs would be available to accommodate the count, and ballots could be made computer readable (Piccard, 1984, p. 520; Macklin, 1989, p. 1). The count would be concluded with dispatch, but those who relish the play of the transfer process would be disappointed if they could not watch it happen. In 1994 the Center for Voting and Democracy conducted a computer recount of the 1991 city council election in Cambridge, Massachusetts, using its PRMaster program on a personal computer with manual data entry. In two minutes the outcome matched the actual results. The data entry step could be eliminated by upgrading voting machines so that voters could record their choices directly. Electronic voting booths from which ballots would be transmitted by modem to the count center provide a promising technology. In order to preserve a community tradition of "watching the count," the program could be written to stop after each count for display of transfer results (Richie, 1994).

Impact of the number of seats. The number of seats on a council or in a multimember district will affect the diversity of representation in a PR/STV system. With a nine-member council, for example, a minority of 10% of the voters has a chance of electing a representative of its choice. A seven-member council would provide the opportunity of representation to a minority of 12.5%. In contrast to LV and CV, a minority-preferred candidate in a PR/STV election is unlikely to defeat another minority-preferred candidate because rank-order voting prevents lower preferences from being counted until higher-ranked preferences are elected or eliminated. Cleveland's 25-member council, elected in four multimember districts, was structured to permit representation of more minorities in that highly diverse community than was possible in the seven- or nine-member councils of the other Ohio PR cities.

Ireland's experience over its more than 70 years of PR/STV elections illustrates the impact of district size in a party-based system. From 1923 to 1977, Dail districts varied in size from three to nine members, depending on district population. Gradually the larger districts were reduced in size to a maximum of five members, and since 1969 the majority have been three-member districts. The number of parties contesting elections declined to a highly stable three-party system in which the third party typically wins less than half as many seats as the second party. O'Leary calls these parties "majority-bent parties with an eye to power" (O'Leary, 1979, pp. 98–99, 110–13).

Some social choice theorists have criticized proportional voting procedures because of a theoretical possibility that changes in individual ordering of preferences could alter the outcome of such elections in ways that negate the "true" choices of voters (Doron and Kronick, 1977; Fishburn and Brams, 1983). This possibility, a condition called "non-monotonicity," suggests that the opportunity exists for strategic voting (often called insincere voting or manipulation) to determine the winner or winners of such elections.

However, strategic voting is possible in all electoral systems, and strategic choices may actually reflect a voter's true preference. For example, in a plurality election with several candidates, a voter who knows that her first choice cannot win may vote for a less preferred candidate in an effort to keep an even more disliked alternative from winning. Her true preference, then, is to keep the least liked candidate out of office. Successful strategic voting depends on understanding how the voting system works, as well as knowing something about the choices other voters are likely to make. The knowledge required to vote the PR/STV ballot strategically is far more intricate than with plurality voting (Reeve and Ware, 1992, pp. 160–61). Hence the STV ballot is more "resistant to manipulation" than other methods of voting that are more widely practiced. For all practical purposes, this is a "non-issue" (Merrill, 1988, p. 66; Austen-Smith and Banks, 1991; Bartholdi and Orlin, 1991).

Summary and Conclusion

Electoral systems are a little-recognized link between the voters' acts of choice in democratic systems and the kind of representation that they win. Electoral systems have political consequences. Plurality voting systems, whether at-large or in small districts, tend to overrepresent the majority and underrepresent or exclude the minority. While malapportionment and gerrymandering may exacerbate this outcome of plurality voting, the manufactured majority commonly occurs in the absence of such egregious tactics simply through the effect of the winner-take-all decision rule.

Semi-proportional systems, the most common of which are limited voting and cumulative voting, are based on at-large or multimember district voting and can be used with either partisan or nonpartisan ballots. By preventing the electoral sweeps of plurality voting systems, these decision rules are likely to result in some representation of a minority party or group. The principal disadvantage of LV and CV is that in the absence of well-organized strategic voting, minority candidates may lose because their support is diffused among too many candidates.

Full proportionality can be achieved by true proportional systems, with ballots organized by party list or by single transferable vote. While PR/PL is necessarily associated with a partisan ballot, PR/STV is adaptable either to partisan or nonpartisan elections. In order to prevent extreme fragmentation in a decision-making body, most PR/PL systems today set a minimum percentage of the vote that is required for a small party to gain any representation at all. Fragmentation is not a major issue in PR/STV elections since size of the elected body (or district magnitude) sets a structural limit below which minorities cannot achieve representation.

The choice of electoral systems has real consequences both for voter behavior and for governance. In systems governed by plurality elections, the winner-take-all result forces candidates and parties to build coalitions in the electorate before the election, if victory is the goal. This is one reason why two-party systems are generally associated with plurality voting patterns. In proportional systems, although coalition building before an election is useful and may indeed produce a working majority in the elected body, it is also possible to build a majority coalition in the policy-making body after the election. For this reason, proportional systems may encourage the formation and persistence of more than two parties in partisan polities and produce more diverse representation in nonpartisan bodies.

The electoral system is only a part of the larger system of representation that is supposed to make democracy a government of, by, and for the people. Recruitment of candidates, organization of parties and interests, and electoral campaigns are other inputs into the process of creating a representative government. Structures of government and decision rules within those structures shape the policies produced as outputs, but the electoral system is a critical and often unrecognized link between the more visible forces of politics in a democracy and the actual governing of a society. The choice of an electoral system should be made deliberately and with full understanding of its consequences for representation and governance.

FOUR

■ ■ ■

Ashtabula: The Pioneer Community

Ronald J. Busch

> The Ashtabula experiment with proportional representation
> has promise beyond the domain of city government. The cities
> are . . . making the largest contributions to our knowledge of new
> governmental devices. This is especially true of the cities in
> those states which, like Ohio, have granted their municipalities a
> large measure of freedom. . . . There is now a noticeable tendency
> for the states to draw their inspiration from the cities. It is pos-
> sible that Ashtabula has started a movement which will end in
> reform of the present inequitable and demoralizing method of
> choosing the members of state legislatures and the lower house
> of Congress.
>
> Hatton, "Making Minorities Count," 1915

ASHTABULA, OHIO, in 1915 the first city in the United States to
adopt proportional representation for its elections, was fertile ground
for the reforms advocated by Progressive thinkers in the early twentieth century. As were other American cities at the time, Ashtabula was
plagued by corruption and waste in municipal government, inefficient
and inadequate delivery of public services, and a Republican regime
too long in power. The Progressive call for honesty and efficiency in
government, neutral administration, and social reform resonated
among a group of leaders who sought to eliminate what they saw as the
evils of partisanship.

*Appreciation is expressed to Sandy Judnick and Richard Marsh for assistance in the
collection and tabulation of data. Special gratitude is owed to Edward Bolte, a
knowledgeable and interested native of Ashtabula, whose insights were invaluable.*

In an election held on 10 August 1915, the city of Ashtabula adopted PR by single transferable vote to elect its city council. Its use three months later, in the November 1915 municipal election, was the first of eight PR elections conducted in the city. After a tumultuous and contested existence, sharpened by ethnic and religious differences, PR was replaced in 1929 by plurality/at-large elections.

Temperance eclipsed party differences in the life of the community, intruding with a disturbing frequency, and agitated by the growing presence of Catholics in the community. Religious and ethnic cleavages were reinforcing rather than cross-cutting. Irish and Italian Catholics were liberal, that is "wet," on temperance, whereas the descendants of British, Swedish, and Finnish immigrants were Protestant and "dry" on temperance. The division between the "wets" and "drys" in the city was deep and implacable. In time, the coalition of Protestants in the city prevailed and the city voted itself "dry" in 1916. Instead of settling the issue, however, local prohibition propelled a continuing struggle. Combative organizations formed in 1917 to defend prohibition included the Guardians of Liberty and the Allied Defenders. In 1923 the Ku Klux Klan, staunchly Protestant in membership and militantly anti-Catholic, joined the fray.

Controversies surrounding these issues increased public impatience with "politics" and created support for those Progressives who sought to improve government. The Progressive spirit in Ashtabula was welcomed by many of the city's leaders, as expressed in the city's leading newspaper: "The Progressive county candidates stand on a platform never heard of in this county before. It means economy and efficiency in the county offices. They are everyone of them honest, up-right businessmen and farmers. They are not hangers-on at the political trough. The people are with them" (*Beacon Record,* 10 Oct. 1914, p. 4).

Efficiency was equated with dollars saved. A more effective government was to be achieved by the adoption of PR, and by the fiscal restraint that minority representation was expected to provide against the flagrant spending practices of an unchecked majority. In Ashtabula, PR and the city manager charter were closely linked as Progressive themes.

National proponents of PR saw in the city a test site from which experience and insight were to be gained and then applied to efforts to win PR charters elsewhere in the United States. Infused with a belief in human perfectibility, PR's advocates assumed that changes in political structures would produce better individuals and, collectively, a more responsible citizenry. Although this optimistic goal proved to be elusive, it was generally conceded that, during the PR era, public services expanded and improved even while taxes were reduced. This positive performance of "reformed" city government was overshadowed, however, by the social conflict that accompanied demographic change.

The Framework for Analysis

To examine the experience of proportional representation in Ashtabula, three electoral periods are analyzed here: 1909–14, encompassing three elections before PR's adoption; 1915–30, during which eight city councils were elected under the PR system; and 1931–36, a post-PR period including three elections.[1]

The impact of PR as an electoral system will be examined by comparing the characteristics of PR-elected council members with those chosen before and after the PR years. The impact of PR on political participation is examined by comparing electoral turnout and competition for office for PR and non-PR councils. Finally, the effect of PR on governmental stability is examined by comparing the extent of divided voting on PR councils to that on non-PR councils.

In the pre-PR period, seven members of city council were nominated in partisan primaries and elected by partisan ballot in a mixed ward/at-large system (four wards, three members at-large). A council president, who presided over meetings and could vote only in case of ties, and the mayor were separately elected at-large. With the adoption of PR, nomination by petition replaced the primary, a nonpartisan ballot was introduced, the separate offices of council president and mayor were eliminated, and the council both elected one of its own as mayor and appointed a city manager. The PR/STV ballot provided for the election at-large of seven council members by numbered choices. The only change in the post-PR electoral system was the substitution of a plurality ballot that allowed the seven candidates with the most votes to win. The differences among electoral systems are summarized in table 4.1. There were 21 elected council members and one appointed replacement in the pre-PR period; 56 elected and two replacements during PR; and 21 elected in the post-PR period.[2]

Although the methodology resembles the classic before-and-after design, differences in the before and after periods may have produced effects independently of PR. The multiple reforms of 1914–15 represented a sharp break with the past, whereas the only change in 1929 was the substitution of plurality voting for the ranked choices of the PR/STV ballot. The office of city manager was retained long after PR was repealed.

TABLE 4.1

ASHTABULA'S POLITICAL SYSTEM, 1909–1937

	1909–15 Pre-PR	1915–31 PR Period	1931–37 Post-PR
Primaries	Yes	No	No
Partisan elections[a]	Yes	No	No
Executive	Mayor	Manager	Manager
Size of council	7[b]	7	7
Council president	Elected by voters	Elected by council	Elected by council
Council districts	Ward and at-large	At-large	At-large

[a]Parties slated candidates throughout the three electoral systems, but the same candidates occasionally ran on different slates in different elections.

[b]This does not include the council president, who was separately elected and could vote only to break ties.

Ashtabula before the Adoption of PR

Ashtabula is located on the southern shore of Lake Erie, in northeastern Ohio, 52 miles east of Cleveland. As a port city it was well situated between the iron ore ranges of Minnesota to the northwest and the steel mills of Youngstown, Pittsburgh, and Johnstown to the south. Lake freighters and railroads provided the essential transport. With slightly more than 12,000 residents in 1900, Ashtabula's population almost doubled by 1930, in a period of rapid growth encompassing most of the political events analyzed here.

Demographic Characteristics

Although the city's greatest expansion had occurred between 1870 and 1900, the population continued to grow rapidly in the first decade of the twentieth century. Between 1910 and 1930 the growth rate declined, owing to the hazards of transatlantic travel during World War I and, later, the restrictive quotas imposed by the Immigration and Naturalization Act of 1924. Further reducing the flow of immigrants was the widespread unemployment following the 1929 collapse of the stock market and the depression, which dampened expectations about the availability of work.

Prominent in the early settlement of Ashtabula were people of Anglo-Saxon origin from Connecticut, upstate New York, and Pennsylvania. Augmenting the "Yankees" were later immigrants, who came in search of economic opportunity in a rapidly industrializing economy. Irish immigrants were the first major group to follow the original settlers. Driven out of Ireland in the 1840s and 1850s by the potato famine, they followed the Erie Canal and the lakeshore west to a better life. In Ashtabula, some would succeed. English-speaking, they settled in homes located throughout the city. Class differences did exist and were evident in references to the "depot" working-class Irish and the better-off "lace-curtain" Irish. In time the Irish would be outnumbered by other European immigrants in Ashtabula.

In the meantime, abolitionist sentiment in the city led to the establishment of an Anti-Slavery Society in 1832, and, like many other Ohio communities, Ashtabula became a link in the underground railroad. For escaping slaves, the city was a point in transit, a way-station between slavery in the South and freedom in Canada. Only a few stayed; the 1920 census estimated the city's African-American population at 239. In the late 1920s African Americans were transported from Florida to work in area orchards, and their population registered an increase to 323 in the 1930 census.

It was during the period of the most rapid population growth, between 1870 and 1900, that the Finns, Swedes, and Italians arrived in Ashtabula. By 1910 new immigrants and their immediate offspring constituted the city's majority, accounting for 57% of its population. One in four (26%) residents were foreign-born, and another 31% had at least one foreign-born parent. By 1910 only 43% of the population was "native white."

The Finns were the largest ethnic group in the city. A contingent of 25 Finns, 24 men and 1 woman, arrived in 1872 as part of a section gang for the Pennsylvania Railroad. Others followed. Largely agrarian in background, these Finns were predictably conservative in politics and Lutheran in religion (Kolehmainen, 1977). By 1874 a permanent Finntown was established in Ashtabula, similar to Finnish settlements in the other Ohio shoreline communities of Conneaut and Fairport Harbor. By 1884 Finns were numerous enough to warrant publication of Ashtabula's first Finnish newspaper, the *Yhdyswaltain Sanomat* (American Finn), renamed the *Amerkan Sanomat and Suometar* in 1897.

The Finns were hard working and dependable, generally engaged in strenuous manual labor. Their culture included communal meeting halls and a common religion and language. They were also dedicated imbibers of alcoholic beverages, a habit that was promoted by the lack of a safe water supply during their earlier years in the city. As alcohol adversely affected the more important values of work and family, the

Finns grew committed to temperance, even to the point of militancy. Finnish temperance societies were established in 1884, 1887, 1892, and 1897. The Kunto and Turva temperance societies were consolidated, and replaced by the Sovento Society in 1910. Their Protestantism and position on temperance made them natural political allies of native white Protestants.

Later-arriving Finns were both less religious and less conservative in their politics. Escaping a rigid class system under the Russian czar, these Finns were influenced by the doctrines and ideals of socialism, a movement that was spreading among the working classes in Europe. The Social Democrats won Finland's first parliamentary election in 1907. By 1911, "the red flag was waving boldly in no less than 217 Finnish settlements in the United States" (Kolehmainen, 1977, p. 180). Religious skepticism accompanied these political views, a reaction to the Lutheran church's historical support for the established class structure in Finland.

A few Swedish immigrants had arrived in 1869, but not until the Swedenborg family settled in 1874 did their community become permanent. Italians were the last of the major ethnic groups to arrive. Their initial settlement in 1880 was the result of the initiative of a *padrone,* a contractor who imported 400 Italian workers from Buffalo, New York, as laborers on the city water works. By 1930 the Italians surpassed the Scandinavians in numbers.

The Economy

Ashtabula was a small lake-port city in a largely agricultural county. In the early years, manufacturing was related to local needs, but after the Civil War a "pipeline" economy developed. Production and distribution needs of a distant steel industry determined the city's economic life, and its fortunes fluctuated with those of steel. Not surprisingly, shipbuilding was an important activity in Ashtabula.

The small size of the city and its dependence on transportation had political implications. Economic activity was a common enterprise shared by all. Interaction between managers and workers was frequent and often direct. Consequently, class differences were more muted than in larger cities where management was often removed from the workplace.

Political Setting

In the early twentieth century, formal governmental arrangements in Ashtabula yielded a system of diffused political power with shared authority and responsibility. In this fragmented system the opportunity for conflict was great. Under the pre-PR mayor-council system, the mayor was "the chief conservator of the peace." He shared executive powers, however, with four other elected officials—the president of the council, the auditor, the solicitor, and the treasurer. The mayor could veto proposed ordinances, but the city council could override a veto by a two-thirds vote. Legislative authority was vested in the seven-member city council, one council member from each of four wards and three council members elected at-large. The main duty of the separately elected council president, who voted only in case of a tie, was to act as moderator. Each voter, therefore, cast five votes for council: one vote for a ward council member, three votes for the at-large council members, and a vote for council president.

Politics in Ashtabula before PR mirrored the political climate of the period. It was a Republican age in the nation and the state, and so it was in the city; yet deep divisions between Progressive Republicans and more conservative mainstream party loyalists often led to Republican electoral losses. The 1913 municipal election illustrates this fragmentation in the majority party. In 1912, owing to the popularity of the Progressive gubernatorial candidate (running in tandem with Theodore Roosevelt's presidential campaign), the "regular" Republican gubernatorial candidate had failed to obtain the minimum 10% of the city vote required in Ohio to assure the party a place on the ballot in the next election. Consequently, local Republican candidates were forced to run independently the following year under such rubrics as Charter Commission candidates, Independents, Conservatives, Independent Republicans, Progressive Conservatives, and Progressive Citizens. Still, Republicans of various persuasions could usually cobble together a majority on council for purposes of local policy and patronage.

Opposition in local politics came from Democrats and Socialists. The Democratic Party provided the major opposition in the city, slating candidates and regularly contesting elections, but Democratic candidates were conspicuously unsuccessful at the ballot box. Socialists were organized and vigorous participants in Ashtabula politics but won office even less frequently.

Socialism had emerged as a set of beliefs whose time had come. Its slogans, "Fraternity," "Freedom," and "Equality" were highly evocative, and they were augmented by proposals calling for the public ownership of utilities, restrictions on corporations and capital, and reform in the workplace. These positions generated sympathy for the

Socialists among working-class Ashtabulans, but competing values such as religion had greater valence. Religious loyalties were deeply rooted in the city, and the Marxist dismissal of religion as "the opium of the masses" proved to be an abhorrent element to those of religious conviction. Its effect was to discount Socialist political and economic ideas, regardless of their merit, and undermine Socialist attempts to gain public office.

Nor was this the Socialists' only liability. Alternative claims to doctrinal purity fragmented Socialist groups, further weakening their cause. Among Finnish Socialists, for example, there were divisions between old world Socialists and their American counterparts, both of whom claimed to be the voice of true Socialism. Labor was the primary clientele group for Socialists, but there were also divisions in the labor movement. Followers of the Industrial Workers of the World (IWW) opposed others who claimed to be the vanguard of social democracy.

Devoid of a firm foothold in the local electorate, the Socialist Party was unable to fashion a meaningful alternative for those who were dissatisfied with conservative politics, corruption, and the condition of the working class. Two Socialist victories at the polls, both before the Russian Revolution of 1917, are in part attributed to the personal popularity of the Socialist candidate, R. W. Earlywine. After the revolution, the Socialist Party was stigmatized in Ashtabula as elsewhere by its opposition to World War I and by the excesses of Bolshevism.

Disgruntled Republicans and frustrated Democrats increasingly turned to the Progressive reformers. The major political parties had been saddled with the incubi of waste and corruption, and they found themselves ill equipped to counter the Progressive appeal for institutional reform as a means to restore the integrity of the political system.

The Adoption of PR

Passage of the home rule amendment to the Ohio Constitution in 1912 heightened local political activity in the state. In many Ohio communities, alternative forms of governance and electoral systems were discussed, among them PR. For change to occur, Ohio law required that a charter commission be established for the purpose of studying and making recommendations to the voters. Upon recommendation of the charter commission, individual issues or whole charters could be placed on the ballot for popular vote.

The Proportional Representation League in New York City had closely followed the home rule debate in Ohio, anticipating the opportunity to demonstrate the benefits of PR/STV and to allay fears of its impracticality. C. G. Hoag, a Quaker from Haverford, Pennsylvania, and general secretary-treasurer of the Proportional Representation League, made several trips to Ohio in 1912 and 1913, introducing the idea of PR first to William E. Boynton, a local labor leader who had formerly served as city council president. In November 1913, after speaking to charter commissions in Cincinnati, Columbus, and Sandusky, Hoag appeared before the newly elected Ashtabula Charter Commission, of which Boynton was a member, to promote the adoption of PR (*Beacon Record,* 12 Nov. 1913, p. 1).

Boynton, like other prominent union men in Ohio, was an ardent Progressive and went on to serve as a member of the national governing council of the Proportional Representation League. He led the effort to get PR adopted in Ashtabula, and in this exerted a prodigious influence. Boynton's role provided local credibility, and Hoag's reception in Ashtabula encouraged the P.R. League to target the city for a campaign to adopt PR. That this drive for PR in Ashtabula was the result of a concerted coalition of forces within and beyond the city is suggested in a letter written in 1915 by Lent D. Upson, formerly director of the Dayton Bureau of Municipal Research and a member of the P.R. League's advisory council, to the editor of the *Proportional Representation Review.* After praising PR, Upson remarked, "I am only sorry that my own city of Dayton should not have been chosen to make the experiment" (*Equity,* Oct. 1915, 17.4:256).

Some local citizens clearly opposed change and thus the proposed charter commission, whereas others just as vigorously favored reform. A fortnight before the election, Boynton urged the public to vote "Yes" on the question of electing a charter commission. He stressed the potential for saving dollars and impugned the motives of the opposition, claiming that "only those who don't believe that the people should be allowed to govern themselves but think they should be ruled by the politicians will object to any move toward Home Rule" (*Beacon Record,* 23 Oct. 1913, p. 4).

On 5 November 1913 Ashtabula voters, by a 69% majority, passed the proposal to elect a charter commission and chose 15 members from a list of 29 candidates. The vote on the question, however, was relatively small ($N = 1,745$), compared to the votes cast for mayor in the same election ($N = 2,848$), a fall off of 1,103 voters (see table 4.2).

TABLE 4.2
VOTING ON ASHTABULA CHARTER QUESTIONS, 1913–1929

	Charter Commission (Nov. 1913)	PR Vote (Aug. 1915)	Repeal #1 (1920)	Repeal #2 (1926)	Repeal #3 (1929)
Yes	69%	60%	46%	46%	58%
No	31%	40%	54%	54%	42%
N^a	1,745	988	5,111	4,194	4,574

Sources: *Beacon Record,* 1913–15; *Ashtabula Star-Beacon,* 1920–29; Bloomfield (1926); and *PRR,* 1913–29.
[a]N = number of voters.

The entire City Council Chamber of Commerce Committee was elected to the commission, as was Ashtabula's leading Socialist, Earlywine. As its president, the commission elected P. C. Remick, and as its first vice president, W. E. Boynton. After meeting regularly for several months to study the charters of other Ohio cities, the commission proposed for voter approval the city manager plan, the initiative, referendum, and recall, and nonpartisan councilmanic elections. However, Boynton, PR's strongest ally, was unable to win majority support for PR, and nine of the 15 members voted to shelve the issue for further discussion. Despite Boynton's efforts and the endorsement of the local chamber of commerce, PR had attracted only a modest level of citizen interest.

Some commission members balked at an electoral system they thought was too complicated for the average citizen to understand. Others suggested that public interest in PR was simply overshadowed by more salient issues in the community, particularly temperance (Bloomfield, 1926). The editor of the *Beacon Record* wrote that there had been too many elections in too short a period of time to expect much public interest in PR.

The proposed city manager charter was adopted by popular vote in the election of 1914. Undaunted by the lack of support for PR in the charter commission or among the public at-large, Boynton rededicated himself to the task of educating the citizenry and gaining public approval of PR before the 1915 municipal election. With the support of the four other members who had fought on the commission for PR, Boynton enlisted Professor Augustus R. Hatton of Western Reserve University in Cleveland. Hatton, an enthusiastic advocate of PR, agreed to work for its adoption in Ashtabula. His effort was not an isolated gesture, for he was involved in the promotion of proportional representation throughout the state. Boynton and the minority commission members waged an intensive campaign.

The earlier strategy to get PR adopted had linked the electoral system to the manager plan as a means to curb the rising costs of government. Concern for efficiency and economy were themes echoed in the newspapers. The header "Mayor Costs City Too Much" (*Beacon Record,* 30 Jan. 1913, p. 1) reflected not only the sentiment of the *Beacon Record's* editor but also that of a growing number of citizens in the city. Councilman C. H. Gallup was unequivocal in his opinion: "The present form of government is too expensive. We have too many officials and most of them receive too much pay for what they do. It is necessary to cut salaries of officials" (*Beacon Record,* 13 Feb. 1913, p. 7).

Now a new, loftier campaign theme was developed: democracy and its requirements. This new theme emphasized the necessity for minority representation for a truly democratic government. The rationale for the theme was that the existing system of electing council members, based on a combination of districts and at-large seats, was defective in failing to provide for representation of the variety of interests essential to democracy. The achievement of diversity in opinion, it was said, would promote a better amalgam for public policy. In a campaign flyer sent to Ashtabula voters, Boynton listed advantages of the PR system:

1. It will give any minority comprising one-eighth of the voters a chance to be represented on council.
2. By requiring the support of different quota of voters for election of each member of council, it makes it impossible for any party or faction to elect a majority of council by focusing its vote on four candidates.
3. It will ensure a continuity of policy in city government.

(Bloomfield, 1926, p. 12)

Because the "best" public decisions had to take into account both minority and majority opinion, a PR-elected council was the appropriate mechanism to appoint the "best man" as city manager, who would in turn ensure efficient administration of the city's business.

Despite efforts on both sides, the 1915 campaign for PR failed to evoke much public interest. The most visible activity consisted of two mass mailings of literature on behalf of PR and one mailing sponsored by the opposition and cosigned by the nine-member majority of the charter commission. Less than a thousand votes were cast at the special election on 10 August 1915, a turnout of only 20% of the eligible voters (Bloomfield, 1926, p. 18), confirming general lack of interest in the electoral system. By a 60% majority, however, PR won (see table 4.2).

PR's adoption can be attributed to a number of factors. Government at all levels was becoming more expensive, and impending tax increases in the city made proposals promising economy more attractive. The national P.R. League's involvement enhanced the campaign. The league's stated purpose was to introduce everywhere "the proportional system of representation—representation by unanimous constituencies" (*PRR*, Oct. 1915, 3rd ser., 36:2). It sought to provide a better foundation for public decision making by including the opinions of minorities in representative assemblies and by eliminating what it saw as the progeny of partisanship: favoritism and graft.

The league was a prestigious organization. On its governing council were many notable American figures, among them Ashtabula's own W. E. Boynton. Instilled with an intense spirit of dedication, league members were convinced that by changing the structures and processes of politics they could improve human beings as citizens and, through them, government. The league had decided to make Ashtabula the test case, to commit energy and resources in the campaign to adopt PR, and to aid in its defense in what can only be described as a difficult existence. PR's small cadre of local citizens, led by Boynton, testified to the power of moral righteousness in American politics. Their perseverance eventually overcame a largely indifferent electorate.

There was, finally, the weakened condition of the political parties. The party organizations could have opposed PR and other reforms, if for no reason other than the uncertainty they posed to the system. But the parties were scarcely viable entities, and they rallied only feebly in opposition to change.

The Abandonment of PR

Opposition to PR during its sixteen-year existence in Ashtabula produced three repeal attempts, in 1920, 1926, and 1929. Defenders of the PR system were able to ward off the first two repeal movements, but support for PR declined and it was repealed by popular vote in 1929.

1920. Five years after its adoption, a single amendment to the city charter was proposed with a dual purpose: to abolish both PR elections and the city manager. The goal was to secure the turnout of a coalition of discontented citizens large enough to defeat both reform features at one stroke.

H. D. Cook, a former member of council and twice mayor of the city, led the repeal drive for both political and philosophical reasons. As an announced candidate for Congress, Cook sought higher office by exploiting public discontent with the city's inadequate supply of gas and its poor public streetcar service. Moreover, he was "an aggressive businessman, who represented the old school of political leadership with its skeptical attitude towards reform in organization and methods of government" (Bloomfield, 1926, p. 19). Under the city manager plan, the solicitor's office had become an appointed and depoliticized position. Joining Cook in the repeal effort were a number of prominent lawyers who favored an elected city solicitor to restore access to and rewards from that office, which they had enjoyed under the old political order.

Discontent with the manager form of government, however, failed to carry the day. With only 46% of the voters in favor of amending the charter again, it was clear that the single-amendment strategy had backfired (see table 4.2, above). Those who wished to preserve one of the reforms had to vote for both, an outcome foreshadowed by the *Star-Beacon* urging: "We are not in favor of the proportional form of voting, but we would rather have it than to lose the manager form of city control" (*Ashtabula Star-Beacon,* 27 Oct. 1920).

Class differences were visible in patterns of voting. The city's wards differed in size and in socioeconomic composition. Wards 1 and 2, the smaller working-class harbor wards, voted for repeal. Wards 3 and 4, however, the predominantly middle-class "up-town" wards on the south side of the city, contained larger numbers of voters, and their support for reform offset the repeal sentiments in the harbor area. Ward 4 alone cast 45% of the total turnout on the repeal issue.

1926.   A second attempt to repeal PR in 1926 was led by Clyde Shaylor, head of the local Republican Party and former solicitor. Because of the failure of the 1920 strategy, repeal forces separated the city manager from PR by placing two issues on the ballot, each proposing two changes. One amendment proposed to abolish PR and substitute election by plurality vote in a mixed ward and at-large system. The second amendment called for the direct election of both the city manager and the auditor.

To defeat both amendments, the Charter Defense Committee of over 150 influential citizens was established, headed by M. C. Robinson, a prominent businessman who for 16 years had been Ashtabula's leader in the crusade for temperance. In the ranks of PR's defenders were former council member F. R. Hogue, who served as secretary of the committee, and Charles A. Bloomfield, then a teacher at Ashtabula High School and later a professor of political science at the University of Illinois. Outsiders on the Charter Defense Committee were, again,

Augustus Hatton of Western Reserve University and George H. Hallett Jr., successor to C. G. Hoag as executive secretary of the national Proportional Representation League.

Perhaps most important to the preservation of PR and the city manager plan was the continued support of the *Star-Beacon*. The editor endorsed both in stark language, reminiscent of the earlier rationale for the adoption of the charter:

> During the past four years there has been a determined effort to annoy, harass, hamper, and obstruct the city manager. Ashtabula needs the city manager plan. Under the old plan of electing councilmen, some political minority machine usually gains control. It could name a political manager and make the whole city administration a political organization. Proportional representation may be complicated, but what of it? A watch is complicated but works beautifully. P.R. does not give any minority control. (*Ashtabula Star-Beacon,* 29 Oct. 1926, p. 10)

At this time, the city manager, William M. Cotton, was indeed under attack from members of the council who objected to his administrative policies. In the hope of saving PR, Cotton, perceiving himself personally to be an issue, announced his resignation before the election.

The amendment to change the electoral system lost, again with only 46% voting to repeal; a similar minority of the voters supported the proposed plurality system. The issues to elect the city manager and the auditor also lost, both attracting about 44% of the vote. Defeat of these issues must have evoked jubilation among members of the Charter Defense Committee and buoyed the spirits of reformers elsewhere. But in this vote there was a foreboding message. Although the percentage of support for PR remained the same in 1926 as in 1920, the turnout declined. More than 500 fewer voters supported PR in 1926 than in the 1920 repeal effort.

In the subsequent three years, the local press highlighted council strife. Conflict among council members and between a few council members and the city manager centered on the enforcement of Prohibition and laws against "vice." Councilman Nick Corrado, who was a saloonkeeper before Prohibition, had converted his establishment to a "confectionery" store, but it was known locally as a "speak-easy." Councilman Arthur Rinto's brother-in-law was arrested for possession of alcohol. Councilman J. J. Garner, a furniture store owner, was allegedly involved with a "house of ill repute" across the river. Successive city managers were charged with enforcing the liquor and vice laws, essentially a political task, given the illegal activities of some public officials. At the same time, city managers were expected to stay out of politics. Inevitably, these hapless administrators became flash points of controversy. Yet public sympathy seemed to lie on the side of the managers, and opponents of PR were able to turn public dismay against the electoral system that appeared to produce the offending representatives.

1929. The last and successful effort to repeal PR came in 1929. A charter commission was established to consider various proposals for improving the city charter. Its members voted 14 to 1 (Boynton dissented) to include repeal of PR among the six issues to be submitted to the voters. For the first time in the succession of anti-PR efforts, the editor of the *Ashtabula Star-Beacon* and the local chamber of commerce supported repeal. Shaylor, now a member of the Committee to Abolish PR, identified PR as the source of the city manager's problems: "Minorities are over represented and set up their own camps for the benefit of their peers, resulting in constant changes in the manager. . . . PR or minority representation is the root evil of bad government in Ashtabula" (*Ashtabula Star-Beacon,* 4 Nov. 1929, p. 10). The charge of "bad government" was highlighted by continuing evidence of corruption, which was readily, if unfairly, tied to the electoral system. Although local law-enforcement agents seemed unable to prosecute Councilman Corrado, federal agents raided his home in 1929, seized liquor and beer, and secured his conviction and imprisonment, forcing his removal from the council.

Despite publicity surrounding these events, turnout on the 1929 repeal of PR was light, with barely 50% of those registered voting on this issue. Significantly more voters cast first-choice preferences for council races in the same election. Wards 3 and 4, earlier strongholds of PR support, experienced a dramatic drop in turnout on the repeal issue, substantially below the turnout in Wards 1 and 2, the working-class wards that were previously less supportive of PR. Opponents carried the day, with 58% of the voters saying "yes" to repeal (see table 4.2).

In the years between 1915 and 1929, a number of factors had converged to bring the experiment with PR to an end. Initial support for PR was weak, despite Boynton's vigorous effort to educate the public on its merits. Low turnout, from the initial election of the charter commission in 1913 through subsequent votes on the issue, suggested public indifference, a frail base upon which the house of reform was to be constructed in Ashtabula. If the system were to survive as a lasting feature of the city's political landscape, a foundation of political support had to be built; but the reformers acted as individuals, neglecting the work of political organization. At the same time, advocates had raised public expectations of a better political system that did not seem to materialize.

Confusion about the procedures of PR/STV voting lent credibility to the critics' charge that PR was too complicated for the average citizen to understand. In each of the eight PR elections, the *Ashtabula Star-Beacon* published lengthy descriptions of how to vote the PR ballot. After each election at least as much space was allocated to describing the count and the transfer process. Such press coverage at the outset of reform, in 1915 or 1917, might simply have fulfilled the informational needs of the community. The appearance of such articles in 1929, however, after the experience of 14 years and seven PR elections, suggests that the public was still unsure about how its electoral system worked.

In part, public confusion stemmed from the opportunity to express preferences for seven candidates when the ballot would count only once. This feature was not neglected by opponents of PR, who emphasized that as late as 1929 exhausted ballots accounted for 15% of the votes cast. Although proponents could have pointed out that in a two-person plurality race almost half of the ballots, or in a three-person race almost two-thirds, may be wasted (that is, cast for a loser), they failed to do so.

Critics were quick to claim that PR created not just public misunderstanding but even bewilderment for election board staff and officials who should be familiar with elections and vote counting. The practice of counting "X" for a preferred candidate was deeply rooted. When only one mark, an "X," was used on the STV ballot, the law required that it be counted as the voter's first choice. If the voter combined an "X" with numbered choices, the ballot should have been invalid. However, election officials in Ashtabula apparently chose to ignore the law and counted as a first choice the candidate designated by an "X" even when other preferences were expressed.

Errors in the count and the elapsed time between election day and the report of final results were also cited by critics as evidence of the system's complexity. In 1919 the election board announced that the count would take two hours, and it spent five hours counting ballots because of errors by precinct workers and election board officials. Results were often not available until two or three days later.

Invalid ballots were also subject to debate. Opponents of PR charged that in each of the four PR elections preceding that of 1929, there had been an increase in the number of invalid ballots. This was an allegation of questionable merit. The average number of invalid ballots cast in Ashtabula's first three PR elections was estimated to be 10%. The high, in 1919, was 13% of the total vote (Atkinson, 1920, p. 12). In subsequent PR elections the number of invalid ballots averaged 3.5%. The proportion of invalid ballots under PR was actually *smaller* than that under the earlier system replaced by PR (Moley and Bloomfield, 1926, pp. 651–60).

There was also an element of chance in the election of council members, acknowledged by proponents and critics alike, resulting from the way in which transfer votes were counted. Poll workers were to count all first-preference votes in the precincts, record the count on envelopes, and then transmit the envelopes with ballots to the board of election for the tally of transfer votes. The element of chance could influence the outcome by the order in which the precinct counts came in. The chance of attaining the quota was increased if those precincts most favorable to a candidate were physically brought to the board first for the count and transfer of votes. Conversely, a candidate whose popularity was greatest in precincts that came in last to the board of elections could be denied a seat on council (*Ashtabula Star-Beacon,* 31 Oct. 1929, p. 4).

This problem was not a defect of the PR/STV system itself but of the procedures prescribed in the Ashtabula charter. The allegation of chance was a persuasive criticism, however, serving as a better campaign weapon than the riposte that a change in the order of winners was an unlikely occurrence.

Minority representation itself became an issue in Ashtabula. Proportional representation was intended to enhance the representation of minority groups. Citizens had been promised that including "unanimous constituencies" of opinion in their council would produce better city councils. PR did accomplish minority representation, but the results were not always welcome to the native white population, which was accustomed to holding a majority on council in spite of its numerically minority status. Disagreement among members of the council was viewed as ethnic discord as early as 1920: "The lack of cooperation between the members of the council themselves and between the council and the manager is believed to be the result of a system of election which produces such a variety of interests and nationalities [that] . . . it lacks what may be called a sense of collective responsibility to the public" (Crecraft, 1920, p. 624).

Demographic changes in a community frequently create public anxiety. Ashtabula's minor wave of immigration after World War I became significant because of the changing ethnic mix. Italian gains in the 1919 municipal election seemed to adversely affect PR. R. C. Atkinson, a Western Reserve University professor, observing the scene from Cleveland, wrote: "There remains a surprising amount of opposition to proportional representation. Opposition arises from two causes—the method of voting and counting of ballots and unwillingness of many of the 'better' citizens to see certain groups, especially organized labor and the Italians, secure representation in the council" (1920, pp. 11–12). When Italian Catholics won two of the seven councilmanic seats in 1919, 1925, and again in 1929, the Italian community was felt to be overrepresented. Yet Italian representation increased during a period of growth in the Italian Catholic population (by 1930 Italian Americans surpassed the Finns as the city's largest ethnic group). The swelling Italian and Catholic character of the population renewed tension among "drys" in the city, manifested earlier in the 1917 organization of both the Guardians of Liberty and the Allied Defenders, and in the 1923 Ku Klux Klan slate of council candidates, two of whom were elected. Ethnic prejudice was fomented by the press. The *Star-Beacon,* for example, headlined a murder that had occurred, not in Ashtabula, but in nearby Geneva, Ohio. The banner read: "Mystery Murder: Investigation Points to 'Black Hand' Plot" (27 July 1927, p. 1).

Given these reinforcing cleavages of ethnicity and religion on the issue of prohibition, it is not surprising that repeal of PR and restoration of winner-take-all elections in 1931 virtually eliminated Italian representation on Ashtabula's council for a number of years. Only one Italian candidate, A. H. Candella, the son of Genaro Candella, a barber, was able to win election in the plurality/at-large system that replaced PR. This occurred in 1933, but Candella served for only a single term.

Ideologies of the left were also targeted by the opponents of PR. Public anxieties were raised by the Central Labor Union's endorsement of five men in the councilmanic elections of 1919. "That organized labor might gain control of the city council filled . . . the minds of a few good people with visions of bolshevism" (Atkinson, 1920, p. 9). At a meeting attended by approximately 300 people, mostly Finns, a resolution was passed condemning Communists, Socialists, and Anarchists as un-American. In 1924 the Socialist leader Eugene V. Debs obtained permission to use an Ashtabula public school auditorium for a speech. However, public outrage led school authorities to withdraw their permission, forcing Debs to a smaller Socialist hall in the city.

Thus was PR tarred by the brush of European ideology. Letters to the editor in the local press referred to PR as a "European system," a scheme that was "un-American," and on more than one occasion as "a system that smacks of bolshevism" (*Ashtabula Star-Beacon,* 7 Aug. 1922, p. 1). These epithets proved to be liabilities for the defenders of PR. Again, fact was not permitted to intrude too heavily on these observations, since PR/STV was actually developed by Thomas Hare, an English attorney, and Ashtabula's system was often called "the Hare system of voting."

Ashtabula's leaders, however, seem to have been most concerned about what they saw as the adverse effects of PR on the city manager plan of governance. Except for one outside professional, William Cotton, who was from Dayton, Ohio, the city managers appointed in the PR period were local political amateurs. Despite their lack of expertise, the managers compiled a positive record. One manager reduced taxes while improving city services. Another manager kept the city within budget at a time when many Ohio cities were in deep financial trouble. Services in Ashtabula had improved, and Ashtabulans seemed generally satisfied with these achievements under the city manager (*PRR,* 1917, 43:63). Proponents of reform had hoped that such accomplishments would insulate the office of city manager from the bitter acrimony that sometimes gripped the city council.

Controversy, however, had surrounded the office of the city manager from 1915, when the first PR council found itself deadlocked over the selection of the city manager. The deadlock prompted the three "drys" on council to caucus, in camera, to consider candidates for the manager's job and to discuss strategy for electing him. Upon learning of this meeting, an incensed council president, J. J. Hogan, retaliated by nominating one of the members of council, Fred A. Briggs, for the manager's job (Boynton, 1917, pp. 87–90). To obtain a majority of four votes, Briggs, a weaver by trade, had to vote for himself, which he did. It was an inauspicious beginning for reform, igniting a firestorm of criticism. A number of community leaders convened to consider the legality of both the appointment and PR, since Ohio law forbade a public servant to hold two public positions simultaneously (*Ashtabula Star-Beacon,* 18 Jan. 1916, p. 1).

The *Star-Beacon,* a proponent of PR, lamely regretted that the council did not do better in its search for a city manager. The newspaper also reminded its readers that the city manager plan was promoted on the assumption that the "best qualified man" would be chosen to manage the affairs of the city. The most qualified person was expected to be found through an "outside" search and to have command of engineering skills. Councilman Briggs, overcome by controversy, resigned from his position as city manager 18 days after his appointment.

The council selected the next manager only after more than 100 ballots, when Socialist member Earlywine agreed to join the council's three "wets" to appoint Warren Prine. This situation was a precursor of future difficulties when the cleavage between "wets" and "drys" repeatedly influenced the selection of managers. William Cotton, the outside expert who was committed to scientific management and neutral administration, was appointed in 1922, over the opposition of Councilmen Corrado and Rinto. His management style would win him, not surprisingly, not only "warm friends, but bitter enemies" (*PRR*, 1927, 81:5).

The council hired and fired six managers in the course of just 13 years.[3] For this Ashtabula was ridiculed in the national press and embarrassed at home. Divisions on council over moral issues (gambling, vice, Sunday closing, and liquor), patronage, and the letting of contracts affected evaluations of the city manager, whatever his administrative performance. Shaylor wrote to the editor of the *Star-Beacon*: "A whole nation points its finger with ridicule at Ashtabula because of its continual changing of city managers. Despite public welfare, despite individual protest, despite a scandalized community, a few councilmen go ahead and do as they please, and give no reason for their act" (*Ashtabula Star-Beacon*, 4 Nov. 1929, p. 3). Cotton, the former city manager, echoed Shaylor's criticism: "Lack of leadership and too many 'minority clan' representatives working for their own selfish interests were responsible for the present conditions under the city manager form of government in Ashtabula" (*Cleveland Plain Dealer*, 4 Jan. 1929, p. 10).

The business community, whose hopes to attract industry and new business to the city were founded on their progressive efforts toward political reform, were particularly vexed. Minority representation was achieved, but it appeared to introduce implacable elements into council. Against the philosophical value of guaranteeing minority representation in government, the time-tested principle of majority rule was underscored during the repeal campaign of 1929 (*Ashtabula Star-Beacon*, 31 Oct. 1929, p. 4).

The promise of a better government had been founded on two assumptions. First, the at-large provisions of the PR/STV system would improve the character of the council by electing people with community-wide standing who would reduce if not remove the baneful influence of parochial concerns. Second, the greater diversity of a PR-elected council would lead members to cooperate with one another and to find allies among those with different interests, leavening the self-serving interests of individuals. Both assumptions were brought into question.

Contrary to popular expectations as well as to the promises of PR's proponents, PR and the city manager plan failed to expunge "politics" from local government. Qualifications of those elected to PR councils were troubling as well. A former council member noted that it was frustrating to have on the council persons for whom such terms as *sinking fund* or *depreciation* were incomprehensible. Doubts about the quality of men elected to council were not limited to adversaries of PR. Raymond Moley, later a prominent New Dealer, who was sympathetic to PR, wrote disdainfully about Councilman Corrado's election to the first PR council. "His [Corrado's] election in 1915 did not add much to council, but it was evident that he was chosen by interests sufficient to be represented" (Moley, 1918, p. 31). The outcome of the same election elicited a direct challenge from one community leader to the citizens: "You people adopt a new form of government and then put in the same men to operate it and expect different results. . . . If you elect the right mayor and the right council under the old form of government, you will have the right kind of government. If you men of Ashtabula allow the wrong men to slip into office you will always have what you have now" (*Ashtabula Star-Beacon,* 18 June 1916, p. 1).

Citizen apathy, antipathy between religious and ethnic groups, a conflictual city council, and an unflagging opposition overcame political support for PR in the end. To understand the actual effects of proportional representation, however, we turn to an examination of turnout, candidate interest, characteristics of council members, and patterns of dissensus in council voting.

Did Proportional Representation Make a Difference?

Exaggerated claims are a common feature of reform movements, and the campaign in Ashtabula was no exception. The gap between promise and performance is always a threat to the persistence of reform measures (Moley and Bloomfield, 1926, p. 660). But what was the record of performance? PR was expected to increase political interest, largely because of the greater opportunities of groups to elect their candidates to public office. Heightened political interest, in turn, was expected to promote turnout. It was also believed that at-large voting would stimulate the civic interest of men of standing in the community, inducing them to become candidates and thus promoting competition for these offices. To what extent were these expectations fulfilled?

Political Interest

Voting Turnout

Psychological predispositions have long been recognized for their effect on political behavior, especially on the act of voting. Voters are more interested in politics, more attentive to political events, and feel more effective in public life than do nonvoters. The proportion of eligible citizens who exercise their right to vote is an important indication of political interest. Table 4.3 shows turnout over the three time periods: before, during, and after PR.

When turnout is measured as the percentage of registered voters who actually voted, a few differences among electoral systems do show up. During the pre-PR period, turnout averaged 66% of those registered. Turnout rose in the first several PR elections, but the average for the eight-election PR period was slightly lower, at 64%. For the post-PR period, the mean turnout rose to 73%.

However, features other than PR may also have been operant. Turnout in Ashtabula's mayoral races had averaged more than 70% in the 10 years before the abolition of the popularly elected mayor, even exceeding the turnout in gubernatorial contests. Since the separately elected mayor was replaced by an appointed city manager, turnout in the PR period could have declined because of the absence of a mayoral race (Moley and Bloomfield, 1926, p. 653).

Furthermore, registration increased dramatically between 1919 and 1921, owing to the extension of the franchise to women. Lower turnout among women who were voting for the first time would be expected in Ashtabula, as elsewhere. Indeed, mean turnout for the first three PR elections (before women won the vote) was 66% of those registered, a figure identical to pre-PR turnout, whereas the five PR elections in which women voted showed a slightly lower mean turnout of 62.6% (see table 4.3).

Nonpartisanship, introduced with the city manager plan and the PR system, has also been associated with lower turnout in municipal elections. In Ashtabula, parties played a less overt role during the PR period than they had previously, when council candidates were nominated in party primaries and elected on partisan ballots. The party affiliation of almost a third of the candidates was not even reported in the press in the era of PR elections (*Beacon Record*, 1915; *Ashtabula Star-Beacon*, 1917–29).

Turnout rose in Ashtabula's council elections after the repeal of PR, although other reform features such as nonpartisanship and the city manager plan were retained. However, the shift to plurality/at-large

TABLE 4.3

TURNOUT IN ASHTABULA MUNICIPAL ELECTIONS, 1909–1935

Year	Registration	Council Vote	Turnout (%)
Pre-PR			
1909	3,979	2,878	72
1911	4,625	2,971	64
1913	4,148	2,575	62
Mean			66
PR/STV			
1915	4,420	2,972	67
1917	4,815	3,438	71
1919	4,668	2,849	61
1921	7,000	4,998	71
1923	7,800	5,018	64
1925	8,491	4,544	54
1927	9,940	5,881	59
1929	9,000	5,880	65
Mean			64
Post-PR			
1931	8,600	6,486	75
1933	9,793	7,110	73
1935	9,639	6,743	70
Mean			73

Sources: Calculated from data published in *Beacon Record,* 1909–15; and *Ashtabula Star-Beacon,* 1917–35.

elections coincided with a national surge in turnout that is commonly attributed to the major party realignment of the New Deal era. There is no clear evidence that the changes in the electoral system in Ashtabula affected turnout.

Candidate Interest

Advocates of electoral reform had long believed that at-large elections would encourage prominent citizens to run for office. PR's enhanced opportunities for minorities to win representation should also have stimulated candidates of previously underrepresented groups to run, leading to greater competition in council races. Competition is also increased when fewer incumbents run for reelection. Table 4.4 shows the number of candidates for council and the proportion of incumbents seeking reelection in the three periods examined.

TABLE 4.4
NUMBER OF ASHTABULA COUNCIL CANDIDATES AND INCUMBENCY
RATE, 1909–1935

	Mean N of Candidates	Mean % of Incumbents
1909–13	27	40
1915–29	16	39
1931–35	17	71

Sources: Calculated from *Beacon Record,* 1909–15; and *Ashtabula Star-Beacon,* 1916–35.

The average number of candidates running in the three pre-PR elections was 27, a substantially larger group than those seeking office in the PR and post-PR periods, when the averages dropped to 16 and 17 respectively. The significant drop occurred with the change from the mixed ward and at-large system of pre-PR to the at-large plan of both PR and post-PR elections. The at-large provision itself appears to have dampened competition. This result is not surprising, since at-large elections, which require candidates to campaign throughout the city, tend to be more complex and costly than ward races.

However, the impact of changing electoral systems on incumbents' decisions to seek reelection follows a different pattern. As table 4.4 shows, there is virtually no change in the proportion of incumbents who sought reelection in the pre-PR and PR periods, 40% and 39% respectively. However, the proportion of incumbents seeking reelection in the post-PR period increased sharply, to 71%. The advantage of a familiar name in the free-for-all of plurality/at-large voting must have played a part. Moreover, the abrupt rise in incumbency could reflect the hardships of the Great Depression, which may have induced more incumbents to seek reelection in the belief that some salary is better than none. Still, the reward was small. In 1929 the council sought unsuccessfully to stimulate interest in council service by raising council salaries from $100 to $600 per year. Competition for council seats in Ashtabula appears to have been shaped by factors other than the electoral system.

Minority Representation

Another expectation entertained by advocates of PR was that PR would achieve more "representative" councils. To explore this question, the characteristics of council members in Ashtabula, by partisan, religious, ethnic, and occupational differences, were examined for each of the three electoral periods.

Party

Ashtabula was a Republican community, as was much of the state, with Democrats and Socialists as minor parties. Although the adoption of nonpartisanship in 1914 limited the information available for the PR period, some conclusions may be drawn.

Electoral system change did not substantially alter the political dominance of the Republican party in the city. Republicans maintained their majority on council in each of the three periods. They controlled 69% of the council seats in the pre-PR period. Their share dropped to 55% of the seats on PR councils, a majority even if all of the members for whom party affiliation is missing were Democrats. In the post-PR period, the Republican majority grew to 71% of the seats in spite of the national surge toward Democratic hegemony in depression-era politics.

In fact, Democratic candidates steadily lost ground in Ashtabula, winning 18% of the seats in the pre-PR period, 12% (as far as is known) during the PR years, and only 9% in the post-PR period. In this small Ohio city, Republican allegiance was not easily shaken.

The Socialist Party was the second minor party in the city, a visible organization maintaining itself as a political entity in Ashtabula and a number of surrounding communities. Before World War I, Socialist candidates won even some plurality elections in northeast Ohio. The Socialist Party was most active during the pre-PR period and was popular for its stands in favor of the public ownership of utilities, the regulation of corporations, and ethics in government. In an at-large contest in the 1911 Ashtabula election, a Socialist candidate, Van Tassell, lost by a single vote. Two other popular local politicians, Boynton and J. D. Knowlton, had at one time run as Socialist Party candidates for office. In the PR years the only minor party candidate known to be elected to council was Socialist Earlywine, a leading citizen of Ashtabula and member of the charter commission. His election in 1915 was the last for this party, whose members were too small an electoral minority to benefit from PR.

Religion

In addition to the overwhelmingly Protestant host population, the Finns, Swedes, Danes, Canadians, and German Lutherans were also Protestant. Together these groups constituted the religious majority in

TABLE 4.5
RELIGIOUS AFFILIATION OF ASHTABULA COUNCIL MEMBERS,
1910–1937 (%)

	Protestant	Catholic	Unknown
1910–15	59	18	23
1916–31	67	33	—
1932–37	86	14	—

Sources: Data are based on candidates' statements to the *Beacon Record*, 1910–15; and the *Ashtabula Star-Beacon*, 1916–37.

the city. Protestants accounted for 59% of the council membership whose religious affiliation was known in the pre-PR era, 67% under PR, and 86% in the post-PR period. Roman Catholicism was the faith of other ethnic minorities—the Italians, the Irish, and those Germans who came from Bavaria and the Rhineland.

Catholic representation increased during the PR years, and only under PR, as is evident in table 4.5. In pre-PR councils, Catholic representation, sustained by the popularity of ward representative Nick Corrado, the saloonkeeper, stood at 18%, grew to 33% under PR, and then dropped to 14% in the post-PR period.

Ethnicity

Although identification based on nationality ran counter to the early twentieth-century American notion of the melting pot, ethnicity was a powerful influence among citizens in Ashtabula. Ethnic groups enjoyed the solidarity of a common heritage, language, religion, and customs. However, durable differences among members of various groups, including Scandinavian clusters, were less pronounced than those defined by the Protestant/Catholic cleavage. By endorsing Scandinavian Protestants such as Amsden, Mack, Rinto, and Swedenborg, the anti-Catholic Guardians of Liberty helped to increase ethnic representation from 1917 on. Given their numbers in the city's population, Italian and Irish ethnic minorities should have gained representation on PR councils. Table 4.6 shows the ethnic distribution of council membership from 1910 to 1937.

As these data show, those citizens of Anglo-Saxon origin—the "native whites" who made up only 43% of the population in 1910—held 66% of the council seats in the pre-PR period. With PR, this group's share of seats dropped to just under half, and it rose only slightly in post-PR plurality voting. The leading ethnic minorities won significantly more seats on the PR ballot, with Irish Americans as the principal

TABLE 4.6
ETHNIC BACKGROUND OF ASHTABULA CITY COUNCIL MEMBERS,
1910–1937 (%)

	Native Americans	Italians	Finns	Swedes	Germans	Irish
1910–15	66	15	4	4	8	4
1916–31	49	18	9	7	—	16
1932–37	52	5	19	—	14	10

Source: *City Directory,* 1910–37, Ashtabula Public Library.

beneficiaries; Finns, Swedes, and Italians followed in that order. Only German Americans lost representation in the PR era, undoubtedly owing to the anti-German sentiment surrounding World War I.

Ethnic successes were as short-lived as the PR system itself. Three of these ethnic groups lost representation in the post-PR period, demonstrating that the electoral system accounted for the temporary growth of ethnic representation. Only the Finns appear to have established themselves firmly enough under PR to gain representation in post-PR plurality elections, although German Americans made a comeback, perhaps owing to declining hostility as the emotions of World War I receded.

It appears that Italian-American voters were more cohesive in support of their candidates than other ethnic groups in the city. Their residential concentration enabled them to achieve some representation in the ward elections of the pre-PR system. Under PR, "bullet" voting by the Italian community is indicated by a relatively high proportion of exhausted ballots in the Italian Ward 2. However, on the PR ballot, limiting choices to one's own group is not necessary to achieve representation; lower-ranked choices cannot take precedence over higher-ranked candidates on the same ballot. Bullet voting should have been more effective in the plurality/at-large elections of the post-PR period, yet a dramatic decline in Italian-American representation occurred. This decline may be attributable to the Prohibition-related scandals cited earlier, as well as to the impact of the plurality/at-large ballot on a residentially clustered minority.

Occupation

Advocates of PR had envisioned a "better" council under PR. They believed that the election of prominent individuals would create councils whose actions would promote the interest of the community as a whole rather than the narrower interests of the old wards.

TABLE 4.7
OCCUPATIONS OF ASHTABULA CITY COUNCIL MEMBERS,
BY PERCENTAGE DISTRIBUTION, 1910–1937

	Blue-Collar	Managerial/ Supervisory	Professional	Business	Other
1910–15	13	25	8	46	8
1916–31	16	39	29	16	—
1932–37	24	48	10	10	—

Sources: *Beacon Record,* 1910–15; and *Ashtabula Star-Beacon,* 1916–37.

Prominent individuals did seek office, most notable of whom was the superintendent of the Harbor Special Schools, W. E. Wenner. In the 1927 election, Wenner obtained the highest number of first-choice votes ever cast, with strong showings in both working-class and "up-town" wards (*Ashtabula Star-Beacon,* 9 Nov. 1927, p. 1). Undoubtedly the type of person the reformers had hoped to recruit, Wenner had an exceptional reputation for honesty, competence, and civic service. He had served on the city's charter commission in 1914 and would serve again on subsequent charter commissions into the 1940s, as well as in the state legislature (*Ashtabula Star-Beacon,* 14 Jan. 1949, p. 1). Wenner resigned from council shortly after his election in 1927, however, purportedly for health reasons, although it was noted that his resignation came after a bitter division over the dismissal of manager Carey S. Sheldon in 1928, and a deadlock in the election of the council president (*Ashtabula Star-Beacon,* 4 Jan. 1928, p. 1). Were the expectations of PR's supporters otherwise satisfied? Table 4.7 shows the data for occupational backgrounds of members of council.

Members of the professions did increase in numbers under PR. Doctors, dentists, lawyers, and educators all fared well in PR elections. From 8% of pre-PR councils, the proportion of professional members more than trebled to 29% of PR councils. Ethnic groups benefited from these outcomes with the election from the Irish community of both the physician Hogan and a dentist, Dr. Robert Goggin. The rise in professional representation, however, was achieved at the expense of small businessmen. In the pre-PR period, grocers, saloonkeepers, nursery operators, and hardware store owners accounted for almost half (46%) of the council membership, but such entrepreneurial representation declined to 16% during PR. In the post-PR period, the trends were reversed, with small businessmen increasing their share of seats to 19%, while professionals declined to 10% of the total.

Council members from both blue-collar and managerial or supervisory occupations showed a steady increase in their representation across the three time periods. Blue-collar membership of council began at 13%, increased to 16% under PR, and grew again to 24% after PR. Nonprofessional white-collar occupations reveal a similar trend. Managerial and supervisory occupations accounted for 25% of the members before PR, 39% during PR, and almost half of the seats after PR.

The evidence thus shows that representation of minority interests increased under PR for Italian and Irish Ashtabulans, Catholics, and members of the professions. Some of these categories overlap. Increased Catholic representation on PR councils was largely due to the success of Irish candidates who were professionals, not working-class "depot" Irish. The Irish were a special case because their homes were scattered throughout the city. The ward feature of the pre-PR electoral system had inhibited Irish opportunities for representation, and the group was not numerous enough to win the few at-large seats. With the introduction of PR the Irish could pull together in the "unanimous constituency" Hare had envisioned, and they chose professionals to represent them. In the winner-take-all races of the post-PR system, their minority status again limited their electoral opportunity.

Decision-Making Patterns

Proponents of PR maintained that the preferential voting required by PR/STV would reduce the personal conflict on the council, which seemed to grow out of traditional head-to-head electoral contests in the wards and the at-large free-for-all of the pre-PR period. With PR, almost all successful candidates needed second-, third-, or subsequent-choice votes from the supporters of other candidates, and therefore they were less likely to use personal attack as a campaign strategy. Proponents also argued that minority representation would bring previously excluded interests into the decision-making process where their demands could be effectively mediated.

Sixty or 70 years ago, local issues were expected to be handled with local resources. The Ashtabula council during this period faced the problems of a semirural community under pressure to provide urban amenities. Construction and maintenance of streets, sewers, and sidewalks; provision of a safe water supply; an ample supply of electricity from its municipal light plant; protection of the citizenry; and the enforcement of vice and gaming laws were the basic concerns of the council.

TABLE 4.8
ASHTABULA CITY COUNCIL WORK LOAD, 1910–1937

	Ordinances[a]			Resolutions		
	N	Avg.	% Unan.	N	Avg.	% Unan.
1910–15	365	61	88	139	23	94
1916–31	1,244	77	83	326	20	81
1932–37	240	40	84	129	22	85

Source: *Council Record*, 1910–37, available in the city auditor's office. The yearly average is the sum of the total number of ordinances and resolutions for the period divided by the number of years.

[a]First and second readings of proposed ordinances were excluded from tabulations.

More peripheral issues were also addressed, such as regulations to deal with noise (from radios), the keeping of fowl or hogs (prohibited), the location of water closets, the rendering of livestock, and the "moving of offal and dead animals through city streets and alleys." Less urgent needs were not ignored, like the letting of contracts to cut "noxious" weeds on city streets. Revenues were as important then as now, and licenses (for automobiles) and permits (for boxing exhibitions) were routine issues of council business.

To measure differences among the three electoral periods in workload and patterns of decision making, the average number of ordinances and resolutions passed in each of the periods was calculated, as well as the percentages of the total that were unanimous (see table 4.8).

On average, PR councils did handle a larger number of ordinances than did non-PR councils, passing an average of 77 ordinances per year, compared to 61 for pre-PR councils and only 40 for post-PR councils. Examination of the *Council Record* reveals that the greater volume of ordinances during the PR years fell largely between 1925 and 1929, when major street improvements were made and the city's municipal light plant was sold to the Cleveland Electric Illuminating Company.

Disharmony and conflict, so frequently the topic of press coverage in Ashtabula, do not appear to have been significantly more characteristic of PR councils than those before or after. The vast majority of all measures were passed unanimously by councils in all three periods. A slight decline is seen in the percentage of unanimous ordinances, from 88% in pre-PR to 83% and 84% in PR and post-PR respectively. A somewhat larger decline is seen in unanimous resolutions from the pre-PR period, at 94%, to the PR and post-PR periods, at 81% and 85% of the total.

Closer examination of specific councils enables us to examine the degree of consensus that existed when more Catholics served on the council. If council diversity were the basis of conflictual relations, and therefore of nonunanimous voting on the issues, we should expect a decline in unanimous voting on the councils of 1920–21, 1926–27, and 1930–31. Tabulation of unanimous votes for these three councils, however, yields scores that are only slightly below the average for all PR councils.

The *Council Record* does show that Councilman Corrado voted against the majority more often than any other member, casting the lone dissenting vote on many ordinances in the pre-PR and PR years. He opposed ordinances to pave Main Street, to issue bonds to purchase a building and equipment for the fire department, to hire detectives (they were often hired to detect "wet" operations), to regulate firearms (Corrado had once carried a weapon), to levy special assessments, and to limit the sale of alcohol. His behavior was unique and even seemed to be defiant of the community's interests.

There were other dissenters too, but there is no record of Hogan, also a Catholic, joining Corrado in dissent. More often Rainnie or Rinto, both Protestants, accounted for other split decisions. Arthur Rinto, a formidable adversary of the manager, was a trial lawyer whose work on behalf of defendants charged with violating "dry" laws may have generated conflict in council business.

One might legitimately ask how press reports of dissent and intransigence on council could be so at odds with the findings related to actual council voting. The best explanation seems to be that the issues voted on by council were believed to be less newsworthy than the social issue that had divided the community for so long. On temperance, the council reflected intense divisions in the city itself. William Boynton commented: "Numerous wet and dry elections had divided the people into opposing factions to such an extent that municipal elections had come to be in the main simply contests between wets and drys for the control of city government" (1917, p. 88). Because Ashtabula voted itself "dry" the year after adoption of PR, virtually the entire electoral experiment with PR was dominated by divisions over prohibition. These divisions explain the conflict between members of council and the chief administrator of the law, the preference for local managers over outsiders, who might have been insensitive to local needs, and the resulting high casualty rate for city managers.

Conclusion

A number of observations are suggested by this study. First, the system of proportional representation did benefit some, but not all, of the significant minorities in Ashtabula. Representation of Irish and Italian Catholics increased under PR, as did representation of Scandinavian Protestants. Professional and blue-collar occupations were more heavily represented, at the expense of small business people, who had been the largest single occupational grouping on the pre-PR council. Partisan minorities such as Democrats and Socialists, and after 1920 women, won either little or no representation on PR councils.

Second, the divisive social issue of temperance, aggravated by reinforcing cleavages of ethnicity and religion, created conflict in a legislative body that reflected the diversity of the community. It is possible that a strong mayor, acting as political leader, instead of the supposedly neutral expert administrator, could have managed the tensions more effectively. It appears that linking electoral system reform to the city manager plan was at least problematical in this case.

Third, the failure of PR's advocates to build an effective and organized constituency to support the new electoral system left PR vulnerable to repeal initiatives. Support for repeal was organized by former office holders and interests seeking to restore lost perquisites and old ways of doing the public's business. The press's penchant for emphasizing the council's bellicosity toward the city manager further undermined the already fragile public support for PR.

Although political parties and their corrupt bosses had been the topic of scathing press commentary in the period leading up to reform, the parties failed to play a significant role in the events detailed here. Little evidence was found of the parties being engaged in the recruitment or election of candidates, the definition of issues, or the governing of the community. As functional institutions they were totally ineffective. Perhaps the press had been successful in stigmatizing both politics and political parties. Perhaps the depoliticization attempted in 1914 through nonpartisan elections and the city manager plan achieved its goal. Whatever the reasons, a void was left to be filled by other interests and organizations. Some, such as Independents for Earlywine and the Finnish Voters' League, were transient. Others, such as the Guardians of Liberty, the Allied Defenders, and the Ku Klux Klan, persisted and exacerbated the political life of the community, serving as surrogates for party. These groups recruited candidates, contested elections, and stimulated anti-Catholic sentiments and ethnic hostilities that thwarted the agenda of democratic politics.

Ashtabula, the pioneer PR community in the United States, was also the first of 22 American PR cities to abandon its electoral experiment. In the post-PR period, plurality dominance returned to Ashtabula in the form of plurality/at-large elections. Although the Yankees were only the largest of this small city's many demographic groups, they captured the majority of council once more. The city's public policies would be made by a body overwhelmingly Protestant, Republican, and, after the first post-PR election, composed largely of incumbents.

PR indeed made a difference in Ashtabula, bringing previously underrepresented ethnic, religious, and labor groups onto the council. This electoral experiment, conducted for 16 years under the pressure of a deep cleavage in the community over prohibition, was not a failure in terms of governance of the city. The diversity it produced, however, was not necessarily valued in the political culture of the 1920s, and its friends were incapable of building majority support for its continuance.

FIVE

■ ■ ■

PR and Boss Rule:
The Case of Cleveland

This election [of 1921] was a most inspiring event for those of us
who like to believe in government not only of and for the people,
but by the people. Our faith has been none too strong at times,
and frequently we have been tempted to fear that "the struggle
naught availeth" and that the labor and the wounds are indeed
vain. But Cleveland has shown us that the people will rise to a
great challenge, that they will not shrink before the big and constructive task, and that they can deal with principles as well as
with men. And if Cleveland, with her 800,000 people of every
race and color and creed, can accomplish such a thing, what may
not democracy dare to hope!

Maxey, "Cleveland Revolts," 1922

THE ACCOMPLISHMENT of Cleveland's voters, acclaimed by reformers across the country in 1921, was the adoption of a city charter
amendment that embraced two key Progressive features: the city
manager plan and proportional representation elections for city council. This triumph was particularly joyous for the reform movement
because Cleveland, then the "Fifth City" in the United States, was the
most populous yet to adopt either the city manager plan or PR/STV.
Moreover, Cleveland's population was "polyglot," brimming with
immigrants whose poverty, illiteracy, and lack of experience with
democracy were believed to pose a severe test of whether or not
democratic institutions could work.

The author acknowledges the assistance of Dan Obermiller for statistical analysis and
Richard Marsh for collection of data.

For almost a decade, Cleveland would govern itself in this reform mode. Five PR/STV elections (1923–31) were accompanied by five repeal initiatives, which culminated in the charter opponents' success in 1931. "Returning the city's government to the people" was the theme of both the 1921 campaign to adopt the PR charter and the 1931 campaign to abandon it.

Cleveland's experiment in municipal reform was conducted within the framework of traditional party institutions of control. As were other large cities in Ohio at the time, Cleveland was governed informally by a Republican machine, with the subservient but cooperative assistance of the Democratic organization. Although "boss rule" was the principal target of the reformers who sought better government in Cleveland, the parties adapted themselves to reform institutions and continued to operate in many ways as they had since the late nineteenth century.

Moreover, although the parties survived administrative reform and electoral system change in Cleveland in the 1920s, for the most part doing business as usual, the reforms did make a difference. This chapter will look at the differences proportional representation elections made, and at why the system was adopted and then repealed within a decade. This chapter will also examine representational outcomes under PR/STV in comparison with the outcomes of the electoral systems used before and after PR/STV. Their impact on consensus or conflict in the operations of the city council will also be assessed.

The "Polyglot" City

By the end of the nineteenth century, Cleveland was the largest city in Ohio and its leading commercial, industrial, and financial center. Cleveland's industrial growth depended on the confluence of lake-shipped iron ore from the north and coal brought by rail from southern Ohio and Appalachia. Although Cleveland had been settled by New Englanders, significant numbers of Irish and German immigrants arrived before the Civil War. Between the Civil War and World War I, hundreds of thousands of immigrants came from southern and eastern Europe, providing labor for the city's factories and steel mills. Labor shortages during World War I led the managers of major Cleveland companies to recruit black workers from the deep South. These new migrants and their families augmented Cleveland's small African-American population, which had migrated north largely from the border states before the turn of the century.

By 1920 the city's population was close to 800,000, more than two-thirds of whom were foreign-born or of foreign parentage. Although European immigration declined during the 1920s as a result of the national quotas of the 1924 Immigration Act, the number of black residents would double again before 1930 to eight percent of the total (Green, 1931, pp. 5, 14–15; Kusmer, 1976, pp. 10, 158).

As in other large manufacturing cities during this period, population growth in Cleveland was accompanied by annexation and suburbanization. Early in the century, the city aggressively annexed outlying parcels of land in order to grow. The business community demonstrated its commitment to growth by establishing the Chamber of Commerce Committee on Annexation in 1916 to promote urban expansion (Richardson, 1986, p. 165). Significant movement of east side residents to new eastern suburbs, however, began at about the same time. To protect the independence of their small residential communities on the fringe of the city, business leaders who had moved out stopped promoting annexation. The chamber of commerce began to urge adoption of a two-tier metropolitan government to advance the efficiency of area-wide operations while maintaining separate local control of core public functions in the city and its suburbs. In 1924 the Committee on Annexation became the Committee on Co-operative Metropolitan Government.

By 1929 reformers would note regretfully that the "best citizens who should afford the political leadership of the community" had moved to the suburbs. Not one member of the executive committee of the Cleveland Bar Association, for example, was a resident of Cleveland (Harris, 1930, p. 354). While Cleveland's population grew 13% between 1920 and 1930, the population of the county outside of Cleveland more than doubled (*Greater Cleveland [GC]*, 20 Oct. 1930, 6:10).

The Political Setting

From the late nineteenth century on, Cleveland's rapid population growth seemed to create a crisis in service delivery and opportunities for new kinds of corruption in government. Republican mayor Robert E. McKisson, elected in 1895, had consolidated power through traditional practices of patronage, graft, and favoritism in the granting of city contracts and utility franchises. Opposition within the mayor's own party to these modes of governing led to the founding of the Municipal Association in 1896. Principal organizers were Harry A. Garfield, son of the late president; Frederic C. Howe, attorney and former student of Woodrow Wilson at the Johns Hopkins University; and Rabbi Moses Gries, leader of the Reform Jewish community (Campbell, 1988, pp. 302–3). Although this initiative arose within the dominant Republican party, it would become bipartisan with the success of Democratic mayor Tom L. Johnson and his four-term reform administration (1901–9).

In the early twentieth century, muckraker Lincoln Steffens celebrated Mayor Tom Johnson's reforms, calling Cleveland "the best-governed city in the United States" (Steffens, 1906, pp. 161, 183). Community leaders felt restricted, however, by state legislative control and were instrumental in furthering the cause of municipal home rule. The Cleveland Municipal Association led the movement for home rule in Ohio, and pursued "good government" issues both locally and in the state legislature (Campbell, 1988, p. 310).[1] Their efforts were rewarded by the adoption in 1912 of the home rule amendment to the Ohio Constitution, which allowed Ohio cities to choose their own form of government (Warner, 1964, pp. 330–32).

Cleveland acted quickly to adopt a home rule charter. A charter commission, elected in 1913, heard extensive arguments on the most controversial issue, the question of ward versus at-large council elections. The city was divided at the time into 32 wards, each ward electing a single member to council by plurality vote. An unlikely coalition composed of the Progressive Constitutional League, the chamber of commerce, and the Cleveland Federation of Labor advocated a small at-large council to represent better the "interest of the whole city" instead of small, parochial segments of it. Party leaders, defenders of the ward system, argued that a small, at-large council was intended to and indeed would operate to exclude Catholics and representatives of the foreign-born from the council as effectively as they had been excluded from the school board in 1892, when its election from 20 wards was replaced by a small board elected at-large by plurality voting (Campbell, 1988, p. 313; Miggins, 1988a, p. 352).

The class character of the debate between advocates of ward and at-large elections is reflected in reformers' fears of lower-class dominance of ward councils, seen as "government by the least educated, the least interested class of citizens" (Hays, 1964, p. 164). Daniel Morgan, a former Republican councilman and member of the charter commission (who would later become Cleveland's second city manager) defended the ward system as necessary to ensure the representation of Cleveland's ethnic citizens—who made up three-fourths of the city's population—by people like themselves. Morgan had lived and worked in Goodrich Settlement House in a densely populated immigrant area, where he had seen the scope of human needs and the importance of assistance provided to dependent people by the ward bosses and precinct workers (Campbell, 1988, pp. 313–14).

C. G. Hoag of the American P.R. League explained to the commission how the PR/STV ballot, which was then not yet in use anywhere in the United States, could be used in Cleveland (*Equity,* Jan. 1914, 16.1:52). Some members of the commission knew of this system because of Tom Johnson's advocacy of PR in the 1890s for electing members to the U.S. House of Representatives. The commission chose instead to introduce the preferential ballot, which was adaptable to ward voting. This choice was viewed as an acceptable compromise, for which credit was given to commission members Morgan and Newton D. Baker, a Democrat, with the help of Mayo Fesler, the secretary of the Municipal League (Mingle, 1974, pp. 42–44).

Named the "Bucklin" ballot for its inventor, this preferential mode of voting was briefly a popular mechanism in the antiboss strategy of the reformers. Nominations by petition replaced the party primaries, which had enabled organization leaders through their loyal voters to control access to public office. On the preferential ballot, with one ward representative to be elected, voters could indicate their first, second, and "other" choices of candidates for election. A candidate with a majority of the first-choice votes would be declared the winner. If the leading candidate won only a plurality, second choices would be added to the candidates' totals. Again, a majority winner would end the count. If there were still only a plurality candidate in the lead, "other" choices would be added to the totals, and a majority or plurality winner would be declared the victor (Warner, 1964, p. 442).[2]

The proposed charter also provided for a nonpartisan ballot; administration by a strong mayor; a civil service code; initiative, referendum, and recall; and the power to purchase and operate utilities. This municipal reform plan was overwhelmingly approved by the voters in July 1913.

In the years to follow, the Republican and Democratic parties constantly attacked the preferential ballot, even as they learned to use it to their own advantage (*Cleve. Plain Dealer,* 18 Nov. 1915). By instructing their regular voters to cast first-choice votes only, the parties denied second- and other choice votes to independent candidates. Independent voters tended to mark two or more choices, thus helping to elect the parties' candidates over their own first choices (Maxey, 1922a, p. 85).

This first home rule charter lasted less than a decade. In the two administrations of Mayor Newton D. Baker (1912–16), the reformers appeared to be in charge; but by 1916 the Republican organization gained control for the remainder of the decade. Maurice Maschke, a Harvard-educated attorney who had learned his politics as a precinct worker in McKisson's machine, became "the boss."

In the continuing struggle to diminish the influence of political parties, civic and reform leaders organized the Committee of Fifteen to evaluate the potential of further charter reform. The city manager plan and PR/STV elections for council, which the National Municipal League had endorsed as a package in 1914, garnered the support of the committee. A few members objected to the city manager plan on the ground that an appointed administrator could not be held accountable to the people, but PR/STV had unanimous support. To some, the single transferable vote simply corrected the manipulability of the preferential ballot. Wider choices for the voters and diversity of representation could be achieved by the more structured rules of the STV count without risking the occasional fluke victory that occurred with preferential voting (Mingle, 1974, pp. 11, 59).

Reform efforts were dormant during World War I and its aftermath, but in 1921 the majority recommendations of the Committee of Fifteen were embodied in a charter amendment written by Augustus Hatton of Western Reserve University, by then a national consultant on municipal charters. The amendment was placed before the voters by initiative in November and the Committee of One Hundred was formed to promote a new charter.

Adoption of PR: Political Dynamics

The urban reformers of the first two decades of the twentieth century in Cleveland were among the most diverse of the nation's Progressives. The legacy of Mayor Tom Johnson was a blend of moral uplift, civic idealism, and the practical exercise of power. Unified principally by their opposition to a corrupt alliance of local party leaders (bosses) and businessmen seeking favors (special interests), the Cleveland reformers included business and professional leaders, social reformers, populists, and labor leaders. Contradictory reform goals did not prevent the coalition from uniting in support of the 1921 charter amendment proposal.

The diversity of the reform coalition was demonstrated by the selection of Peter Witt to chair the Committee of One Hundred. A protégé of Tom Johnson, Witt was viewed as a radical populist, and therefore with suspicion, by the business community. Although a Democrat, Witt was neither regular nor predictable, and he identified himself as an Independent after 1915. Upon becoming head of the Committee of One Hundred, he said that the new charter could not eliminate the parties from city government, but it would relegate them to "proportional" power (*Cleve. Press,* 1 June 1921).

Support for the committee came from both outside and local sources. George Hallett, associate director of the P.R. League, came from New York City to campaign for the charter. Although the Cleveland Federation of Labor opposed the charter, a Union Labor P.R. Club was formed by members of at least 15 Cleveland unions who disagreed with the Federation's stance. The Brotherhood of Locomotive Engineers was particularly active, printing and distributing hundreds of thousands of pro-charter leaflets directed to workingmen (*PRR,* 1922, 61:4–5). A column allocated to the Union Labor P.R. Club in the city's Socialist newspaper, the *Cleveland Citizen,* urged readers to vote for the proposed charter primarily in order to secure PR, to "take the 'lid' off all the real but now repressed opinions of the voters of this city" and to "give every voter and interest perfect justice and freedom" (*Cleve. Citizen,* 5 Nov. 1921, p. 3).

Organized women also played an important role in the charter battle. In 1894 Ohio women had won the right to vote in school board elections. In Cleveland this right was widely exercised, becoming a stimulus to further political activity. By 1920, 80,000 women had joined local suffrage groups in the city, an unprecedented mobilization of political feminism (Scharf, 1986, pp. 75, 81). After the vote was won in 1920, the Cleveland League of Women Voters, following in the footsteps of its national parent body, endorsed PR. League volunteers worked tirelessly to win its adoption. In the league's spirit of educating voters, public, open-air debates on PR and the city manager plan were sponsored, and these major events were both preceded and followed by house-to-house canvasses, which women organized and carried out by ward and precinct to promote the charter (Abbott, 1949, pp. 107–19; Morton, 1988, pp. 341–42).

The city's newspapers were divided. The *Cleveland Press* waged an active campaign for the charter, printing daily supportive cartoons and editorials on the front page, as well as straw polls favorable to passage. The *Press* also conducted a contest for the best answer to "why you intend voting for the City Manager Plan at the November 8 election," with prizes for the winners (*Cleve. Press,* 25 Oct.–8 Nov. 1921, p. 1). A spirited campaign was conducted on the theme of wiping out the evils of boss rule. Special appeals were directed to newly enfranchised women, including such pro-charter testimonials by women as: "We deplore methods and results in city housekeeping which would never be accepted as efficient in individual businesses or in a home" (*Cleve. Press,* 29 Oct. 1921, p. 1). The *Press* reported that women were "worrying the political bosses" by attending meetings about the charter in large numbers, listening intently and making no public commitments (*Cleve. Press,* 13 Oct. 1921, p. 4).

PR/STV elections triggered the opposition of the *Cleveland Plain Dealer,* both political parties, the chamber of commerce, and the Cleveland Federation of Labor. The *Plain Dealer* called PR/STV "complicated, undemocratic and dangerous" because it would lead to the fragmentation of council into many small interests (*Cleve. Plain Dealer,* 22 Oct. 1921, p. 21). If the city manager plan were desirable, it could be submitted to the voters later "without the PR incubus" (*Cleve. Plain Dealer,* 7 Nov. 1921, p. 14). The chamber feared destruction of the two-party system and introduction of unstable coalition government (Cleve. Chamber of Commerce, 1921).

In the campaign little attention was paid to the unusual combination of PR elections with a multimember district system. By 1921 PR/STV was in use for municipal elections in Ashtabula, Boulder, Kalamazoo, Sacramento, and West Hartford. Of these, only one small community, West Hartford, used districts (Moley, 1923, p. 652). Professor Hatton, undeterred by novelty, tried to avoid the acrimonious debate of a decade earlier between defenders of the wards and advocates of citywide election.[3] He combined the wards into four large districts, each of which would elect five, six, or seven members. These large districts were proposed as an ingenious middle ground between the extremes, enlarging the scope of representation beyond the ward, yet allowing for some territorial ties.

District lines were said to be drawn to reflect "social and economic homogeneity" (Maxey, 1922a, p. 84). District 1, west of the Cuyahoga River, and District 4 to the "far" east (around University Circle), containing "one of the city's best residential districts," were allocated a total of 14 seats. Districts 2 and 3, including "the principal foreign and colored elements of the city's population," had a total of 11 seats. Because these district lines created unequal populations, additional seats were assigned to the more populous districts (*PRR,* 1924, 69:19, 24).

The allocation of seats to districts was also influenced by the variance in the number of registered voters in the respective districts; a smaller proportion of residents of Districts 2 and 3 registered to vote.[4] But political values also appear to have shaped the distribution of power. Since the Second and Third Districts were also the strongholds of the political parties, the districting plan, skewed to the advantage of the First and Fourth Districts, favored independents and upper-status, better-educated voters. Furthermore, candidates were permitted to run in any district, regardless of their district of residence, a feature that emphasized the "quality" of the individual candidate, rather than geographical representation.

Since local opinion leaders were deeply divided over the proposed charter, and their views highly publicized, its defeat could have been anticipated. Instead, victory ensued. The adoption of the charter on 8 November 1921 was welcomed by PR advocates everywhere. Not only was Cleveland the largest U.S. city to adopt both the city manager plan and PR, but its diverse population provided a unique test case. Cleveland would become "the nation's greatest experiment station for attacking the problem of efficient democracy" (Maxey, 1922a, p. 84). With a turnout on the charter issue of 81.4% of registered voters, the new charter was approved by 57.2% of those voting on the amendment. Although the turnout of registered voters was high, the number voting on the charter actually represented only 27% of Cleveland's voting age population. Still, the charter passed in 29 of the 32 wards. Support was high in wards heavily populated by native-born whites, with high levels of school attendance and high voter participation rates. Significantly less support for the charter was shown in wards where black and foreign-stock residents lived, political party organizations were strong, illiteracy rates high, and school attendance rates low (Mingle, 1974, pp. 81–88). Since the political parties were explicit targets of the reformers, it is not surprising that wards with populations more dependent on the machines would be less supportive.

Opponents of the new charter promptly carried their battle to court, challenging the new mode of voting under both state and federal constitutions. As discussed in chapter 2, the Ohio Supreme Court rejected the argument that PR/STV violated an alleged state right to vote for all seats in a multimember election (*Reutener v. Cleveland,* 1923). Furthermore, the allegation of federal protection of plurality voting through the republican form of government guarantee (art. 4) and the equal protection of the laws (amend. 14) was also rejected (*Hile v. Cleveland,* 1923; writ of error dismissed, 1924). Cleveland's own Judge Florence Allen, who before her judicial career had been a vigorous advocate of Progressive reform, wrote the opinions in both cases (Tuve, 1984, pp. 92–93).

Abandonment of PR

The five PR elections in Cleveland (1923–31) were interspersed with five repeal attempts. Dissatisfaction was common to all, although each repeal effort had unique features. Opponents changed; the parties even switched sides. By the fifth repeal campaign, a reform faction seeking to achieve "a better council" was ready to abandon Cleveland's four-district PR system to seek a smaller council elected at-large by PR/STV.

The turnout of voters for the five repeal initiatives was not significantly related to the outcome of the vote. Turnout for these initiatives swung dramatically from a low of 19.5% of registered voters on the first repeal attempt to a high of 84.2% on the second. A steady and substantial opposition vote was cast (47.2% to 49.3% voting for repeal) until the successful repeal effort of 1931, when slightly over half the registered voters (50.6%) participated and endorsed repeal by 54.2% of the vote (see table 5.1).

TABLE 5.1

ADOPTION AND REPEAL OF CLEVELAND'S 1921 CHARTER AND CITY OF CLEVELAND VOTE ON 1935 COUNTY HOME RULE CHARTER

Election Date	Issue	Registration[a]	Total Vote[b]	Turnout as % Registration	Yes Vote[b]	% Yes
11/8/21	Adoption (Cleve. charter)	167,125	136,092	81.4	77,888	57.2
8/11/25	Repeal #1	211,828	41,271	19.5	20,353	49.3
11/8/27	Repeal #2 (Davis)	182,770	153,880	84.2	73,732	47.2
4/24/28	Repeal #3	n.a.	85,012	—	40,890	48.1
8/20/29	Repeal #4	150,082	97,272	64.8	47,134	48.4
11/3/31	Repeal #5	224,203	113,379	50.6	61,448	54.2
11/5/35	Adoption (county charter)[c]	372,022	232,929	62.6	125,930	54.0

[a]Data for 1921 from *Cleveland Press*, 24 Oct. 1921, p. 10; 1925, 1927, 1929 from *Greater Cleveland*, 13 March 1930, 5.24; 1931 and 1935 from Ohio, Secy. of State, *Vote Polled in the Several Counties of Ohio*, Registration in Cities of Ohio, 1930, p. 53 and 1934, p. 89. Permanent registration replaced annual registration in 1930. From that date forward, registration data are available only for even-numbered years. The volume of *Vote Polled* for the 1928 primary is missing from the official records, and no other contemporary source for this datum has been located.
[b]Cuyahoga County Board of Elections, *Municipal Election Vote*, 1921, 1925, 1927, 1929, 1931, 1935; *GC*, 3 May 1928, 3.32:145.
[c]Data shown for City of Cleveland only. The total Cuyahoga County vote was as follows: Total Vote, 315,577; Yes Vote, 167,061; % Yes, 52.9%. This PR/county manager charter was subsequently invalidated by the Ohio Supreme Court. *State ex rel. Howland v. Krause et al.*, 130 O.S. 455 (1936).

"Why doncha use this broom?" *Cleveland Press,* 4 August 1925, p. 8

Only in the first repeal attempt was PR tested alone. Initiated in 1925 by the Cuyahoga Club (young Democrats) and former Democratic mayor Newton D. Baker, the proposal was to substitute a nonpartisan 33-ward, plurality-elected body for the PR-elected council. To prevent a second PR election in November, its sponsors placed the issue on the ballot at a special August election. The strategy was designed also to draw a light vote, which ward leaders could presumably control. Both

"Digging up the old stuff." By Hal Donahey. *Cleveland Plain Dealer,* 2 August 1925, p. 1

political parties supported the issue, as did 17 of the 25 PR-elected council members (N. Shaw, 1925, p. 593).

Opposing repeal were the major newspapers, including the *Plain Dealer,* which had opposed adoption of PR in 1921, and the Charter Defense Committee, an autonomous organization led by independent council members Augustus Hatton (author of the charter), Peter Witt,

"The lion and the lamb!" By Hal Donahey. *Cleveland Plain Dealer,* 5 August 1925, p. 1

and Marie Wing, joined by labor leader James J. Hoban, president of the Cleveland Typographical Union (N. Shaw, 1925, p. 590). Although the Cleveland Federation of Labor continued to advocate a return to ward-based elections, other labor organizations joined the fray in support of PR: the Worker's Party, the Cleveland District Council of the Brotherhood of Railway Clerks, the Czechoslovak Workers Council, and the Union Labor P.R. Club. The national P.R. League again sent an

"The Swat Brothers, keepers of the gate!" By Hal Donahey.
Cleveland Plain Dealer, 7 August 1925, p. 1

organizer from New York to assist in the campaign, and helped to raise money in what was viewed as a nationally significant struggle to save PR (*PRR,* 1925, 76:93).

Two charges against PR were made in this first repeal campaign: first, that voting the PR/STV ballot was cumbersome and complicated, leading to declining turnout and unpredictable results; second, that

PR interfered with geographical representation, leaving some wards "unrepresented" in the council. The proponents of PR responded to these attacks by arguing that Clevelanders, already accustomed to the preferential ballot, could understand the PR/STV ballot as an expansion of their choices and a correction of the preferential ballot's flawed count. Moreover, freedom to choose a preferred candidate from outside of one's ward was an advantage, not a loss.

In August 1925, the small turnout resulted in the closest division of the four unsuccessful repeal efforts, the amendment losing with 49.3% voting to repeal PR. Fewer people voted for the alternative ward-based 33-member council plan than had signed petitions to put it on the ballot (*PRR*, 1925, 96:91).

The four subsequent repeal efforts (1927, 1928, 1929, 1931) were aimed at the entire charter, and the principal focus of controversy shifted from the electoral system to the city manager plan. The eventual success of repeal in 1931 may be attributed to factors of political corruption, controversy over the city manager, fragmentation of the major party alliance, and race.

Political Corruption

While the 1921 charter was hardly responsible for the political corruption that flourished in Cleveland during the late 1920s, voters who had been promised "good government" were disillusioned by the new system's failure to prevent partisan deals, patronage, bribery, and graft.

In 1928 the electorate was jolted by the eruption of scandals in the county board of elections. A special grand jury investigating alleged irregularities and fraud in the 1927 municipal election discovered that all the ballots had been (illegally) destroyed (*GC*, 19 Jan. 1929, 4.16:70). This and other wrongdoing led the state to replace the members of the county board (*PRR*, 1929, 90:32). That same year, three Republican council members and the city clerk were indicted for fraud, bribery, and graft. Two of these officials were acquitted, two convicted. Sent to the penitentiary were Liston G. Schooley, (white) chairman of the finance committee, and Thomas W. Fleming, a (black) council member of 20 years and chairman of the police and fire committee, both important leaders in the Republican machine (Harris, 1930, pp. 350–51; P. W. Porter, 1976, p. 43). Those indicted had originally been elected under the ward system. If the election system were related to the character of successful candidates, a return to the ward system would be irrational, an irony not lost on the advocates of PR (*PRR*, 1929, 91:50; Huus and Cline, 1929, pp. 289–94). However, the popular impulse for structural reform to get "better government" was reinforced (*PRR,* 1932, 101:5), and the effort to abolish PR gained impetus from the publicity surrounding the prosecutions of public misdeeds.

In 1930 the public learned that Republican leader Maurice Maschke and Democratic leader W. Burr Gongwer (the bosses) had secretly chosen William R. Hopkins as the first city manager. The public also learned that the choice hinged on an agreement, which Hopkins endorsed and adhered to, that all city jobs from directors of departments to street sweepers would be divided between the two parties in a ratio of 60% Republican to 40% Democratic (Campbell, 1966, p. 100; *PRR,* 1932, 101:5). The ratio approximated party strength on the pre-PR council, a division that persisted throughout the twenties. The agreement was revealed only because of a split between Hopkins and Maschke that forced Hopkins to resign in 1930. Daniel Morgan, chosen by Maschke to succeed Hopkins, repudiated the agreement, fired a number of Democrats and hired only Republicans at city hall (P. W. Porter, 1976, p. 45; *GC,* 5 Apr. 1934, 9.28:127). This resumption of past patronage practices, like the repudiated 60:40 deal, violated the spirit of the reform charter, if not its words, and alienated many Cleveland voters. By 1931 a new charter amendment committee could argue persuasively: "The unparalleled list of land scandals, bribery of councilmen, corruption of public officials, inefficient and extravagant administration . . . have shown how meaningless and empty council manager plan promises are (Charter Amendment Committee, *Cleve. Press,* 2 Nov. 1931, 6:3).

Controversy over the City Manager

Hopkins, a Republican business leader of great energy and ability, was a controversial city manager from the start. In the debate over adoption of the charter in 1921, reformers tried to distinguish policy (the council's job) from administration (the manager's job). After Hopkins' appointment in 1924, Mayo Fesler of the Citizens League urged Hopkins to respect his limited role as a professional administrator of the city's affairs (Fesler, 1924). Hopkins, however, quickly assumed political leadership of the city and made policy and implemented it, frequently informing the mayor and council only after his initiatives were under way (F. Shaw, 1966, p. 13). Disillusionment with reform was intensified by the perception that this office was not filled as intended.

Organized labor, divided over the merits of the charter at the outset, became more unified in opposition to Hopkins's labor practices, particularly his refusal to enforce the local laws that required the city to hire union labor and to fix a minimum wage (Harris, 1930, p. 347). Furthermore, the city manager plan stood in the way of men who believed they could be elected by the people to be mayor, particularly former Republican mayor and one-term governor of Ohio Harry L. Davis and Democratic prosecutor Ray T. Miller. Both campaigned against the charter. Davis sponsored three of the repeal initiatives himself in opposition to his own party, appealing for the workingman's vote. Indeed Davis and Miller were each elected mayor for a term in the 1930s (F. Shaw, 1966, pp. 20–26). In the end Hopkins himself believed that it was the manager plan, not PR, that caused abandonment of the charter under which he served (Hopkins, 1935, p. 29).

Partisanship

Although both parties opposed the 1921 charter at the time of its adoption, their leaders quickly adapted to the new political structure. The Maschke-Gongwer maneuver to control the appointment of the city manager was possible because the Republican majority retained its control of the first PR-elected council, and the Democratic leader was willing to make a deal. City clerk Fred Thomas was assigned the responsibility for allocating municipal jobs according to the ratio agreed upon (Campbell, 1966, p. 100).

Still, four independents had been elected to council in 1923, and they apparently raised enough questions about contracts and allocation of jobs to make the party leaders uncomfortable (Harris, 1930, pp. 344–45). In 1925, when only the PR sections of the charter were on the ballot for repeal, both parties supported repeal. By 1927, however, Hopkins was working well with both party leaders, and both parties opposed Davis's repeal initiative. Maschke's opposition was based not only on his support for Hopkins but also on his need to suppress factionalism in his party.

In 1928 Davis initiated charter repeal at the April presidential primary. This time, Maschke remained silent on repeal in order not to alienate the Davis faction from Herbert Hoover's candidacy for president, a priority for Cleveland's powerful Republican leader (Harris, 1930, p. 349). The Democrats opposed repeal, as they had in 1927 and would again in 1929. Not only did Gongwer support Hopkins, but he recognized that the Democratic minority on council was strengthened by PR voting. By 1929 Maschke was losing control of Hopkins on downtown development issues. He swung the Republican Party's support to repeal in order to get rid of "his" increasingly independent city manager. The strategy failed with defeat of the repeal effort.

Only in the 1929 election was a party-like independent organization created to raise money, defend the charter, and elect reform-minded candidates. The Progressive Government Committee (PGC) was organized by community leaders from the Citizens League, the Cleveland League of Women Voters, pro-PR labor groups, and other civic entities. Over $70,000 was raised, and the PGC earned credit for "saving" the charter and electing 12 of its endorsed candidates (Hallett, 1940, p. 126). Although PGC's efforts may have been critical to the fourth successful electoral defense of PR/STV, the actual impact on election outcomes is difficult to measure because of overlapping endorsements. Nine of its winners were Democrats; three were Republicans. Furthermore, eight were incumbents, including the council-elected mayor.

By 1931 the PGC could raise only $3,000 to support its endorsed candidates and to fight repeal of the charter. The parties, switching sides on repeal, were active. Maschke, who had forced Hopkins's resignation in 1930, was pleased with his new handpicked city manager, Daniel Morgan, and he opposed repeal. The Democrats were in transition. No longer controlling access to a guaranteed share of the city patronage, Gongwer was losing control of his party to Ray T. Miller, the successful county prosecutor. Miller was building Democratic strength at the grass roots in Cleveland by prosecuting corrupt Republican officeholders. He also rode the crest of the Great Depression–era shift in voter allegiance from the Republican to the Democratic Party. With a Democratic majority taking shape on the city's political horizon, Miller saw no stake in the reform charter. He persuaded his party to support repeal for the first time since 1925.

Race

Black political leaders played a significant but little-known role in the struggle over structural reform in Cleveland in this period. In the nineteenth century, the educational and socioeconomic status of Cleveland's small black community was similar to that of the white community, and blacks were generally integrated into housing, schools, and public institutions. Settlement of the Western Reserve by New Englanders had created an antislavery climate of opinion in northeastern Ohio long before the Civil War, and egalitarian attitudes remained dominant through the nineteenth century. In the 1890s two black representatives and one black senator were elected to the Ohio Assembly from largely white districts in Cuyahoga County (Kusmer, 1976, pp. 3–9, 55–64).

Between 1890 and 1910, the black population of Cleveland increased only from 1.2% to 1.5% of the total. By 1920, recruitment of southern black workers to fill industrial jobs during World War I had led to an increase of the black population to 4.3% of the total. Residential segregation developed gradually during this period, and by the 1920s job discrimination and exclusion from public facilities limited the upward mobility of both impoverished and middle-class blacks. Skilled industrial employment was barred, once the war was over, by the exclusionary policies of most of the trade unions. Moves out of the older areas of the city became difficult for black residents of all classes, and the modern urban ghetto was born. Between 1920 and 1930, as the total population of the city grew by 13%, the black population doubled to 8% of the total. Housing and school segregation intensified (Kusmer, 1976, pp. 42–46, 67–69; Miggins, 1988a, p. 366).

From the Civil War to the New Deal, Cleveland's black voters were loyal Republicans. Their support was recognized and rewarded by the Republican organization. In the late nineteenth century, the successful black legislative candidates were nominated by the Republican Party and elected by mostly white voters who would vote for their party's candidates. In 1907 the introduction of the direct primary in Ohio narrowed political opportunities for black candidates, for few could win primaries against white candidates of their own party in largely white districts. In intraparty contests, Republican voters failed to adopt the integrationist strategy that party leaders had used so successfully when they controlled nominations (Kusmer, 1976, p. 143).

Thomas W. Fleming was a barber and successful businessman who earned a law degree and in 1903 organized the Twelfth Ward Republican Club "to combine and solidify the Afro-American voters" (Kusmer, 1976, p. 145; Wye, 1973, pp. 390–94). In 1906 he founded a citywide organization, the Attucks Republican Club, which became the focus of black political activity within Maschke's organization. With Maschke's help, Fleming was elected to city council in 1909 and reelected (with the exception of two terms) until 1929. His electoral successes included three PR elections.

Fleming was the only African-American member of council until 1927, when two other black members were also elected on the PR/STV ballot. By the late 1920s, however, the growing pattern of segregated housing in Cleveland left the black community with little to lose from the return to a ward-based council. Reform was not a high priority in the African-American community, and the black wards generally voted the Republican position on charter repeal.

The city manager's actions, however, were important to black political leaders. During Prohibition, vice and bootlegging were protected by the police, and city services were neglected in the increasingly densely populated black wards (Kusmer, 1976, pp. 177, 221). City manager Hopkins not only failed to deliver city services equitably but resisted black leaders' efforts to reverse the segregation of staff at City Hospital, refusing even to meet with the black councilmen to discuss the exclusion of black doctors and nurses from the public hospital (Campbell, 1966, p. 104; Wye, 1973, pp. 21–22). The issue festered for several years before Maschke's break with Hopkins. In 1930, when Maschke was arranging the selection of a new city manager, he brought Daniel Morgan together with the African-American leadership and secured assurances from Morgan that the issue would be resolved. The black council members supplied the necessary margin of votes for Morgan's appointment, and Morgan as city manager reversed the discriminatory policy of the hospital (Campbell, 1966, pp. 104–5). It was too late, however, to make "good government" a priority in the black community.

Little evidence can be found of cooperation between African-American community leaders and the reformers. Although the Citizens League endorsed black council candidates from the first PR election until its repeal, the "preferred" rating was bestowed because each "would make a satisfactory representative of his people," as distinct from "preferred" white candidates who "would make a satisfactory councilman" (GC, Nov. 1923, 1.1:5; GC, Oct. 1925, 2.6:2ff; 2 Nov. 1927, 3.8:37–41; 28 Oct. 1929, 5.7:35–45).

In 1923, a year during which the Ku Klux Klan was active throughout Ohio, the Citizens League also listed as "preferred" six Cleveland city council candidates who were endorsed as well by a Klan-supported electoral organization called the Ohio State Good Government Club (PRR, 1924, 69:11–14). Not only were reformers' endorsements questionable in the black community, but reformers failed to use what would seem today to be an obvious strategy for preserving their charter: to publicize the increase in black representation under PR to secure African-American voting support against repeal.

The Reformers Themselves

The national P.R. League attributed the repeal of the reform charter in Cleveland to the continued dominance of the bosses and the revelations of corruption in council that reform government had failed to prevent. The P.R. League's unshaken faith in structural reform was

Clayborne George, 1927.
Courtesy of *The Cleveland
Press* Collection of the
Cleveland State University
Archives

Maurice Maschke, 1930.
Courtesy of *The Cleveland
Press* Collection of the
Cleveland State University
Archives

Marie R. Wing, 1926.
Courtesy of *The Cleveland
Press* Collection of the
Cleveland State
University Archives

demonstrated by its attack on Cleveland's district system of election as a fatal defect for a PR plan, making it difficult "to organize and focus attention on a city-wide independent campaign." Furthermore, the low councilmanic salaries ($1,800 per year), the league argued, made it difficult to attract and keep the "quality" candidates that the PR system purportedly brought to municipal elections (*PRR*, 1932, 101:6).

The P.R. League did not note that the fragmentation of reform efforts contributed to the 1931 abandonment of PR. While the League of Women Voters remained steadfast, once more organizing its membership to conduct a house-to-house canvass on behalf of the charter (Abbott, 1949, p. 118), the efforts of others in the reform coalition flagged. From at least 1928 on, a significant group of PR/STV proponents in Cleveland spent its time and money promoting a charter amendment to elect a nine or 15-member council at-large by PR (*PRR*, 1928, 85:19; 1929, 91:49; 1930, 96:76). Although these reformers were unlikely to vote for the ward-based council of the proposed 1931 charter, their attacks on the multimember district-based PR council system undermined its defense.

In the early 1930s, the Great Depression rapidly overwhelmed the city government. City workers were paid in scrip and the unemployed stormed city hall for jobs. People in distress looked for a strong political leader, not an efficient administrator. They wanted a ward representative to turn to for personal help, not one with the interests of "the city as a whole" at heart (F. Shaw, 1966, p. 27). In 1931 the voters went to the polls in what reformers saw as a negative mood. The voters not only repealed the 1921 charter but also defeated both the "good government" candidates for municipal court judge (endorsed by the bar association) and city board of education members (endorsed by the Citizens Committee for the Schools).

Comparative Analysis of Three Periods

As in the chapters on Ohio's other PR cities, the analysis here of differences among the three electoral periods will focus on characteristics of council members, geographic representation, "effective" voting, turnout for council elections, and stability in council decision making. Patterns of transfer votes will also be explored. The reader will recall that in the pre-PR period a ward-based preferential voting system was used, whereas following the PR/STV period, voting was by plurality in the pre-PR wards, with a nonpartisan primary to reduce the number of candidates. During the pre-PR and PR periods, nominations were by petition; the preferential and PR/STV ballots served both to narrow the field of candidates and to elect the winners. In all three periods the election ballot was nonpartisan. The three elections immediately before and after the PR period were chosen for comparison with the period of Cleveland's five PR elections.

Characteristics of Council Members

It was the firm expectation of the champions of PR/STV elections that "better men" would be elected by this new method. Generally "better" was understood to mean independent and better educated than the council members traditionally elected from small wards. PR-elected members were expected to be drawn from the ranks of business and the professions, people who would achieve low-tax, efficient government. There were policy-oriented reformers who hoped for council members committed to expansion of city services that would alleviate the degrading consequences of poverty.

Table 5.2 shows political variables of party affiliation and incumbency, and demographic variables of race, sex, occupation, and education, of all Cleveland city council members from 1917 to 1937. Differences in members' characteristics among electoral periods have been tested for significance.[5]

Election of a Republican majority represents the most important thread of continuity in Cleveland municipal politics through the three periods. The political parties regularly endorsed candidates for council, and a majority of Republicans won until 1937, when equal numbers of Republicans and Democrats and one independent were elected. The pre-PR wards remained the basic political unit of the city throughout the 1920s and 1930s, serving as single-member electoral districts before and after PR, and providing the building blocks of the four multimember PR districts during the PR period. The failure of the council to redistrict (as required by the charter) after the 1930 census left these basic party building blocks undisturbed through the post-PR period, easing the parties' adjustment to the new electoral system.

Independents (or, in 1917, Socialists) were elected in all three periods. The election of four Citizens League–endorsed independents in 1923 and 1925 was believed at the time to vindicate the predictions and hopes of the reformers for more efficient government under PR. These independents had little staying power, however. The effectiveness of their service was hampered by short tenure, the party lock on council and on the city manager, and the lack of an independent support group over time.

TABLE 5.2

CHARACTERISTICS OF CLEVELAND CITY COUNCIL MEMBERS, 1917–1937

Election Year	Political Variables						Demographic Variables									
	Party					Occupation[b]				Education[c]			Race: Black	Sex: Female
	Rep.	Dem.	Soc.	Ind.	Incumbent[a]	Prof.	Bus.	Blue	Other	GR/HS	College	Unknown		
1917	14	10	2	0	17	8	15	2	1	4	10	12	1	0
1919	17	9	0	0	20	10	13	2	1	7	12	7	1	0
1921	19	11	0	2	18	14	14	3	1	11	15	6	1	0
Pre-PR (N = 84)	50 59.5%	30 35.7%	2 2.4%	2 2.4%	55 65.5%	32 38.1%	42 50.0%	7 8.3%	3 3.6%	22 26.2%	37 44.0%	25 29.8%	3 3.6%	0 0.0%
1923	15	6	0	4	17	10	10	3	2	12	12	1	1	2
1925	15	6	0	4	21	10	12	1	2	12	12	1	1	2
1927	17	7	0	1	18	13	9	0	3	10	15	0	3	1
1929	14	10	0	1	14	12	12	0	1	11	14	0	3	2
1931	15	8	0	2	12	16	7	1	1	3	22	0	3	1
PR (N = 125)	76 60.8%	37 29.6%	0 0.0%	12 9.6%	82 65.6%	61 48.8%	50 40.0%	5 4.0%	9 7.2%	48 38.4%	75 60.0%	2 1.6%	11 8.8%	8 6.4%
1933	16	12	0	5	11	14	13	4	2	14	19	0	3	0
1935	17	15	0	1	21	15	9	6	3	12	21	0	3	0
1937	16	16	0	1	16	19	7	4	3	9	23	1	3	0
Post-PR (N = 99)	49 49.5%	43 43.4%	0 0.0%	7 7.1%	48 48.5%	48 48.5%	29 29.3%	14 14.1%	8 8.1%	35 35.4%	63 63.6%	1 1.0%	9 9.1%	0 0.0%

Sources: Civic League of Cleveland, *Civic Affairs*, no. 10 (Nov. 1917); no. 23 (Oct. 1919); no. 30 (Nov. 1921); *Greater Cleveland*, Nov. 1923, 1.1:2; Oct. 1925, 2.6; 2 Nov. 1927, 3.8:37–41; 28 Oct. 1929, 5.7:35–45; 22 Oct. 1931, 7.6:24–30; 28 Sept. 1933, 9.2; 2 Nov. 1933, 9.7; 17 Oct. 1935, 11.5; 23 Sept. 1937, 13.2; and 21 Oct. 1937, 13.6.

[a]"Incumbent" is defined as a member of the previous council, whether previously elected or appointed to a vacancy. Calculated from Cuyahoga County Board of Elections, *Municipal Election Vote*, 1915–35 (Cuyahoga County Archives), 1937.

[b]Occupational categories are Professional, Business, Blue-collar, and Other. "Other" occupations included government employees, such as inspectors, and housewives.

[c]Educational category "GR/HS" combines grade school and high school; "College" includes some college, college graduate, and postgraduate. Before 1923 education was often not reported.

The decline in number of Republicans elected from the PR period to the post-PR period is statistically significant ($p < .0398$). However, factors other than the electoral system contribute to this outcome. The twenties marked a shift of partisan loyalties, particularly in industrial cities such as Cleveland, from Republican to Democratic. The fact that presidential candidate Robert M. LaFollette (Independent Progressive) carried Cleveland in 1924 foretold Cleveland's shift to the Democratic party in state and national politics. From 1926 through the post-PR period, Democratic candidates for governor and president swept Cleveland. During the depression in the early 1930s, these partisan loyalties changed at the local level as well.

The PR period witnessed a significant correlation between votes for partisan candidates and seats won by each major party. During the PR period both Republicans ($p < .0216$) and Democrats ($p < .0233$) were significantly more likely to win "their share" of seats, as measured by percentage of votes cast for their winning candidates, than before or after PR.[6] Although this result would be expected from the PR ballot, it was scarcely noted at the time.

Given the continuity of Republican control of the council for most of these years, it is not surprising that there was no significant difference in the incumbency factor between the pre-PR and PR electoral periods. The importance of incumbency was clear. As seen in table 5.2, a comfortable majority of incumbents was elected to each council, until the last PR election. In 1931 the defeat of five regular Republicans and the reelection of the fewest incumbents since the adoption of PR led reformers to celebrate the "best" council yet, ironically elected simultaneously with the repeal of PR (*PRR*, 1932, 101:7; *Cleve. Press*, 4 Nov. 1931, 1:6).

In the transition to single-member district plurality voting in 1933, incumbents became vulnerable. Whereas the 1935 election returned a majority of new incumbents to council, the growth of Democratic loyalties in Cleveland caused more turnover in 1937. Overall, in the post-PR period, only 48.5% of the council members elected were incumbents, compared to over 65% in both the pre-PR and PR periods. This fact suggests that changes in electoral systems had less impact on the tendency of voters to reelect incumbents than had shifts in partisan loyalty.

Limited change in education and occupation of council members occurred over the three periods. Significant exceptions were a decline in business representation between pre-PR and post-PR ($p < .0476$) and an increase in blue-collar occupations between PR and post-PR ($p < .0286$). The abandonment of PR in favor of a ward-based single-member-district council appears to have facilitated the election of working-class representatives.

In light of this finding, it is perhaps surprising that the reformers' success rate, measured by election of candidates endorsed by the Citizens League, increased in the post-PR period, from an average of 52.3% of those elected in the pre-PR period and 52.8% during PR to 60.4% in the post-PR years.[7] However, as the reform literature reiterated, the endorsements were made among available candidacies. The reformers' goal of achieving higher-status councils was defeated more by their failure to recruit higher-status candidates than by voter rejection of such candidacies.

Developments that were statistically significant also occurred in characteristics of race and sex. African-American representation on Cleveland's council increased significantly from pre-PR to the PR period ($p < .0414$). However, this increase also corresponded to an increase in the black population, from 4.3% in 1920 to 8% of the total in 1930. Black representation on council, averaged for each of the three periods, corresponds rather closely to the black proportion of the population: 1918–23: 3.6%; 1924–33: 8.8%; and 1934–37: 9.1%. The shift to single-member districts in 1933 did not prevent election of a proportional share of black representatives to council, because of the increasing segregation of the growing black population within the city. Indeed, African-American candidates began to run against each other in the inner-city wards.

The representation of women reflected a different set of phenomena. Significant change occurred in the PR period ($p < .0102$). No women were elected either pre- or post-PR, but women were elected eight times in the PR period. Factors other than the electoral system were involved here as well. Not until 1921 were women allowed to vote or to run as candidates in municipal elections. On the preferential ballot in 1921, 13 women ran for council seats, but none was successful (Cuyahoga County Board of Elections, 1921, *Vote*).

When the new charter was in effect, the Citizens League urged citizens to recruit and organize campaigns for "men and women of standing and influence" (*GC*, 1925, 2.2:4). The league maintained stoutly that "the council of a city of a million population calls for men and women of character, training, experience, ability and capacity for leadership" (*GC*, 1925, 2.6:2). Although the extent of individual recruiting efforts is unknown, between four and eight women ran for council in each municipal election of the PR period, with one or two winning seats each time.

Did the PR ballot encourage women to enter local contests? Research in other electoral settings has shown that voters were more likely to vote for a female candidate as one of several choices in a multimember district than in a head-to-head contest for one seat (Rule, 1987). The multiseat feature of Cleveland's PR elections may have facilitated women's victories, apart from the ranking of choices on the PR ballot. Furthermore, the success of women candidates in Cleveland municipal politics coincided with a period of heightened feminist consciousness developed in the suffrage campaigns.

In 1933, with the return of ward primaries and elections, there were four women candidates in the primaries; two former councilwomen were nominated but neither was elected. In 1935, and again in 1937, three women ran in the primaries but none was nominated. In single-member districts, female opportunities appeared to evaporate. The shifting political culture reinforced the negative impact of ward elections after 1931. As the depression deepened in the early 1930s and jobs grew scarce, working women experienced intensified employment discrimination. The number of women entering politics and the professions declined (Lemons, 1973, pp. 230–31; Scharf, 1986, pp. 86–88). Feminist political momentum was lost, and in Cleveland women disappeared from council for the next 16 years.

The representation of immigrant groups on council was not an issue in Cleveland for at least two reasons. First, the Republican party had incorporated immigrants into its organization for decades, developing effective precinct captains and ward leaders, and electing council members in the "immigrant wards" (Moley, 1923, p. 663). Second, the nonpartisan preferential ballot used from 1915 through 1921 had facilitated ethnic voting, and the ward-based council provided access to power and patronage for the neighborhoods. Polish, Hungarian, Slovenian, German, Irish, Russian, Ukrainian, and Italian ethnic groups elected "their" council members under each electoral system. These groups were often the source of the business and professional presence on council—small merchants, undertakers, real estate and insurance salesmen, lawyers educated in night law schools, each advancing up the political and economic ladder. As incumbents under the old system, many of these white ethnic council members were reelected on the PR ballot and triumphed again in their old wards after 1933.

The Impact of Transfers in the PR/STV Count

One of the most effective arguments used by PR opponents seeking repeal was the complexity of the ballot count, although voting itself was simple; ordinal ranking of candidates was but a refinement of the choices Cleveland voters were accustomed to making on the preferential ballot. The count was more complicated. In Cleveland it was conducted in public, presenting an exciting opportunity for interested citizens to watch the changing fortunes of candidates, as surplus votes and second and subsequent choices from the ballots of hopelessly trailing candidates were posted on an enormous board.

Most of the time the PR/STV ballot produced first-count winners who were final winners. From the official record, four types of candidacies unique to PR/STV can be identified and analyzed:[8] strong winners, who achieved a surplus on the first count (12.8% of council seats filled in the PR period); transfer winners, who did not rank among the leaders on the first count but won on transfer votes from others (9.6% of the total); polarizing winners, who dropped more than three ranks during the transfer process (2.4% of the total); and viable losers, who ranked among the leaders on the first count but lost in the transfer process as the transfer winners moved up (9.6% of the total). It is clear from these relatively low percentages that, although there were 73 changes in rank order from first to final count among the 125 winning candidacies, few of these changes were significant. Characteristics of the four types of candidacies are shown in table 5.3.

The strong winners, candidates who won surpluses on the first count, tended to be incumbents and persons with higher education. They were more likely than other candidates to be independents, and less likely to be endorsed by the reformers (less than a third). Although no women were among the strong winners, a disproportionate share of African-American candidates was found in this group. Those of the strong winners who were not independents were party organization candidates, a characteristic that helps to explain their ability to attract surplus votes as well as their low rate of reform endorsement.

The 12 transfer winners, who moved up in the transfer process to capture the places held on the first count by the viable losers, were significantly less likely to be incumbents (only a third) and more likely to be Democrats. The Citizens League had endorsed 83.3% of the transfer winners. Occupational differences from the other types of candidacies were not significant, but transfer winners were significantly more likely to have higher education than the viable losers they replaced in the final count. Like the viable losers, the transfer winners were all white, but unlike them, one was a woman, Helen M. Green. Green was a teacher by occupation, an independent Republican, president of the Cuyahoga County Women's Christian Temperance Union, and backed by the Ohio State Good Government Club.

TABLE 5.3
Comparison of All PR-Elected Cleveland Council Members with Special Subgroups for Selected Characteristics, by Percent

| | Political Variables | | | | | Demographic Variables | | | | | | | |
| | Partisan ID | | | | | Occupation | | | | Education | | Race: | Sex: |
	Rep.	Dem.	Ind.	Incumbent	Reform-Endorsed	Prof.	Bus.	Blue	Other	GR/HS	College	Black	Female
All candidates elected by PR (N = 125)	76 60.8%	37 29.6%	12 9.6%	82 65.6%	66 52.8%	61 48.8%	50 40.0%	5 4.0%	9 7.2%	48 38.4%	75 60.0%	11 8.8%	8 6.4%
"Strong winners" (N = 16)	8 50.0%	4 25.0%	4 25.0%	11 68.7%	5 31.2%	10 62.5%	6 37.5%	0.0%	0.0%	6 37.5%	10 62.5%	3 18.8%	0.0%
"Transfer winners" (N = 12)	5 41.7%	7 58.3%	0.0%	4 33.3%	10 83.3%	7 58.3%	5 41.7%	0.0%	0.0%	4 33.3%	8 66.7%	0.0%	1 8.3%
"Polarizing winners" (N = 3)	2 66.7%	1 33.3%	0.0%	2 66.7%	2 66.7%	2 66.7%	1 33.3%	0.0%	0.0%	1 33.3%	2 66.7%	2 66.7%	0.0%
"Viable losers" (N = 12)	8 66.7%	3 25.0%	1 8.3%	5 41.7%	4 33.3%	5 41.7%	5 41.7%	0.0%	2 16.7%	10 83.3%	2 16.7%	0.0%	0.0%

Notes: "Candidates" is used here to mean "candidacies," since some individuals had multiple candidacies. "Unknowns" have been omitted, leaving an N of 123. "Strong winners" are candidates who were elected on the first count and had surpluses to transfer. "Transfer winners" are candidates who were not among first-count "winners" but who received enough second- and other choice ballots to win. "Polarizing winners" are successful candidates who dropped at least three ranks from the first count to the final count. "Viable losers" are candidates who were first-count "winners" but lost on transfers by the final count.

The polarizing winners, those winning candidates who dropped at least three ranks between the first and final counts, share with the viable losers a narrow base of support. The three candidacies that fell into this category represented just two individuals. One, John P. McGreal, white, an undertaker by profession and a Democrat, first ran for council in 1927 and was elected, despite the Citizens League's characterization of him as incompetent and lacking in leadership potential. By the time he ran for reelection in 1929, he may have lived down to his potential, since he became a viable loser, dropping from second rank on the first count to loser. In 1931 McGreal was reelected on transfers (perhaps an instance of sympathy voting), rising from tenth rank on the first count to fifth on the final count.

The other polarizing winner was Clayborne George, the first successful African-American candidate in the Fourth District, known as the "East End" or "better residential district." An attorney, and from 1924 to 1926 president of the Cleveland chapter of the National Association for the Advancement of Colored People, George first ran unsuccessfully in 1925, when he was rated "qualified" by the Citizens League. In 1927, rated "preferred," he was elected but only after dropping from fifth to seventh rank. He met the criterion of polarizing winner in 1929 by dropping from fourth to seventh place, and in 1931 from second to fifth in the transfer process. In 1933 he resigned from council to run citywide for municipal court judge. George's experience under PR differs from that of other black council members of the 1920s, because he won three times in a largely white district. For the black council members of the 1920s, it was the Third District, with its significant African-American population, that offered a secure base for Thomas W. Fleming, Dr. E. J. Gregg, Dr. Leroy N. Bundy, and Lawrence O. Payne, all of whom were elected either with surplus votes or with enough transfer votes to stay within one ranking (up or down) of their first-count position.

The viable losers, who were among the leaders on the first count but were replaced at a later stage by transfer winners, had to be the first choice of a significant number of voters, but support in their districts was narrow. They received few transfer votes either from surplus votes of strong winners or from weak candidates who were eliminated in successive transfers. All 12 were white men, none of blue-collar status but all less educated, less likely to be incumbents, and less likely to gain reform endorsements than the winners. Their names suggest a scattering of nationalities as well as the native born. Half of these viable losers were successful in the next election. This delayed success

TABLE 5.4
CLEVELAND CITY COUNCIL, PERCENTAGE DISTRIBUTION OF VOTE
TRANSFERS, BY PARTY, 1923

Ballots Transferred	From Republicans	From Democrats	From Independents[a]
To Republicans	74.6	41.0	63.1
To Democrats	13.8	39.9	14.3
To Independents	11.6	19.1	22.6
Total	100.0	100.0	100.0

Source: Calculated from data reported in *PRR*, 1924, 69:8.
[a]Independents included two Socialist Party candidates and three Workers' Party candidates.

suggests a sympathy vote from an electorate in which substantial opposition to PR persisted throughout Cleveland's PR experience.

The P.R. League reported the transfer votes by party in the first (1923) Cleveland PR election, showing the numbers of votes transferred from independents and candidates of each party to independents and those of the other party. Also reported were partisan and independent transfers to the winning candidates by party. The P.R. League concluded (apparently from the fact that transfers crossed party/independent lines at all) that voters had ranked their choices on the basis of candidates' "individual qualifications" (*PRR*, 1924, 69:8– 9). However, a simple percentage distribution of transfers shows a significant pattern, as evident in table 5.4.

Almost three-quarters of transfers from Republicans went to other Republicans, whereas fewer than two out of five transfers from Democrats went to other Democrats. In fact, a plurality of Democratic transfers went to Republican candidates! Moreover, over three out of five transfers from independent candidates went to Republicans. The P.R. League offered its explanation of this dramatic Republican success in the transfer process: it was "apparently due in large measure to [Republican] sagacity in endorsing candidates who could command support on their own merits" (*PRR*, 1924, 69:8). In 1925 the P.R. League reported that more ballots were transferred from Democrats to Republicans than from Democrats to Democrats; and more from independents to Republicans than from independents to independents. Republican transfers to other Republicans were not mentioned and no individual transfer data were provided. The P.R. League proclaimed: "Party Lines Disregarded" (*PRR*, 1925, 75:81).

TABLE 5.5
CLEVELAND CITY COUNCIL, PERCENTAGE DISTRIBUTION OF BALLOTS
ELECTING WINNERS, 1923

Ballots Received	15 Republican Winners	6 Democratic Winners	4 Independent Winners
First choice	59.1	68.7	82.8
From Republicans	16.8	7.6	2.6
From Democrats	6.7	15.0	4.9
From Independents	17.4	8.7	9.7
Total	100.0	100.0	100.0

Source: Calculated from data reported in *PRR*, 1924, 69:9.

It could not have been irrelevant, however, that the Republican party in Cleveland was well-organized, active in instructing its voters, firmly in control of the lion's share of city patronage, and therefore positioned well to use the STV ballot effectively. The ability of a well-organized party to benefit from the PR ballot is shown by the percentage distribution of ballots received by the winning candidates. In table 5.5, the 1923 winners are shown by party and by the percentage of their votes derived from first choices and from transfers of votes from Republican, Democratic, and Independent candidates. Republican winners received a lower share of their votes from first choices and a significantly larger share from transfers than did either Democrats or independents (*PRR*, 1924, 69:9).

Individual transfer data from the Third District are reported in Moley's review of the first PR election (1923, pp. 668–69). There were 18 candidates, with six to be elected. Herman H. Finkle, Republican floor leader, was the only candidate with a surplus to transfer. Fleming, the Maschke organization's African-American incumbent who had come in second on the first count, received enough of Finkle's second-choice transfers to be elected. Bronstrup, another Republican regular, received almost half of Finkle's surplus, and the rest were transferred in small numbers to all other candidates. Heinrich, a Workers Party candidate, was first to be eliminated. The largest single recipient of his transfers was Marie Wing, a white independent reform candidate. When Dr. Joe T. Thomas, an independent black candidate, was eliminated, only one out of five of his effective second choices went to the other African-American candidate, Howard E. Murrell, president of the Empire Savings and Loan Company, a reform-endorsed independent, with the rest scattered among the remaining (white) candidates. Murrell was the last candidate to be eliminated, on the thirteenth count. Wing received half of his effective second-choice votes, reaching the quota, and the rest were divided among the remaining contenders, both Democratic and Republican. The end result of the transfer process in the Third District was the election of three regular Republicans, two regular Democrats, and Wing.

Partisanship and ethnicity competed for the loyalty of voters in the transfer process. Polish voting patterns exemplify the differential impact of PR and plurality voting. In 1919 and 1921, Bernard Orlikowsky, a Polish Democrat, had been elected on the preferential ballot in the Fourteenth Ward. Under PR the Fourteenth Ward was absorbed by the Second District, where Orlikowsky was reelected by PR in 1923 and 1925. In 1927, however, he was defeated. A second Polish candidate in the Second District race, Republican Stanley F. Szczuka, also lost because a majority of Orlikowsky's second-choice votes went to non-Polish Democrats (*PRR*, 1928, 85:15). In 1929 Szczuka was elected as a transfer winner over W. S. Piotrowicz, an independent Republican and a "preferred" Citizens League candidate from the Polish community. In 1931 Szczuka did not run, but Democrat E. P. Lewandowski, also identified as Polish in the Citizens League's endorsement, was elected in the Second District, and then was reelected in the plurality elections of 1933, 1935, and 1937 from the old Fourteenth Ward. Hence Polish representation persisted, with the exception of a single term, through three electoral systems.

Partisanship overcame ethnicity in an example of voting in the First District in the 1931 election. Two "Irish places" had been established by tradition in previous PR elections in what was called the "Irish Derby." After the election of one Irish Republican in the First District and the elimination of all but two of the other Irish candidates, enough transfer votes from an Irish Democrat went to a German Democrat to elect him rather than to the Irish Republican still in the running who was also close to the quota (*PRR*, 1932, 101:9–10).

The 1929 election was significant because it was the only instance in Cleveland's experience with PR in which a PR "party," the Progressive Government Committee (PGC), organized, endorsed candidates, and raised money to support a slate campaign. In the Fourth District, George W. Furth, an independent Jewish Republican candidate, PGC-endorsed, edged out another Jewish candidate, Herman E. Kohen, a Maschke ally who had been attacked in the newspapers as "a symbol of all that is worst in machine politics." Furth's margin of victory was provided by transfers from Lockwood Thompson, an Anglo-Saxon Democrat, also endorsed by the PGC and the last candidate to be eliminated in the Fourth District (*PRR*, 1930, 93:12–13).

Minor parties did not benefit from the PR/STV ballot in Cleveland, although the city had a significant history of minor party activity and was an important center of Socialist Party strength between 1910 and 1920. In 1917 the Socialist candidate for mayor, Charles E. Ruthenberg, an American of German-Lutheran descent, won a third of the vote (Campbell, 1988, pp. 315–16). Socialist candidates also ran for council in 21 of the 26 wards, and J. G. Willert and Noah Mandelkorn were elected on the ward-based preferential ballot, both defeating incumbents. However, they were expelled from council in 1918 for "disloyalty to the United States" because of their vocal opposition to American participation in World War I (City of Cleveland, *City Record,* 3 Apr. 1918). After a hiatus in 1919, Socialist candidates ran again in 1921, this time unsuccessfully.

Throughout the twenties and thirties, doctrinaire small parties, including the Socialist, Workers, and Communist Parties, ran candidates for Cleveland city council. During the PR period, these candidates were on the ballot in all four districts, but none was elected. Willert was regularly rated "qualified" by the Citizens League, as was Socialist Joseph Martinez in 1929. In the 1929 election, 2,636 of the 3,322 ballots giving Socialist candidates first-choice votes were transferred to non-Socialists, with anti-Maschke candidates (independent, Republican, or Democratic) benefiting from the transfers (*PRR*, 1930, 93:8).

These fragments of transfer evidence tell us that, under a variety of circumstances, the factors of partisanship, race, ethnicity, and the activity of an organized reform party all contributed to electoral success in the transfer process of the PR system. The minor parties of the left were apparently too weak to benefit from PR at all.

Geographic Distribution of Representation

Localism, a traditional force in Cleveland political culture, continued to shape much of its municipal politics throughout the PR period. The 33 pre-PR wards were used by the party organizations for dispensing patronage, recruiting candidates, and focusing the organization's electoral activity. The 1923 reduction in council size to 25 members elected from four districts determined that ward representation would not continue as before. Yet the 1923 PR/STV election produced resident council members in 17 wards. The "unrepresented wards" became a rallying cry for the opponents of PR, who attacked "taxation without representation" (N. Shaw, 1925, p. 593). Broader freedom of candidate choice, however, was one of the advantages that proponents of PR had promoted in the campaign for the new charter. Reformers felt vindicated in the first PR election, when voters of the Fourth District elected both Professor Hatton, author of the new charter, and John D. Marshall, later the council-elected mayor, although both lived outside the district in the Nineteenth Ward. Peter Witt, popular heir of the tradition of Tom Johnson, lived and voted in the Fourth District, but ran for council in the First District "at the other end of town," where he had grown up; he was elected with more first-choice votes than any other candidate in the city received (*PRR*, 1924, 69:29).

By the fourth PR election in 1929, 63.2% of voters cast their first-choice votes for nonresidents of their respective wards. Although a majority in all four districts preferred nonresident candidates, different patterns emerged. In the First and Fourth Districts (the west side and the east end), 67.0% and 69.9% respectively of the voters preferred nonresidents of their wards. Voters of the Fourth District even elected a nonresident of the district, independent Democratic attorney Susan Rebhan, who lived in the Third District but ran in the Fourth (*PRR*, 1930, 93:17). In the Second and Third Districts (southeast and downtown), where ethnic and black votes were concentrated, 51.8% and 57.4% of the voters gave their first choices to nonresidents of their wards. This difference in localism may be attributable to the greater strength of party organization in the working-class districts, and more dependence on the benefits of ward politics than in the "better residential" areas.

In 1931 the recently fired city manager, William R. Hopkins, who lived in the same Fourth District ward to which Mayor John D. Marshall had moved, ran for council in the Second District and was elected, leading in both the first and final counts. Marshall, although running third in first-choice votes in his new ward of residence, was reelected from the Fourth District.

Although the pre-PR charter had permitted council aspirants to run outside their wards of residence on the preferential ballot, few candidates did because the strategy was seldom successful (*PRR*, 1930, 93:17). The large-district-based PR charter moved the city partway toward nongeographic representation. In each PR election, 12 to 16 of the 33 wards went "unrepresented" because residents voted for nonresident candidates, and at least one council member was elected from a district in which he or she did not live.

"Effective" Voting

The advocates of PR argued that the system would waste fewer votes than plurality elections, in which a large minority or, in a three-candidate race in a single-member district, a majority of voters may not be able to elect a candidate. For the five PR elections in Cleveland, the P.R. League tabulated the number and percentage of voters whose first choice was elected and whose votes by transfer helped to elect members of council (*PRR*, 1930, 93:15; 1932, 101:8). These shares of effective votes are shown in table 5.6.

It is clear that PR significantly increased the share of effective first-choice voters over the preferential ballot, and dramatically increased the percentage of voters (including those whose ballots were transferred to second or subsequent choices) who actually elected a council member. In the post-PR period the use of council primaries reduced most races to two candidates, effectively forcing a majority winner. This two-stage system performed about as well in enabling voters to be effective as PR had done on first-choice votes, but there were no successive choices to expand the pool of effective votes as PR did with transfers. Only 20% of the voters in the five PR elections cast ineffective votes, compared to over 40% in the post-PR period.

Turnout for Council Elections

The impact of PR/STV on voting turnout was debated throughout its existence. Registration was required annually in Cleveland through the 1920s. Because the number of both registrants and actual voters declined in the first two PR elections, opponents of PR argued that the complex ballot with multiple choices drove voters away from the polls. PR proponents attributed the 1923 and 1925 declines in voting to the absence of a contest for mayor, presumptively more salient than the council races. Both registration and voting rose sharply, however, in the third PR election and fluctuated for the remainder of the PR period.

To compare participation among the three electoral periods, turnout is measured by the percentage of registered voters who actually voted, shown in table 5.7. No statistically significant difference in voting turnout for Cleveland council is found among the three electoral periods. Although turnout rose and fell within each period, the average turnout for the three pre-PR elections—at 77.4% of registered voters—was about the same as the average turnout for the five PR elections (77.5%). A decline of 10 percentage points in the average council turnout of the post-PR period, to 67.6%, may be an artifact of the state's 1930 change to biennial registration.[9] At least it is clear that

TABLE 5.6
"Effective Votes" in Cleveland Municipal Elections,
1917–1937

Election Year	% of Voters Whose First Choices Were Elected[a]	% of Voters Whose Votes Helped Elect Council Member
Pre-PR		
1917	42	46
1919	50	53
1921	42	46
Mean	44.7	48.3
PR/STV		
1923	58	81
1925	59	82
1927	68	80
1929	56	78
1931	51.6	77.1
Mean	58.5	79.6
Post-PR		
1933	59.2	—
1935	58.1	—
1937	58.4	—
Mean	58.6	

Note: An "effective vote" is one that counts toward the successful election of a candidate, including successful transfer votes in preferential or PR/STV elections. An "ineffective vote" is a vote for a losing candidate in a plurality election or, in a preferential or PR/STV election, a ballot on which all marked candidates are eliminated in successive counts.

[a]*PRR*, 1930, 93:15; 1932, 101:8. Percentages for the post-PR elections are calculated from Cuyahoga County Board of Elections, *Municipal Election Vote*, 1933, 1935, 1937. Because primaries were instituted for these post-PR elections, voters had only one choice for council member in the plurality-based general election.

the return to ward elections ("restoring power to the people") did not stimulate higher political participation. The rise and fall of turnout must be explained by factors other than the electoral system, such as interest in particular issues or candidates and effectiveness of parties and other organizations in turning out the vote. The presence or absence of a popular mayoral race does not appear to have influenced council turnout. While it is true that the pre-PR and post-PR mayoral races drew higher participation than the council races of the same election year, the separate mayoral races did not induce higher council voting (table 5.7).

TABLE 5.7
TURNOUT FOR CLEVELAND MUNICIPAL ELECTIONS, 1917–1937, BY
PERCENTAGE OF REGISTRANTS VOTING

Election Year	Council Vote as % of Registrants	Mayoral Vote as % of Registrants	Difference between Mayoral and Council Turnout
Pre-PR			
1917	73.9	87.1	+13.2
1919	80.1	88.8	+ 8.7
1921	77.9	90.0	+12.1
Mean	77.4	88.8	+11.4
PR/STV			
1923	79.8	—	—
1925	79.9	—	—
1927	80.3	—	—
1929	82.3	—	—
1931	69.3	—	—
Mean	77.5		
Post-PR			
1933	79.0	88.0	+ 9.0
1935	66.9	72.6	+ 5.7
1937	59.3	62.5	+ 3.2
Mean	67.6	73.3	+ 5.7

Source: Calculated from registration data in Greater Cleveland, 13 Mar. 1930, 5.24; Cleveland Press, 24 Oct. 1921, p. 10; Ohio, Secretary of State, Vote Polled in the Several Counties of Ohio, Registration in the Cities of Ohio, 1930, p. 53; 1932, p. 93; 1934, p. 89; 1936, p. 123 (permanent registration replaced annual registration in 1930). Voting data in Cuyahoga County Board of Elections, Municipal Elections, 1917–37; GC, 23 Nov. 1925, 2.7:1–2. Council voting is based on first-choice votes under preferential (1917–21) and proportional (1923–31) voting systems, and all votes in plurality elections (1933–37). Mayoral voting is based on first-choice votes in preferential elections (1917–21) for mayor and total general election votes in plurality elections for mayor (1933–37). The mayor was elected by council from 1923 to 1931.

Turnout patterns within the city of Cleveland varied more than turnout under different electoral systems. Analyses of turnout by the Citizens League found higher turnouts in the "foreign district"—that is, among naturalized foreign-born or foreign-stock voters—than in the "better residential" wards. In the 1925 election, for example, almost twice the proportion of eligible adults voted in the Polish ward and in other "congested wards of foreign-born residents" as in the "east end" (GC, 23 Nov. 1925, 2.7:3). By the end of the decade, the Citizens League would conclude that citizens of foreign birth "prize their right of franchise" more than native voters (*GC,* 28 Nov. 1930, 6.11:56). Any putative role of party organizations in turning out these voters was not credited in the reformers' analysis.

Stability in Decision Making

A frequent claim of PR opponents has been that a PR election system, whether party list or STV, fragments a legislative body by facilitating minority representation. Conflict, instability, and deadlock are the operative features posited for PR-elected governments (Hermens, 1941, 1985). No evidence of these dire consequences could be found in the Cleveland PR experience. The search for evidence included a tabulation of nonunanimous votes as a percentage of total council votes on ordinances and resolutions for alternate years in the pre-PR, PR, and post-PR periods. A mean percentage of nonunanimous votes was calculated for each period. The results are shown in table 5.8.

It is clear that the electoral system was not related to conflict on the Cleveland city council between 1918 and 1938. Dissensus overall was extremely low, and the differences among electoral periods are not significant. The only tendency that can be extracted from the data is a very small trend toward increased conflict, as measured by means of nonunanimous votes for the periods, from pre-PR (1.4%) through PR (2.2%) to post-PR (3.7%). Since no minor party candidate was elected to Cleveland municipal office in the PR period, partisan factional conflict was confined to the major parties. In fact, the highest proportion of divided votes (7.5%) occurred in 1936, in the ward-based plurality-elected council. The election of the council president was a notable source of conflict in this period. In 1934, eight divided ballots and, in 1936, 15 such ballots were required to elect a leader.

These leadership contests can be attributed not to the electoral system but to the disintegration of the majority party organization that had controlled Cleveland government for much of the first third of the century. During the 1930s, the transition from Republican to Democratic control of the city featured both internal party disputes and interparty conflict that erupted in council decision making. However, the fears of fragmentation of power in Cleveland's governmental process through the workings of PR proved to be unfounded.

Did PR Make a Difference in Cleveland?

Moving beyond quantitative measurement, did PR make a difference in Cleveland? The obstacle to confident claims that "it mattered" is the simultaneous adoption of the city manager plan. Cleveland's two city

TABLE 5.8

CLEVELAND CITY COUNCIL, PERCENTAGE NONUNANIMOUS VOTES ON
ORDINANCES AND RESOLUTIONS, 1918–1938

Council Session	No. of Ord./Res.	% Nonunanimous
Pre-PR		
1918	1,257	1.9
1920	1,393	.4
1922	1,397	1.9
Mean		1.4
PR/STV		
1924	1,773	3.3
1926	2,061	2.5
1928	1,871	.6
1930	1,132	2.3
1932	843	2.7
Mean		2.2
Post-PR		
1934	460	3.4
1936	976	7.5
1938	1,308	.8
Mean		3.7

Source: City of Cleveland, *City Record,* 1918–38, alternate years.
Note: Excluded from the tabulation are nonsubstantive motions, such as approval of minutes and resolutions honoring individuals and groups, all of which were unanimous. Ordinances on second and third reading and resolutions relating to the operation of the city are included.

managers, Hopkins (1924–31) and Morgan (1931–32), were dynamic individuals with clear agendas. Efficient management of city services was a high priority for both. Capital improvements became the other leading concern of Hopkins, whereas Morgan, by force of circumstance and short tenure, had to deal with relief of economic distress. Hopkins clearly usurped the role of political leadership and took policy initiatives that he believed were needed, whereas Morgan was more respectful of the council-elected mayor and of council (*GC,* 19 Jan. 1929, 4.16:70–72; 5 Apr. 1934, 9.28:125–28).

Contemporary accounts give the performance of the PR-elected council a mixed review. Throughout the decade the Maschke machine organized the council after each election. The first mayor to be elected, Clayton C. Townes, was the previous Republican president of council; he was succeeded in 1925 by Republican John D. Marshall. The first

PR-elected council chose the chairman of the Republican county executive committee to head the Civil Service Commission, providing powerful support for Fred Thomas, the city clerk whose job it was to carry out the 60:40 patronage agreement. Herman H. Finkle, first elected to council on the preferential ballot in 1917 with Maschke's help, served on council until he died in 1952; was majority floor leader from 1921 throughout the PR and post-PR periods; and survived the reformers' constant attacks on his machine-style tactics.

Evidence of bipartisan cooperation abounds. In the first PR council, committee chairmanships were allocated to 12 Republicans, five Democrats, and one Independent (*PRR*, 1925, 75:82). A joint Republican-Democratic caucus met regularly to make decisions about council actions; the independents did not participate (Harris, 1930, p. 344).

By 1931, although PR advocates argued that the electoral system was gradually improving the independence and ability of council members (*PRR*, 1932, 101:7), its critics attacked both PR and the manager plan as "the boss plan," dominated by "the invisible government of Maurice Maschke" (*Cleve. Press*, 2 Nov. 1931, 6:3).

Still, the reformers' goal of economy had been achieved. The city property tax rate, which had increased by 56.6% between 1917 and 1923 (the pre-PR period), decreased by 7.2% during the PR-city manager years. Despite lower taxes, significant public improvements were undertaken and completed, including the municipal airport, the stadium, swimming pools in the neighborhoods, park improvements, sewage treatment works, and street paving (*GC*, 8 Oct. 1931, 7.4:16–17). Public interest in city operations increased, as shown by the growth in attendance at council meetings from fewer than 50 people before 1924 to more than 500 during the PR period (Tugman, 1924, p. 257).

In contrast, the post-PR period, which coincided with the Great Depression, was marked by deterioration of government services as the plurality-elected mayor and ward-based council emphasized patronage. The filling of 200 unskilled jobs allocated to each member of council occupied both the Republican majority and the Democratic minority. Among the policy issues not addressed by council under what the Citizens League called this "vicious small-ward system" were welfare relief, budget deficits, an expiring street railway franchise, and refinancing of bonded debt (*GC*, 15 Sept. 1935, 11.1:1–4).

Experienced politicians who were disappointed by the ineptness of the post-PR council joined the reformers in attempts to restore PR elections. Former friends of PR such as Peter Witt and council member Ernest Bohn joined former opponents such as council president

Alexander DeMaioribus to propose charter amendments for election of an at-large council of nine or 15 members by PR/STV. Several proposed amendments would have restored the city manager; others provided for a separately elected mayor. None reached the electorate, but the ongoing drive for further reform demonstrated persistent dissatisfaction with city government in the post-PR period (*NMR*, 1933, 22:337–39; 1935, 24:184, 490; 1937, 26:43).

In the 1930s a county home rule charter was promoted to deal with issues of metropolitan governance. PR/STV elections were viewed by many as an essential method to achieve fair representation county-wide. In 1935 Cuyahoga County voters did adopt such a charter, providing for a nine-member county council to be elected at-large by PR/STV, with a county manager plan as well (Hallett, 1940, pp. 128–29; *NMR*, 1935, 24:513–14, 702–3). Cleveland, the largest of 60 cities in the county, supplied a significant margin of votes for its adoption (see table 5.1). For Cleveland voters, reform that included a PR electoral system was again a viable option. Before it could be put into effect, however, the entire county charter was invalidated by the Ohio Supreme Court, for reasons unrelated to PR.[10]

In a retrospective evaluation of PR/STV as it had worked in Cleveland, former city manager Hopkins wrote in 1935 that the PR-elected councils were "the best . . . in many years . . . truly representative of the people of Cleveland as a whole." Because they were "truly representative," they were not as outstanding as the advocates of PR had promised, according to Hopkins, but were better than the "professional controllers of government for their own purposes" wanted. Hopkins argued that the large-district base for elections led council members to "take a broader view of all questions." He was confident that PR would prevail in the long run as a "better form of representation" (Hopkins, 1935, pp. 27, 41).

Conclusion

The Cleveland PR experience was similar in many ways to the adoption, operation, and abandonment of PR/STV in other American cities in the first half of the twentieth century. The PR electoral system was but one feature of a municipal reform package promoted by the National Municipal League. The city manager plan was the more prominent feature, and much of the controversy at the time of both adoption and abandonment swirled around the change in executive management rather than the election of the legislative body.

The Cleveland experiment with PR was unique in Ohio in the use of large multimember districts instead of a small at-large council. Proposed in order to ease voter acceptance of the PR system, the districts were a compromise between ward-based localism and the broader view reformers sought of the interest of the whole city. Cleveland voters made use of their wider geographical choices by freely electing council members who lived outside their wards or even beyond their districts.

Political and demographic characteristics of Cleveland council members did not change dramatically under PR. The Republican majority of the pre-PR period retained firm control through the PR period, and a substantial majority of incumbents was reelected in each municipal election except in the turmoil of 1931. Because of continuity in both partisanship and incumbency, change was inevitably gradual.

The predominant pattern of representation throughout the PR years was that of white businessmen or professional men with at least some higher education. The significant differences PR elections brought to the Cleveland council include the election of women and an increase in African-American representation proportional to the increase in the African-American population.

Turnout was not significantly affected in Cleveland by PR elections, in spite of opponents who saw the ballot as too complex for voters to understand, or proponents who believed that better representation would profoundly kindle interest in voting.

Since PR elections in Cleveland did not result in a factionalized council, it is not surprising to find a high degree of consensus in the working of the PR-elected council. The decade of PR/city manager government in Cleveland was marked by high civic energy and significant accomplishment of public improvements, both for downtown and for the neighborhoods.

Drawing lessons for the present from the Cleveland PR experience may be risky because the political and economic context powerfully shaped the way the electoral system worked. Yet Cleveland politics were not unique. Patronage and political corruption are not rare features of local government in the United States; local economies rise and fall over time; urban populations generally are diverse. At least it is clear from this case study that partisan, racial, and ethnic groups can be fairly represented in a large-district PR/STV system. Furthermore, with PR elections, fair minority representation does not depend on the preservation of segregated neighborhoods as with the single-member district system. And, finally, a severely underrepresented majority, women, can improve their access to political power without handicapping minorities. The opportunity for voluntary constituencies to coalesce and secure representation in policy-making bodies remains PR's most attractive political asset.

SIX

■ ■ ■

PR in Cincinnati: From "Good Government" to the Politics of Inclusion?

Robert J. Kolesar

> Before the introduction of proportional representation in Cincin-
> nati, the plan of voting under the so-called majority system per-
> mitted the control of government by a minority. . . . The last two
> elections in Cincinnati have conclusively demonstrated that the
> once vaunted majority is, and probably always has been, a mi-
> nority disguised as a majority by an unfair and fallacious system
> of counting the vote.
>
> Bentley, "What PR Has Done for Cincinnati," 1929

CINCINNATI'S EXPERIENCE with proportional representation has
long been regarded as one of the most notable in the nation. Between
1925 and 1955, the city elected its council by the Hare system of
proportional representation (the single transferable vote). PR was only
one element of a package of reforms adopted in 1925; others included
placing executive powers in a city manager and reducing the council's
size. Before 1925 the city council consisted of 26 ward representatives,
elected by plurality vote from single-member districts, and six at-large
members. Until 1917 members served a two-year term; a charter
amendment that year changed the term to four years. The PR council
numbered nine members, elected at-large, for a two-year term. The
only change made on its repeal was to substitute a plurality/at-large
ballot (9X) for the single transferable vote. City manager government
and the small at-large council were both retained.

"Good government" sentiments animated the 1920s reforms. Before
reform, Cincinnati had the reputation of being one of the nation's
worst-governed cities. Its reformed government soon earned it praise as

160

one of the best. One of the major reasons was that the 1920s reform movement precipitated the formation of a durable local political party, the Charter Committee. Despite its self-perception of nonpartisanship, the Charter Committee acted as a local political party throughout the PR era, uniting Democrats and independent Republican reformers against the Republican organization. The longevity of PR in Cincinnati, the durability of the reform coalition, and the praise Cincinnati's PR governments garnered, were each noteworthy aspects of Cincinnati's experience with PR. Also notable was African-American representation on Cincinnati's PR councils. With PR's demise in 1957, the city's black community lost representation that it had long enjoyed under PR, thus bolstering PR's reputation as a mechanism of political inclusion.

Social and Political Setting

Several social characteristics of the city help to explain reform's longevity and its institutionalization in the Charter Committee. Reformed urban political structures generally have been associated with educated, upper-middle-class constituencies and relatively homogeneous midsized cities. Cincinnati did not experience the problems and conflicts of rapid growth in the twentieth century. Its 1920 population of 401,247 took 30 years to reach its high point of 503,998 in 1950 (population growth was 12.4% in the 1920s, 1% in the 1930s, 10.6% in the 1940s, and −0.3% in the 1950s). Jon Teaford's recent comparative work has shown that suburbanization had less impact on Cincinnati than on other older northeastern and midwestern central cities. The major reform constituency, the city's upper middle class, remained concentrated in city neighborhoods such as Clifton, Hyde Park, and North Avondale. The city's immigrant population in the 1920s and later was also comparatively low. In 1920, foreign-born residents constituted 12% of the city's population, only one-half the proportion of 30 years earlier. Although the African-American population rose steadily, the increase was not concentrated in one particular period. From 7.5% of the city's total population in 1920, the black proportion rose to 10.5% in 1930, 12.2% in 1940, 15.6% in 1950, and 21.6% in 1960 (Silberstein, 1982, p. 306; Teaford, 1990, pp. 14–15, 124–25).

Most powerfully, the memory of the machine helped to sustain reform. Before 1925 the Hamilton County Republican organization controlled the city's government. One of the few durable machines, it gave Cincinnati a national reputation for bad government and malrepresentation. In 1921 only one Democrat had managed to win election to the otherwise solidly Republican council of 32 members. The conventional wisdom remained, long after the initial burst of reform enthusiasm had passed, that "Cincinnati was a sick city" in the final years of machine rule. Its government was in thrall to the Republican organization, heir to the legendary Boss Cox; the council "capable only of blind obedience"; the mayor "almost equally helpless"; the city starved for funds because "the people persistently refused to vote extra tax levies to be spent by a government they did not trust" (Reed and Reed, 1944).

Some of this was myth. Boss Cox's machine had been an adaptable organization, which served as a mediator and in many instances brought "positive government to Cincinnati" (Miller, 1968, p. 239). By the 1920s machine rule had been weakening for years. At the 1926 retirement of Rudolph Hynicka, its boss, one local political writer noted that he "has reigned but not ruled." Hynicka had long spent more time in New York than in Cincinnati. As a result, "the Cincinnati Republican organization suffers not from too much bossism but from too little. . . . There has been an absence of direction and of discipline" (Henderson, 1926). Furthermore, the party's internal harmony had been upset profoundly in 1920, when Hynicka ordered delegates at the national convention to desert Ohio's own Warren G. Harding after the first ballot (Millard, 1924).

Reformers argued that "certain peculiarities" of the city's pre-PR charter had helped the Republican organization maintain control. First, council candidates could run only on a party ticket. Second, Cincinnati was the only city under home rule in the state to retain party symbols (the eagle and the rooster) on the ballot. "This made it much easier for the organization in control to poll the ignorant vote," one of the city's leading reformers wrote. Third, although municipal elections had been separated from state and national elections, the county partisan committees continued to be elected on state and national primary ballots. Partisan considerations were thus paramount in the selection of "the real governing body of the city," the Hamilton County Republican organization. Gerrymandered wards also helped to protect the Republican machine from the threat of popular dissatisfaction, blunting the potential effectiveness of reform mayors (Bentley, 1925).

Republican organization hegemony between 1910 and 1930 was more a result of the weak alternative offered by the local Democratic party and of the divisions among reformers than of the Republican party's own strength. Nevertheless, although the local Democratic party remained an empty shell, surely scarred in the minds of many reformers by a history of sharing patronage with the Republican organization, progressive Democrats did take an active role in reform efforts. One of these, Herbert Bigelow, helped win Ohio's initiative, referendum, and municipal home rule provisions. In Cincinnati, Bigelow used his People's Church as the nucleus for a People's Power League. In 1916 another Democratic reformer, Edward Alexander, brought the People's Power League together with a number of prominent civic leaders to support a home rule charter for Cincinnati. Their pressure forced the Republican organization to accede to a new charter, adopted in 1917. The charter made few significant changes in the city's government, but reformers saw it as opening the door to additional reforms (Miller, 1968, p. 164; Alexander, 1988).

Boss Hynicka also had begun to reform the Republican organization itself. To do so he formed the Republican Executive and Advisory Commission, which included a number of businessmen and professionals long associated with civic reform. Its most important member, John R. Holmes, had been affiliated with reform movements dating back to the 1880s. Apparently Hynicka was grooming Holmes to succeed Hynicka himself, but Holmes died before the opportunity arose. Despite these changes, the machine continued to provide reformers with a convenient target far into the future. "The partially reformed organization with the Cox tradition still alive, but the bullying, fear-inspiring methods of the Big Boss largely eliminated," Charles P. Taft admitted a few years after reformers had won their battle, "was a far different machine from what it was at its height in 1905, whatever the public might continue to think about it" (Taft, 1933, pp. 19–20).

Adoption of PR

Reform initiatives in the 1920s came from two distinct sources. The first and most important group, independent Republicans, favored city manager government and a small, nonpartisan council elected at large. They hoped to see the election of a "better" class of councilmen who were removed from the control of party managers. A second group was essential to the inclusion of proportional representation in the charter proposal that went to the voters in 1924. Generally made up of progressive Democrats, this group wanted most to win mechanisms of minority representation. Proportional representation was the price they extracted from Republican reformers for supporting city manager government and a small at-large council. They had important popular organizational support to offer in return.

The impetus for reform was the fiscal collapse of the city's government. The collapse was partly due to restraints in state law on the city's ability to raise taxes, and partly due to reformers' appeals to voters to defeat necessary tax levies. As part of its effort to solve the city's ongoing fiscal problems, the Republican organization itself commissioned a broad ranging survey of municipal governance, published in 1923. The resulting reports, particularly on the caliber and performance of the city council, provided reformers with all the ammunition they needed to launch their municipal revolution.

Birdless Ballots, the Upson Survey, and Taxes

A small group of young men, for the most part Republicans, provided the primary impetus toward reform. Through the Cincinnatus Association, organized soon after World War I, these men conducted investigations of the city's government, held meetings twice a month, and, in doing so, garnered much newspaper publicity. As a result of one of the papers read at their meetings, the Birdless Ballot League was formed to remove partisan symbols from the city election ballot (Bentley, 1925, pp. 69–74; Taft, 1933, p. 54).

Through the initiative of the birdless ballot, they hoped to "improve" the electorate by reducing the influence of "ignorant" voters. Henry Bentley, the major proponent of the ballot, compared the results of a city election for auditor with "birds" on the ballot to a school board election without "birds" on the ballot. In the "residence sections of the city," he showed, 95% of the voters had cast ballots for both offices; in the central wards, however, where "the instruction of the Republican workers to certain types of voters was to vote for the bird with pants (referring to the eagle)," the number voting in the "birdless" school election was only 40%–65% of the number voting for auditor. A birdless ballot, Bentley argued, "would require the parties to appeal to the more intelligent part of the population and not to the element that votes the straight ticket without knowledge or consideration" (Taft, 1933, pp. 52–53).

In this antiparty climate, a major report on the city's government quickened interest in broader reform. A special advisory subcommittee of the Republican Executive and Advisory Committee, which included among its members Murray Seasongood, Charles Taft, and other reform stalwarts, had commissioned a full-scale survey of Cincinnati's government, coordinated by Lent Upson, a University of Michigan political scientist. The survey's major recommendations covered the coordination of city and county government, proper city financing, reduction of county and city expenses, and increased efficiency.

Although certainly critical of machine politics, the report need not have been taken as an indictment of the city's governmental structure. Constraint on its revenue was the major cause of Cincinnati's problems. "Final solution," Upson noted, "lies in state legislation permitting the city to tax itself sufficiently for ordinary purposes. . . . Were the city of Cincinnati governed by the most high minded and efficient administrators in existence, they could not possibly, with the funds now available, give the citizens the type of government to which they are entitled. It must not be believed that the administrative side of the city and county governments does not compare favorably with that of other cities and counties,—it does" (Upson, 1924, pp. 36–37).

Given their aversion to partisanship in local affairs, reformers found it easy to see the survey as an indictment of Republican machine rule. They focused their attention on Thomas Reed's section of the survey, his report on the city council. Reed, then a professor of political science at the University of Michigan, and formerly a city manager of San Jose, California, painted a damning portrait of a council wallowing in routine administrative matters "devoid of general popular interest"; a council with only six members on key committees who had "the intellectual activity, knowledge, and interest to be active councilmen"; a council composed of "mere voting automata" subservient to the Hamilton County Republican organization; a council that offered "very little incentive for any man of real ability to seek a place." Although he briefly noted that the six members elected at-large were of somewhat higher station than the members elected from wards, he attached little importance to the fact. He feared that a small council elected at-large by plurality voting would merely enhance the position of the Republican party. For that reason he noted with favor Cleveland's experiment with PR, and forthrightly asserted that proportional representation "of some sort is the only thing which will meet squarely the needs of Cincinnati" (Upson, 1924, pp. 189–98).

Although Upson's conclusions did not embrace PR, his summary echoed Reed's characterizations of the weaknesses of the large ward-based council. According to Upson, Cincinnati's large council was incapable of "intelligent planning." Planning was essential to the modern city, but "ward representatives in the very nature of things are likely to over-emphasize the requirements of their localities to the detriment of the City as a whole." He recommended reducing the council's size and electing its members from large districts rather than wards to attract "men of wider experience and accomplishment to Council." He also urged nomination by petition instead of primary elections. He made no specific recommendation for proportional or plurality voting, but he insisted that a reorganized council needed to be limited to no more than nine members elected on a nonpartisan ballot (Upson, 1924, pp. 19–20, 30, 43, 45).

Upson's chief target was partisanship. In this sense, the report inescapably pointed to the need for some mechanism to provide for minority representation. "Until there exists in Cincinnati a strong, intelligent, critical minority, so dangerous to the life of the dominant party that the latter is constantly urged to its best efforts, the maximum of effective government cannot be expected," Upson concluded. "I am convinced that great improvement in the government of Cincinnati will come from the introduction of a strong and critical minority into council, the independence of that council from national party affiliation, and the destruction of the theory under which the political organization in power usurps the authority and annuls the independent judgment of elected administrative and legislative officers" (Upson, 1924, pp. 38–39).

Resentment of taxes, not political theory, proved to be the vehicle that made reform a popular movement. The Upson Survey refused to recommend the approval of special bond issues because of the debt the city already bore. It also castigated the city administration for diverting auto license fees designated for street repairs to other purposes. However, it strongly supported a special tax levy designed to cover the deficit and support current city services (Upson, 1924, pp. 7–23). Voters rejected it. Reformers urged them to do so. A speech against the levy given by Murray Seasongood to the Cincinnatus Association gained wide publicity and made him the leader of the campaign to defeat the tax levy. The speech marked Seasongood's full-scale engagement in local politics and the reform cause. To politics Seasongood brought a "strict moral rectitude" and "uncompromising ethical code." A Republican himself, his slashing attacks on the Republican organization left little room for nuanced discussion of the burdens imposed by state fiscal restraints on Cincinnati's government. Voters followed with ease an explanation of the city's fiscal plight cast in terms of morality. Seasongood's rhetoric turned a vote against the tax levy into a moral condemnation of the machine (Baughin, 1988; Taft, 1933, pp. 33–39).[1]

Given Seasongood's new prominence, Democrat Edward Alexander turned to him as a potential leader of a movement to bring PR to the city council. Cleveland's experiment with PR intrigued Alexander; earlier he had tried to interest Herbert Bigelow. At first, neither Bigelow nor Seasongood indicated much interest in PR. By early 1924, however, Bigelow, then leader of the LaFollette Conference for Progressive Political Action (CPPA), asked Alexander to prepare a petition for a city manager-PR charter amendment (Alexander, 1988).

The varied sources of reform sentiment soon came together. A Democrat involved with the birdless ballot initiative asked Alexander to approach Bigelow for help in gathering signatures to support a proposed charter amendment. Bigelow and the CPPA refused. Alexander then attended a meeting of the birdless ballot group and pointed out the weaknesses of their proposal. It would only keep party designations off the ballot; Cincinnati's charter still would not allow independent candidacies (Alexander, 1988; Millard, 1924).

Discussion soon turned to more far-ranging reform. Charles Taft suggested city manager government. Alexander replied "that the group which I represented would not support a city manager amendment unless it included proportional representation." Alexander prepared a draft modeled on the Cleveland charter, including a 25-member council elected from large districts by PR. Alexander's insistence on PR dismayed the others, Taft recollected. Seasongood objected to the number of councilmen and the districting provisions. He wanted a nine-member at-large council elected by PR. A small council, he argued, would limit the number of groups represented, curbing the potential for group conflict and the formation of "racial, geographical, religious, and other blocks." Although Alexander still wanted a larger council and districting, "the preference did not seem vital and I agreed that Seasongood's proposal could be accepted" (R. A. Burnham, 1990, pp. 35–37; Alexander, 1988, pp. 24–25; Taft, 1933, pp. 54–55).

The Organization of Charter Forces and the 1924 Campaign

Reformers soon launched an effort to secure city manager government, a small council elected at-large, and proportional representation. On June 9 the Birdless Ballot League disbanded, superseded by a new City Charter Committee. Alexander joined five former members of the Birdless Ballot League on its executive committee, and they quickly built a "thoroughgoing and systematic" campaign organization. Alexander made a trip to Cleveland to study techniques reformers had used there three years earlier to win adoption of PR. Bigelow's CPPA, as well as the Charter Committee, furnished headquarters for gathering signatures to put the proposed charter amendments on the ballot. The committee recruited middle-class women to serve as ward leaders, but they themselves did most of the remaining organizational work. The committee also made special efforts to supply newspapers with favorable copy; as a result, they won much better support from the local press than reformers had in Cleveland in 1921. The organizational efforts brought in 22,000 signatures in four weeks, far more than the required 13,000 (Millard, 1924; Alexander, 1988; Bentley, 1925, p. 72; Taft, 1933, pp. 54–55).

Henry Bentley, from the Birdless Ballot League, coordinated the fall campaign, but Murray Seasongood was "naturally the outstanding protagonist," Alexander later recalled. "Above all, [Seasongood] possessed the power of righteous indignation. He was a hell-raiser par excellence." Women, however, provided the organizational backbone, drawing on 30 years' experience with reform causes in Cincinnati. With the help of the League of Women Voters and the Woman's City Club, women ward leaders organized 20 of the 26 wards with 465 precinct workers. A speaker's bureau coordinated appearances before some 300 meetings. Reformers seized upon specific irritants—a streetcar fare increase, the poor conditions of the streets and the diversion of auto license fees from street repairs, a gas rate increase, organized labor's suspicion that labor-endorsed candidates had been cheated in the August Republican primaries—in their "appeal for a small council, business management, and honest elections" (Alexander, 1988, p. 26; Bentley, 1925, pp. 71–73; Miller, 1968, pp. 118–20).

Reformers emphasized the benefits of a small council and at-large representation. The Republican organization offered ineffective replies, concentrating instead on PR as the most "dangerous" aspect of the reform package. PR was, they charged, an "assault on Americanism" that would heighten "religious and racial distinctions." Council members "would sit 'not as Republicans or Democrats, not as adherents of this or that policy, but as Catholics, Protestants, or Jews, or as white men or negroes.' " PR would subvert the two-party system that had been "designed to obliterate and soften" racial and religious differences. The Republican organization prepared two alternatives to the package designed by the City Charter Committee. Both called for nine-member councils. One alternative would have council members nominated from wards, but elected at-large, the other would have members elected from districts. Both would have retained partisan elections, the organization's overriding concern (Taft, 1933, pp. 54–55; Henderson, 1926; R. A. Burnham, 1990, pp. 31–33, 36–42; Millard, 1924, p. 604).

It fell to Seasongood to defend PR against the organization's attacks. Although Seasongood and most other advocates of a smaller at-large council had embraced PR with only moderate enthusiasm, it was still an essential component of their alliance with Alexander and Bigelow. Ignoring the group categories that Republicans stressed—race and religion—Seasongood emphasized Cincinnati's relative ethnic homogeneity. The position was less than a full defense of the principle of group representation (R. A. Burnham, 1990, pp. 33–36).

The election was not even close. Cincinnati voters adopted the reformers' package by a vote of two to one (92,510 to 41,105) in the November election. Voters' party affiliation was of little importance; in the same election, the Republican national, state, and county tickets carried the city easily. The margin of victory exceeded two to one in 17 of the city's 26 wards, including wards with significant foreign-born populations. Although low-income and lower-middle-income wards in or near the inner city gave the amendment a smaller margin of victory than did middle- and upper-middle-income wards on the periphery, even there the margin of victory was generally substantial. Only four wards failed to return a majority for the amendment. Three contained the majority of the city's black residents, where the amendment lost by a vote of 5,693 to 3,878, despite the support of an African-American newspaper. Reformers had made some efforts to extend their campaign to the black community, but little evidence suggests that they saw much hope of breaking the hold of the Republican machine on its votes. Ward 6, an inner-city, poor white ward (and Hynicka's home ward), also voted against the reforms (R. A. Burnham, 1990, pp. 44–49).

Yet the magnitude of the reform victory did not necessarily represent an embrace of reform ideology by the majority of the city's voters. Reform leaders recognized that their victory was most properly attributed to simple disgust with the current state of city affairs. It did not represent a reasoned preference for either city manager government or proportional representation. Walter Millard's analysis of the probability of the reform victory, made a month before the election, holds up well: "It will not be because every citizen understands that a city manager is technically a 'controlled executive,' nor because a Hare count has become as popular as Mahjong. . . . when a meeting breaks up, the same old remark that has done service in every other city manager campaign is heard on every side: 'We don't understand all of this new scheme, but nothing could be worse than what we've got' " (Millard, 1924, p. 605). What was needed was a permanent charter committee.

The Permanent City Charter Committee and the First PR Election

The Charter Committee's transformation into a permanent political organization following its 1924 victory was crucially important to the longevity of reform in Cincinnati. The organization was built on a tradition of "nonpartisan" reform politics in Cincinnati that united independent Republicans and both organization and "radical" Democrats (Miller, 1968, pp. 179–80). At a victory dinner held in November 1924, "it was felt that unless an organization was effected to secure the election of proper men for council, the victory might prove futile." Five new members were added to the executive committee and a permanent headquarters secured. This committee's charge went beyond the usual prescription of study, investigation, and publicity, to the creation of an organization "which will endeavor to perfect the ward and precinct organization of the city so as to have a human telephone system whereby facts of political significance can be carried direct to the voters." It was not clear at first whether the new organization would itself nominate candidates, but its organizers hoped, at the least, to encourage candidacies by "men of the proper type" through emphasis on "the importance of the position of councilman and the dignity and honor of the position." Reformers felt confident that they stood a fair chance of remaking the council in the image they desired because of Cincinnati's relatively small foreign-born population. Yet they were also well aware that voters in 1924 had voted "against the existing government rather than in favor of the new government." Voters still needed to be converted to the cause of "good government and constructive policies." That was to be the work of the permanent Charter Committee in its first test, the 1925 council election (Bentley, 1925).

In April the Charter Committee decided to endorse specific candidates. Disavowing partisanship in local affairs, they feared that too many independent candidacies would divide the reform vote. The nomination of candidates "was something of a ticklish job." The Charter Committee was still "little more than a somewhat alliance of groups that did not have too much in common. The conservative independent Republican group controlled the board, but there were a few Democrats including two labor men, friends of Herbert Bigelow," who needed to be satisfied. The nominating committee asked the Democratic organization to name three candidates. The other six slots were reserved for independent Republicans. The committee also wanted to balance the ticket by geography, religion, ethnicity, and economic class, a balance made easier by the nomination of a full slate of nine candidates. Suggestions solicited from civic groups "were classified, for purposes of consideration, by political affiliation, nationality (German, Irish or American descent), residence and religion" (Alexander, 1988; Bentley, 1926, p. 466; Taft, 1933, pp. 76–78).

Careful attention to political considerations marked the campaign. Henry Bentley supervised the committee's ward and precinct organization, which remained particularly strong in middle-class areas of the city. The organization was tested first by a voter registration campaign, then by the collection of signatures for candidates. The committee also made special efforts to enforce campaign unity. It required each endorsed candidate to accept nomination in writing and to promise to support the entire ticket, helping to foreclose the effectiveness of selective Republican endorsements. Yet, even as the Charter Committee acted as a political party in each of these respects, reformers continued to campaign on the antiparty premise that PR "permitted the citizens to think of candidates as individuals and not as units in a block" (Taft, 1933, pp. 74–75; Bentley, 1926, pp. 466–69).

The Republican organization in contrast waged an inept campaign. Rather than nominate a full slate, they chose only six candidates. They "districted" the city among the six, but, "as the fight got hotter and the Republican nominees saw that the machine could not assure the victory of all six candidates, they commenced to fight among themselves. Friends of Republican candidates sought first choice votes in districts that had been apportioned to other Republican candidates" (Bentley, 1926, pp. 467–68; Taft, 1933, pp. 79–80). The Charter Committee elected six of its nominees to the council; the Republican organization, only three. The election had fundamentally altered the partisan alignment in Cincinnati's council.

Abandonment of PR

In September 1957 a significant majority of Cincinnati's voters voted to repeal PR, effective with that fall's municipal election. It was the fifth time they had been asked to do so. The Republican organization was the leading impetus behind each of the repeal efforts. In each campaign, opponents attacked only proportional representation. They made no efforts to change city manager government, the small at-large council, the nonpartisan ballot, or nomination by petition. In 1936, 1939, 1947, and 1957, the proposed substitute was a nine-member council, elected at large on a plurality ballot, with each voter having nine votes (9X). The 1954 repeal issue proposed a limited voting

TABLE 6.1
ADOPTION AND REPEAL OF PROPORTIONAL REPRESENTATION

Year	Issue	Registration	Total Vote	Turnout as % of Registration	Pro-PR Vote	% for PR
1924	Adoption	n/a	133,615		92,510	69.2
1936	Repeal/9X	243,241	72,469	29.8	36,650	50.6
1939	Repeal/9X	228,912	95,858	41.9	48,300	50.4
1947	Repeal/9X	246,671	155,003	62.8	81,365	52.5
1954	Repeal/6X	245,429	150,416	61.3	75,544	50.2
1957	Repeal/9X	242,348	119,843	49.5	54,097	45.1

Sources: Registration figures are from Ohio, Secretary of State, *Vote . . . Polled,* various years. Even-year registration figures have been used to provide a consistent base. Voting figures are from R. A. Burnham (1990); the *National Municipal Review;* and the *Cincinnati Times-Star,* 4 Oct. 1957.

alternative that would have allowed each voter six votes for a nine-member council (6X), an attempt to diffuse fears that PR's repeal would bring a return to the partisan hegemony characteristic of pre-1925 councils. Submitted alone, PR never received the overwhelming support that the entire reform package had garnered in 1924. Three times, in 1936, 1939, and 1954, PR survived with narrow majorities; only once, in 1947, did a significant majority support PR's retention. In 1957 racial polarization, Republican and Democratic partisanship, and business community dissatisfaction with governance each contributed to PR's repeal. Although certain unique circumstances existed in 1957, particularly the racial situation, the final success of PR's opponents was the culmination of their previous four efforts. In each of the repeal campaigns PR's opponents reiterated many of the same arguments.

First, PR's opponents charged that the single transferable vote operated as a lottery, capriciously altering the outcome. In 1957 Republicans pointed to the fact that they had polled 51% of first-choice votes in 1955 but had failed to win a majority of seats on the council. PR's defenders countered with long explanations of a recount held in 1955 that closely mirrored the initial count. The defenders also denied the truth of the assumption that first-choice votes reflected partisan preferences. Reminding voters of Republican party hegemony on the pre-PR council, the defenders argued that to repeal PR while retaining a small at-large council would produce a Republican clean sweep of all nine council seats. PR's supporters hammered at the "distinctly political sources" of the repeal effort, discounting "the character and aims" of its opponents as "self-serving" (Heisel, 1982; Reed et al., 1957, pp. 39–51).

Second, opponents argued that PR contributed to stalemate on the council. In 1957 they pointed to the 1954 council's lack of a working majority, and its inability to name a mayor, because of the defection of a Charter member. That situation had brought back memories of prolonged wrangles on the council in the late 1930s and early 1940s that were a result of the election of independent candidates to the council. Defenders of PR replied that such disputes had little effect on the city's essential business (Heisel, 1982; Reed et al., 1957, p. 38).

Third, opponents consistently charged that PR fostered block-voting. In 1957 that argument took on distinctly racial overtones. Two years earlier, an African-American Charter Committee candidate, Theodore Berry, had led all other Charter Committee candidates in the first-choice vote, running second among all candidates, and had thus almost become Cincinnati's first black mayor. The city's social characteristics also had changed enough to highlight the racial issue. Between 1950 and 1957, the city's nonwhite population, 15% of the city in 1950, had risen more than 35%, while the white population had grown by less than 2%. Urban renewal projects made the city's growing African-American population evident to whites who had little previous contact with blacks. Furthermore, the repeal vote took place as the racial crisis in Little Rock dominated headlines. Open charges that a black patronage machine existed in city hall, along with a whispering campaign, exacerbated racial fears and hostilities. The racial aspects of PR's repeal were quite evident. In predominantly white precincts, PR lost by more than a two to one margin; in African-American precincts, it won by four to one. Little more than a month later, Theodore Berry was the only incumbent Charter councilman to lose a bid for reelection on the plurality ballot (Gray, 1959, pp. 1.4, 2.10–11; Frank, 1957).

Two other factors were present as well in 1957. At least some Democrats had "long been grumbling that P.R. means the submission of their party in the Charter party" and was an obstacle to the Democratic party's growth in the city. The repeal effort also included business and community leaders impatient "with what seems to them the slow progress of the city in dealing with such major projects as expressways and off-street parking" (Reed et al., 1957, pp. 47–49).

Racial polarization, partisanship, and dissatisfaction with governance each contributed to PR's repeal in 1957. That partisanship was a key factor was rooted in the initial motivation of Cincinnati's reformers in the 1920s, when their chief target had been the Republican organization. The political struggle between the City Charter Committee and the Republican organization had continued since then. What was new was the equivocal position of the city's Democratic politicians. In the 1920s they had much to gain from alliance with independent Republicans in the Charter Committee. In the 1950s that was no longer the case, for by then Democrats ran stronger races than did independent Republicans as Charter candidates. There was some irony in PR's identification with black representation in 1957. In 1924 African Americans had been the only group in the city to vote against PR, but by 1957 black identification with the Republican party had waned as a result of the New Deal realignment and the Charter Committee's recognition of the need for black representation. There was also irony in the business community's dissatisfaction with the city's governance in the 1950s. In the 1920s reformers had harped on the old government's inability to pave the streets. By the 1950s Cincinnati seemed to be falling behind in the urban redevelopment race; its government no longer seemed "dynamic" to members of the business community. Some "went so far as to say that they would prefer a corrupt government which is dynamic to what they have. They even point to some notoriously badly governed cities which have built more expressways and off-street parking facilities than Cincinnati" (Reed et al., 1957, p. 25).

Proportional Representation and Council Characteristics

Assessment of PR's effect on council characteristics is intrinsically problematic. When adopted in the 1920s, it was only a part of a larger package of reforms. Three decades later, when it was abandoned, many of the city's political and social characteristics had changed. Although significant differences are evident in the political and social characteristics of council members elected before, during, and after PR, few can be attributed solely to PR. The major differences lie between the pre-PR predominantly ward-based council and the small at-large council first elected in 1925 and continued to the present. Under neither PR nor 9X did one-party hegemony reemerge. On its face, PR seems to have moderately improved the chances for success of independent candidacies, but successes were rare. The class status of council members changed dramatically from the pre-PR period (1915–21), but no significant difference existed between the PR (1925–55) and post-PR (1957–61) periods. Women gained no advantage from PR in terms of council representation. African Americans did, but their success also was due to the independent impact of partisan competition for black votes during the PR period.

Partisanship: Republicans, Democrats, and the Charter Committee

The single most striking change after the adoption of reforms in the 1920s was the breaking of Republican hegemony on the council. PR councils much more closely mirrored electoral divisions than had the pre-PR council. That had been one of the most important goals of reformers. The change in the council's partisan composition was due to reduced vote distortion, which measures the difference between a party's proportion of legislative seats and its share of the vote as a percentage of the vote. Positive values signify a party's overrepresentation; negative values, underrepresentation (Argersinger, 1989, pp. 72–73). Although vote distortion in Cincinnati increased somewhat in the post-PR period, the increase was primarily due to the Democratic party's withdrawal from its electoral coalition with the Charter Committee (see table 6.2).

Differences in vote distortion for Republican, Charter, and Democratic candidates across all three periods were quite significant ($p < .0002$, using the Kruskal-Wallis one-way anova test). Much of the difference, however, was due to the Democratic coalition with the Charter Committee during the PR period. If the Charter Committee and Democratic Party vote distortion figures are considered together for the years in which they did not run opposing slates, the difference across all three periods is not statistically significant ($p < .068$). Using adjacent periods only (pre-PR and PR; PR and post-PR) rather than all three periods, differences in vote distortion for Republican, Charter, and Democratic candidates (Charter and Democratic considered both separately and together) are all statistically significant ($p < .0139$). Although independents won four seats during the PR period, the data on vote distortion are not strong enough to support a finding of statistical significance.

It is difficult to disentangle the independent effects of PR and the Charter-Democratic coalition on the reduction of vote distortion and the council's partisan make-up. Reformers attributed the Charter coalition's durability primarily to PR. Henry Bentley argued that PR, the lack of a primary, and the consequent invigoration of the City Charter Committee were intricately linked pieces that "afforded an opportunity for citizens to unite and secure for themselves good government" (Bentley, 1929). William Hessler (1953) also attributed the longevity of

TABLE 6.2

Party Distribution of Seats, Votes, and Vote Distortion, Cincinnati City Council, 1915–1961

Year	Republican No. Seats	% Seats	% Votes	Vote Distortion (%)	Democratic No. Seats	% Seats	% Votes	Vote Distortion (%)	Charter No. Seats	% Seats	% Votes	Vote Distortion (%)	Independent/Other No. Seats	% Seats	% Votes	Vote Distortion (%)
1915																
AL	6	100.0	62.4	60.3	0	0.0	34.5	-100.0					0	0.0	3.1	-100.0
W	25	100.0	60.1	66.4	1	3.8	36.8	-89.5					0	0.0	3.2	-100.0
1917																
AL	6	100.0	50.5	98.0	0	0.0	37.1	-100.0					0	0.0	12.5	-100.0
W	23	88.5	52.4	68.9	3	11.5	37.8	-69.5					0	0.0	9.9	-100.0
1921																
AL	6	100.0	53.7	86.2	0	0.0	30.2	-100.0					0	0.0	16.1	-100.0
W	25	96.2	56.0	71.8	1	3.9	31.5	-87.6					0	0.0	12.5	-100.0
1925	3	33.3	27.8	19.9					6	66.7	63.8	4.5	0	0.0	8.4	-100.0
1927	2	22.2	28.6	-22.3					6	66.7	58.0	14.9	1	11.1	13.4	-17.1
1929	3	33.3	36.7	-9.2					6	66.7	56.8	17.4	0	0.0	6.6	-100.0
1931	4	44.4	39.6	12.2					5	55.6	52.8	5.2	0	0.0	7.6	-100.0
1933	4	44.4	45.6	-2.5					5	55.6	49.7	11.8	0	0.0	4.7	-100.0
1935	4	44.4	41.1	8.1					4	44.4	39.6	12.2	1	11.1	19.3	-42.4
1937	4	44.4	44.0	1.0					4	44.4	36.8	20.8	1	11.1	19.3	-42.4
1939	4	44.4	49.4	-10.0					4	44.4	34.3	29.6	1	11.1	16.4	-32.2
1941	5	55.6	59.3	-6.3					4	44.4	32.4	37.2	0	0.0	8.3	-100.0
1943	5	55.6	54.2	2.5					4	44.4	40.2	10.6	0	0.0	5.6	-100.0
1945	5	55.6	54.8	1.4					4	44.4	44.2	0.6	0	0.0	1.0	-100.0
1947	4	44.4	47.8	-7.0					5	55.6	47.8	16.2	0	0.0	4.4	-100.0
1949	4	44.4	47.1	-5.6					5	55.6	50.8	9.4	0	0.0	2.1	-100.0
1951	5	55.6	52.2	6.4					4	44.4	47.3	-6.0	0	0.0	0.5	-100.0
1953	4	44.4	48.5	-8.4					5	55.6	51.4	8.1	0	0.0	0.1	-100.0
1955	4	44.4	51.0	-12.9					5	55.6	42.9	29.5	0	0.0	6.2	-100.0
1957	5	55.6	50.3	10.4					4	44.4	49.7	-10.6	0	0.0		
1959	5	55.6	40.8	36.2	2	22.2	27.9	-20.4	2	22.2	29.1	-23.6	0	0.0	2.2	-100.0
1961	5	55.6	41.4	34.2	3	33.3	35.7	-6.6	2	11.1	23.0	-51.7	0	0.0		

Source: Hamilton County Board of Elections, *Elections in Hamilton County*, various years.

Notes: AL = councilmen at-large, W = ward council members (1915–21). % Votes based on first-choice ballots for PR elections (1925–55). Vote Distortion has been calculated as (% seats − % votes) ÷ % votes, following Argersinger (1989).

the reform movement in Cincinnati chiefly to PR. Thomas and Doris Reed and Ralph Straetz (1957, pp. 14–16, 23) contended that, in Cincinnati, PR was the only mechanism by which the city could have both election at large and partisan competition. The City Charter Committee "could not have developed into a permanently effective opposition party except under P.R.," because PR had ensured its candidates' representation even after the initial burst of reform had been spent. The vote distortion figures in table 6.2 do show that the Charter Committee benefited from PR even as the committee's electoral support waned in the 1930s, helping to maintain it as a viable party.

Although the adoption of PR in the 1920s provided the initial framework for partisan competition, the organizational efforts of both local parties insured its continuation. Voters did not "unite and secure for themselves good government." They responded to partisan choices.

In 1933 the Republican organization reorganized itself, helping to shed its image of "bossism" and preparing it to take advantage of waning support for the Charter Committee. From 1934 to 1946 it returned solid majorities for Republican gubernatorial candidates in Cincinnati; although Democrat Franklin D. Roosevelt won the city in the 1932 and 1936 presidential elections, he lost it in 1940 and 1944, as did Truman in 1948 (Ohio, Secretary of State, *Vote . . . Polled in the Several Counties*). Throughout the 1930s, Republicans elected four members to each council; in 1941 they gained a majority on the council, for the first time since the 1921 election, retaining it for three terms.

The Charter Committee also revamped itself, concluding that "the honest government idea is worn out" as it saw Republican fortunes improve. It took on more of the attributes of a political party as it recognized the need to broaden its appeal and to solidify its support. It began to exercise greater policy oversight over Charter council members. It also gave ward captains a greater role within the Charter organization as a substitute for patronage. Furthermore, it adopted a specific policy platform, rather than campaigning solely on "good government" principles and its past accomplishments (R. A. Burnham, 1990, pp. 97, 259–69).

As the Charter Committee took steps to regularize itself as a local party organization, its coalition began to change. In 1936 Charter councilmen reached an accord with Herbert Bigelow, elected as an independent, in return for his support for their mayoral choice. Some Charter-Republicans refused to countenance the deal with the "radical" Bigelow and left the Charter Committee. Support for the committee among Republican voters then eroded. Between 1925 and 1935, 35% of Charter-endorsed Republican candidates had won election; that figure dropped to 19% between 1937 and 1947. Tensions within the Charter-Democratic coalition were also apparent. In 1937 a full slate of "Roosevelt Democrats" ran in the council election to try to reestablish the Democratic party in the city. Although the ticket ran poorly, and did not receive the support of the regular Democratic organization, the bolt from the Charter coalition indicated the dissatisfaction of at least some Democratic activists with their party's subordinate place within the Charter coalition (R. A. Burnham, 1990, pp. 97, 259–89).

After World War II, stresses within the Charter coalition became more evident. The Charter Committee could not prevent its most visible council member, Russell Wilson, a Charter-Republican who had served 15 years on the council and eight years as mayor, from publicly mocking its call for an investigation of municipal ownership of utilities. Support among Republicans continued to erode. In 1951 Charles P. Taft formed a special group, the Independent Republicans of Hamilton County, to help win support for Charter-endorsed Republicans, but the group failed to elect any of the three candidates it endorsed. Although the local Democratic organization remained formally within the Charter fold, it undertook vigorous independent campaign efforts for Charter-endorsed Democratic candidates. In 1959, two years after PR's repeal, the Democratic party decided to run its own ticket for the first time since the creation of the Charter Committee in 1925. Republican candidates drew electoral advantage from 9X as Democratic and Charter candidates vied with each other. The contention of PR's supporters that PR had been necessary to the viability of the Charter coalition seemed validated (R. A. Burnham, 1990, pp. 297–304).

Fears that PR's repeal would result in a Republican sweep of the 9X council proved to be unfounded. Higher levels of vote distortion in 9X elections did not approach those of pre-PR elections and were due largely to the split between the Charter Committee and the Democratic party. The change to 9X was one element of the Democratic organization's decision to leave the Charter fold, but there were other reasons. In cities throughout the nation in the 1950s, the Republican Party was collapsing (Teaford, 1990, pp. 62–63); local Democratic leaders were surely hopeful that the same might happen in Cincinnati. In only one gubernatorial election between 1948 and 1958 was the Republican Party able to win a majority for its candidate in the city, a dramatic reversal of its earlier success (Ohio, Secretary of State, *Vote . . . Polled in the Several Counties*). In 1958 Democrats won an impressive victory in state and county races, lending further credence to the possibility of a Democratic resurgence in the city. As the abortive bolt of Roosevelt Democrats in 1937 had shown, there had long been dissatisfaction among at least some Democrats about their status in city politics. As Democratic leaders saw support from independent Republicans for the Charter ticket wane in the 1940s and 1950s, they grew restive about the subordination of their party to the Charter Committee. It is thus not possible to attribute the dissolution of the Charter-Democratic coalition, or the advantages Republican candidates drew from 9X, solely to the abandonment of PR.

Stability: Independent Candidacies, Dissensus, and Incumbency

An oft-voiced criticism of PR government is that PR engenders factionalism, conflict, instability, and deadlock in legislative bodies. In Cincinnati, PR's opponents contended that PR undermined effective majority rule by encouraging the election of independents and giving them an inordinate voice in the council when there was an even division of the major parties (Reed et al., 1957, p. 38). Such circumstances were rare in Cincinnati (see table 6.3). Only four Independent candidacies, one each in 1927, 1935, 1937, and 1939, won election under PR. In 1927 and 1937 the elected independent soon joined the Republicans on the council. Only long-time Progressive gadfly Herbert Bigelow (who in the second and third decades of the century had been instrumental in securing municipal home rule provisions in Ohio and including PR in Cincinnati's revised charter) continued as an independent in office, rejecting the Democratic party leadership's accommodation with the Charter Committee and winning election to the council as an independent in 1935 and 1939. It is important to note as well that three of the four successful independent candidacies occurred in the politically unstable depression years, and that Bigelow also won a plurality election as a Democrat to the U.S. Congress in 1936 (Bentley, 1937).

At least in some respects, one of the goals of reformers in the 1920s was to structure a city government that would allow for more dissensus on the council. The city's government before 1925 allowed little room for the expression of dissent. The pre-PR council held little real authority. The 1923 Upson Survey noted that the mayor held an unusual degree of appointive authority and that an "unusually large amount of administrative authority" was delegated to certain department heads and to a board of control consisting of the mayor, the

TABLE 6.3
CHARACTERISTICS OF CINCINNATI CITY COUNCIL MEMBERS, 1915–1961

Election Year	Political Variables					Demographic Variables							
	Party				Incumbent	Occupation				Education		Race: Black	Sex: Female
	Republican	Charter	Democrat	Other		Professional	Business	Blue-Collar	Other	GR/HS	College		
1915													
AL	6		0	0	5	1	3	1	0	0	1	0	0
W	25		1	0	15	2	16	3	2	2	1	0	0
1917													
AL	6		0	0	3	2	2	2	0	0	0	0	0
W	23		3	0	18	3	15	4	1	2	2	0	0
1921													
AL	6		0	0	0	2	3	1	0	2	4	0	2
W	25		1	0	18	5	14	3	1	2	2	0	0
Pre-PR (N = 96)	91 94.8%		5 5.2%	0 0.0%	59 61.5%	15 15.6%	53 55.2%	14 14.6%	4 4.2%	8 8.3%	10 10.4%	0 0.0%	2 2.1%
1925	3	6	0	0	1	3	4	1	1	1	8	0	0
1927	2	6	0	1	7	4	4	0	1	1	8	0	0
1929	3	6	0	0	3	4	3	0	2	1	8	0	0
1931	4	5	0	0	8	4	3	0	2	2	7	1	0
1933	4	5	0	0	5	5	2	1	1	2	7	0	0
1935	4	4	0	1	6	5	2	1	1	2	7	1	0
1937	4	4	0	1	5	6	2	0	1	1	8	1	0

continued

TABLE 6.3
CHARACTERISTICS OF CINCINNATI CITY COUNCIL MEMBERS, 1915–1961—continued

| | Political Variables | | | | | Demographic Variables | | | | | | | |
| | Party | | | | | Occupation | | | | Education | | Race: | Sex: |
Election Year	Republican	Charter	Democrat	Other	Incumbent	Professional	Business	Blue-Collar	Other	GR/HS	College	Black	Female
1939	4	4	0	1	7	5	3	0	1	2	7	0	0
1941	5	4	0	0	7	5	3	0	1	2	7	1	0
1943	5	4	0	0	8	4	3	0	2	2	7	1	1
1945	5	4	0	0	7	4	3	1	1	3	6	1	0
1947	4	5	0	0	7	5	2	2	0	3	6	1	0
1949	4	5	0	0	6	6	1	1	1	1	8	2	0
1951	5	4	0	0	8	6	1	1	1	1	8	2	0
1953	4	5	0	0	4	4	2	1	2	0	9	1	1
1955	4	5	0	0	8	6	1	0	2	0	9	1	1
PR (N = 144)	64 44.4%	76 52.8%	0 0.0%	4 2.8%	97 67.4%	76 52.8%	39 27.1%	9 6.3%	20 13.9%	24 16.7%	120 83.3%	13 9.0%	3 2.1%
1957	5	4	0	0	7	5	2	0	1	0	9	0	1
1959	5	2	2	0	8	5	2	0	1	0	9	0	1
1961	5	1	3	0	7	5	3	0	0	0	9	0	0
Post-PR (N = 27)	15 55.6%	7 25.9%	5 18.5%	0 0.0%	22 81.5%	15 55.6%	7 25.9%	0 0.0%	2 7.4%	0 0.0%	27 100.0%	0 0.0%	2 7.4%

Sources: Demographic data from Cincinnati Directory (1915, 1917, 1921) for pre-PR council; from Cincinnati League of Women Voters, The Who and What of Elections, various years, for PR and post-PR councils.
Notes: AL = councilmen at-large, W = ward council members (1915–21).

director of public service, and the director of public safety. Although the council attended to "routine functions" such as minor ordinances related to permits and to street and sewer improvements, these were "devoid of general popular interest" and were " 'legislative' in name only." Committees concluded policy matters behind closed doors (Upson, 1924, pp. 183, 189–90).

Reformers hoped that the provision of a smaller council would bring to it members more capable of articulating policy positions because of their higher and presumably more independent status. In Cincinnati, reform augmented the council's policy-making authority and circumscribed the authority of the city manager more than was the usual case. The mayor, elected by the council from its own members, had the authority to appoint (with council approval) the city auditor and members of the board of health, the park board, the housing authority, the board of directors of the city university, a majority of the members of the recreation commission and the city planning commission, and one member of the civil service commission (Reed and Reed, 1944).

In these circumstances, a higher degree of dissensus on the council was to be expected, and perhaps welcomed. Yet Straetz (1958, pp. 62–96) found the large majority of council votes to have been unanimous. Of 727 votes on resolutions and ordinances taken by the 1941 council (on which Herbert Bigelow served as an Independent), 90.9% (661) were unanimous. In 1947, 95.6% (889) of the 930 votes taken on bills and resolutions were unanimous; in 1951, 87.1% (706) of 811 votes. Party was the most important consideration in nonunanimous votes. The most significant sources of dissensus were not policy differences but the political organization of the council itself—the election of the mayor and the filling of council vacancies.

There was some evidence of political dissensus on the reformed council from the start. In 1926 Murray Seasongood was the "inevitable" choice for mayor, but dissident Charter council members delayed his mayoral election. Disagreements among Charter council members in the early years of the reformed government became public because of a refusal to hold legislative caucuses, but by 1930 Charter council members reverted to more usual legislative partisan practices (Alexander, 1988, p. 28; Straetz, 1958, p. 73).

The 1935 election of Herbert Bigelow (then a prominent Coughlinite) as an independent brought a week-long deadlock over the selection of a mayor when the new council took office in 1936. Bigelow used the situation to extract concessions favoring his positions on the municipal ownership of utilities and the Single Tax. The 4-4-1 council split allowed him to do so. Bigelow had set terms to each side for his vote; initially neither Charter members nor Republicans accepted them. Ultimately Russell Wilson, the Charter leader and incumbent mayor, accepted a compromise agreement that "committed the Charter group to nothing inconsistent with its principles and ideals."[2] Despite the innocuous terms of the agreement reached with Bigelow, conservatives opposed to any acceptance of his demands raised a "storm" that they soon directed at PR itself. This, combined with the Charter Committee's loss of a council majority for the first time since its organization, led to the first repeal campaign in 1936 (Hallet, 1936a, b; Bentley, 1937).

If the 1936 mayoral imbroglio illustrated the possibility, however modest, of an enhanced ability to bring independent views to the council under PR, a similar situation in 1940 showed how such views could be quashed. Again Bigelow forced a deadlock over the selection of a mayor. This time Charter members, led by Charles P. Taft, refused to deal with him. Instead, Taft tossed Charter support to the Republican mayoral candidate. In return, the Charter Commission gained the vice mayoralty and other positions. Charter forces proclaimed that they had thus refuted charges that PR "enables one person to select their mayor for the people of Cincinnati." Bigelow was left out. Although he had been able to extract some concessions in 1936, he was not able to do so in 1940 (*NMR*, 1940, 25:71).

A somewhat similar situation occurred in 1954. The incumbent mayor had died in May. One of the Charter council members, Albert Jordan, an official of the steelworkers' union enraged about the council's imposition of an earnings tax on workers, had resigned from the Charter Committee. He refused to support the Charter Committee's choice for mayor, Dorothy Dolbey, but, since Dolbey had already been selected vice mayor, the Charter Committee was not obliged to win Jordan's support. Dolbey simply continued to act as mayor (Frank, 1954a, b).

These are limited examples, but they do support Straetz's conclusions that dissensus was not a significant problem on PR councils, even on the 4-4-1 councils on which Bigelow sat. The dissensus that did exist was due to the electoral system only in that, under PR, relatively close partisan balance generally existed on the council. Only in 1936 did a dissenting minority win concessions, and these were quite modest. In similar situations in 1940 and 1954, the majority was able to transact its business with no concessions whatsoever. Heisel (1980, p. 8; 1982) concluded that although the possibility of minority representation under PR could work against the presence of a working council majority, "with strong political leadership, such as a two-party system which existed in Cincinnati under most of its post-1926 history, a working majority was usually present. This was true under both PR and 9X." He found no evidence of any significant difference in council dissensus between PR and 9X councils.

In defending PR against charges that PR tended to promote instability, its advocates also could and did point to the success of incumbents. The Reeds and Straetz (1958, pp. 22–23) noted that only 48 individuals had served in the 144 seats in PR councils between 1925 and 1955. Only twice, in 1929 and in 1953, did a new council hold a majority of new members; in both cases, the exception was due to incumbents choosing not to run for reelection. The proportion of incumbents reelected under PR was greater than before PR (table 6.3). Again, it is difficult to attribute the change to PR. High rates of incumbency success continued to characterize the council after PR as well (Heisel, 1980; H. D. Hamilton, 1977, table 10). Even the immediate consequences of the change of electoral systems in the 1950s failed to reduce incumbency success, as might be expected. The small at-large council would seem to be the most relevant variable to incumbency success.

Representation: Geography, Class, Gender, and Race

From 1925 to the 1970s, little concern was expressed in Cincinnati about the geographic distribution of representation. The City Charter Committee in its first campaigns took care to balance their ticket geographically. Overall, however, as is to be expected of a small at-large council, council members' residences were concentrated in elite areas. Heisel (1982) found little difference between PR and 9X in this respect. Despite the geographic bias common to small at-large councils, a return to ward representation was not perceived as viable in Cincinnati, because at-large representation after 1925 dramatically reduced the partisan bias of the previous electoral system, restored effective partisan competition, and increased the social class status of council members (H. D. Hamilton, 1977, pp. 17, 98). None of the repeal campaigns directed against PR proposed the elimination of the small at-large council.

To reformers, by far the most damning part of the portrait of Cincinnati's government drawn by the 1923 Upson Survey was Thomas Reed's characterization of the class status of council members. Reed attributed "machine" control of the council to the low status of its members. Seven "were actively connected with the liquor business. Several of them conduct or have conducted resorts of disreputable character." Reed observed that,"with few exceptions, the professional members of council are not leaders in their fields, and the business men are neither successful nor prosperous." He attributed these factors to ward elections. Thirty-four years later, the Reeds and Straetz repeated those characterizations of the pre-PR council verbatim (Upson, 1924, p. 193; Reed et al., 1957, p. 20).

The change brought by reform in the social status of council members was immediate and long lasting. In 1944, the Reeds found that among PR council members "a sizable proportion have been top-flight business and professional men." Straetz (1958, pp. 47–60) similarly laid great stress on the improved social and class status of council members under PR. He noted that more than four out of five had greater than a high school education. Furthermore, broad social and civic involvement, prior government experience, and continuing public careers at higher levels of service characterized PR council members. In 1957, the Reeds and Straetz (pp. 19–21) in their joint report pointed to the "extraordinarily high level of education, experience and ability" of PR council members, particularly when contrasted with the "political hacks who occupied seats in the old council."

Systematic comparison of the occupation and education of council members elected under each electoral system supports their conclusions. The occupational and educational data reported in table 6.3 are significantly different for all three periods ($p < .027$, using the Kruskal-Wallis one way anova test). Restricting the statistical test to adjacent periods, all occupational variables are significantly different between the pre-PR and PR councils ($p < .019$), but not between the PR and post-PR councils. The known educational background of pre-PR council members is too sketchy to permit comparison; between the PR and the post-PR period the difference in educational background is significant ($p < .019$).

The differences between periods owe something to general changes in the populace's occupational and educational profile, but these general changes do not explain the sharp differences between the pre-PR council and the first PR councils. The proportion of college-educated professionals, primarily attorneys, rose dramatically on PR councils. That rise came not at the expense of blue-collar representation but of business representation. The 1921 council consisted primarily of small business proprietors and employees. Only five of 32 members were attorneys. Business proprietors included a butcher, a barber, a grocer, a hay and grain dealer, two plumbers, a restaurateur, two saloon keepers, and a tailor. Business employees included two auto salesmen, a brewery manager, two salesmen, and a clerk. The only "workman," according to the definitions of the Upson Survey, was a metal polisher (Upson, 1924, p. 193).

The Reeds (1944) and Straetz (1958, pp. 21–22) argued not only that PR councils included more "top-flight" professionals but that they had "not failed to represent the common man." To support this, they pointed to union officers on PR councils: "Labor . . . has been represented . . . not merely by rank-and-file workers but by genuine labor leaders." Yet neither study addressed the question of how representative the labor leaders were of labor or of the vast majority of unorganized "common men." It is at least arguable that the petty proprietors on the 1921 council were more representative of common men than were the labor officials on PR councils. The greater representation of labor leaders on PR councils is best attributed to the increased representation of professionals and to partisan competition for the labor vote. Labor organization was unable "by its own efforts to maintain labor representation in council" (Reed et al., 1957, pp. 33–36).

The data in table 6.3 and other sources show little difference in class status between PR council members and those elected under the plurality system in 1957 and later. Heisel (1982) found little difference in occupation or education between PR and 9X council members. H. D. Hamilton (1977, pp. 105–8, 20) attributed the higher status of PR and post-PR council members to at-large elections, and he noted that labor continued to be well organized and represented under 9X. The demonstrable differences in class status between pre-PR councils and PR councils were quite consonant with generally accepted understandings of the effects of small at-large councils in raising the social class status of members above that of ward-based councils.

The proportion of women elected to the council in each of the three periods was not significantly different (table 6.3). Two women sat on the pre-PR 1921 council; not until 1943 was a woman elected to a PR council. In the 16 PR elections, only three female candidacies were successful. The transition to plurality voting in 1957 made no apparent difference, as Dorothy Dolbey, elected under PR in 1953 and 1955, was reelected on the plurality ballot in 1957 and 1959. Heisel (1982) also found no significant difference between PR and 9X in female representation.

The Charter Committee did nominate women a number of times, but Charter nominations may not have been made with the expectation that female candidates would be successful. Edward Alexander (1988, p. 27) recalled that in 1925 Mary Hicks had been nominated "to represent the ladies," but she was "hardly known in the community" and her nomination was an "exception" to a ticket that was otherwise "without doubt the strongest ever nominated for a local P.R. election." She received fewer votes than any other Charter or Republican candidate. Murray Seasongood in 1927 took pains to convince an audience in Atlanta, Georgia, that PR would not mean women's "control." Noting the important role women played in the Cincinnati Charter Committee's organizational work, he assured his audience that they "have been thoroughly unselfish about it, not even aspiring to positions as women and effacing themselves as candidates in the forthcoming election" (1960, p. 76).

Cincinnati women's organizational work did not overcome presumptions against their direct representation on the council. Between 1925 and 1941, 23% of the Charter Committee directors were women. Organized in a separate women's division, women provided the Charter Committee with its most important continuing source of organizational support. Their role, however, was to focus on issues affecting home and family, not such "civic affairs" as "bridge building, road construction, the electric light plant," and "the gas franchise," which were the concerns of "father." After a second female Charter candidate lost in 1931, female board members themselves "voted unanimously not to nominate a woman in 1933." It was 10 years before the Charter Committee nominated another (R. A. Burnham, 1990, pp. 86–95).

Representation of African Americans on the council provides the strongest case for the proposition that PR "made a difference" in Cincinnati. The data reported in table 6.3 for race are significantly different among the three periods, as well as between adjacent periods ($p < .05$, corrected for ties). One of the most compelling arguments of PR proponents is PR's theoretical ability, with a nine-member council, to facilitate the representation of any self-defined group totaling more than 10% of the population through its own votes. Blacks in Cincinnati satisfied that threshold criterion for most of the PR era. Heisel (1982) found black representation to be the only significant difference between PR and 9X. H. D. Hamilton (1977, pp. 42, 55–58, 62) concluded that PR was the only system that guaranteed full representation to blacks in Cincinnati. Before PR and in the three elections after PR, no African Americans were elected to the council. During PR, 13 black candidacies were successful; blacks made up 9% of all PR-elected council members. The abandonment of PR in the 1950s led to the immediate defeat of the incumbent black council member, Theodore Berry. The evidence is strong that PR made an enormous difference in African-American representation. Yet some qualification needs to be made.

PR itself neither awakened black political consciousness nor automatically guaranteed more equitable representation for blacks. The Reeds (1944) noted that "P.R. did not give Negroes ... the idea that their interests call for political action. They have that idea in hundreds of cities where P.R. does not exist." The Reeds went on to argue, however, that PR "gives the Cincinnati Negro an opportunity to get a representative directly at the polls instead of indirectly by pressure on the party slate-makers." The evidence supports the first observation, but not the second.

In Cincinnati, African Americans did not use PR to secure direct representation, if by direct representation the Reeds meant independent election rather than election through partisan nomination; rather they used PR to apply pressure on the Republican organization and the City Charter Committee to include black candidates on their tickets. Blacks won representation only through the dynamics of partisan competition, despite the theoretical possibility under PR that they could win independently of partisan recognition. The general pattern was that a strong but losing independent black candidacy would be followed by a Republican or Charter endorsement of the viable black candidate in the next election. Although black candidates drew overwhelming first-choice support from blacks, that was not sufficient to elect a member of the council, even as late as 1947 (in 1950 blacks made up 15% of the city's population), because two black candidates divided African Americans' first-choice votes. Blacks forced recognition by withholding transfer votes; but bullet-voting is as possible under plurality/at-large voting as under PR. In addition, the contemporaneous national transition of black voters from the Republican to the Democratic parties augmented African Americans' ability to exert leverage on the local Republican and Charter organizations. The PR period stands alone among the periods compared as an era of intense partisan competition for black votes, not only locally but nationally.

Blacks first applied pressure to the Republican organization, which long had drawn the benefit of black votes without extending to African Americans nomination to office. In 1927 Frank A. B. Hall ran well as an independent candidate. In 1929, after the Republican organization refused to give a place on the ticket to a black candidate, a second independent black candidate joined Hall. African-American community leaders exhorted "their people to vote for these two, and then to vote for no further choices." In response, the Republican organization put Hall on its ticket in 1931. Only 1,068 votes shy of the quota on first-choice ballots, Hall gained only slowly from transfers, but was the first Republican elected in that year (Reed et al., 1957, p. 31; Taft, 1933, p. 211; Gosnell, 1930; R. A. Burnham, 1990, pp. 78–86).

The Charter Committee, Charles Taft reported, felt "no great pressure . . . to nominate a negro as one of its ticket" in PR's early years, but Republican nomination of black candidates troubled Charter Committee leaders, for they feared that "when he [a black Republican] was not elected, the regulars should get all his second choices" (Taft, 1933, pp. 180–83). By the late 1930s, black loyalties to the Republican party presumably had waned enough to encourage the Charter Committee to run a black candidate. Perhaps more importantly, Republican fortunes in Cincinnati had improved enough to require the Charter Committee to compete for black transfer votes by placing an African American on its ticket. They did so in 1937 and 1939, but in both elections the Charter-endorsed black candidate ran behind the Republican black candidate. In 1937 the Republicans elected their candidate; in 1939 both Charter and Republican black candidates failed to win election. In 1941 the Republicans picked Jesse Locker to run; he proved to be their most successful African-American candidate, winning reelection five times. In 1941 the Charter Committee offered a black "opponent" to Locker, but they failed to do so in 1943 or 1945 (Reed et al., 1957, p. 31).

In 1947 civil rights activist Theodore Berry repeated the technique that Frank Hall had used a generation earlier. Running as an independent candidate, he garnered a large first-choice vote but few transfers. His challenge to Locker for first-choice votes split the black vote and "compelled [Republican] organization leaders to drum up a minimum of four first-choice votes per precinct for Locker in the solid white neighborhoods in the city in order to insure his survival" (Frank, 1948, p. 227). Berry's impressive showing won him a place on the Charter ticket in 1949 and in succeeding years. In 1949 and 1951 both Berry and Locker won election to the council, Berry as a Charter candidate, Locker as a Republican. The competition between the Charter Committee and the Republican organization for black votes thus allowed blacks to win two of the nine council seats. For a brief time Cincinnati's African-American community experienced a rare instance of "overrepresentation." Blacks, 15% of the city's population, held 22% of council seats.

Two black seats on the council were more than could be sustained under the mechanics of PR. Black candidates depended on blacks for first-choice votes. Since voters could make only one first-choice vote, Berry siphoned away Locker's secure source of support, and in 1951 Locker ran the poorest race of all incumbents. Two years later Locker did not run for reelection; the black Republican candidate who replaced him on the ticket ran poorly, as Berry won easily. In 1955, Berry again won, leading the Charter ticket—and Republicans, for the first time since 1931, did not field a black candidate. Thus an important dynamic underlying black representation in the PR period—the competition between the Charter Committee and the Republican party for black votes—changed dramatically at the very end of the PR period. The election of two black council members, in 1949 and 1951, was not likely to be repeated.

With PR repealed, Berry, despite his very strong showings in previous elections, lost his bid for a fifth term in 1957. Running on the Charter ticket again in 1959, he lost a second time under the plurality system. He chose not to run in 1961. Election observers noted a decided decline in voting participation among blacks, "where an attitude of 'what's the use, we can't win' is becoming more and more entrenched," despite the increase in the size of the city's African-American community to nearly 22% of Cincinnati's total population in 1960 (Frank, 1962). The change to plurality voting undoubtedly hurt Berry. Following on the heels of the successful campaign for PR's repeal, which had brought racial issues into the open, Berry may have suffered from white voters' resentment of national publicity that painted PR's repeal as a racist vote. In 1959 the Charter coalition crumbled, and Berry that year bore the additional burden of competition with Democratic candidates as well as Republicans.

African-American representation was greater during the PR period than either before or after. In the period immediately before the adoption of PR, the partisan biases evident in Cincinnati politics were so great that the Republican Party had no need to recognize African Americans through nomination of blacks to city offices. With PR's repeal, an all-white council was elected in each of the three succeeding elections. Although PR may have encouraged independent black candidacies, these were never successful. National as well as local partisan dynamics contributed decisively to the circumstances, which blacks were able to use to their advantage. Their election as members of broad partisan coalitions, and their need to work within those coalitions, undoubtedly tempered their stands on racial issues as well.

It has been argued that PR elections may produce black council members more representative of the black community, because successful black candidates need fewer white votes than is the case in plurality at-large elections (Heisel, 1980). In Cincinnati, however, Berry and Locker both operated within the framework of their parties. In the two terms that both sat on the council they did not act together. They never voted together as a minority of two. Of 105 votes on which the council was divided in 1951, Barry and Locker voted differently 23 times. Both appear to have held relatively modest expectations of city action on racial issues. Not until 1954 did the city abolish racial questions on civil service applications and dual eligibility lists; a voluntary fair employment practice ordinance failed to be enacted. In the face of such policies, neither Locker nor Berry used obstructionist tactics, preferring to work within their partisan coalitions (Reed et al., 1957, pp. 31–32).

Effective Voting, Turnout, and the Single Transferable Vote

A prime concern of reformers in the 1920s was the issue of "effective" voting. That concern was closely bound to the partisan biases of the previous electoral system. In 1921, partly owing to the entry of a strong Independent slate into the election, the Republican Party won all council seats except one ward seat. Reformers could logically argue that nearly one-half of the city's voters had cast "ineffective" votes; that is, that all those voters who had voted for a losing candidate under the plurality system had no representation in the council. Given the extreme partisan bias of the council at that point, the charge had considerable merit.

PR dramatically increased the proportion of effective votes measured two ways (table 6.4). First, the proportion of voters whose votes went to a winner either on first choice or by transfer averaged 90% with little variation (as a percentage of total valid vote). Second, the proportion of voters whose first-choice vote went to a winner also was impressive, never falling below 60% and eleven times exceeding 70%.

For the post-PR period, PR advocates decried an apparent plunge in the proportion of effective votes under 9X. Yet the figures must be viewed cautiously. Under 9X, each ballot would need to be examined to determine the proportion of voters who cast one of nine allowable votes for any winner, in order to arrive at figures comparable to what is possible to calculate from PR or single-member district returns. A different measure of the comparative effectiveness of votes is provided by the data in table 6.2, which compares the party distribution of seats

TABLE 6.4
"Effective" Votes in Cincinnati Council Elections, 1915–1961

Election Year	Total Valid Vote	% of Voters Whose Votes Helped Elect Members of Council		% of Voters Whose First Choice Was Elected in PR Elections	
		Effective Votes	% of Valid Vote	Total First-Choice Vote of Winners	% of Valid Vote
1915					
AL	540,772	337,365	62.4		
W	92,844	56,117	60.4		
1917					
AL	535,243	270,242	50.5		
W	90,124	49,014	54.4		
1921					
AL	769,282	413,205	53.7		
W	128,973	72,251	56.0		
1925	119,730	107,766	90.0	86,778	72.5
1927	124,287	111,861	90.0	94,236	75.8
1929	138,763	124,893	90.0	92,964	67.0
1931	122,278	110,052	90.0	86,986	71.1
1933	155,370	139,842	90.0	106,405	68.5
1935	137,334	123,608	90.0	97,465	71.0
1937	142,071	127,872	90.0	85,528	60.2
1939	146,319	131,289	89.7	98,601	67.4
1941	144,171	129,762	90.0	100,784	69.9
1943	117,717	105,948	90.0	90,340	76.7
1945	118,812	106,938	90.0	87,573	73.7
1947	162,176	145,962	90.0	119,344	73.6
1949	158,290	142,049	89.7	115,641	73.1
1951	136,111	122,508	90.0	101,736	74.7
1953	143,188	128,811	90.0	108,152	75.5
1955	141,910	127,734	90.0	106,151	74.8
1957	1,157,301	693,478	59.9		
1959	1,124,670	551,108	49.0		
1961	1,097,197	524,501	47.8		

Sources: Data for 1925–55 from Straetz (1958), p. 309; data for 1915–21 and 1957–61 calculated from Hamilton County Board of Elections, *Elections in Hamilton County,* various years.

Notes: AL = councilmen at-large, W = ward council members (1915–21). For at-large and ward elections, the total valid vote reported here is the sum of votes received by all candidates; the effective vote is the sum of votes received by winning candidates.

and votes. Vote distortion did not differ dramatically in 1957 from PR elections, although the distortion under 9X that year favored the Republicans rather than the Charter Committee, which had generally been favored in PR elections. In 1959 and 1961 vote distortion did increase, but much of the increase was due to the running of independent Charter and Democratic tickets, splitting the anti-Republican vote.

The proportion of effective votes did increase under PR, but it is not clear that a significant difference between the PR and post-PR periods can be attributed to the electoral system itself. No clean sweeps occurred in the post-PR period, supporting a conclusion that Cincinnati voters split their tickets and probably continued to see at least one of their choices elected to the council.

It is difficult to attribute significant changes in turnout for council elections to electoral systems. Data presented in table 6.5 show the turnout for council elections for all three periods. The turnout is calculated as a percentage of total registration for the preceding year, which was chosen as the registration base to eliminate the fluctuation of registration totals for council election years; the fluctuation is itself a measure of voter interest in the council election.

Registration figures have not been located for years before 1929. Comparison of the pre-reform council with the PR council thus must be based on raw vote totals. The change from the mixed council of the pre-PR period to the small at-large PR council seems to have reduced voting participation. The decline of turnout from 1921 to 1925, however, could be attributed to other factors, such as generally declining voter participation in the 1920s and a surge-and-ebb effect from the enfranchisement of women first effective in the 1921 election. Generally increased voter participation levels in the 1930s are evident; that again is fully to be expected from general national patterns of voter participation, as is the decline in participation during World War II. A surge in the post–World War II years can be attributed to returning soldiers and perhaps to heightened interest in domestic affairs (Kleppner, 1982).

Some decrease in voter participation is evident in the post-PR period. Heisel (1982) found a slight drop in voting participation from the PR period to the post-PR period. Although the figures are not dramatic they did seem to indicate a general lessening of interest in city elections as compared to those for other levels of government. In the 1954 gubernatorial election, 159,651 votes had been cast in the city; in the 1955 council election, 153,886 (96% of gubernatorial vote).

PR in Cincinnati

TABLE 6.5
TURNOUT FOR CINCINNATI CITY COUNCIL ELECTIONS, 1915–1961,
AND MAYORAL ELECTIONS, 1915–1921

Election Year	Registration	Total Vote	Total Valid Vote	Total Council Vote as % of Regis.	Total Valid Vote as % of Regis.
1915					
Ward	*	*	92,844		
Mayor	*	*	95,127		
1917					
Ward	*	*	90,124		
Mayor	.*	*	93,241		
1921					
Ward	*	*	128,973		
Mayor	*	*	134,659		
1925	n/a	124,091	119,730		
1927	n/a	131,416	124,287		
1929	209,428	145,464	138,763	69.5	66.3
1931	169,809	128,677	122,278	75.8	72.0
1933	230,038	163,749	155,370	71.2	67.5
1935	223,641	145,200	137,334	64.9	61.4
1937	243,241	150,415	142,071	61.8	58.4
1939	228,912	155,017	146,319	67.7	63.9
1941	264,707	154,302	144,171	58.3	54.5
1943	239,572	123,752	117,717	51.7	49.1
1945	234,289	124,347	118,812	53.1	50.7
1947	246,671	171,176	162,176	69.4	65.7
1949	258,772	167,482	158,290	64.7	61.2
1951	263,017	144,482	136,111	54.9	51.7
1953	278,219	152,766	143,188	54.9	51.5
1955	245,429	153,886	141,910	62.7	57.8
1957	242,348	140,825	*	58.1	
1959	242,259	142,867	*	59.0	
1961	254,482	136,737	*	53.7	

Sources: Registration figures are for the prior even-year, from Ohio, Secretary of State, *Vote . . . Polled,* 1930–60. Registration figure for 1929 from list available at the Municipal Reference Library, Cincinnati (1928 figure used). Vote figures from Straetz (1958); Hamilton County Board of Elections, *Elections in Hamilton County,* various years.
*Figures not available. Only for PR elections were invalid and valid vote totals reported separately. No credible evidence suggests that there was a significant difference in the percentage of invalid votes among the three electoral systems.

Theodore M. Berry, 1957.
Courtesy of the Charter
Committee of Greater
Cincinnati

Rudolph K. Hynicka, n.d.
Courtesy of the Ohio
Historical Society

Murray Seasongood, 1937.
Courtesy of the Charter
Committee of Greater
Cincinnati

The difference between the two elections of 1958 and 1959 was much greater. In the 1958 gubernatorial election, Cincinnati voters cast 179,440 ballots; in the 1959 city election, 142,867 (80%); but the difference did not necessarily indicate long-term trends. In 1950 voters had cast 196,678 ballots in the gubernatorial election; in the following year's city election only 144,482 (73%) (Ohio, Secretary of State, *Vote . . . Polled in the Several Counties*). The short-term influences of issues and personalities were undoubtedly more important to varying levels of voting participation than were structural differences between the PR and plurality ballots.

PR vote tallies (see sample, pp. 198–99) lend themselves to further analysis of the impact of the single transferable vote (STV) on council characteristics. The mechanics of the STV reward two different types of candidacies—those that draw enough first-choice ballots to achieve the quota (for a nine-member council, 10% of the vote plus one) on the first ballot and those that win enough transfers from eliminated or elected candidates to achieve the quota during the transfer process. PR's proponents argue that the STV helps to diversify representation; its detractors fear that it promotes factionalism. Analysis of subgroups of candidacies, chosen to illustrate the impact of the STV ballot on the characteristics of council members, lends little support to either PR proponents' hopes or its detractors' fears (table 6.6). Other than among black candidates, STV tended to reinforce the characteristics of a small at-large council.

The 26 "strong winners" (18% of all candidacies), those candidates who achieved the full quota for election on the first-choice ballot, exemplified the characteristics of all candidates in exaggerated form. They were relatively evenly divided between Republicans and Charter candidates and included only one independent. They were more likely to have been incumbents than other candidates. They were overwhelmingly college-educated professionals. With strong first-choice support from the black community, three were black. None were women.

The 15 transfer winners (10.4% of all candidacies) were those candidates who did not run in the top nine in the first count but won enough transfer votes to raise their final count to one among the top nine. These were the candidates who most clearly benefited from the transferable vote. Charter candidacies were more heavily represented in this subgroup than Republican candidacies; no independents were included. Transfer winners also were more likely to have been incumbents than were other candidates, although not to the same extent as strong winners. Their occupational and educational background was close to the norm for all candidates. All were white males; no women

TABLE 6.6

COMPARISON OF ALL PR-ELECTED CINCINNATI COUNCIL MEMBERS WITH SPECIAL SUBGROUPS FOR SELECTED CHARACTERISTICS, BY PERCENTAGE DISTRIBUTION, 1925–1955

| | Political Variables | | | | Demographic Variables | | | | | | | |
| | Party | | | | Occupation | | | | Education | | Race: | Sex: |
	Republican	Charter	Other	Incumbent	Professional	Business	Blue-Collar	Other	GR/HS	College	Black	Female
All candidates elected by PR (N = 144)	64 44.4%	76 52.8%	4 2.8%	97 67.4%	76 52.8%	39 27.1%	10 6.9%	20 13.9%	24 16.7%	120 83.3%	13 9.0%	3 2.1%
"Strong winners" (N = 26)	13 50.0%	12 46.2%	1 3.8%	21 80.8%	21 80.8%			5 19.2%		25 96.2%	3 11.5%	
"Transfer winners" (N = 15)	6 40.0%	9 60.0%		11 73.3%	7 46.7%	7 46.7%		1 6.7%	2 13.3%	13 86.7%		
"Polarizing winners" (N = 3)	2 66.7%	1 33.3%		1 33.3%	3 100.0%					3 100.0%	2 66.7%	
"Viable losers" (N = 15)	9 60.0%	1 6.7%	5 33.3%	7 46.7%	7 46.7%	5 33.3%	1 6.7%	1 6.7%	4 26.7%	10 66.7%	4 26.7%	

Source: Cincinnati League of Women Voters, *The Who and What of Elections*, 1925–55.

Notes: All candidates elected by PR = all successful PR council candidacies, 1925–55. "Strong winners" = candidates elected on the first count. "Transfer winners" = winning candidates not among first nine on first count. "Polarizing winners" = winning candidates who dropped more than three places from first to final count. "Viable losers" = losing candidates who ranked in first nine on first count. Occupation and education missing in one case.

VOTE FOR COUNCIL OF CINCINNATI — 1943
Total Vote Cast, 123,752   Invalid, 6,035

CANDIDATES	First Count	2. Surplus (Stewart)	3. Surplus (Locker)	4. (21)	5. (6)
1. David V. Attig (R)	3,998	4,394	4,424	4,425	4,432
2. Herbert S. Bigelow (I)	6,359	6,595	6,620	6,620	6,656
3. Albert D. Cash (C)	10,776	11,122	11,139	11,140	11,147
4. Wiley Craig (R)	3,887	4,463	4,529	4,529	4,542
5. Willard Irvin Crain (C)	1,247	1,283	1,286	1,286	1,288
6. W. M. Davidson (I)	220	251	256	258	......
7. Charles B. Ginocchio (C)	2,751	2,828	2,830	2,830	2,854
8. Willis D. Gradison (R)	9,195	11,669	11,741	11,743	11,772
9. Albert F. Guethlein (R)	2,655	2,781	2,786	2,787	2,795
10. Alfred R. Hill (R)	1,127	1,244	1,255	1,255	1,258
11. Jesse D. Locker (R)	12,184	12,184	11,772	11,772	11,772
12. D. Beryl Manischewitz (C)	1,809	1,852	1,864	1,864	1,870
13. Robert G. McIntosh (C)	1,679	1,748	1,755	1,755	1,759
14. John M. Molloy (R)	6,717	7,383	7,449	7,449	7,460
15. Elizabeth Cassatt Reid (C)	7,237	7,579	7,607	7,608	7,617
16. George P. Starling (C)	1,626	1,704	1,707	1,707	1,707
17. James Garfield Stewart (R)	19,831	11,772	11,772	11,772	11,772
18. Edward N. Waldvogel (C)	9,734	10,482	10,494	10,496	10,504
19. Charles E. Weber (R)	4,253	5,070	5,090	5,091	5,121
20. Russell Wilson (C)	10,413	11,294	11,322	11,325	11,339
21. Written in Names	19	19	19	......	......
(Accumulative) Ineffective Ballots	......	0	0	5	52
Total Republican Vote	63,847	60,960	60,818	60,823	60,924
Total Charter Vote	47,272	49,892	50,004	50,011	50,085
Total Independent Vote	6,598	6,865	6,895	6,878	6,656
Total Ineffective Vote	......	......	......	5	52
Transfer to Republicans	0	5,172	270	5	101
Transfer to Charter	0	2,620	112	7	74
Transfer to Independents	0	267	30	2	36
Ineffective	0	......	0	5	47
Total Transfer	0	8,059	412	19	258

(R)—Republican; (C)—Charter; (I)—Independent.

ELECTED 1943

James Garfield Stewart (R)   Russell Wilson (C)

Jesse D. Locker (R)   Albert D. Cash (C)

Willis D. Gradison (R)   Edward N. Waldvogel (C)

TOTAL: REPUBLICAN, 5; CHARTER, 4.

Quota, 11,772

6. (10)	7. (5)	8. (16)	9. (13)	10. (12)	11. (9)	12. (7)	13. (1)	14. (4)	15. (2)
4,640	4,696	4,742	4,864	4,904	5,281	5,359	......	......	......
6,678	6,703	7,008	7,096	7,282	7,384	7,631	7,904	8,884	......
11,183	11,314	11,569	11,772	11,772	11,772	11,772	11,772	11,772	11,772
4,651	4,685	4,984	5,152	5,277	5,765	5,796	7,319	......	......
1,319	......	......	......	......	......	......	......	......	......
......	......	......	......	......	......	......	......	......	......
2,869	2,941	2,967	3,097	3,228	3,435	......	......	......	......
11,772	11,772	11,772	11,772	11,772	11,772	11,772	11,772	11,772	11,772
2,847	2,895	2,929	2,993	3,018	......	......	......	......	......
......	......	......	......	......	......	......	......	......	......
11,772	11,772	11,772	11,772	11,772	11,772	11,772	11,772	11,772	11,772
1,888	1,902	1,920	1,970	......	......	......	......	......	......
1,783	1,823	1,860	......	......	......	......	......	......	......
7,631	7,665	7,785	7,964	8,067	8,816	10,359	11,314	11,772	11,772
7,702	8,145	8,231	8,664	9,444	9,615	10,456	11,242	11,772	11,772
1,713	1,727	......	......	......	......	......	......	......	......
11,772	11,772	11,772	11,772	11,772	11,772	11,772	11,772	11,772	11,772
10,545	10,585	10,875	11,110	11,409	11,772	11,772	11,772	11,772	11,772
5,390	5,505	5,572	5,694	5,780	6,237	6,431	8,221	11,772	11,772
11,431	11,673	11,772	11,772	11,772	11,772	11,772	11,772	11,772	11,772
......	......	......	......	......	......	......	......	......	......
111	142	187	253	448	552	853	1,085	2,885	11,769
60,495	60,762	61,328	61,983	62,362	61,415	63,461	62,170	58,860	58,860
50,433	50,110	49,194	48,385	47,625	48,366	45,772	46,558	47,088	47,088
6,678	6,703	7,008	7,096	7,282	7,384	7,631	7,904	8,884	0
111	142	187	253	448	552	853	1,085	2,885	11,769
829	267	566	655	379	2,071	2,046	4,068	4,009	0
348	996	811	1,051	1,210	741	841	786	530	0
22	25	305	88	186	102	247	273	980	0
59	31	45	66	195	104	301	232	1,800	8,884
1,258	1,319	1,727	1,860	1,970	3,018	3,435	5,359	7,319	8,884

John M. Molloy (R)

Elizabeth Cassatt Reid (C)

Charles E. Weber (R)

or blacks won enough transfer votes to overcome their finishing out of the top nine on the first count.

The final two groups, polarizing winners ($N = 3$, 2.1% of total candidacies) and viable losers ($N = 15$, 10.4% of total candidacies), were both hurt by the transfer process. Polarizing winners fell more than three ranks during the count (only three polarizing winners have been identified, thus conclusions based on that category are at best suggestive); viable losers were those who finished among the top nine in the first count but were eliminated during the transfer process. Republicans and independents predominated among viable losers. Only one of the 15 viable losers was a Charter candidate. Among the three polarizing winners as well, Republicans outnumbered Charter candidates two to one. Both polarizing winners and viable losers were much less likely than other candidates to be incumbents. Occupational and educational differences were not dramatically different from the norm for all candidates, but viable losers did seem to be somewhat more likely to have less than a college education and to be engaged in business rather than a profession. Blacks were heavily overrepresented among both polarizing winners and viable losers. That reflected their reliance on strong first-choice votes from the black community. No women were in either group.

In summary, the data indicate that the mechanics of STV reinforced the advantages held in small council at-large elections by reform candidates (endorsed by the Charter Committee), incumbents, college-educated professionals, and white males. Charter candidates were helped by the transfer process and Republicans and independents were hurt. The data do not support the proposition that the transfer process itself helped black candidates, independents, or women.

Analysis of PR vote transfers can also help isolate the relative importance to voters of variables such as party, race, ethnicity, religion, and class. PR advocates argue that the single transferable vote allows voters to form voluntary constituencies along whichever lines they value most. Previous studies of PR in Cincinnati have shown the predominant influence of partisan considerations. Straetz (1958, pp. 97–198), attentive to charges that PR encouraged "block voting," gave considerable attention to transfers among a number of different groups of candidates. He showed that party far outweighed other variables in explaining transfers, although other variables did have some importance.

The most extensive analysis of the vote transfers in any single Cincinnati PR election was offered by Harold Gosnell (1930) soon after the 1929 election. Like Straetz some 30 years later, he found that "the rivalry between the Charter Committee and the organization Republican party outweighed all other factors." More than four out of five transfers went to candidates on the same ticket. Race, however, was of considerable importance as well. In 1929 Hall and Conrad ran as independent candidates, and black leaders urged blacks not to transfer their votes to any other candidates. As a result, three-fourths of the transfers from the first eliminated black candidate went to the second; when the second black candidate was eliminated, over half of his ballots were nontransferable. Ethnic, religious, and class influences were noticeable but insignificant, as both tickets were reasonably well balanced.

Data for all vote transfers by party for all PR elections are presented in table 6.7. It shows percentages to and from each party and independents. Some clear patterns emerge from inspection of the data. First, most transfers from Charter and Republican candidates went to candidates on the same ticket. Second, with a few exceptions, Republican transfers (and to a lesser extent independent transfers) were less likely to be effective than Charter ballots. Third, the Charter Committee ticket retained a greater proportion of transfers than the Republican ticket did. Fourth, transfers from independent candidates did not show a consistent preference for either major party.

Table 6.8 offers additional evidence on the dynamics of PR in Cincinnati. Again, data from all PR elections are given, showing the percentage distribution of ballots received by winning candidates. The table lists winners by party and the percentage of their votes derived from first choices and from transfers from Republican, Charter, and Independent candidates. In nine of 16 elections Republicans received a larger share of their votes from first-choice ballots than did Charter winners. Both Republican and Charter winners received the bulk of their transfer votes from their own ticket. The Independent winners drew few of their votes from Republican or Charter transfers.

The most striking aspect of PR in Cincinnati was the regularity and persistence of party voting. This regularity is particularly striking in the case of the Charter Committee ticket, which each year included both Republicans and Democrats, some of whom were quite visible in national and state Republican and Democratic politics. Despite the changes within the Charter coalition noted above, the Charter Committee forged a durable electoral coalition under PR. The decision of the local Democratic organization to refrain from offering its own ticket

TABLE 6.7
PERCENTAGE DISTRIBUTION OF VOTE TRANSFERS BY PARTY, CINCINNATI CITY COUNCIL, ALL PR ELECTIONS

Year	Transfers from Republican to			Transfers from Charter to			Transfers from Independent to		
	Republican	Charter	Independent	Republican	Charter	Independent	Republican	Charter	Independent
1925	73.0	22.4	0.0	9.1	62.3	3.1	23.0	54.4	14.5
1927	39.0	20.7	10.2	11.6	74.5	10.5	37.3	33.9	14.5
1929	58.0	16.2	1.0	14.6	83.7	0.5	28.4	18.7	8.6
1931	66.8	6.7	0.6	15.6	76.1	1.8	27.0	16.3	34.3
1933	50.8	11.9	0.4	21.0	76.4	1.0	41.2	45.5	4.9
1935	50.5	15.1	0.3	24.1	72.2	1.9	29.6	37.9	23.4
1937	46.6	20.8	6.9	20.8	53.8	10.2	26.9	27.0	34.3
1939	35.1	21.2	8.7	12.1	65.6	8.7	19.6	44.3	22.7
1941	50.6	32.5	6.4	28.8	62.7	4.4	7.0	24.5	3.8
1943	64.6	20.2	6.6	37.9	47.6	8.3	1.2	0.9	0.4
1945	50.1	38.9	0.1	25.1	71.7	0.0	32.0	37.2	2.8
1947	50.5	20.9	0.9	32.7	58.2	2.1	26.1	29.3	43.9
1949	46.9	18.4	0.0	31.9	54.6	1.5	42.0	44.5	3.7
1951	43.6	14.4	0.0	31.5	54.4	0.0	46.5	46.2	0.0
1953	44.8	18.3	0.0	23.9	68.0	0.0	43.8	30.4	0.0
1955	48.8	32.3	6.2	22.9	59.3	12.8	4.5	29.2	0.8
Average	51.2	20.7	3.0	22.7	65.1	4.2	27.3	32.5	13.3
Std. Dev.	9.7	17.6	10.7	8.2	23.0	31.4	13.4	13.5	16.6

Source: Calculated from Hamilton County Board of Elections, *Elections in Hamilton County,* various years.
Note: Remaining ballots were not transferable because either no more candidates had been listed, all remaining candidates on the ballot had been elected or eliminated, or all seats had been filled.

TABLE 6.8
PERCENTAGE DISTRIBUTION OF BALLOTS ELECTING THE WINNERS, CINCINNATI CITY COUNCIL, ALL PR ELECTIONS

Year	Republican Winners First-Choice Ballots	Transfers from Republican	Transfers from Charter	Transfers from Independent	Charter Winners First-Choice Ballots	Transfers from Republican	Transfers from Charter	Transfers from Independent	Independent Winners First-Choice Ballots	Transfers from Republican	Transfers from Charter	Transfers from Independent
1925	58.1	27.9	8.6	5.3	66.3	3.3	23.5	7.0				
1927	63.6	21.8	5.9	8.7	61.4	7.4	27.0	4.2	54.1	17.4	18.6	9.8
1929	58.8	34.5	4.4	2.4	72.4	6.8	18.7	2.1				
1931	61.8	26.5	6.8	4.9	63.2	2.1	31.9	2.8				
1933	61.7	27.2	7.9	3.2	63.6	5.2	27.2	4.0	100.0			
1935	62.2	21.3	6.4	10.1	56.1	7.7	18.5	17.7				
1937	71.3	17.5	4.7	6.5	67.2	8.8	15.6	8.4	47.9	12.5	11.5	28.0
1939	83.9	11.6	1.2	3.4	64.1	9.2	17.0	9.7	60.9	11.4	7.1	20.6
1941	76.7	19.1	3.5	0.7	61.9	19.7	12.4	6.1				
1943	74.3	21.3	4.4	0.1	81.0	9.6	9.3	0.1				
1945	83.8	11.7	3.9	0.6	71.6	10.2	17.6	0.7				
1947	74.3	20.8	3.0	1.9	78.2	8.7	10.3	2.8				
1949	75.9	18.5	4.6	1.0	77.5	7.4	13.5	1.6				
1951	79.5	11.5	8.8	0.2	75.7	3.3	20.8	0.2				
1953	76.3	17.8	5.8	0.0	74.3	5.2	20.4	0.0				
1955	74.2	21.2	4.1	0.5	66.8	16.5	11.5	5.2				
Average	71.0	20.6	5.3	3.1	68.8	8.2	18.5	4.5	65.7	10.3	9.3	14.6
Std. Dev.	8.4	6.1	2.0	3.1	6.9	4.4	6.3	4.5	30.2	5.5	5.3	8.5

Source: Calculated from Hamilton County Board of Elections, Elections in Hamilton County, various years.

made that coalition possible. Voter loyalty to Charter and to Republican tickets left little opportunity for independents or dissident Democrats to win election. It is also evident that there was at least some basis for Republican claims that PR disadvantaged them, at least as measured by the somewhat greater facility of the Charter Committee in retaining the allegiance of its voters during the transfer process, by the larger number of Republican ballots that became ineffective, and by the likelihood of Charter transfer winners replacing Republican viable losers.

Conclusion

The provision for proportional representation in Cincinnati's reform charter did not significantly modify, except in one respect, the essential attributes of manager-council reform government. Even that exception, black council representation, drew on familiar rules of ethnic brokerage and partisan competition. Other social characteristics of Cincinnati's PR councils closely approximated those expected of a small at-large council elected by a plurality ballot.

PR advocates often pointed to the success of Cincinnati's government as evidence of the success of PR itself. In the 1920s reformers had not appealed to voters on theoretical grounds of group representation, but on the more immediate need to create a city government capable of repairing potholes. The new reform government created such a city government. The rebuilding of the city's streets was its major accomplishment. PR advocates, however, faced difficulty in separating the impact of PR from the other reforms adopted in the 1920s, most notably the city manager and the small council. Also, although Cincinnati's reform governments quickly won a reputation for effective governance, some fortuitous circumstances attended their early success. First, a long-running dispute with the city's privately owned street railways had been settled. The railway company, whose general counsel was Robert Taft, brother of Charter leader Charles Taft, had delayed maintenance on the lines, arguing for higher fares. Once the dispute was settled, the company synchronized its own reconstruction program with the city's street rebuilding program. Second, the state tax laws that the Upson Survey had identified as the major obstacle to effective city government were revised. The new laws removed sinking fund and interest charges from all limitations on the tax rates. The city was also released from the county budget commission's control. The power to fix its own tax limit also was added to the home rule charter.

Charles Taft concluded that, "without these laws the new councilmen and city manager would have been greatly handicapped" (1933, pp. 111–17).

After its early successes, reform government was perhaps more attentive to process than to results. Reform brought Cincinnati "decent, honest and representative government," Thomas and Doris Reed noted in a major report in 1944, but it had not broken with "the habit of civic parsimony." Noting the broad acceptance of the manager plan in the city, the Reeds recited a lengthy list of the reformed government's accomplishments. First, it had "replaced a politics-ridden, inefficient, slovenly administration with one which performs the routine activities of a modern city economically, efficiently and with a minimum of political interference" and thus had maintained a high credit rating, low taxes, and low cost direct operations. But while "routine operations" had attained "in many cases a degree of perfection unusual in American cities," weak areas of service and deferred physical improvements remained. The police force was understaffed. Funding for park and playground activities was insufficient. The hospital stood in need of maintenance. The water supply needed attention. Twenty years earlier, the Reeds concluded, the question had been " 'Can Cincinnati have a decent government?' Now it's 'Can Cincinnati overcome the legal obstacles and popular inertia which have prevented her from pursuing some of the higher goals of civic ambition?' "

In the 1920s voters' refusal to support necessary taxes had been a major impetus to reform. In the 1940s voters still seemed ill-disposed towards new initiatives. Bond issues and special levies required a 65% majority; from 1933 to 1943, 52 city, county, and school bond issues and tax levies had been put to the voters: only five had won the necessary majority. Although the Reeds generally praised the city's reduction of debt and real estate taxes since 1923 (the city's tax burden was in 1944 only 62.7% of the average American city's), they added that "it is not enough . . . for a city to live within its means. There are occasions—and this is eminently true of Cincinnati today—when a city needs to enlarge its resources to meet new needs."

In 1957 the Reeds and Straetz, proponents of PR, defended Cincinnati's PR council against complaints of the business community that it had not "secured the adoption of an adequate program of physical development for the city." They argued that much progress had been made since the 1940s. Although much of it had been confined to planning and programming, and the city's "achievements in the way of major capital improvements have been less notable than in the more routine fields of municipal housekeeping," they concluded that "a system of government which produces honesty and efficiency in the routine operations, sound planning and progressive financing on a long-term developmental level, provides as satisfactory a combination of governmental qualities as can be found anywhere" (Reed et al., 1957, pp. 25–29). Ralph Straetz echoed the joint report's observations on governance in his own well-known book. The city's PR governments provided "efficiency and economy but no dynamic change." PR had produced city councils in Cincinnati best characterized as "conservative, harmonious, experienced" (Straetz, 1958, p. 96).

PR did make an enormous political difference in Cincinnati. Placed in the 1920s reform package to attract Democrats to the banner of "good government," it held together the subsequent Charter Committee coalition of independent Republicans and Democrats. Before PR, much of the Republican organization's electoral advantage derived from its divided opposition. The opposition did not factionalize under PR because effective campaigning required candidates to seek transfer votes, thus encouraging balanced tickets and campaign unity. After PR's repeal, renewed Republican biases evident in the 9X system followed on the dissolution of the Charter-Democratic alliance. After Charterites and Democrats allied again in 1969, they regained the electoral advantage (Heisel, 1980, p. 7; Lieske, 1989). PR's chief triumph had been to hold their alliance together for an extraordinarily long period, despite PR's alleged propensity to foster political factionalism. As long as the 1920s charter remained intact, that triumph may have been due as much to their shared memories of having slain the machine as to the mechanics of PR itself, which did facilitate cooperation. In any event, and somewhat ironically, given the hopes of PR's advocates that PR would diversify representation, and the fears of its opponents that it would fragment politics, PR strengthened the two-party system in Cincinnati, albeit a local version of the system.

In the 1980s new efforts were launched to return to PR. Groups dissatisfied with continuing black underrepresentation on the 9X council have focused their efforts on PR's return rather than on district representation (Stephens, 1987, 1988). One factor that may help explain lack of concern about the geographic distribution of representation is the symbiotic relationship that has developed between at-large council members and neighborhood councils in Cincinnati. H. D Hamilton (1977, p. 66) has shown the strength and importance of local neighborhood councils and their interaction with city council members. At-large council members have performed an array of ombudsman services to neighborhoods. Perhaps because ward representation would reduce the influence of neighborhood councils as an intermediary between neighborhoods and the council, most neighborhood council leaders favored the retention of the at-large council in Hamilton's survey.

In 1988 the return of PR was put before Cincinnati's voters. The issue did better than observers predicted, winning 45.4% of the vote. Analysis indicated that 75%–80% of black voters supported PR. Whites, however, remained "very cool" to its return, only one-third supporting it. Even white neighborhoods generally considered to be "liberal" failed to return a majority for its return, suggesting "that it will be very hard to create a majority for PR." Increased white support seemed "unlikely" (Tuchfarber, 1989).

An exit poll of voters held in 1989, conducted as a trial PR election, should offer a caution to those who look to PR to provide a more representative council, and should perhaps ease the minds of those who fear its return. The poll offered some evidence that blacks and women would benefit from a return of PR, but for neither group was the evidence conclusive (Petrie and Tuchfarber, 1990). Cincinnati's historical experience with PR also indicates that PR made only a marginal difference in council characteristics as compared to plurality/at-large voting for a small council. As PR was only one element of the reform formula of the 1920s, those interested in reform today might best consider its relationship to the entire structure of representation and governance. Important factors include the size of the council, its authority and its relationship to executive power, and the nature, structure, and organizational base of partisan coalitions.

The essential conservatism of Cincinnati's governance during the PR period was not a function of PR itself. It matched the general characteristics of small at-large councils. PR provided Cincinnati with only very limited exceptions to those characteristics. The combination of PR with the small at-large council was rooted in the efforts of 1920s reformers to "improve" the caliber of council members and to reduce the influence of "ignorant" voters and their tendencies to look to government to attend to their personal and local interests. Furthermore, the PR campaign strategy of seeking transfer votes encouraged the moderation rather than the articulation of competing interests. The Reeds and Straetz noted in defense of PR in 1957 that "the political groupings of Negroes, labor unionists, and coreligionists, to be found in Cincinnati, are moderate in action and in no wise provocative of the bitterness and community disorganization which sometimes occur when racial, class or religious differences are highly accentuated. . . . the Cincinnati council is not made up of the agents of heterogeneous and warring factions. It genuinely represents the city as a whole" (p. 38). To reformers who still believed in the overriding importance of "the city as a whole," their conclusions stood as praise indeed. To those who today are dubious of that notion, and instead desire the actual representation of groups within the city, with all their different and competing interests and desires, their conclusions offer PR but faint praise. Even at its end, PR in Cincinnati remained tied more closely to "good government" than to the politics of inclusion.

SEVEN

■ ■ ■

Hamilton: PR Defeated by Its Own Success

Leon Weaver and James L. Blount

> Perhaps you are one of those who in the past has voted with
> the minority party. And your vote, on that account, has been lost.
> Under the new system of PR, minorities come into their own.
> Only ONE-EIGHTH of all the votes cast is enough to elect your fa-
> vored candidate to Council. Or, you may have always been in the
> majority party, and have neglected to go to the polls, feeling that
> your vote was not needed. Remember, then that a different sys-
> tem is now in effect. Under PR, majorities have lost their power
> of exclusive control. Possibly you have been in still another
> class—of those who have not voted because no satisfactory can-
> didate was offered. This year, with 31 candidates to choose from,
> every voter can surely find at least one whom he is willing to
> support.
>
> Political advertisement, *Hamilton Evening Journal,* 1927

THE PR/STV SYSTEM of elections was adopted by the city of Hamilton in 1926 and used continuously until its repeal in 1960, a longevity
equaled by Cincinnati and exceeded among American cities only by
Cambridge, Massachusetts. The adoption and repeal of PR, and comparative data on council members elected before, during, and after its
use, will highlight issues of class and race and will show that PR
accomplished what it was intended to achieve. The city, however, was
not receptive to those results.

Prior to adoption of the PR system, Hamilton had a mixed electoral
system, choosing three council members and a separately elected
council president by plurality voting at-large, and six council members
from single-member districts. Nomination was by partisan primary

and election was by partisan ballot. The PR system adopted in 1926 provided for nomination by petition, thus eliminating the primary, and election of seven members at-large on a nonpartisan single transferable vote ballot. In the post-PR period, following repeal of PR in 1960, major features of the previous system were retained: nomination by petition, and seven members elected at-large on a nonpartisan ballot; but voting was by plurality instead of by single transferable vote. The framework for analysis here embraces the pre-PR elections of 1921–25, early PR (1927–33), late PR (1953–59) and post-PR (1961–65). Early and late periods of the PR era are selected for statistical analysis from the universe of 17 PR elections in order to provide an empirical ground for understanding how the PR/STV electoral system worked over time. Significant participants and observers of Hamilton politics were interviewed as well.[1]

The Historical and Political Context

Hamilton is a small industrial city north of Cincinnati, about 20 miles from the downtown of its neighboring metropolis. This proximity appears to have influenced Progressive Era political developments in Hamilton including the adoption of PR, but by the late 1950s in the abandonment phase, indigenous influences appear stronger.

At the turn of the twentieth century, Hamilton was well established as a thriving manufacturing center (White, 1940). Following World War II, significant changes in the mix of industries occurred with the development of large automotive manufacturing concerns and their suppliers, a development that was accompanied by industrial unionism. The city's location astride the Great Miami River gave rise to a class cleavage between Ward 1, west of the river, and the rest of the city. Ward 1 held twice the voting strength of any other ward and was the major place of residence of the city's business and professional elite.

The city experienced important changes in the size and mix of its population between 1920 and 1960. These changes were stimulated by the growth of existing industries and by the arrival of new industries and service businesses through the mid-1950s. Hamilton's 1920 population of 39,675 grew to a peak of 72,354 in 1960. The increase resulted, as in other midwestern communities, from annexation of suburban areas, increase in birthrate, and in-migration. In 1930 the population of Hamilton was predominantly native-born and white (92%), with a small foreign-born, largely central European presence (4.2%) and a smaller African-American component (3.8%) (White, 1940).

TABLE 7.1
CHANGE AND CONTINUITY IN ELECTORAL SYSTEMS, HAMILTON, OHIO,
1915–1965

	Pre-PR	*PR*	*Post-PR (7X)*
Council			
Term (years)	2	2	2
Election time	Odd-numbered year	Odd-numbered year	Odd-numbered year
Ballot form	Partisan	Nonpartisan	Nonpartisan
At-large/wards	4 at-large; 6 from wards	7 at-large	7 at-large
Nominations	Partisan primary	Petition	Petition
Votes available to voter	1 vote for ward council member; 1 vote for separately elected council president; 3 votes for 3 at-large council members (3X)	Numbered preferences, counted as single transferable vote	7 votes for 7 at-large (7X)
Winner decision rule	Plurality	PR quota	Plurality
Mayor	Direct election—plurality rule	Election by council	Council member with most votes
Manager	None	Council-appointed professional	Council-appointed professional

Sources: Hamilton city charters; Howard White (1940, pp. 7–27).

By 1960 the black population had grown to six percent of the total, but more significant change resulted from successive waves of in-migration of Appalachian whites from the mountains of southeastern Kentucky. These in-migrants replaced more-established white business and professional people who were moving to newer suburbs, creating by 1960 a class composition significantly different from that of the 1920s (Kindness, 1988).

In contrast to the dominant Republican tenor of Ohio politics in the first two decades of the twentieth century, Hamilton voted Democratic in presidential elections. Indeed, in 1912 the Socialist presidential candidate rather than a Republican was the runner-up (Lehman, 1964, pp. 21–22). The use of partisan primaries and elections for local office linked local outcomes to national political tides.

In the second decade of the century, Hamilton had a taste of reform government and some experience with the Socialist party. Local Socialist tickets had provided the main opposition to the normally dominant Democrats, and a sprinkling of these candidates had been elected to the Hamilton council. In 1913 a Socialist mayor, Fred Hinkel, and a Socialist majority of council were elected, giving the city a reform administration for one term. In 1915, however, the Democrats regained control, holding power until 1923. In 1913 and 1917 there was not even a Republican nominee for mayor. The principal issue in local politics throughout this period was Hamilton's apparently well-deserved reputation as a "wide-open town" for gambling, prostitution, and liquor interests, allegedly protected by the Democratic machine (Lehman, 1964, pp. 21–22, 108).

Reform forces were not dormant, however. Republicans and Socialists, united only by their opposition to Democratic organization politics, struggled to oust the machine. They could not agree, however, even on so mild a measure as calling a charter commission to initiate local structural change, an effort that foundered in 1916 on Socialist opposition (White, 1940, p. 11).

In the early 1920s, divisive social issues were exacerbated by Prohibition. The reform forces were strengthened by the addition of women to the electorate, but Socialist electoral strength had been eroded by the party's antiwar position in the previous decade. In 1921 Democratic attorney Harry Koehler was elected mayor by a narrow margin over Republican corporate executive Harry Kelly, and the city continued to operate "wide open." In 1923 former Socialist mayor Hinkel ran as an Independent, finishing in third place with a respectable share of the vote. He apparently captured enough Democratic votes to throw victory to Kelly, the first Republican mayor in over a decade (Lehman, 1964, p. 22).

Mayor Kelly and the Republicans gave the city another reform administration, but it was marked by turbulence and confrontations with opponents to reform. In the 1925 election Koehler and the Democrats were swept back into power in the first head-to-head mayoral contest between nominees of the major parties in over two decades.

Not surprisingly, elements of the city's leadership outside the party organizations, distressed by sharp partisan swings in control, looked to a new charter as a means of reforming municipal operations and stabilizing the effects of reform. The National Municipal League offered a model charter, which had been adopted by a growing number of cities, including several in Ohio, one of which was Cincinnati, only a short distance away.

The Reform Charter of 1926

The Woman's City Club and business and professional leaders circulated petitions calling for an election that would create a charter commission. The proposition was submitted to voters at the regular municipal election in November 1925, together with a list of nominees by petition. The proposition passed by a vote of 4,435 to 3,519 (56%), with majority support in all wards except the low-income Second Ward (Blount, 1987, p. 39). The women's vote and the decline in Socialist influence were believed to have made the critical difference between this 1925 victory and the 1916 defeat of a similar issue. The voters chose commissioners drawn primarily from upper-status occupations. The exceptions to this were the president of the Trades and Union Council and a carpenter-contractor. Six of the seven losers had blue-collar occupations (*Hamilton Evening Journal,* 30 Oct. 1925, p. 7; 31 Oct. 1925, p. 6; 4 Nov. 1925, p. 16).

The charter commission secured the assistance of Professor Hatton of Western Reserve University, the expert on municipal charters who had drafted the PR/STV-city manager charters for Ashtabula and Cleveland and who was then serving a second term on the Cleveland council under its new charter. Advice was also obtained from political leaders in those cities and from such notables as the National Municipal League's Walter Millard and the P.R. League's George Hallett. PR/STV was the electoral system incorporated in the NML's *Model City Charter* at that time.

The Hamilton Charter Commission unanimously recommended PR/STV elections, accepting the premise that PR was a necessary ingredient of a reform-model council-manager charter (Vaughn, 1936). The charter, drafted by Hatton and submitted to the voters, provided for a seven-member council to be nominated by petition and elected at-large on a single transferable vote ballot.

The PR feature of the charter was subjected to some dialogue at the elite level, but these discussions apparently generated little controversy. A surprisingly broad segment of the city's political leadership, including Mayor Koehler, endorsed the charter. However, nine of the ten council members opposed it. Incumbents may have felt threatened by both the at-large feature and the proposed reduction of council size from ten to seven members.

Neither party organization took a position on the issue. During its study of charter provisions, the Woman's City Club heard presentations on PR voting from Robert Taft, then Republican floor leader in the Ohio House, who opposed it, and from Walter Millard of the National Municipal League, who advocated it (White, 1940, p. 22). Several

TABLE 7.2
PR ADOPTION AND REPEAL ISSUES IN HAMILTON, 1929–1960

Year/Issue	Type of Election	Total Vote	% Yes	Turnout[a](%)
Adoption				
1926	General	10,911	51	38
Repeal				
1929	Municipal	11,762	27	38
1933	Special (May)	10,713	39	33
1933	Regular	14,755	45	46
1944	General	18,843	43	54
1960	General	28,651	56	66

Sources: Blount (1987: for 1924, p. 36; for 1944, p. 98; for 1960, p. 17); *National Municipal Review,* 1933, 22:286–87, 613–14.
[a] Percentage of persons of voting age who voted on the issue.

unions recorded opposition to PR, but the Hamilton Trades and Union Council, whose president had been one of two blue-collar members on the charter commission, supported the entire package (White, 1940, p. 37).

The charter was submitted to the voters at the November election of 1926 and was narrowly passed by a vote of 5,535 to 5,376 (50.7%) (table 7.2). This close margin demonstrated more substantial opposition than was reported in the Hamilton press, which tended to reflect the views of the business and professional community. A harbinger of things to come was the defeat of the charter in the Second and Fifth Wards, both encompassing low-income neighborhoods. The Fifth also contained a concentration of recent Appalachian migrants, a group that would become increasingly important in Hamilton politics (Blount, 1987, p. 39).

For the third time in little more than a decade, reform was in the saddle again. The two previous short-lived reform regimes had been Socialist and Republican respectively; this time "nonpolitical" business and professional leaders who shunned identification with any party were in control.

It is clear in the Hamilton context that the adoption of PR was actually the adoption of a reform charter containing PR. Of the Ohio cities experimenting with the PR/STV electoral system, only Ashtabula, the first, voted on PR as a separate feature of its municipal government. Proportional representation was viewed generally as just one component of a reform package that would take power from party organizations and restore it to the people.

The nonpartisan ballot, at-large election of a smaller council, council election of the mayor, and selection of the city manager were interdependent structural changes. A behavioral change among the voters and in the government of Hamilton is more difficult to assess, but a certain reform élan seemed to prevail, reflecting the optimism inherent in earlier Progressive initiatives.

The Hamilton Experience with PR

Although some observers have concluded that the new regime did not create a sharp break with the past (White, 1940, p. 24), charter implementation transferred power from Democratic organization leaders to a largely business and professional elite whose members tended to be overtly nonpartisan and in some cases antiparty. Only two incumbent council members, Republican ward representatives Leo Welsh and August Biermann, survived the 1927 election.

Reformers claimed that the result was a civic renaissance, characterized by financial honesty, nonpolitical personnel administration, and other hallmarks of city manager government. City government also turned activist, protecting the public ownership and operation of utilities, and developing streets, parks, and sewer systems, issues that previous caretaker governments had not addressed.

The Role of Parties

The cleavages and symbols of the national and state parties had dominated Hamilton politics during the pre-PR years. The partisan ballot and partisan primary were important structural features that assured overt local party government; there were also behavioral factors such as habits of mind. Democratic machine politics had prevailed in the city for two decades with the exception of the one-term council interregnums of the Socialists in 1914–15 and Republicans in 1924–25 (Hallett, 1940, pp. 129–30). The immediate pre-PR period (1921–25) was marked by abrupt swings in party control (table 7.3).

After the first PR election in 1927, Hamilton's nonpartisan elections were dominated by slates that cut across major party lines. In some elections the only identifiable slate was that of the reform forces, often called the "Good Government" slate, espousing standard reform doctrines and law enforcement to "clean up" the "wide-open town." The Municipal Ownership League, which had been organized to prevent the threatened sale of Hamilton's municipal light plant and gas distribution system, presented slates of candidates (Hallett, 1940,

TABLE 7.3
PARTY FORTUNES IN HAMILTON POLITICS

	Partisan Affiliations, City Councils			Party Carrying City in State or National Election	
	Democratic	*Republican*	*Unknown*	*Democratic*	*Republican*
Pre-PR					
1921	7	3			
1923	1	9			
1925	7	3			
Total	15	15		3	1 (pres., 1924)
Avg.	5	5			
Early PR					
1927	1	6			
1929	3	4			
1931	2	5			
Total	6	15		3	1 (pres., 1928)
Avg.	2	5			
Late PR					
1955	5	1	1		
1957	5	2			
1959	4	3			
Total	14	6	1	1 (gov., 1958)	3
Avg.	4.7	2	0.3		
Post PR					
1961	4	3			
1963	3	4			
1965	5	2			
Total	12	9		1 (pres., 1964)	3
Avg.	4	3			

Sources: Newspaper reports; interviews; and White (1940, pp. 15, 30).
Chi-square test (council data) = 10.854; df = 6; $p < .093$

p. 130). These reformers had little overt competition from the parties. Opposition was provided by "Independent" candidates who ran with the endorsement and support of their respective party organizations.

These "Independent" candidates failed to constitute an effective opposition because they lacked the common programmatic approach to issues that characterized the reform slates. The fluidity of slates and antislate candidacies gave an edge to reform forces in the transfer-vote dynamics of the PR count, as will be explored below.

During the first several PR elections, with the exception of Republican holdovers Biermann and Welsh, the PR councils consisted of members who emphasized their distance from national and state parties. These members were not organization Republicans or Democrats; rather they regarded the influence of national and state parties in local affairs as pernicious. More significant cleavages among council members in both the PR and post-PR eras were based on ideology and economic interests. These were defined to a large extent by class-oriented preferences on social issues and the reform approach to municipal affairs (P. Davis, 1982).

Analysis of party identification of council members, however, does reveal the ebb and flow of party fortunes and the relationships between municipal and state and national politics during the periods of three electoral systems.

Pre-PR (1921–25) councils were dominated by Democrats, except when a significant third force (Independent/Socialist) threw a plurality victory to the Republicans. This Democratic dominance at the municipal level was matched at the state and national levels in Hamilton's voting patterns, with the exception of the presidential race of 1924.

In the early PR years, Republicans won a substantial majority of the council seats (table 7.3). Evidence suggests several reasons for this outcome: reform slates, recruited largely from business and professional people, tended to be disproportionately Republican; the nonpartisan ballot enabled Republicans to run without the handicap of the minority party label; and the support of slating organizations was effective. Koehler Democrats ran a few candidates in 1927 under the surprising label of the "Hamilton Proportional Representation Organization." They failed to draw significant support and their lack of success signalled a decade of decline in local Democratic influence.

Under the new charter, the insulation of city politics from the state and national levels led to more split-ticket voting. Hamilton voters chose Democratic state and national candidates, with the exception again of presidential voting, this time in the presidential race of 1928.

The partisan balance began to swing in the depression years, and by the 1950s, "late PR," Democrats captured the majority on council once again. In this period, however, Republican candidates tended to carry the city in state and national elections. This apparently paradoxical voting behavior may be attributed to dual forces: the growth of industrial unions that locally endorsed labor-oriented, mostly Democratic slates, and the persistence of Republican state and national loyalties among increasing numbers of Appalachian migrants from Kentucky.

The cross pressures on these voters, suggested by election data, must have been great, but were perhaps dampened by election timing. In local politics their lifestyle preferences were shared by "anti-establishment" slates that contained a preponderance of Democrats. Voting for these candidates in the odd-year municipal election on a nonpartisan ballot and voting for Republicans in the even-numbered years would require a minimum of strain. However, coalitions were complex, and little seemed to unite these anti-establishment forces except their opposition to Hamilton's "movers and shakers." The latter were men and a very few women who owned local industries and businesses, were officers of the chamber of commerce, served on the boards of trustees of the YMCA, YWCA, local charities, and hospitals. In most cases, they were also members of prominent families, all white, and mostly Protestant. They supported the charter and sought to end gambling, prostitution, and profligacy in Hamilton.

The anti-establishment forces, on the other hand, included at least four identifiable, and sometimes conflicting, groups: those who distrusted people with money, power, and social prestige; labor interests who distrusted their own leaders; those who favored an open city with no police interference in gambling or prostitution; and members of the Ku Klux Klan. Klan members reached their peak of strength in the early twenties (pre-PR) in Hamilton, as elsewhere in Ohio. Unlike other groups in the anti-establishment array of forces, Klan members opposed gambling, prostitution, and liquor, along with integration, immigration, internationalism, and the influence, if not the very presence, of Catholics and Jews (Blount, 1990a). Whereas those who favored an open city supported Democratic candidates for local office, Klan members tended to support Republicans (Blount, 1990b).

The Democratic advantage that developed in municipal elections in the late PR period persisted into the post-PR era in spite of plurality/at-large voting. As in the late PR period, Hamilton voters favored Republicans at the state and national level with the exception of the presidential election of 1964.

Although it appears that, during the early PR period, PR aided Republicans as members of the minority party, the nonpartisan ballot could also achieve this effect and indeed did so in many non-PR cities (Adrian, 1959). Actually the principal cleavage in Hamilton politics during the PR and post-PR periods was not partisan but reform versus traditional politics, across and independent of party lines. Reform forces may have exercised disproportionate power because they tended to be cohesive and programmatic. These qualities also attracted support on occasion from nonreform members of the council.

Participation

Political participation in the three electoral systems will be analyzed by examination of both voter turnout and the number of candidates competing for election.

Because of the lack of consistent and reliable registration data for Hamilton, the measure used for turnout is the percentage of the population over 21 years of age who voted for council. No significant differences in turnout can be identified for the four periods (pre-PR, early PR, late PR and post-PR) of the study. Turnout ranged from a low of 37% in 1931 (early PR) to a high of 50% in 1963 (post-PR), but participation within each period varied independently of electoral system change.

The popular perception was that turnout declined in the PR period. Opponents of PR variously attributed this perceived decline to the alleged complications of the STV ballot, absence of a head-to-head contest for mayor, and the loss of ward representation. In the pre-PR system, there were significantly more votes cast for mayor than for the council at-large candidates, and slightly more for ward representatives than for the at-large seats. But there was actually no discrepancy in turnout to explain, since the differences in turnout among elections and electoral system periods were patternless and marginal.

The number of candidates running for council may also indicate citizen interest, although like turnout this measure fluctuated within and between electoral system periods. The average number of candidates for council seats increased from pre-PR (21 candidates for 10 seats, an average of a little over 2 candidates per seat) to 22 for 7 seats (slightly over 3 per seat) during the PR period. The higher average number of candidates in PR elections may have resulted from the opportunities presented by nomination by petition, compared to the previously constricted access through partisan primaries. However, in the post-PR (7X) system, in spite of continued nomination by petition, the average number of candidates seeking council seats dropped below 18, to about 2.5 candidates per seat.

Although turnout and the number of candidacies may both be measures of citizen interest, they are interdependent variables because the number of candidacies may influence turnout. Indeed, with the exception of the first PR election, the two measures exhibit some rough parallels.

Incumbency

Turnover of council members did change significantly over the three electoral systems, declining from the volatile swings of the pre-PR period's mixed system to the PR period, and declining again, although less precipitously, in post-PR plurality voting.

During the pre-PR period incumbents fared poorly. Turnover averaged 7.7 members of the 10-member council. Partisan swings, together with the combination of at-large and ward seats, meant that slight shifts in voting behavior could result in reversal of party control. In contrast, in five of the 17 PR elections all the incumbents who ran were reelected. During both the early-PR and late-PR periods, an average of three members of the seven-member council were new following an election.

Under the plurality/at-large system of the post-PR period, turnover dropped to an average of 2.3 members per term. Defeat of an incumbent became the exception rather than the rule, a significant change from pre-PR (table 7.4).

Characteristics of Council Members

One of the key questions to ask in comparing and contrasting electoral systems is whether there were any systematic differences in the kinds of candidates elected under the different systems. Characteristics to be examined here include occupation, as a rough measure of socioeconomic status (SES), race, gender, religion, and place of residence.

Class

Councils of the pre-PR period were composed primarily of men who worked with their hands, albeit in skilled industrial jobs. The exceptions were Democratic small businessmen. The advent of reform government in 1927 created major changes in these characteristics. Blue-collar members became a minority, while business and professional people became a majority of the PR councils. Corporate managers were especially prominent in the early PR council majorities, but blue-collar representation, although still a minority, increased in the late PR period (table 7.5).

Blue-collar participation declined again in the post-PR period, a renewal of the trend from pre-PR to PR. Because an increase in

TABLE 7.4

INCUMBENCY SUCCESS RATE OF HAMILTON CITY COUNCIL MEMBERS
UNDER THREE ELECTORAL SYSTEMS, 1921–1965

	A. Status of Council Members	
	% Who Were New Members	% Who Were Reelected Incumbents
Pre-PR (1921–25; council of 10)	77.0	23.0
Early PR (1927–31; council of 7)	43	57
Late PR (1955–59; council of 7)	43	57
Post-PR (1961–65; council of 7)	33	67

	B. Electoral Fate of Council Incumbents		
	% Who Were Reelected	% Who Ran But Were Defeated	% Who Didn't Run
Pre-PR (1921–25; council of 10)	22.3	24.3	53.4
Early PR (1927–31; council of 7)	50	25	25
Late PR (1955–59; council of 7)	57	10	33
Post-PR (1961–65; council of 7)	66	5	30

Section A: Chi-square = 11.639; df = 3, $p < .009$
Section B: Chi-square = 13.504; df = 6, $p < .036$

representation of business and professional elites occurred in other reform cities without PR, it can be argued that the trend in occupational characteristics of council members found in Hamilton resulted from the nonpartisan ballot and the at-large election of a smaller council, virtually universal features of "reformed" cities. What follows, then, is that PR in Hamilton saved blue-collar and other lower-SES candidates from the electoral sweeps of plurality/at-large systems, such as occurred in post-PR Hamilton.

Appraising the role of organized labor in the politics of Hamilton under the various electoral systems is fraught with complications. In the 1920s "Labor" meant craft unionism, many of whose rank-and-file members probably voted Republican in state and national politics. By the 1950s and 1960s, "Labor" meant preponderantly industrial unionism, oriented to the Democratic party. In the PR period, some blue-collar members of the Hamilton council were recruited, nominated, and supported by the managers of reform slates. Furthermore, some

TABLE 7.5
OCCUPATIONS OF HAMILTON COUNCIL MEMBERS UNDER
THREE ELECTORAL SYSTEMS

		Occupation (%)					
		Business		Clerical	Blue-		
	Professional	Small	Corporate	& Sales	Collar	Other	Total
Pre-PR (1919–23; council of 10)		10.0		30.0	60.0		100.0% (30)
Early PR (1927–31; council of 7)	14.3	9.5	28.6	28.6	19.0		100.1% (21)
Late PR (1955–59; council of 7)	14.3	23.7	4.8	19.0	33.0	4.8	100.0% (21)
Post-PR (1961–65; council of 7)	19.0	4.8	14.3	23.7	19.0	19.0	99.8% (21)

Sources: Press reports; directories; and White (1940, pp. 15–30).
Note: Numbers in parentheses are *N*s.
Chi-square = 32.950; df = 15, $p < .0005$

council members, who were classified under small business at the time they were elected, retained labor ties from earlier occupations and used these ties in campaign appeals.

Despite such complications, some generalizations can be made. In the early PR councils, no blue-collar members were union officials. In fact, one prominent union leader, Louis Nau, president of the AFL Trades and Union Council, was defeated in spite of his yeoman work on the drafting of the new charter, getting it passed, and running on the charter commission's 1927 slate. During these early years several Independent candidates endorsed by labor and campaigning on their labor affiliations were also unsuccessful. In the late 1930s some Independent and anti-establishment slate members bore the labor label and used labor rhetoric. In 1937 the first such candidate was elected, an independent Democrat who was not endorsed or supported by the Democratic organization (White, 1940, p. 30).

By the 1950s anti-establishment slates were increasingly using the rhetoric of labor and implicitly of class. Independent blue-collar candidacies were occasionally succeeding. Late in the decade a leading role was played by Robert Westfall, both as a council candidate and ironically as a leader of the anti-PR campaign. The increasing political consciousness and role of organized labor in Hamilton politics must account in part for the increase in blue-collar representation in the late PR councils. Still, the sudden decrease in such occupations in the post-PR councils indicates a significant electoral system effect as well.

Gender

By the mid-1920s women were being elected in Hamilton to the nonpartisan board of education and to the partisan office of treasurer. Women ran for council in 1923 (pre-PR) and 1935 (PR) but were not elected. In 1943 the first woman to be elected to the Hamilton council used her initials on the ballot, appearing as E. W. Frechtling, but she was reelected in 1945 as Eleanore Frechtling. A woman was elected again under PR in 1951, and under the post-PR plurality system in 1961 and 1963 (*Hamilton Evening Journal,* 5 Oct. 1923, p. 14; 7 Nov. 1923, p. 12; 4 Nov. 1925, p. 16; Butler County Board of Elections, *Abstract of Votes,* 1943–63).

The paucity of female candidates contrasts, today we would say starkly, not only with their numbers in the electorate but also with the prominent role played by women who were civic leaders in initiating and securing the adoption of Hamilton's reform charter. However, nomination by petition and election by PR/STV appear to have increased opportunities for women to participate in local politics as candidates. Their infrequent success in the post-PR period suggests that the plurality/at-large system diminished those opportunities.

Race

African Americans made up less than four percent of Hamilton's population in 1930, a fraction that increased only to six percent by 1960 despite significant population growth. Race did not appear to play a role in the organized politics of the city in the pre-PR period. After PR was adopted, a few black candidates were elected through coalition strategies.

In the first PR election (1927) a black candidate ran as an Independent but did not attract enough support either on first choices or transfers to win. The first successful black candidacy was that of Dr. L. L. Hunter, a dentist, in 1949. Hunter had run in 1947 as an Independent, and on his second try was recruited for the reform slate, his key to victory. The slate strategy was to prove successful for the second black council member as well. Fred Grant, a foreman in a manufacturing plant, ran eighth in the 1955 election and as runner-up

was appointed to a vacancy on council in 1957. He was elected to a full
term that November when he ran on an anti-establishment "United
Hamilton" slate. In 1959 he ran as an Independent and, like Hunter,
was defeated after one term (*Hamilton Evening Journal,* 10 Nov. 1927,
p. 15; White, 1940, p. 31).

Thus, by the end of the PR epoch, the score for African Americans
consisted of two full elected terms, one partial appointed term. Both
wins occurred with slate endorsements; both candidates subsequently
failed as Independents. This experience confirms the effect of PR/STV
on minorities whose electoral strength is less than a PR quota. In
Hamilton's seven-member system, approximately 12% of the total vote
constituted a Droop quota. With two percent of total council seats held
in the 34 years of PR government, blacks in Hamilton were underrepresented. Only a coalition strategy could bring success for so small a
minority.

Despite this limitation, black community leaders vigorously supported the PR system, as early as the repeal campaign of 1933 (*Hamilton
Journal News,* 28 April 1933, p. 11; 28 Oct. 1933, p. 18). Their stance
was vindicated by the failure of any African-American candidates to be
elected in the post-PR (plurality/at-large) period (1961–65).

Religion

Although religious cleavage was an important factor in Ohio politics in the first half of the twentieth century, influencing social issues
such as prohibition, gambling, Sunday closing laws, and aid to parochial schools, religion does not appear to have been an important issue
in Hamilton council elections. In a comment about the city's first six
PR councils, White wrote:

> Division of the electorate along religious lines was not accurately re-
> flected in the council. The proportion of Roman Catholics was somewhat
> larger in the council in 1938 (about 57 percent) than among the voters
> (about 40 percent); in the six [PR] councils, however, five Catholics and
> eleven Protestants had been elected. Only one Catholic was elected to
> the first charter council. Consequently, religion could not have been the
> basis for the preferences expressed by most voters. (1940, p. 31)

Since systematic information about the religious affiliation of neither
council members nor the electorate can be ascertained, defining the
role of religion in Hamilton politics of the era is an elusive task.
However, the overt anti-Catholic, anti-Jewish activity of the pre-PR
period—hooded and masked Klan parades, cross-burnings, and acts of
violence against individuals—declined after 1925 (Blount, 1990a;

1990b). At least it is noteworthy that religious hatred did not prevent the adoption in Hamilton in 1926 of a political reform, PR/STV, that would facilitate the election of minorities.

Geographic Distribution

The distribution of council members' residences throughout the city inevitably becomes an issue in the transition from a small-district to an at-large electoral system. Traditional neighborhood representation is pitted against the reform vision of representation of the city "as a whole." In Hamilton, as elsewhere, class issues underlay the debate.

The pre-PR system combining ward and at-large representation assured at least one council member for each of the city's six wards. Ward boundaries changed little between 1910 and 1960, so comparisons of electoral system effects can be made across time. Ward 1 west of the river was both the most populous and the most prosperous. In contrast, Ward 2 in the central city was the lowest-income ward and provided the principal base of Democratic strength.

Because of Democratic local voting patterns in the pre-PR period, Ward 1 and Ward 2 were equally represented in the council through at-large as well as ward seats. Since PR voting was conducted at-large, its introduction freed council representation from the ties of residence. In the early PR period, Ward 4 secured more than "its share" of representation through the success of long-term incumbent Leo Welsh, while Ward 1 fell to second place.

By late PR, Ward 1 was the place of residence of a majority of council, a concentration of geographical representation which continued in the post-PR period. Ward 2 fared even less well in the post-PR period than it had under PR, losing its representation altogether in plurality/at-large voting. Ward 3, a mixed-income ward, was represented only in the pre-PR period, gaining no representation under either the at-large PR system or plurality/at-large voting (table 7.6).

Ward 1's record of disproportionate representation in the late PR and post-PR periods is consistent with findings elsewhere that at-large elections favor upper-SES groups in the electorate. However, it must be noted that Ward 1 contained twice the population of any other ward, so that later under the standards of one person-one vote its share of council members would not be so lopsided.

Furthermore, anomalies of residence complicate the notion of geographical representation. For example, low-income Ward 2 was a focal point of anti-charter and anti-PR strength, yet in the early PR period it contained the residence of Dr. Mark Millikin, a reform council

TABLE 7.6
GEOGRAPHIC DISTRIBUTIONS OF RESIDENCES OF
HAMILTON COUNCIL MEMBERS, 1921–1965

	Council Size	Average No. of Council Members per Ward					
		Ward 1	Ward 2	Ward 3	Ward 4	Ward 5	Ward 6
Pre-PR (elections of 1921–25)	10	2.0	2.0	1.3	1.3	1.3	1.3
Early PR (elections of 1927–31)	7	1.3	1.0	0	2.0	1.0	1.3
Late PR (elections of 1955–59)	7	4.7	.3	0	1.0	.7	.3
Post-PR (elections of 1961–65)	7	4.7	0	0	1.0	.7	.7

Sources: Newspaper reports and Hamilton city directories.

member and leader of reform activities. Another example is found in upper-income Ward 1, by late PR still a bastion of pro-PR voting strength. Two leaders of the 1960 campaign to repeal PR, council member Mark Petty and 1959 runner-up Robert Westfall, both resided in Ward 1 (Kindness, 1988). These apparent anomalies could, however, be recognized as natural outcomes in a PR electoral system, which facilitates self-selected constituencies unrestricted by residence.

Consensus and Conflict in Decision Making

A persistent question in the evaluation of electoral systems is whether or not the method used to elect members of a legislative body influences its operations. Multipartyism, factionalism, exacerbated conflict, and paralysis are among the charges brought by critics against governments elected by proportional representation (Hermens, 1941, pp. 406–34; Hermens, 1985, pp. 9–10; Duverger, 1963, p. 239; Riker, 1982, p. 754). Although most of these criticisms are directed at national parliaments elected on party-list ballots (PR/PL), they have also resonated throughout the debates about use of PR/STV in nonpartisan municipal elections in the United States (Price, 1941, pp. 575–78). Therefore consensus and conflict in decision making on the Hamilton council will be examined over three electoral systems.

Press reports create perceptions of divisiveness because consensus seldom merits coverage. A more objective measure of conflict is the

TABLE 7.7
CONSENSUS AND CONFLICT IN COUNCIL VOTING PATTERNS,
1922–1967

| | Division on Substantive Roll Call Votes | | |
	Split (%)	Unanimous (%)	N
Pre-PR (mixed system)	74.8	25.2	103
Early PR	9.6	90.4	125
Late PR	11.2	88.8	715
Post-PR (7X)	18.8	81.2	760

Source: Tabulated from Hamilton city council minutes. Substantive Roll Call Votes include all roll-call votes of council and the Committee of the Whole in the specified time periods, excepting procedural votes.
  Chi-square = 250.014; df = 3, *p* < .0001

percentage of substantive roll call votes which were nonunanimous. Excluding votes on procedural matters, this statistic has been calculated for the four periods of this study (table 7.7). The findings produce no evidence of either more factionalism or more deadlock in the functioning of PR councils than that experienced by councils elected by other means.

In fact, PR-elected councils demonstrated significantly higher consensus patterns. In early PR, for example, 90.4% of the roll calls were unanimous; in late PR 88.8%, a proportion higher than either before or after the PR period. Under the combined ward and at-large system (1922–27) only 25.2% of the roll call votes were unanimous. After the repeal of PR/STV (1962–67) unanimous votes by the councils elected on plurality/at-large ballots fell from the PR period high to 81.2%, a level significantly more consensual than in the pre-PR period, but still more conflictual than during PR.

In all three periods, divided votes occurred on such issues as enforcement of antigambling ordinances and political-level personnel decisions, such as electing a mayor or manager and occasionally selecting a department head. Evidence of deadlock or paralysis in municipal operations under PR is, however, lacking. Although difficult to quantify, contemporary accounts portray PR councils as activist in orientation, accomplishing civic advancement, maintaining and improving services such as city-owned power, reducing bonded debt, and revising the municipal code to respond to new demands on government (*Hamilton Evening Journal,* 31 Dec. 1931, p. 20; *Hamilton Journal News,* 3 Nov. 1955, p. 48; 5 Nov. 1955, pp. 7, 24).

White argued that PR in Hamilton contributed an integrative rather than a divisive effect:

> Critics of proportional representation often stress its tendency to divide
> the electorate into distinct factions. Results in Hamilton tended strongly
> toward unifying the electorate. Almost all of the successful candidates
> avoided concrete, sharply defined issues. They were for honesty, effi-
> ciency, and economy. They did not want to take a stand antagonistic to
> any bloc of voters that might otherwise give them even third-, fourth-, or
> fifth-choice votes. (p. 32)

Whatever the validity of the proportionalism/deadlock thesis at the level of national parliaments, at least evidence from Hamilton discon-firms its applicability to small municipal councils. Opportunities for conflict along class or ideological lines existed in Hamilton, but they did not result in consistent or fractious cleavages in the functioning of PR councils.

Features of the PR/STV System

Although the PR/STV electoral system was subject to constant criti-cism for its complexity, it is the count rather than the ballot itself that is the issue. In this section, effectiveness of the ballot and the respective roles of first-choice and transfer votes will be explored.

Effective Ballots

The issue of the effective ballot is seldom raised in discussions of plurality voting, yet in a winner-take-all election, the only effective votes are those cast for the winner in a single-member district or multiple winners in at-large elections. Votes marked incorrectly (such as two X's in a ward election) are invalid, and votes for losers are wasted. In a two-person plurality election, as few as 50% plus one of the ballots may be effective. In a three-person race the percentage of effective votes may be even lower because only one can win.

Because the ballot itself changed in systems adopting PR/STV, a great deal of attention, in Hamilton as elsewhere, was focused on invalid and ineffective votes. In 17 PR elections in Hamilton, an average of less than one percent of the voters failed to vote for council while casting votes for other local offices or issues (calculated from Butler County Board of Elections, *Abstract of Votes*).

Invalid ballots for council members were cast by an average of less than four percent of the voters. These ballots were spoiled by markings that failed to make the intent of the voter clear to counting officials.

One "X" on a ballot would be counted as a single first-choice vote, but multiple X's instead of numbered preferences could not be counted.

Ineffective PR votes include also the exhausted ballots, on which all of the preferences marked have been either already elected or eliminated. In the 17 Hamilton PR elections, an average of less than five percent of the voters cast ballots that were exhausted by the end of the count (calculated from Butler County Board of Elections, *Abstract of Votes*).

The share of ballots ultimately counted for an elected candidate under PR—the effective votes—therefore totaled between 89% and 91%. Thus, under the conditions of Hamilton PR elections, few votes were wasted. Approximately nine out of every ten voters could see at least one candidate on the council for whom they had voted. This linkage has been identified as important in minimizing feelings of alienation on the part of voters in municipal elections (Heilig and Mundt, 1984). In contrast, in the post-PR period when plurality/at-large voting was the rule, the percentage of total votes cast for elected candidates was significantly lower, at an average of 56.3% (calculated from Butler County Board of Elections, *Abstract of Votes*). Although this figure meets the criterion for majority rule, it still shows that 43.7% of the votes were cast for candidates who were not elected, compared to 10% of the votes under PR/STV voting.

First-Choice Votes

The limited but still important role of first-choice votes is sometimes unappreciated by those unfamiliar with the workings of the STV ballot. It is true that a transfer vote counts as much as a first-choice vote and that transfers can change a candidate's standing as determined by first choices; however, a candidate must still do well enough on first choices to avoid being eliminated. It is sometimes said that to be a viable candidate on the PR/STV ballot one need only be "everyone's second choice." This is not true. Such a candidate would be eliminated early in the count.

In Hamilton's 17 PR elections, elected candidates' first-choice votes ranged from a high of 72% to a low of 44% of the total votes cast. This percentage is a function of voters' concentration of their first-choice votes on ultimate winners, which is in turn partly a function of the number of candidates in the race. In the same 17 elections the runner-up candidate (ranking eighth in the final count) received first-choice votes ranging between 4% and 6% of the the total vote cast. This is about half the total number of votes not recorded for an ultimate winner.

Finally, eliminated candidates received a share of first-choice votes that varied between 24% and 51%, depending again on the number of candidates running. An apparent winner on first-choice votes may be converted to a loser in the transfer process.

Transfer Votes

Transfer votes are of two kinds: surplus votes of strong candidates elected on first-choice votes; and votes transferred from candidates who rank too low to have a chance of election and are therefore eliminated during the count. In 11 of the 17 PR elections, surpluses were recorded and ballots were transferred to second or subsequent choices. In every PR election ballots were transferred from eliminated candidates to second or subsequent preferences, thus accounting for most of the action in Hamilton counts.

As in most electoral systems, strategic voting appears to have affected outcomes. Over time surpluses of popular candidates seemed to shrink as their supporters learned to give their first-choice votes to candidates less assured of election. Slates were designed to maximize intraslate transfers; furthermore campaigns were often directed toward encouraging interslate transfers. These effects of the single transferable vote were often noted by PR advocates as features that reduced the more typical personal attacks and mudslinging of head-to-head con-tests.

There is impressive evidence that reform groups were more suc-cessful than their rivals in strategic use of the transfer process. In six out of eight instances in which the transfer process turned first-choice leaders into losers, and lower-placing candidates into winners, it was a reform candidate who benefited (table 7.8).

These transfer winners were integrating candidates, that is, their support was broader than a single group in the electorate. The transfer losers, on the other hand, showed strong support at the outset but were unable to broaden their base through second and subsequent choices by other voters. Not surprisingly, given the small number of black voters in Hamilton, the two African-American incumbents who were elected when they were part of the reform slate became transfer losers when they ran for reelection as Independents. In 15 out of the 17 PR elections, Independent candidates or those backed by an anti-establishment slate would be the last candidate eliminated and therefore be left as runner-up (Butler County Board of Elections, 1927–59).

TABLE 7.8
Transfer Winners and Viable Losers in Hamilton PR Elections,
1927–1959

Year	Candidates	Order of First Choices	Order of Finish	Difference (col. 2 – col. 3)
1933	Winner: Welsh	8	5	+3
	Loser: Biermann	6	9	−3
1943	Winner: Spaulding	9[a]	3	+6
	Loser: Bruck	6	8	−2
1947	Winner: Radcliffe[b]	14	7	+7
	Loser: Hunter[b]	7	8	−1
1949	Winner: Radcliffe[b]	12	5	+7
	Loser: Blumenthal	7	9	−2
1951	Winner: Blumenthal[b]	8	6	+2
	Loser: Burnett	7	8	−1
1953	Winner: Fiehrer[b]	8	7	+1
	Loser: Lakeman	7	8	−1
1955	Winner: Bartels[b]	8	6	+2
	Loser: Grant[c]	7	8	−1
1959	Winner: Blumenthal[b]	8	7	+1
	Loser: Westfall	6	8	−2

Source: Butler County Board of Elections, 1933–59.
Note: The chance of six successive wins by reform-endorsed candidates is 1 in 64 or .0156.
[a] Tied for ninth place.
[b] Candidate was on a "good government" slate.
[c] Black candidate.

The Repeal Campaigns

After four unsuccessful initiatives to repeal PR/STV in Hamilton, the fifth succeeded in 1960. These campaigns reflected different phases of political activity in Hamilton and can be distinguished by different sets of actors and issues.

Resurgence of the Old Guard: 1929 and 1933

The first three attempts to repeal PR, in November 1929 and May and November of 1933, were clearly efforts of the Koehler faction of the Democratic Party, the old machine, to abolish an electoral system in which its candidates failed to get elected. Proponents of PR viewed these repeal efforts also as the first stage of an attack on the entire city manager plan of government.

In 1929 the petition-initiated amendment to the charter provided for retaining the at-large council and nomination by petition, but abolished the PR ballot and substituted election by plurality vote. Both 1933 repeal attempts added the nomination of candidates in a nonpartisan primary if necessary to narrow the field to 14 contenders. All three of these efforts were supported by both major party organizations and opposed by reform groups, by the local Socialist Party, and by the major daily newspaper in Hamilton, the *Evening Journal*. Labor forces were neutral.

The 1933 campaigns were somewhat more complex than the initial effort in 1929. In 1933 the Municipal Ownership League joined the repeal side, and national Socialist leader Norman Thomas persuaded local Socialists who had opposed repeal in 1929 to remain neutral. The Woman's City Club took the leading role in defense of PR, supported by the most prominent political organization in the small African-American community.

The campaigns elicited attacks on PR as "impossible to understand," bewildering to the voters who "did not know for whom their votes would be counted." Pro-PR literature cited the low rate of invalid ballots (2.7% to 5.6% at the time) as evidence that voters understood how to vote on a single transferable ballot, and it argued that "the regular re-election of so many councilmen indicated that the voters were persistent in the expression of their choices" (White, 1940, p. 32). Proponents of PR also defended the electoral system as the "heart and soul" of the new charter, thus stressing its linkage with the city manager plan.

Although anti-PR forces won increasing support in each of these three campaigns, all three issues failed (table 7.2). Furthermore, from 1927 through 1933 the Koehler forces failed to muster enough votes to elect even one council candidate with a PR quota.

Different Actors, Changes in the Script: 1944

Eleven years passed before repeal of PR was attempted again. The original cast of characters had passed from the scene and Hamilton had changed. New voters, mostly of Appalachian origin, were said to be a factor in encouraging anti-PR forces to submit a repeal amendment to the charter (*National Municipal Review*, Dec. 1944, p. 630). Elements of both continuity and change are found in the 1944 repeal campaign.

Once more, as in 1929, the amendment proposed to substitute for PR a plurality election at-large of seven council members on a nonpartisan ballot, without a primary. A new feature was to provide that the highest vote getter would become mayor, thus taking the mayoral election away from the council. The amendment also provided for the election of a new council (if the issue were to pass) at the same election in which the voters were deciding on the proposed change. This provision was viewed by many as a confusing technical flaw, since the issue was on the ballot in a presidential, not a municipal, election year, and a plurality ballot that was not yet authorized would have to be printed.

Opponents of PR called PR unconstitutional and un-American, arguments that must have resonated in the midst of World War II (*Hamilton Journal News,* 19 Oct. 1944, pp. 6, 19). Although unions were growing in strength, organized labor did not take a position on the charter amendment.

Proponents of PR organized a Hamilton Nonpartisan Council Committee, in which the Woman's City Club and a group of ministers took leading roles. Since reform forces had elected only three members of council in 1943, they put forward minority-representation arguments in favor of PR with renewed vigor. They also pointed to the manipulability of plurality voting. If a majority of voters casts votes for all seven seats in a plurality/at-large election, a minority interest, if successful in teaching its supporters to limit their choices to four, could capture a majority of seats on the new council. This possibility surfaced in the campaign through the "social issue." Pro-PR forces warned that plurality voting would allow a determined minority opposed to enforcement of laws against gambling and prostitution to win a majority of the council seats (*Hamilton Journal News,* 1 Nov. 1944, p. 4, editorial).

The proposed amendment was defeated in the relatively small (wartime) presidential election turnout, with 43% of the voters supporting the issue (table 7.2). The defeat laid the repeal question to rest once more, this time for 16 years.

A New Ball Game: 1960

By 1960 conditions had changed enough in Hamilton to enable the forces of repeal to prevail. Changes in the composition of the electorate, organized labor's active participation, and the successful decoupling of the PR issue from the city manager plan all contributed to the success of repeal. By this time the other Ohio PR cities—Ashtabula, Cleveland, Cincinnati, and Toledo—had all abandoned PR, but only Cleveland had given up its city manager. The historic linkage between the city manager plan and PR elections appeared to be broken.

However, the politics of the 1959 municipal election and its aftermath may have been the deciding factor in the ultimate outcome.

Over three decades had passed since the adoption of the city manager/PR charter. The electorate had doubled in size, but more important, a generational turnover had occurred and the fervor of the reform impulse in Hamilton had dissipated. Many upper-status voters who had been significant proponents of the reform agenda had moved to suburbs and had been replaced in the city by migrants from southeastern Kentucky. These new residents were likely to be influenced by a growing anti-establishment constituency.

Since the late 1930s, candidates from blue-collar occupations had been increasingly successful under PR/STV, bringing with them the symbols and rhetoric of labor, although not necessarily the endorsement of labor organizations. Unions took no official stand on candidates or ballot issues, but by the 1950s "Labor" was a label affixed to candidates by press reports and used at times on the masthead of slates. The year 1960 marked the peak of Hamilton's industrial unionism as well as of its population growth.

In the 1959 municipal election, Mark Petty, an Independent candidate, ran on a repeal-PR plank. Robert Westfall, president of the newly combined AFL-CIO Council, ran as an Independent with labor support. An emotional dimension was added to the campaign literature by increasing appeals to class antagonisms in a city already noteworthy for them (P. Davis, 1982). Events of the transfer process and a subsequent appointment to a vacancy exacerbated these appeals.

Westfall finished sixth on the basis of first-choice votes but eighth on the final count, edged out by 19 transfer votes that went to Jack Blumenthal, a candidate on the reform slate. Blumenthal's election gave the reform forces a majority of the new council. Westfall demanded a recount; minor discrepancies were found but did not change the outcome. Meanwhile, Donald Grammel was the last reform-slate candidate to be eliminated, but he ranked lower than Westfall in the final tabulation.

After the election one of the newly elected candidates resigned, and in January 1960 both Westfall and Grammel applied to the new council for appointment to the vacancy.[2] Westfall's supporters argued his claim to be the runner-up. They also argued that the reform forces had already won four seats, and a fifth would amount to overrepresentation. Grammel's advocates responded that the reform majority was entitled if not obligated to choose Grammel because of the principles on which they were elected. The charter clearly gave the council discretion to act. Grammel was subsequently appointed by a vote of four reform members to two Independents (Frank, 1960).

Meanwhile, because of increasing attacks on PR in the community, the previous council had asked its successor council to evaluate the electoral system. The old council authorized the appointment of an advisory committee and compiled a list of nominees from which the next mayor was to make these appointments. The mayor acted early in 1960, asking the committee to report on PR and on possible alternative electoral systems. Robert Westfall was one of the 13 appointees. The committee rendered its report in July 1960. PR led the list of electoral systems considered to be "recommended" or "acceptable"; only one member (presumably Westfall) considered it "undesirable." The city council voted five to two not to place the question of repeal on the ballot.

Petitions were immediately initiated by a repeal committee organized and chaired by Robert Westfall, and the issue reached the ballot by initiative for the fifth time, scheduled for the presidential election of 1960. The proposed alternative was the same plan that had been defeated in 1944: nomination by petition, with at-large election of seven council members by plurality voting on a nonpartisan ballot. The council member with the most votes would become mayor.

The Westfall committee led the campaign to repeal PR. Council member Petty played a prominent role. Democratic workers were active in the campaign, and organized labor for the first time formally endorsed repeal. A three-county AFL-CIO Council adopted a resolution calling PR "unfair to minority groups" and pointing out that "other cities are abolishing this form of voting" (*Hamilton Journal News,* 18 Aug. 1960, p. 18).

A "small but militant unit" of the League of Women Voters, with help from Cincinnati friends of PR, campaigned vigorously for its retention. The defense of PR by Hamilton's other reform groups appears to have been limited to voter education. The Citizens' Government League sponsored a public meeting at which Professors Howard White and James Woodworth of nearby Miami University lectured, attempting to present fairly all sides of the question. According to press reports, White made the case for PR; Woodworth pointed out its limitations and disadvantages as he perceived them, but concluded that in view of the flaws in the proposed plurality voting system, he preferred PR (*Hamilton Journal News,* 4 Nov. 1960).

Although the advocates were decorous in their campaign—indeed, some said "feeble and faint-hearted"—other important actors remained neutral. The Republican Party organization took no stand. The *Journal*

News, which in previous campaigns had been a stalwart defender of
PR, took a carefully worded position intended to be neutral but
interpreted by others as a renunciation of its former support:

> [W]ith the passing of . . . years, in spite of arguments favoring . . . PR
> . . . there has developed confusion from the many ramifications in its
> makeup—the many complications in the manner in which votes are cast
> and . . . counted. Hamilton has stood by PR longer than most cities.
> Cincinnati recently made a change when the people there found it too
> complicated. So, it is . . . proper . . . that the matter should be brought to a
> vote . . . so that voters can decide. . . . Proportional representation has been
> challenged four times since its adoption in 1926. On all occasions . . . this
> newspaper advocated retention. Today, however, with attendant confusion
> increasing in an increasing population, the matter becomes one in which
> people again should express their desires. (19 Oct. 1960, editorial)

In the highest turnout of any repeal vote (66%), PR was rejected by
a 56% majority. The vote was decisive and fairly evenly distributed;
only a few precincts favored retention of PR (*Hamilton Journal News,* 8
Nov. 1960, p. 32; 9 Nov. 1960, editorial). No significant pattern of class
or racial voting can be identified. Because of the large turnout associated with the presidential election, it is possible that anti-PR sentiment was disproportionately characteristic of less politically attentive
voters who participate in presidential elections only. Ironically, repeal
was accomplished by a turnout significantly larger than had voted in a
municipal election on either the pre-PR or PR ballot.

It appears, however, that the election was not so much won by repeal
advocates as it was lost by the failure of reform forces to organize and
campaign. Their credibility had been damaged by the reform incumbents' appointment to the council vacancy, passing over the runner-up
who probably would have been elected by plurality voting.

Weakened by the successive repeal efforts in Hamilton and demor-
alized by the abandonment of PR in other Ohio communities, PR's
friends dissipated their strength. Confident now that the city manager
plan was separable from PR elections and relatively secure, they gave
up the fight.

The Post-PR System: "7X"

With the introduction of plurality/at-large voting in the 1961 municipal election, the council candidates with the most votes won (winner-
take-all). Voters could mark their ballots with up to seven X's, hence

"7X." The winner with the most votes became mayor, taking mayoral selection out of the hands of council. It appears that a period of some political fragmentation followed the three decades of PR elections.

Surprisingly in light of their defeat on the retention of PR, reform slates were successful in gaining council majorities in the first two post-PR elections. The persistence of reform majorities may have been influenced by the tendency of incumbents to win reelection. Yet newcomers also fared well with the voters, and the provision that the leading vote getter became mayor produced first-time winners in the mayor's office in the early plurality/at-large elections.

This feature, intended to give the voters more power and perhaps to preempt interest in a popularly elected mayor, introduced conflict and unpredictability into the operations of the council. Although the position of mayor in a city manager government is largely ceremonial, its occupant presides over council meetings and can presumably shape consensus on difficult issues. In the free-for-all of plurality voting on a nonpartisan ballot, however, the voters could not or did not elect a leader with a working majority on the council.

For example, in 1961 Robert Westfall, the disappointed runner-up of the 1959 election who had been passed over for appointment to a vacancy, ran again and as recipient of the highest vote became mayor. His visibility as leader of the anti-PR campaign undoubtedly contributed to this outcome, but at the same time, as noted earlier, the voters returned a reform majority to the council.

The resulting council (1962–63) was described as being characterized by "chaotic . . . conduct" and protracted "bickering," a pattern that reportedly persisted through the 1963 campaign. The daily fare of the campaign, the *Journal News* noted, was made up of "personal remarks, assumptions, personalities, grievances and the political type of propaganda best described by the word 'smokescreen' " (1 Nov. 1963). "Incredible, wild, irresponsible accusations" were made, and "hateful . . . insinuations designed to injure the reputation of others" (2 Nov. 1963).

A further element of confusion in the post-PR politics of Hamilton was the use of slate designations. In 1963 the reform candidates preempted the label "United Hamilton," which in previous elections had been used by anti-establishment slates (*Hamilton Journal News,* 6 Nov. 1963, p. 44).

Lack of satisfaction with the plurality/at-large electoral system resulted in a proposal to abandon it and substitute a single-member-district council of nine members, each elected from a ward. This plan, initiated in 1965 by neighborhood groups on the east side of the city, was targeted to eliminate the concentration of a council majority from one ward, to reduce the cost of citywide campaigns, and to counter allegedly discriminatory policies of the current council, such as the lack of a swimming pool on the east side of town (*Hamilton Journal News,* 21 Oct. 1965, pp. 50, 52). Hamilton voters decisively rejected this proposal, which would have combined ward election with a partisan ballot (not used in Hamilton since pre-PR days) and election of the mayor by council (*Hamilton Journal News,* 2 Nov. 1965).

At the same election in 1965, the reform slate elected only three candidates. The voters, however, produced no alternative majority on council, since the other four seats were divided between two members elected on an opposition slate and two Independents. It is difficult to demonstrate that this political fragmentation would have been avoided if PR/STV had still been in effect, but at least it should be noted that such a fractured council had not been elected in the previous 17 elections.

Evidence from the PR elections between 1947 and 1959 shows that reform-slate candidates tended to benefit from the transfer process (table 7.8). In the 1960s, however, when Democratic and labor groups in the city became better organized, they could have used intraslate transfers as well to strengthen their representation on council if PR had been retained.

In a plurality/at-large system the share of effective votes depends both on the number of candidates and the number of votes cast per voter. This latter number is in turn affected by the voter's information about and preferences for candidates. However, votes cast for less-preferred candidates may help defeat more-preferred ones. For those voters who understand this feature of plurality voting, strategic voting leads to restricting the number of choices made. A knowledgeable voter with a single strong preference may act by "plunking," or voting for one candidate only.

In the first three "7X" elections, Hamilton voters typically voted for six candidates out of their seven available choices (Butler County Board of Elections, *Abstract of Votes,* 1961–65). Over time this number might decline as voters experienced defeat of a more preferred candidate by a less valued one for whom they had also voted.[3] With bare electoral data it is impossible to distinguish between lower knowledge or interest and strategic voting as an explanation of the number of choices made by voters.

In these same three elections, the 7X system produced plurality rather than majority winners, as its critics had predicted. Distribution of the vote over winners and losers is to some extent a function of the number of candidates. The fewer candidates there are, the more easily winning candidates obtain a majority. Most of the candidates winning with a plurality would have obtained a quota under the previous electoral system, thus becoming winners. However, the transfer process of PR would probably have enabled an occasional first-choice runner-up to displace a plurality winner.

The post-PR increase in professional and corporate representation on council and the corresponding decline in the blue-collar presence, identified earlier, suggests that the 1960 electoral system change benefited upper-status groups in Hamilton.

Conclusion

In the press or in contemporary polemical materials originating in Hamilton, few clues are provided to the kind of polity PR advocates attempted to create. Reformers who supported PR, the inheritors of the Progressive tradition, sought more responsive as well as more efficient government. But diverse and perhaps even conflicting motives underlay the efforts of what came to be called the Good Government movement in this small industrial city.

At least since the second decade of the twentieth century, Hamilton has been riven by significant class cleavages, while racial cleavages have been less salient. Proponents of PR argue that divided societies are best served by an electoral system built on the proportional principle rather than the winner-take-all principle of plurality systems (Weaver, 1982, pp. 1, 7).

Indeed, Hamilton's experience in the PR period shows evidence of some cooling off of social conflict. Campaigning in PR elections by candidates angling for second- and lower-choice votes was somewhat muted. Before and after PR, more contentious campaigning prevailed. Minority representation guaranteed by PR may have vented social conflict through the council, conflict that plurality systems before and after PR suppressed.

The transfer of preferential votes is the heart of the PR system. Its financial costs are minor when viewed as a fraction of the cost of the entire electoral process; but PR has political costs as well, such as delays at the counting stage and controversies generated by candidates (and interest groups they represent) who consider themselves disadvantaged by transfer votes. Political reformers in Hamilton failed to educate the public as to the *how* and *why* of PR, and therefore it was ultimately rejected. Among the American cities that used PR, only in Cambridge, Massachusetts, did the proponents of PR conduct a significant educational campaign, and there PR is still in use (Weaver, 1982, 1986).

The Hamilton electorate that adopted PR in 1926 was considerably smaller and more homogeneous than the body of voters that abandoned the system in 1960. Yet this latter decision seems to reflect not so much public discontent as it does the enmities of political leaders who lost out in the transfer-vote dynamics of PR.

The composition of the electorate had changed by 1960, but despite PR opponents' rhetoric about confusion, voters exhibited considerable continuity in local political participation. Ironically, the antiestablishment forces, representing generally lower-status groups, were approaching an effective level of competitiveness in their use of slating strategies under PR when disappointed political leaders launched their final attack on the system. At that point the fainthearted support of PR's friends left it vulnerable.

However, the demise of PR in Hamilton can be attributed primarily to the political consequences of transfer votes giving expression to voters' political values more effectively than had the previous electoral system. PR was not defeated by the inability of voters to use it, or by multipartyism or by governmental indecision, but by being successful at what it was designed to do: reflect voters' values and preferences.

EIGHT

■ ■ ■

PR in Toledo: The Neglected Stepchild of Municipal Reform

Dennis M. Anderson

> Basically the city manager plan has much to commend it. Under such a plan there is much greater promise and opportunity for stability, for continuity of policy, and for long range planning, than under any charter which requires the election of the city's chief executive every two years. . . . I regret that next Tuesday we shall not have an opportunity to vote for a city manager charter providing for a council elected at least in part by districts, and without the bewildering, fortuitous, and un-American features of proportional representation.
>
> Walter F. Brown, *Toledo Blade*, 1934

TOLEDO'S ADOPTION of proportional representation elections for its city council grew out of the city's Progressive tradition of municipal reform. More immediately, reform was precipitated by corruption and incompetence in local affairs. In 1934 the voters of Toledo adopted PR/STV as an integral feature of the charter for a city manager plan. Eight PR elections were conducted over a 16-year period. As in other Ohio PR cities, politicians who had lost power repeatedly challenged Toledo's new electoral system, achieving its repeal in 1949.

An industrial city with a population of 290,718 in 1930 (U.S. Census, 1930), Toledo had known earlier waves of municipal reform under the leadership at the turn of the century of Mayor Samuel M. "Golden Rule" Jones (1897–1904) and his Progressive successor, Brand Whitlock (1905–13). Viewing political parties as vehicles of special interest domination and corrupt practices, these early reform mayors pursued nonpartisanship as their chief goal. Whitlock organized his own Independent Party, which became a proving ground for future reformers, but it did not survive his departure in 1913 from Toledo politics (Emch, 1938, p. 188).

Statewide adoption in 1912 of a home rule amendment to the Ohio Constitution, however, set in motion forces to elect a charter commission whose work would lead to the adoption of a new city charter. Approved in 1914, the new charter provided for nonpartisan primaries and elections for 20 ward-elected members of council and a separately elected mayor (Stinchcombe, 1968, p. 37).

By the 1920s, the Lucas County Republican Party, led by Chairman Walter F. Brown, had gained control of the council and municipal administration. Public discontent over cost overruns on uncompleted bond issues led to new demands for reform of city government. In addition, successful campaigns to adopt the city manager system in Cleveland, Cincinnati, and Hamilton in the mid-1920s served to encourage Toledo reformers and to legitimize the idea of a city manager (Emch, 1938, p. 121; Jones, 1954, p. 31).

The Adoption of Proportional Representation

Conditions seemed ripe for reform in the late 1920s. By 1927 an independent City Manager League (CML) had taken shape, and it vied with a Republican Party slate for places on a new charter commission. All candidates, however, were pledged in advance to support the city manager plan. Proportional representation was not an issue at this time, but it was an idea circulating among civic elites. A committee of the Toledo Chamber of Commerce recommended the adoption of both the city manager plan and PR. After addresses by three nationally well-known advocates of municipal reform, Augustus R. Hatton, Leonard D. White, and Lent D. Upson, the chamber of commerce endorsed these recommendations by a vote of 985 to 34.

Elected to the 1927 charter commission were eight City Manager League candidates and three members of the Republican slate who had also been endorsed by the league. The commission proposed to the voters a plan calling for a city manager and a small council elected at-large by the single transferable vote system of proportional representation (PR/STV). The council was to select one of its own members as mayor. Although the commission was unanimous in favor of the city manager plan, its vote on PR was 8 to 4; the four who voted against PR also opposed the final draft of the charter submitted to voters.

The city council promptly submitted an alternate charter revision plan to the voters, featuring a city manager but retaining ward elections in council's hands for all but one at-large seat. This competing proposal introduced confusion into the campaign for reform and, not surprisingly, in the November 1928 election, both plans were defeated. The Proportional Representation League, which had sent staff to assist in the Toledo campaign, maintained that real majority support for the reforms had been obscured by the Republican organization's "political trick" of placing on the ballot at the same time the second charter amendment for a city manager plan (*PRR*, 1928, 89:3–4). Voters could vote for either, neither, or both of the plans, but because it was said in the campaign that a vote "yes" for one's second choice would help defeat one's first choice, few people voted for both (table 8.1). The large number of candidates and referenda on 10 separate ballots in this presidential year also took a toll on support for reform (Shenefield, 1929, pp. 735–37).

In 1931, undeterred by defeat, Toledo reformers again submitted to the voters a city manager plan, this time with a council to be elected in part at-large and in part by wards. Again, the council submitted an alternative proposal calling for a city manager but making no change in the now 21-member ward-elected council. Once more both plans were rejected. Of the four city charter amendments defeated by Toledo voters in 1928 and 1931, the proposal that included proportional representation elections received the highest approval, at 41% of those voting (table 8.1). This suggests that PR was not necessarily an impediment to obtaining public approval of the city manager system.

The Great Depression hit Toledo with devastating impact. The city defaulted on its bonds, curtailed or suspended city services, and paid its employees in scrip. Now economy became an important watchword for reform efforts. In late 1933 the *Toledo Blade* ran a series of articles supporting the manager plan. The City Manager League organized a broad-based citizens' group to promote a new city charter amendment. In 1934 seniors at the University of Toledo, under the leadership of political science professor O. Garfield Jones, gathered over 25,000 signatures to place a charter amendment on the ballot by initiative petition. Since these depression-era students "lacked funds," the petition campaign was their departing gift, "a spiritual rather than a concrete memorial," one that would "morally strengthen" the bond between the university and the city (Jones, 1954, p. 51). The proposal embodied the city manager plan and a nine-member council elected at-large by PR.

The City Manager League led a formidable campaign. The charter amendment was supported by the civic establishment and endorsed by the *Toledo Blade*. Debate this time focused on the size of the council

TABLE 8.1
SUMMARY OF VOTES ON TOLEDO CITY CHARTER
AMENDMENTS, 1914–1949

Year	Proposal	For	Against	% For
1914	Elected chief executive Council elected by wards Nonpartisan ballot	21,028	16,466	56
1928	City manager Small council, by PR	36,445	52,604	41
	City manager Council of 11, 10 by districts and 1 at-large	27,634	59,232	32
1931	City manager Council of 9, 5 by districts and 4 at-large	23,493	39,359	37.5
	City manager Council of 21, by wards	22,712	39,701	26.5
1934	City manager Council of 9, by PR	33,229	28,014	54
1935	Elected chief executive Council of 21, by wards	18,338	27,624	40
1937	City manager Council of 21, by wards	19,150	37,107	34
1945	City manager Council of 9, at-large without a primary	21,441	38,481	36
1946	Elected chief executive Council of 21, by wards	40,076	48,565	46
1949	City manager Council of 9, at-large with a primary to reduce candidates to 18	56,751	30,378	65

Source: Lucas County Board of Elections, *The Abstract,* 1914–49.

and the method of its election. Donovan Emch, a founding member of the CML, believed that by now the voters were well-educated about the manager plan. The students had answered voters' questions when they canvassed door-to-door with their petitions, and press coverage was positive (Emch, 1938, pp. 145–46, 149).

Opponents focused on proportional representation. The Central Labor Union was opposed to any form of at-large elections. The

Republican organization did not oppose the new charter at the outset, but late in the campaign Chairman Brown praised the manager plan while denouncing the proposed election system as "un-American." The embattled ancien régime in city hall conducted a covert campaign against the proposal, urging city workers and their families "to vote against the amendment" because their "jobs probably would be abolished or their wages reduced if the manager plan carried" (Emch, 1938, pp. 145–46, 149; Johnson, 1934, p. 554).

The financial difficulties of the city, however, and the ineffective administrations of recent mayors had inspired a "throw-out-the-old, try-anything-new" mood among the voters (Emch, 1938, pp. 149–90). In the November 1934 election, the new proposal won approval from 54% of the voters, and the first of eight PR/STV elections was held in 1935.

Repeal Issues and the Abandonment of PR

During the 15 years of PR elections in Toledo, repeal efforts were mounted by opponents on five occasions: 1935, 1937, 1945, 1946, and 1949. After successfully fending off four repeal attempts, the friends of reform went down to defeat in 1949. By then, the repeated repeal campaigns themselves had made PR controversial.

1935. Even before the new charter could take effect, the outgoing ward-elected city council called for a special election the following spring to repeal the new city charter. This first repeal issue pitted the City Manager League against the remnants of the old city power structure and its allies whom it had vanquished just five months earlier. Mayor Solon T. Klotz and the City and County Employees Union focused their fire on PR, claiming that it was a "lottery system of voting" and renewing the charge that it was "un-American." Some elements of organized labor attacked the City Manager League as "backed by vested interests with ulterior motives." The credibility of these opponents, however, was damaged by the revelation of fraudulent signatures on repeal petitions. The newspapers vigorously attacked the opponents of reform.

This first attempt to repeal the newly adopted city charter was beaten back by a three to two margin (table 8.1). The charter's defenders attributed their victory to the CML's vigorous campaign; continuing concern about the "deplorable condition of municipal affairs," which had prevailed the previous November; and indignation over the "extra cost of an unnecessary special election" (Gladieux, 1935, p. 357; Stinchcombe, 1968, p. 42; Report of Campaign, 1935).

1937. The second repeal attempt separated the city manager from PR. The city manager would be retained, while the small PR-elected council would by replaced by a return to the old 21-member ward-elected council. A special election was called for September 1937. Surprisingly, PR was a subordinate theme in news stories about this campaign. The size of city council was highlighted as the major issue. Fifteen of the 19 news stories on the special election that appeared from four days before to four days after the election contained no mention of PR whatsoever. In those mentioning PR, the drawbacks of ward elections were featured. Headlines also gave the impression that the two sides were arguing over the size of city council. The supporters of PR were referred to as "9-Man Council Supporters," supporters of the "9-Man City Charter," "The Manager Government," "The Manager League," or supporters of "The Edy Government," after John N. Edy, Toledo's first city manager (*Toledo Blade,* 1937: 4 Aug., pp. 8, 12; 13 Aug., pp. 1, 6; 16 Aug., p. 1; 26 Aug., sec. 2, p. 17; 27 Aug., p. 3; 6 Sept., p. 3). Opponents of PR, some of whom had been leaders of the 1935 repeal campaign, were labeled the "larger-Council Group," or the "Guitteau Group" after Josephine Guitteau, leader of the repeal forces.

There were, however, substantive arguments. Guitteau charged that under PR minorities would "dominate" the council. Furthermore, it was alleged that a larger council would be "more representative" and thus "more democratic." Although some pro-charter labor representatives contended that labor had received "a fair deal" under PR in other cities, most leaders of organized labor in Toledo argued that workers would fare better with a system of ward elections (*Toledo Blade,* 8 Sept. 1937, p. 15; 11 Sept. 1937, p. 5). Supporters of the CML viewed labor as greedy for more than the minority representation they could win in elections conducted by proportional representation (Emch, 1986).

The principal defense by City Manager League's spokesmen was that the repeal of PR (the "small 9-member council") would undermine the city manager. Although the proponents of repeal claimed they were not opposed to the city manager plan, reform forces argued that election of 21 council members from wards would bring back parochialism, log rolling, partisanship, and political interference with administration. Opposition to such "politics" was a major tenet of the creed of the national City Manager League. As the campaign arguments became simplified, PR's supporters and the newspapers were able to define the election as being about "good government" at "lower cost, higher efficiency," honest management, and a "successful drive against vice" (*Toledo Blade,* 18 Sept., 1937, p. 10).

The league and the newspapers were also successful in pinning negatives to the opposition. Guitteau was dubbed "Empress Josephine." She and William Cahill, one of her chief deputies and a former Ku Klux Klan leader, were labeled "enemies of good government." Repeal forces were alleged to be fronts for gambling interests and the "old gang" at city hall, which would reinstate "boss rule, waste, inefficiency, extravagance, nepotism and graft" (*Toledo Blade,* 11 Sept. 1937, p. 9; 31 Aug. 1937; *Toledo Times,* 9 Sept. 1937; *Toledo News-Bee,* 26 Aug. 1937, p. 6).

The new charter survived the challenge by nearly a two to one ratio. Repeal forces lost in 17 of the 21 wards. The only wards carried by repeal were populated primarily by Polish, Hungarian, and African-American voters who, theoretically, would gain representation through PR (table 8.2). But the CML had not mobilized minorities, nor had issues of representation been prominent in the debate. The pro-reform forces were so successful in tying PR (through the small council) to the manager that their overwhelming victory was only tenuously connected to PR itself. This was strikingly illustrated by a post-election headline that erroneously trumpeted "$12,884 Spent to Retain City Manager Form!" (*Toledo Blade,* 2 Oct. 1937, p. 3).

The CML's effectiveness as a municipal political party was tested and honed in these two repeal attempts. As a campaign organization, the league could boast of a mailing list of 4,000 people, 1,500 dues-paying members, and the ability to field over 500 volunteer campaign workers (Emch, 1938, p. 187; Stinchcombe, 1968, p. 43). CML endorsees made up a majority of the first two PR-elected city councils. In 1935, in a field of 58 candidates, the CML elected 5 of its 9 endorsees to the first PR council, 8 of 12 endorsees in 1937, and 4 of 9 in 1939, only 2 of whom were incumbents.

Candidates endorsed by the league were called upon to pledge themselves "to abide by all the principles of good government . . . under the city manager-small council charter." Typical of the self-confidence of the reformers is a 1939 report that "Dr. A. R. Hatton, authority on city manager government . . . explained to the prospective councilmen methods and practices which should be followed to obtain the best results from city manager government" (*National Municipal Review [NMR],* 1939, 28:747).

The CML was an effective municipal political party that also functioned as an alert guardian of good government, of which the city manager system was deemed a major and PR a minor part (as confirmed by the omission of PR from the pledge). When Edy, the first city manager, accused two newly elected council members of interfering with administration, the press and the league mobilized public support to ensure his continuing autonomy. Again, the league mobilized the city's establishment on Edy's behalf when Addison Q. Thacher, a veteran council member and pre-PR mayor, introduced a resolution to remove him. Edy was an outside professional hired in accordance with the mandate of the new charter. Civic and service clubs and churches passed resolutions denouncing the Thacher motion. At a council meeting attended by an overflow crowd of the manager's supporters, the motion was defeated by a vote of two to seven. Thacher was denounced in the press as "a front for selfish, greedy men . . . planning . . . to reestablish the spoils system" (Willoughby, 1938, pp. 505–6, 517).

The association of the reform ethos with civic pride was evident in a "municipal exhibit" sponsored by the CML and the Toledo League of Women Voters in June 1938. Thousands of citizens toured public buildings and exhibits, and listened to radio shows with question-and-answer sessions on "government in action." The manager addressed a crowd of 2,000, on hand for the exhibition's closing, and Percy C. Jones, son of the late mayor, "Golden Rule" Jones, presented certificates of merit to longtime city employees. It was reported that the "municipal exhibit reflected the pride of the citizens as well as city employees in the quality of city government" (Seed 1938, pp. 400–404, 428).

Toledo's reform spirit persisted through the late 1930s and early 1940s. Although CML endorsees won only four seats in 1939, a league-endorsed council member was elected mayor, the fifth vote coming from a council member who had won the league's endorsement in 1937. After the 1941 election, in which the league again won control of council, public hearings were held on a proposal to resubmit the electoral system to the voters. The council tabled the proposal on the grounds that those who wanted another vote on the issue could and should obtain it by initiative petition. In 1943 the election of three new members resulted in a diverse council that was representative of most areas of the city. Most of the council candidates known to be opposed to proportional representation went down to defeat (NMR, 1944, 33:100).

By 1941 CML supporters seem to have felt secure about the reforms embodied in the 1934 charter, including PR (Yager, 1984; Britt, 1984).[1] During that critical year, the City Manager League ceased to function as a municipal political party and transformed itself into the Toledo Municipal League (TML), a civic research organization eligible to

1937. Courtesy of the Corporation for Effective
Government, Toledo

receive tax-exempt contributions (*NMR,* 1942, 31:57–58). In retrospect this was a watershed event, signaling the loss of an organized and politically active constituency for reform.

1945. After World War II, the challenge was posed again by organized labor. As part of a larger strategy to test its electoral strength, in 1945 the local Political Action Committee of the CIO launched a repeal campaign. Its proposed amendment retained the city manager but provided for the plurality/at-large election of a nine-member council (9X) without a primary to narrow the field of candidates. Although this amendment provided a frugal alternative to PR, the omission of a primary proved to be ill-advised. Defenders of PR elections quickly pointed out that such an election, especially in a crowded field of candidates, could result in winners chosen by a very small segment of the electorate.

Although by 1945 many voters seemed to be looking for an alternative to PR, the "cure" of a plurality/at-large election with no primary looked "as bad or worse than the illness it seeks to treat" (*Toledo Blade,* 2 Nov. 1945, p. 22). Press reports suggest that PR was given a temporary extension "until we find something better." There were frequent calls for studies to find something better after the election (Jewell, 1945, p. 15; *Toledo Blade,* 23 Oct. 1945, p. 3).

Reporting on electoral system issues had grown far more sophisticated over the decade, as the question of an alternative method kept coming back to the voters, and by 1945 PR was no longer bathed in the protective glow of reform. Although nearly two-thirds of the voters opposed the one-stage plurality/at-large election, defeat of the issue was less a resounding endorsement of PR than a practical assessment of a flawed alternative. A heavy agenda on the ballot—several bond issues and tax levies, four-year terms for council members, and the council elections themselves—did not distract the electorate from this decision (*Toledo Blade,* 19 Oct.–3 Nov. 1945).

1946. After the 1945 election the city council responded to perceived public dissatisfaction with city government in general and PR in particular by ordering the city's Commission on Publicity and Efficiency to study the charter and to recommend needed changes. However, before this commission could act, Josephine Guitteau and her husband, William B. Guitteau, longtime opponents of city manager government, filed an initiative petition for a charter amendment. This initiative, presented to the voters in November 1946, proposed the elective mayoralty and a 21-member ward-elected city council. This was the first attempt since 1935 to restore the old order in its entirety.

Defenders of the existing charter organized themselves into the Committee Against the Guitteau Amendment and successfully characterized the proposal as "a return to the spoils system, to graft, waste, log-rolling and lax law enforcement" (Jenks, 1946, p. 1). Once again, voters who may not have supported PR opposed the issue because they disliked the alternative. There were also misgivings about the campaign's sponsors, the Guitteaus. However, an ambivalent defense of PR was mounted. The co-chairman of the committee, Edward A. DeAngelo, said he "would not oppose elimination of PR if the essential features of the present charter were preserved" (Jenks, 1946). This indication that PR was no longer considered an "essential feature" of the system of governance did not bode well for its future. Still, the committee conducted an ambitious campaign, raising and spending more money than did the repeal advocates, whose campaign was handled almost entirely by the Guitteaus (*Toledo Blade,* 6 Nov. 1946, p. 1). Although the Guitteau plan was defeated, it won a surprising 46% of the vote, the highest support for repeal to date (see table 8.1).

In the meantime, a changing partisan landscape introduced a new factor into Toledo's municipal politics. The major parties were relatively inactive in Toledo through the 1930s, although the Republican Party was clearly dominant. After the adoption of the new charter in 1934, the Democratic Party had initially endorsed slates that included not only Democrats but also Independents and Republicans, on the grounds that this position was consistent with the nonpartisan character of municipal elections. Union organizing, however, and particularly the Democratic loyalties of the United Auto Workers, stimulated greater activity in both parties as links between local politics and state and national issues developed.

By the early 1940s partisanship was growing more open in Toledo's "nonpartisan" council elections. In the 1946 repeal campaign, although most citizen attention was focused on the election of county, state, and federal officials, neighborhood workers of both parties tried to persuade regular party voters to oppose PR (Jones, 1954, p. 57). As a rising force, Democrats led the way in tearing aside the facade of nonpartisanship. By the mid-1940s, local Democrats were campaigning openly for a council slate of partisan loyalists.

The Democratic Party had never actively supported PR in Toledo, although individual Democratic council members who won election under PR in the early 1940s were cognizant of its benefit to minority party representation. In 1947 Democrats won control of city council for the first time. During the years of local Republican hegemony, majority party power had been wielded in council, but in a covert fashion. This situation changed as the Democratic Party took control. The selection of the vice mayor, for example, became a strictly partisan vote in the two councils in which the Democrats held a majority, and once in the majority, the party took over leadership of the opposition to PR.

1949. By 1949 reformers had abandoned PR as an essential element in their package of "good government" reforms; but it was John P. Kelly, chairman of the Lucas County Democratic Party, who sponsored this final and successful challenge to proportional representation. According to Kelly, the local Republican Party wanted to join the Democrats in this attack on PR but were told not to by the state Republican organization (Kelly, 1984).

The 1949 plan called for retaining the nine-member at-large council, but for nominating candidates in a nonpartisan primary and electing them by plurality voting. While the Republican Party remained publicly neutral, organized labor and both newspapers joined the Democrats in urging the repeal of PR. A few individuals who had been associated with the former City Manager League spoke in favor of retaining PR, but no committee of citizens was organized to defend it. The Toledo League of Women Voters was the lone organization to oppose repeal.

In calling for a primary to reduce the field of candidates to 18, the 1949 plan avoided the flaw of the 1945 proposal. Furthermore, unlike the 1946 alternative, this plan was not vulnerable to the charges of parochialism associated with ward elections. The reformers could be confident that the citywide perspective would be preserved. The issue of the campaign could not be framed as "good government" versus the spoilsmen, a successful theme in earlier repeal initiatives, because PR was now bereft of its critical linkage to the city manager plan. The verve and passion of the "good government" jihads of 1935 and 1937, waning in 1945 and 1946, had vanished by 1949. Newspaper accounts of the campaign portray a tepid contest (Douglas, 1949, sec. 1, p. 3; Jenks, 1949a, p. 1; Jenks, 1949b, sec. 2, pp. 1, 3).

The old arguments for PR were, however, given full airing: PR guaranteed minority representation and made 90% of voters' ballots effective in electing one winner. Its repeal would put an end to the opportunities of independent candidates, destroy nonpartisan city government, and cause the return of mismanagement and the spoils system to city hall. These arguments from the shrunken ranks of its defenders had lost their power.

The Democratic Party claimed that PR was "a phony way of voting . . . [because] all a voter's votes should count, not just one or two choices." Not every ballot cast for "a good man" is counted, the party charged. Years later party chairman Kelly, basing his objections on its complexity and unfairness, would deny that his opposition to PR involved party advantage. "I never could get the point of it," he said (Kelly, 1984).

The *Toledo Blade* turned traditional good government appeals against PR by contending that it encouraged "lax administration" because citizens could not hold responsible council members who were elected by only a few thousand voters. Whereas PR's defenders assumed the superiority of nonpartisanship, its opponents (ignoring the nominally nonpartisan character of Toledo municipal elections since 1914) asserted that PR undermined party responsibility by encouraging each candidate to run on his own. The "hocus pocus" of the long count and PR's alleged complexity as a "highly technical device" were denounced, and PR was labeled a "lottery" because of the random drawing of surplus votes in the transfer process.

Contemporary newspaper accounts provide little evidence for the empirical propositions in these campaign arguments. For example, PR had not prevented either party from running well-publicized slates, as both were doing by the late 1940s. Furthermore, the ballot language was both imprecise and flagrantly biased. The amendment did not juxtapose a choice for voters between plurality/at-large election and PR, which was also conducted at-large. Instead, the ballot defined a vote "FOR THE AMENDMENT" as one that "provides for the election by popular vote and eliminates proportional representation (PR)"; the alternative box "AGAINST THE AMENDMENT" was simply explained, "retain proportional representation (PR)." PR's enemies had gained control of the definition of terms. So one-sided was the debate that repeal forces won acceptance of their slogans, "Popular Voting," and "PV versus PR," in the media. The oversimplification of campaign rhetoric put a complex system such as PR at a competitive disadvantage.

Not surprisingly, the plurality/at-large election, mislabeled "Popular Voting" (PV), buried PR decisively with a 65% majority (see table 8.1). The sorrowful words of Ronald E. Gregg, executive secretary of the Toledo Municipal League, were not far from the mark:

> The election system change is simply the natural turn of the events under existing circumstances, for political power never goes begging.
> Briefly, the reformers tired, allowed the City Manager League to die, and did not rally against the accumulated opponents, and more voters with short memories came to believe that they were as confused about P.R. as they were told by newspapers and politicians these last three years. (Gregg, 1950, p. 49)

TABLE 8.2
Vote by Groups on Proportional Representation in Toledo (%)

Group	Adoption, 1934		Repeal,[a] 1935		Repeal,[a] 1937		Repeal, 1945			Repeal,[a] 1946			Repeal, 1949		
	Pro-PR	Anti	Pro-PR	Anti	Pro-PR	Anti	Pro-PR	Anti	Roll-Off	Pro-PR	Anti	Roll-Off	Pro-PR	Anti	Roll-Off
Citywide	54	46	60	40	66	34	64	36	-15.8	54	46	-5.4	35	65	-6.3
Polish, Wards 4 and 14	26.8	73.2	26.2	73.8	28.1	71.9	67.6	32.4	-21.2	31.8	68.2	-6.1	36.9	63.1	-6.9
Hungarian, Ward 20	38.8	61.2	41	59	51.5	48.5	63	37	-15.6	41.1	58.9	-5.5	29.3	70.7	-6.1
Black, Ward 8	36.9	63.1	35	65	36.2	63.8	47.8	52.2	-46.0	61.1	38.9	-12.9	56.4	43.6	-23.6
"Silk Stocking," Wards 10 and 12	75	25	83.5	16.5	86.3	13.7	70.3	29.7	-9.4	68.6	31.4	-3.9	38.3	61.7	-4.0

Source: Calculated from Lucas County Board of Elections, The Abstract, 1934–49.
Notes: A "Pro-PR" vote is a "no" vote on the repeal proposals. "Roll-off" is the percentage of voters who received ballots in the election but failed to vote on these proposed city charter amendments pertaining to the method of electing city council.
[a] The proposed alternative to proportional representation was election by wards as opposed to plurality/at-large election of council.

In retrospect, when the reformers put the City Manager League out of business as a municipal political party in 1941, they acted from complacency and perhaps boredom with their exotic electoral step-child. Their growing indifference could be attributed in part to migration to the suburbs of middle-class people who had provided much of the early support for PR (Emch, 1986).[2] Opposition leader Kelly agreed, describing the supporters of PR derisively as people from "Sylvania, Ottawa Hills and Perrysburg," upscale suburbs of Toledo. By the 1940s, he noted with an overtone of class antagonism, PR lacked significant support among "real" Toledoans (Kelly, 1984).

Although the ardor of PR's friends had cooled, the enmity of organized labor and the political parties had not waned. The parties had an obvious interest in opposing a system designed to enhance the ability of independents or a motivated single interest group to carve out a share of power on city council. Union and party leaders succeeded in casting PR as alien and strange, whereas its defense was generalized to "good government" in 1937, conceded to be merely a "lesser evil" than its alternative in 1945, and detached in 1946 from the protection of the city manager plan.

PR failed in Toledo because its original supporters failed to develop either an enduring reform constituency or other constituencies among minority groups that benefited from PR's electoral opportunities. When the league mobilized the public against council members who interfered in administration or proposed to fire the city manager, PR was not mentioned. Only incidental references to PR appear in accounts of the "municipal exhibit" of 1938 in which public enthusiasm for reform ran high. These instances illustrate the subordinate position of proportional representation in the Toledo reform package (Crane, 1935, pp. 79–80, 97).

Still, PR had potential constituencies with a vested interest in its survival. The electoral record of the repeal campaigns by identifiable ward-based groups is shown in table 8.2. Support for the reform package including PR was strong among voters in middle- to upper-middle-class wards during the early PR elections. This early backing, more than 20 percentage points higher than the city average, presumably reflects the values of clean, efficient, neutral, expert municipal government associated with reform. By 1945, when the campaign focus is less on "good government" versus self-serving spoilsmen and more on the pros and cons of different election systems, the support for PR from these wards drops to a level only six percentage points higher than for the city as a whole. This decline in middle-class support heralds detachment of PR from the earlier reform tradition as well as the waning of the reform impulse itself.

Other constituencies, however, could have been mobilized on behalf of an electoral system that effectively guaranteed minority representation. Voters of Polish origin are most distinctive among Toledo's white ethnics. Concentrated in two geographically separated neighborhoods, they were subject to prejudice and discrimination by the native white majority. The minutes of early meetings of the City Manager League show concern about developing support among white ethnics, and the league endorsed both Polish and Italian candidates for council in the first two PR elections. Nonetheless, Polish voters were strongly opposed to PR in the three repeal elections when a return to ward elections was the alternative, even though their residential dispersal made success unlikely. In 1945, however, faced with a choice of PR or a 9X system, the Polish wards favored retention of PR by percentages higher than or equal to the citywide average. PR victories by Polish candidates must have contributed to this outcome. Similarly, voters of Hungarian extraction who lived in an eastern section of the city, primarily the Twentieth Ward, gave majority support to PR only after election of one of their own. By 1949, however, the support for PR collapsed among ethnic Toledoans as it did among the white population generally (table 8.2).

As in other northern cities, housing segregation in Toledo led to the concentration of African Americans in a few wards, primarily the Eighth. No black council member had been elected, however, in the ward elections of the pre-PR period. Constituting only five percent of the population of Toledo in the 1930s, under PR the black community would be unlikely to reach the minimum required total vote for one council member (one-tenth plus one on a nine-member council) without white support. It is not surprising then that in 1934 almost two-thirds of the voters in Ward 8 opposed the new charter, which included PR elections, and favored its repeal in 1935 and 1937. However, it was a much reduced majority that supported repeal in 1945, the critical year in which the first African-American member, James B. Simmons Jr., was elected to the Toledo City Council.

Although black voters came to support PR in the end, Simmons believed that many had experienced confusion over the procedures for voting and counting PR ballots. His recollection is supported by the abstention of a substantial minority of black voters in 1945, 1946, and 1949 on the issue of repeal of PR, voters who nevertheless cast votes

Walter F. Brown, 1931.
Courtesy of *The Cleveland
Press* Collection of the
Cleveland State University
Archives

James B. Simmons Jr., n.d.
Courtesy of the Cleveland
Public Library Photograph
Collection

on other issues and candidates (see "roll-off" column, table 8.2). Ward 8 abstentions dropped significantly, however, in 1946, following Simmons's 1945 victory.

Simmons, an attorney, supported proportional representation, believing that it would be the key to black representation. At the same time he recognized the black community's enthusiasm for ward elections. Under any at-large system, he said, African-American voters feared that "nobody would represent them as individuals" (Simmons, 1984). Even so, in the repeal referendum of 1946, with a 21-ward election plan as the alternative, Ward 8 registered its highest level of support for PR, with 61% voting against repeal. The impact of Simmons's victory on the black community's perception of PR was clear. In 1949, by which time the African-American population had grown to eight percent of the total (U.S. Census, 1950), Ward 8 again turned out a majority in favor of PR. With the plurality/at-large election as the alternative, the black community was the only identifiable group of voters in Toledo that supported PR when the majority finally rejected it (table 8.2).

City Council Elections and Toledo Politics

Citizen Participation

The effect of PR on citizen participation was an issue widely discussed. Proponents expected voter turnout to rise because PR's ability to promote group representation would mobilize previously underrepresented clusters of the population. Moreover, up to 90% of the ballots would count toward the election of a council member, unlike in the former plurality system in which up to half of the votes could be wasted—that is, cast for a loser in a winner-take-all election. Republicans in Democratic wards and Democrats in Republican wards, for example, would have a new incentive to go to the polls. Opponents, on the other hand, feared that the unfamiliarity of the new system would raise the motivational threshold that prospective voters would have to surmount. Other elements of the new charter could have depressing consequences for turnout as well. Although Toledo had absorbed the depoliticizing effect of nonpartisan elections two decades earlier, the city manager feature of the 1934 charter wiped out the excitement of a mayoral election, and the at-large character of PR destroyed the intimacy of neighborhood politics that had prevailed in ward contests.

To what extent did Toledo's different electoral systems enhance or diminish participation of the citizenry at the ballot box? Table 8.3 shows voter turnout as a percentage of the adult population (age 21 and over) for Toledo city council, presidential, and congressional elections before, during, and after the period of proportional representation.

Toledo's voter turnout in presidential and congressional elections rose, as did national turnout with the New Deal realignment, a phenomenon particularly marked in the industrial cities of the East and Midwest. Turnout in Toledo municipal elections, in contrast, dropped to 40% during the PR period from a pre-PR average of 47% of the adult population. Moreover, the discrepancy between Toledo's municipal and national election turnouts is greater during the PR era than during the pre-PR era. Indeed, Toledoans' pre-PR turnout in city council elections was actually six percentage points higher than turnout in the pre-PR congressional elections. During the PR period congressional elections drew a turnout five percentage points above municipal elections. The decline in turnout for Toledo city council elections between the last ward-elected council and the first PR election in 1935 was nearly 14 percentage points. In the first six elections conducted under PR from 1935 to 1945, turnout remained in

TABLE 8.3
TOLEDO MUNICIPAL VOTER TURNOUT, 1926–1957 (%)

| | *Type of Election* | | |
	City Council	*Presidential*	*Congressional*
Pre-PR[a] (1926–34)			
	1927 46.0		1926 35.7
	1929 46.0	1928 60.6	
	1931 45.6		1930 42.0
	1933 51.4	1932 53.4	
			1934 44.9
Mean	47.3	57.0	41.2
PR/STV[b] (1935–49)			
	1935 37.0	1936 59.0	
	1937 33.2		1938 47.8
	1939 46.2	1940 66.9	
	1941 35.3		1942 38.7
	1943 35.5	1944 65.0	
	1945 36.8		1946 48.8
	1947 46.5	1948 62.3	
	1949 47.3		
Mean	39.9	63.3	45.1
Post-PR[c] (1950–57)			
	1951 38.6		1950 55.0
	1953 46.4	1952 74.6	
	1955 45.7		1954 52.1
	1957 44.7	1956 68.9	
Mean	43.8	71.8	53.6

Notes: Voter turnout is measured by percentage of population age 21 and over that voted. U.S. Bureau of the Census, 1930, 1940, 1950. For the years between censuses, the eligible electorate is calculated by linear interpolation. This calculation assumes a constant rate of growth within each decade. The number of voters is taken from the Lucas County Board of Elections, *The Abstract,* 1926–57.

[a]Large ward-elected council; directly elected mayor.
[b]Small PR/at-large-elected council; council-elected mayor.
[c]Small plurality/at-large-elected council; council-elected mayor.

the mid-30% range rising above 35% only in 1939 when a statewide pension referendum stirred unusual interest. In the 1947 and 1949 PR elections, when the political parties reactivated their participation in municipal contests, local turnout rose again, reaching the level of congressional turnout in nonpresidential years.

In the post-PR period, with the implementation of plurality/at-large council elections, another sharp drop in turnout occurred, this time nine percentage points below the last PR election. Some observers attributed this drop to a heavy, unseasonable snowstorm on election day. In the subsequent three plurality/at-large elections, turnout rose moderately so that an average turnout of about 44% of the voting-age population characterized the post-PR period. This level of participation fell midway between the higher level of pre-PR and the lower turnout of the PR years.

The drop in municipal turnout during the PR period suggests that substantial numbers of voters found the new system of proportional representation daunting, particularly in contrast with the familiar pre-PR ward system. Except in 1939, turnout persisted at a modest level, between 33.2% and 37.6% through 1945. Toledo voters apparently grew comfortable with at-large voting during the PR years, however, since the last two PR elections and all but one of the post-PR plurality/at-large elections brought to the polls numbers comparable to three of the four pre-PR (ward) elections. Since by 1947 PR was under serious political challenge, the rise in turnout would appear attributable more to the resumption of partisan activity in local politics than to acceptance of proportional representation.[3]

Two other factors might plausibly account for some of the turnout decline associated with five of the eight PR elections. These are the disruptions caused by World War II, and the removal of the election of the mayor from the ballot with the implementation of the city manager plan. Upon further exploration, neither factor is persuasive.

Because of the mobility of workers in war industries and of armed service personnel and their families, World War II is often cited as a cause of low voter turnout in the United States during the war years. In Toledo, however, municipal turnout had already dropped to the mid-30% range in three of the four PR elections preceding America's entry into the war. Furthermore, turnout in wartime city council elections (1943 and 1945) is only marginally lower than the average for the preceding four municipal elections (1935–41).

The end of direct popular election of the mayor in 1935 is another potentially depressing influence on turnout. Because the election of a single executive is easily understood and focuses the attention of the public and the media on a limited number of candidates (usually two), it could stimulate higher turnouts than elections that merely select members of a legislative body. However, with the restoration of a popularly elected mayor, 16 years after Toledo jettisoned PR, turnout did not increase. Surprisingly, voter participation actually dropped by six percentage points.[4] The failure of these alternative explanations of voter decline leaves PR as an apparent culprit.

We may conclude, then, that ending ward elections eliminated a stimulus to voter turnout. Furthermore, the greater gap between municipal and national elections during the PR era suggests that the amount of voter motivation required to participate in council elections was greater under PR than under ward-elected councils. The concurrent rise in voter turnout for congressional and presidential elections suggests that the municipal turnout decline in the PR era occurred among occasional or peripheral voters rather than within the core partisan electorate.

Another measure of participation is the number of candidates who contested council seats under each electoral system. Ward elections clearly outdrew the at-large systems in this respect. In the 20 pre-PR wards (21 after 1930), there was competition in about 90% of the wards in most elections; in many wards three candidates would run. This meant that typically 40 to 50 candidates ran for council. A neighborhood campaign, especially one based on traditional ward lines, facilitates candidacies built on modest resources. Neighborhood notables are advantaged, but new candidates do not face insuperable barriers.

In contrast, both PR and plurality/at-large systems require serious candidates to be able to raise resources for a citywide campaign. The prospective candidate under PR needs a solid base of first-place votes and, unless these constitute a quota, widespread name recognition in order to attract enough transfer votes to win. In post-PR plurality/at-large elections in which "first-choice votes" have no tangible meaning outside the mind of the voter, a committed base of single-minded supporters is less crucial than widespread favorable name recognition. By its very logic PR offers more incentive for well-defined interests and groups to field candidates of their own, because in a nine-seat contest 10% of the voters can elect their candidate. In contrast, in a plurality/at-large election where voters may use nine nonpreferential votes (9X), 10% of the votes will not elect a candidate. In a final field of 18 candidates in a 9X election, winning candidates need a majority or near majority of the votes to win. The candidates' own resources and strategic situation (in particular, the firmness of group support) will determine whether it is more difficult to get a first-choice vote from 10% of the electorate or to get 40% to 50% of the voters to give them one of nine votes.

For the eight council elections conducted under proportional representation, the average number of candidacies was 28, with a range of from 19 to 58. The average for the first eight elections under plurality/at-large was also 28, but with a narrower range of 23 to 36 candidates. Although there is no discernible difference in the averages, the greater range under PR suggests a greater variety of electoral opportunities and the likelihood that minority groups tried to launch their own candidates, or independents launched themselves, in the PR context.

In summary, PR in Toledo is associated with generally lower turnout, particularly in contrast with ward elections. The number of candidates was fewer under PR than in ward elections because of the significantly smaller council, and equal to the average under plurality/at-large. However there was a greater range in the number of candidates under PR than in the plurality/at-large elections that followed.

Winners and Losers: What Difference Does PR Make?

The municipal reformers who made PR part of their recipe for good government wanted to even the odds between the civic-minded but busy citizens and the ever-active but self-serving political bosses. A manipulation-proof election system such as proportional representation would put these two groups on a more nearly equal footing (Hallett, 1940, p. 33). Another concern of the early reformers was to achieve broad-based representation, presumably including all significant elements in the community. The analysis that follows is an examination of the characteristics of successful candidates under three electoral systems.

Characteristics of Council Winners

To compare the results of ward-based, PR/STV, and plurality/at-large elections for Toledo city council, demographic, political, and socioeconomic characteristics of members were collected from newspapers and other contemporary sources. Partisan affiliation and educational attainment for pre-PR council members were not reported in original sources, but summary data have been recalculated from tabulations in Bast (1973), and are shown in table 8.4, along with more complete data from the later councils.

Ohio was a predominantly Republican state from the Civil War to the New Deal, and not surprisingly its major cities, including Toledo, tended to elect Republicans to office. Municipal elections in Toledo had been nonpartisan since the adoption of the city's first home rule charter in 1914, but Democrats, Independents, and Progressive Republicans contended for council seats with the Republican organization's candidates. Bast reports that Republicans dominated the ward councils elected between 1919 and 1935 (including what is defined here as the pre-PR period), with more than four Republicans elected for every Democrat among those whose partisan affiliation is known. During these same years, three Socialists, one Communist, and one Independent were elected by plurality from wards (Bast, 1973, p. 36).

Commenting on the "halt in the influx of new and younger workers in the wards," George Jenks, political reporter for the *Blade,* saw the at-large feature of PR as a leading cause of the deterioration of both (major) party machines (*NML,* 1951, 40:493). Yet Republicans continued to dominate the council in the PR period, holding 64% of the seats. Democratic representation increased to 33% of the seats, and Democrats actually won a majority of seats on the last two PR councils (1947 and 1949). This accomplishment reflected the relatively late consolidation of the New Deal party realignment in this northwestern corner of Ohio (Sternsher, 1987, p. 96). In Toledo only one Independent was elected by PR, and no minor party candidate ever won in a PR election.

In the first post-PR election, the winner-take-all effect of plurality/ at-large voting in a low-turnout election enabled Republicans to take advantage of short-term political forces, sweeping all but one of the council seats; but the new Democratic majority regained control for the remainder of the post-PR period (see table 8.4).

The force of incumbency in council elections shows a somewhat different pattern. Nearly two-thirds of the council members who served in the PR period had immediately prior service, whereas only half of the pre- and post-PR plurality-elected councils consisted of incumbents. The partisan volatility found in occasional ward and 9X elections contrasts with the more gradual partisan turnover in the PR period, perhaps because stable group and personal loyalties were expressed in the voters' rankings of preferred candidates (table 8.4).

Education and occupation are used here as measures of socioeconomic status. Given the citywide character of both PR and post-PR electoral systems, and the greater resources needed for at-large races, higher socioeconomic status would be expected of council members in the later two periods. Indeed, raising the "quality" of people elected to council was an explicit goal of the early twentieth-century reformers as they battled the corruption and "lower-class" dominance of political machines. At the same time, educational levels have risen steadily in twentieth-century America; certainly not all change can be attributed to changing electoral systems.

TABLE 8.4

CHARACTERISTICS OF TOLEDO CITY COUNCIL MEMBERS, 1927–1957

Election Year	Political Variables				
	Political Party				Incumbent[a]
	Rep.	Dem.	Ind.	?	
1927					15
1929					12
1931					10
1933					4
Pre-PR					41
(N = 82)	37.3%[d]	8.0%	1.3%	53.4%	50%
1935	5	2	1	1	1
1937	7	2	0	0	6
1939	7	2	0	0	6
1941	7	2	0	0	8
1943	7	2	0	0	6
1945	5	4	0	0	7
1947	4	5	0	0	6
1949	4	5	0	0	7
PR	46	23	1	1	47
(N = 72)	63.9%	33.3%	1.4%	1.4%	65.3%
1951	8	1	0	0	4
1953	4	5	0	0	3
1955	3	6	0	0	8
1957	3	5	0	1	4
Post-PR	18	17	0	1	19
(N = 36)	50%	47.2%	0%	2.7%	52.7%

Sources: The Toledo City Journal; Toledo Blade, 4 Sept., 6 Oct., 13 Oct., 1937; Toledo Public Library, Local History and Genealogy Department: Name File, Toledo Bibliographical Scrapbooks, and Toledo History Scrapbooks—Elections.
[a]Incumbent is defined as a member who served on the previous council whether by appointment or election. Calculated from the *Toledo City Journal,* 1925–57.
[b]Occupational categories are Professional, Business, Blue-Collar, and Other. Most "Other" are government employees. For the 1931 and 1933 councils, see Emch (1938, p. 211).
[c]GR/HS combines council members with grade school and high school education; Coll. includes some college, college graduate, and post-graduate education. Toledo Public Library files include no information on years of schooling for pre-PR council members. The summary figures are from Bast (1973, p. 27).
[d]Percentages recalculated from Bast (1973, p. 36).

| Demographic Variables | | | | | | | | |
| Occupation[b] | | | | | Education[c] | | | Race: Black |
Prof.	Bus.	Blue	Other	?	GR/HS	Coll.	?	
0	4	5	0	11				0
0	10	4	0	6				0
1	18	2	0	0				0
1	14	5	1	0				0
· 2	46	16	1	17				0
2.4%	56.1%	19.5%	1.2%	20.7%	79%	21%	0%	0%
3	4	2	0	0	2	7	0	0
5	2	2	0	0	1	8	0	0
4	4	1	0	0	2	6	1	0
4	3	2	0	0	2	6	1	0
3	3	2	0	1	3	4	2	0
3	3	2	0	1	3	4	2	1
4	3	2	0	0	3	6	0	1
4	3	2	0	0	3	6	0	1
30	25	15	0	2	19	47	6	3
41.7%	34.7%	20.8%	0%	2.7%	26.4%	65.3%	8.3%	4%
2	5	0	0	2	2	7	0	0
4	2	0	2	1	2	7	0	1
5	1	0	1	2	1	7	1	1
6	2	0	0	1	0	9	0	1
17	10	0	3	6	5	30	1	3
47.2%	27.7%	0%	8.3%	16.7%	13.9%	83.3%	2.7%	8.3%

The rise in educational attainment of council members over the three electoral periods is indeed striking. In the ward elections of pre-PR, almost 79% of council members had not gone beyond high school, whereas only 21% had some college education, were college graduates, or had post-graduate education (Bast, 1973, p. 27). With PR elections, the educational level of council members soared to over 65% with higher education, whereas only 26% had high school level or less schooling. In post-PR, and with post–World War II educational opportunities, educational levels rose again. More than 83% of plurality/at-large-elected members had at least some higher education, whereas just 14% had high school or fewer years of schooling (table 8.4).

Occupational variations mirror to some degree the educational changes. A shift from primarily business to professional occupations marked the transition from ward to PR elections; with the implementation of plurality/at-large elections, the shift became more pronounced. Council members from blue-collar occupations constituted about one-fifth of the ward-elected and PR councils, but those disappeared completely in the post-PR period (table 8.4).

The categories in table 8.4 do not capture the rich contrasts in occupations between the large ward-elected councils and the post-1935 councils. On the last 21-member ward council, there were two confectioners, two barbers, a railroad clerk, a plumber, a draftsman, a machinist, an automobile club adjuster, a city railroad freight agent, and the chief deputy in the county recorder's office (Emch, 1938, pp. 210–11). These members were hardly drawn from the traditional civic elites.

The category of "business" also conceals some differences between the pre-PR and PR councils. Although there is considerable representation of retail merchants in all three types of councils, office managers swell the business category during the ward elections. Others among the neighborhood business people during the era of ward elections were the proprietor of a billiard parlor and the manager of a cab company.

The category "blue collar" masks another difference between ward elections and the PR elections that followed it. Under the ward system, blue-collar members were typically workers such as conductors, plumbers, and machinists; under PR, however, labor representatives tended to be union leaders, such as union business representatives and CIO officials. This was precisely the kind of change that PR's advocates believed would benefit both the city and workingmen. The fact that blue-collar representatives dropped from a fifth of the council in both earlier periods to none in plurality/at-large elections seems to demonstrate that the change in representative character was not merely the result of moving from ward to at-large campaigns but can be attributed to PR as well. Although PR elections were conducted at-large, the preferential ballot enabled organized labor to achieve a significant minority presence.

The concept of broadly based representation, promoted by the advocates of PR, was extended also in Toledo to ethnicity and race.

The election of Polish and African-American members to the city council was noted earlier. Ethnic names have not been reduced to numbers in table 8.4, but the category of race is more easily identified. In 1945 PR greatly facilitated the election of James Simmons Jr., the first African-American member of council. Since Toledo's black population made up only seven percent of the total at that time, Simmons had to attract white support to win. He was reelected twice by PR. In 1951 he lost under the new rules of the plurality/at-large electoral system. In part owing to publicity about the 1951 loss, but also because of the high regard in which he was held by the community, Simmons was reelected in the remaining plurality/at-large elections of the post-PR period. By this time endorsed by the *Blade,* the Democratic Party, the United Labor Committee, and by reformers formerly active with the City Manager League, he had won the support of a significant share of the white community (Stinchcombe, 1968, pp. 193–94).

In Toledo the implementation of PR did not signal a new day for the representation of women on council. No women had been elected by ward in the pre-PR period. During the eight PR elections, only four women were even candidates—out of 238 candidacies that were held by between 160 and 170 different people. Eighteenth place was the closest any female candidate came to victory. Indeed, the only woman whose name figured prominently in the history of city elections in Toledo during the PR era was Josephine Guitteau, an opponent of PR. The change from PR to 9X in 1951 brought no immediate change in the all-male character of the city council. Not until the 1960s were women represented on the Toledo council.

Although there are occasional references to individual women candidates in election news stories during the PR period, women's representation was not formally raised as an issue. The occasional woman candidate earned no feature stories, but references were made to activities of the "Women's Auxiliary" of the City Manager League. The low status of women in politics at that time is confirmed by this organizational separatism. The headlines of the day, such as the "9 Men Council" references of 1937, are also revealing. Without organization, independent resources, or a significant level of self-awareness, a group is unlikely to gain representation even from an election system designed to facilitate such an outcome.

The political, socioeconomic, and demographic data that characterized Toledo council members between 1927 and 1957 demonstrate the advantages of small-scale (ward) elections to lower-status candidates, and of at-large contests to candidates with greater resources. However, not all benefits flowing from electoral system change can be attributed to the citywide feature of PR and plurality/at-large elections. Polish, African-American, and labor union representation were all facilitated by PR and became to some degree an accepted part of the political landscape in Toledo because of access won in PR elections.

Transfer Votes and Political Advantage

Records at the Lucas County Board of Elections make it possible to analyze in detail the flow of transfer votes in Toledo's eight PR/STV elections. The transfer data tell us who benefited from transfers and how PR worked to provide seats for previously underrepresented groups. Table 8.5 lists all candidates elected to the Toledo city council during the PR period and lists the losers among the top nine on the first count who were displaced in the transfer process. "First-Place Vote Winners" (column 1) lists those who reached the quota on the first count, thereby winning election. This group constituted 25% of the 72 places filled by PR. "First Nine Finishers Dependent on Transfers" (column 2) lists those among the first nine who won by transfer votes; this category accounted for 62.5% of the total seats. "Come-from-Behind Transfer Winners" (column 3) did not place among the first nine but were advanced into the winning circle by transfer votes, only 12.5% of all seats. Finally, "Fast Starters, Transfer Losers" (column 4) were displaced by the "Come-from-Behind Transfer Winners," having placed among the first nine at the outset, only to lose by the end of the last transfer. The numbers following each name in columns 2 through 4 indicate the candidates' rank order of finish on the initial count of first-choice votes and their ultimate rank order of finish.

Endorsements are indicated by (ML) for the City Manager League, (L) for organized labor, (R) for Republican, and (D) for Democratic. Labor had fewer candidates than the CML to start with, and although they fared well in the transfer process, there were not enough Labor candidates to provide later transfers to other like-minded candidates. Generally the only Labor endorsees to win were those jointly endorsed by the Democrats. More league than Labor candidates won either on first-choice votes alone (column 1) or by starting out among the first nine finishers (column 2) and obtaining enough transfers to stay to the end among the top nine. However, *among candidates who were strong enough to reach this competitive level,* league candidates enjoyed no special advantage over Labor candidates. Therefore, it is reasonable to conclude that the league owed its success to an initial broad base of support, not to a disproportionate mastery of the transfer process.[5]

TABLE 8.5
WHO WON AND HOW UNDER PR?

Election Year	1. First-Place Vote Winners	2. First Nine Finishers Dependent on Transfers		3. Come-from- Behind Tranfer Winners		4. Fast Starters, Transfer Losers	
1935	Goodwillie (ML)	Thacher	2-3	Cohn (ML)	10-9	*Klotz	7-11
		Carey (ML)	3-2	Hoover	11-8	Czelusta (ML)	8-10
		*Consaul (ML)	4-7	Murphy (L)	12-4	*King (L)	9-12
		Start (ML)	5-6				
		DeAngelo (L)	6-5				
1937	Czelusta (ML)	Cohn (ML)	5-6	King (ML-L)	10-8	Beckett (ML)	9-10
	Start (ML)	Bame	6-5				
	Carey (ML)	Consaul (ML)	7-9				
	Thacher (ML)	Hoover (ML)	8-7				
1939	Thacher	Czelusta	3-3	Hoover	11-8	*Lehman (ML)	8-12
	Carey (ML)	Roulet (ML)	4-5				
		Bame	5-4				
		Kelly (ML)	6-6				
		Etchen	7-9				
		Consaul (ML)	9-7				
1941	Carey (D)	Thacher (R)	2-2	Hoover (R)	12-5	*Lehman (R)	6-10
		DiSalle (D)	3-3	Bame (I-R)	10-9	*Biniakiewicz (D)	7-11
		Czelusta (R)	4-4				
		Jurris (R)	5-6				
		Roulet (R)	8-7				
		Etchen (R)	9-8				
1943	Roulet (R)	Burke (D)	3-4	Bame (I-R)	11-8	*Biniakiewicz (D)	7-10
	DiSalle (D)	Thacher (R)	4-3				
		Jurris (R)	5-5				
		Lehman (R)	6-7				
		Czelusta (R)	8-6				
		Millard (R)	9-9				
1945	Roulet (R)	Czelusta (R)	4-5				
	DiSalle (D)	Jurris (R)	5-4				
	Burke (D)	*Simmons (D)	6-9				
		Thacher (R)	7-6				
		Lehman (R)	8-7				
		Donovan (D)	9-8				
1947	DiSalle (D)	Simmons (D)	3-4	Czelusta (R)	10-8	Sturm (D)	9-11
	Roulet (R)	Galvin (D)	4-3				
		Burke (D)	5-5				
		Degnan (I-R)	6-6				
		Jesionowski (D)	7-9				
		Jurris (R)	8-7				

continued

TABLE 8.5
WHO WON AND HOW UNDER PR?—*continued*

Election Year	1. First-Place Vote Winners	2. First Nine Finishers Dependent on Transfers		3. Come-from-Behind Transfer Winners	4. Fast Starters, Transfer Losers
1949	DiSalle (D)	Jurris (R)	4-4		
	Roulet (R)	Kirk (R)	5-7		
	Simmons (D)	Berlacher (D-L)	6-8		
		Czelusta (R)	7-6		
		Galvin (D)	8-5		
		Jesionowski (D)	9-9		
%	25	62.5		12.5	(12.5)
N	18	45		9	(9)

Sources: Lucas County Board of Elections, *The Abstract*, 1935–49; *Toledo City Journal*, 1935–49. Endorsements and party identification are from the *Toledo Blade*, 1935–49.
Notes: *= polarizing candidate, ML = City Manager League, L = Labor, D = Democratic Party, R = Republican Party, I = Independent.

The effectiveness of different groups' use of the process can be seen by examining the actual pattern of transfers for candidates backed by different parties or groups. Table 8.6 provides a sampling of transfers from several of Toledo's PR elections.[6] The selected transfers are chosen to suggest the range and typicality of the patterns of transfer votes. The importance of slates in Toledo PR elections is demonstrated by transfers of ballots to similarly endorsed candidates. A large number of candidates (N) remaining on a slate increases the chance that the slate as a whole will capture a larger percentage of transfer votes.

On transfers where there were at least five or six City Manager League candidates remaining—and the exhausted votes for that transfer are not much over 20%—the league normally could expect between 50% and 80% of its voters to continue marking choices for its other candidates. The pass-on percentages of Labor voters were lower, but, as noted earlier, there were fewer back-up candidates available to them. "Labor" in table 8.6 includes both those candidates who were endorsed by Labor only and those candidates jointly endorsed by Labor and the Democratic Party. When the Labor-only candidates are separated out, their transfer percentages are often very low. However, the transfer option enabled Labor to maintain its pre-PR representation in the small PR-elected council, representation that would disappear with the 1951 transition to plurality/at-large elections.

Party voting is discernible, with Republicans more successful than Democrats in winning seats with transfer votes. However, Democratic voters increased their transfer success rate over time, confirming the increasingly partisan character of late-PR elections. No evidence of an effective common effort among Independents emerges from the transfer data. Seven or eight times as many of those who voted for eliminated Independent candidates cast their next choice for one of the party-endorsed candidates as for another Independent.

Finally, ethnicity is the most striking relationship in the transfer data. When a candidate with a Polish name is eliminated, usually from 59% to 65% of the subsequent choices go to one of the two or three remaining Polish candidates out of the 10 to 20 candidates still in the running. The transfer process clearly worked to facilitate entry of ethnic minorities to the Toledo council.

The distribution of surplus votes from "First-Choice Vote Winners" shows an even more significant partisan pattern than those found in transfers from the ballots of eliminated candidates. An example is shown in table 8.7. Michael DiSalle, a Democrat, and Lloyd Roulet, a Republican, were leaders of their respective parties; each had served as a council-elected mayor in the 1940s when his party held a council majority. In 1947 each of these candidates had more than 4,000 surplus votes. Sixty-three percent of DiSalle's and 65% of Roulet's surplus ballots were transferred to fellow partisans. The weaker intraparty transfers from the eliminated candidates (table 8.6, C and D) suggests that the also-rans were less identified with their respective parties in the public mind and that their sparse support was more idiosyncratic.

Polarizing Candidacies

One of the ostensible purposes of PR is to enable distinct and self-conscious minorities to elect one of their own to represent them. This outcome seldom occurs in a plurality/at-large system. Such minority candidates could readily appear as "First Nine Finishers Dependent on Transfers" (table 8.5, column 2) or among "Fast Starters, Transfer Losers" (column 4) with substantial declines in ranking from first choice to last transfer.

A polarizing candidacy is defined here as one that has strong support from a minority of voters but wins few transfer designations from the remainder of the electorate. A polarizing candidate will make a strong showing of first-choice votes, but will be the subsequent choice of few voters, thereby achieving a higher rank order standing among all candidates on the first-choice count than on the final rank order standing. As an operational indicator of a polarizing candidacy, a

TABLE 8.6
TOLEDO PR/STV ELECTIONS: VOTE DISTRIBUTIONS ON SELECTED TRANSFERS

Transfer No.[a]	Elec. Year	N of Remain. Cands.	% of Votes Won by Remaining Candidates Endorsed by:										Exhausted Ballots[b] (%)
			CML		Labor		Demo-crats		Repub-licans		Polish		
			%	N	%	N	%	N	%	N	%	N	
A. On transfers on which CML-endorsed candidates were eliminated													
2 CML,L	1937	13	60	7	39	4	40	3	43	7	-	-	6
8 R	1937	7	81	5	9	2	5	1	83	5	-	-	8
12 P	1939	20	17	7	3	2	-	-	-	-	64	2	8
22	1939	10	47	6	-	-	-	-	-	-	-	-	14
B. On transfers on which Labor-endorsed candidates were eliminated													
4	1937	11	28	7	71	1	35	5	18	6	-	-	6
9	1937	4	72	4	42	1	42	1	30	3	-	-	28
5	1939	28	15	8	59	3	-	-	-	-	-	-	4
8 P	1949	17	-	-	6	2	34	6	53	9	65	3	10
C. On transfers on which Democratic candidates were eliminated													
5	1937	10	66	7	44	3	39	2	36	6	-	-	15
7 CML, L	1937	8	64	6	33	2	26	1	59	6	-	-	8
2	1945	15	-	-	-	-	35	5	53	8	-	-	7
6	1947	12	-	-	-	-	54	6	25	5	-	-	7
17	1949	8	-	-	18	1	54	3	32	5	-	-	14

continued

TABLE 8.6
Toledo PR/STV Elections: Vote Distributions on Selected Transfers—continued

Transfer No.[a]	Elec. Year	N of Remain. Cands.	% of Votes Won by Remaining Candidates Endorsed by:										Exhausted Ballots[b] (%)
			CML		Labor		Democrats		Republicans		Polish		
			%	N	%	N	%	N	%	N	%	N	
			D. On transfers on which Republican candidates were eliminated										
1	1937	14	44	8	15	4	11	4	48	7	–		23
3	1937	12	68	7	7	2	6	3	76	6	–		5
5	1945	12	–		–		16	4	72	7	–		6
5	1947	13	–		–		27	7	49	5	–		7
14 P	1949	11	–		6	1	46	4	42	6	59	2	9
			E. On transfers on which Independent candidates were eliminated								Independent		
											%	N	
2	1947	16	–		–		37	7	37	7	17	3	8
3	1947	15	–		–		27	7	50	6	10	2	12
4	1947	14	–		–		47	7	34	6	11	1	10

Note: Complete transfer data are on file at the Archival Center of the Jerome Library, Bowling Green State University. Read the table as follows: "% of votes won by remaining candidates endorsed by," then the endorsing group or identity, and then the lettered headings, A, B, etc. For example, on the 8th transfer in 1937 (second line under heading A), 81% of the voters who voted for the CML-endorsed candidate who was eliminated on that transfer voted their next choice for one of the remaining five candidates of the CML. Reading to the right, 9% of these voters voted next for a Labor-endorsed candidate. Because of multiple endorsements of the same candidate, these categories may total more than 100% across. Here, the eliminated candidate was also a Republican, as indicated by the "R" in the first column.

[a]Letters following the transfer no. in the first column indicate additional endorsements/identity of the candidate eliminated in that transfer: L = Labor or joint endorsement by Labor and Democratic Party, R = Republican, D = Democratic, CML = City Manager League, P = candidate of Polish origin.

[b]"Exhausted ballots" are ballots with no more usable numbered choices on them. The reciprocal of the percentage of exhausted ballots is the remaining proportion of the pool of transfer votes actually available for transfer.

TABLE 8.7
DISTRIBUTION OF SURPLUS VOTES, 1947

	N of Candidates	% of Surplus from Leading Democrat (Michael DiSalle)	% of Surplus from Leading Republican (Lloyd Roulet)
Second choice for			
Democratic candidate	7	63	22
Independent candidate	6	12	13
Republican candidate	7	24	65
Total %		99	100
N pf surplus votes		4,308	4,132

Source: Calculated from Lucas County Board of Elections, *The Abstract,* 1947.

drop of three places in the rank order of candidacies from first count to last transfer is used here. Polarizing candidates will also have a disproportionately small share of the pool of transfer votes. Finally, a smaller proportion of their total votes will come from transfer votes. Candidates who dropped three or more places in rank order of finish are indicated in table 8.5 by an asterisk before their names.

In Toledo PR elections, only six different candidates in eight races fit this definition of polarizing candidacies, and only two of those won in a polarizing race: Consaul in 1935 and Simmons in 1945 (table 8.5). Clear ethnic or racial identification was a significant source of polarizing candidacies.

Simmons's election in 1945 is a clear example. Ranking sixth in first-place votes, he dropped to ninth, receiving only 6% of the transfer votes on the third from last transfer, when each of the other five candidates who eventually won claimed from 17% to 22% of this pool of votes.[7] At his election on the last transfer, only 18% of his total vote came from transfers,[8] and he was nearly 300 votes short of the quota. Thus Simmons won in spite of being the second, third, or fourth choice of far fewer voters than other winning candidates. He could not have been elected by black votes alone, given the small size of the African-American community in Toledo at that time. His concentrated support in the black community (over 80% of his first-place votes came from the four wards with the highest black population), however, enabled him to win with minimum support from white voters. It seems fair to conclude that at least his initial election could not have occurred in plurality/at-large voting.

In contrast, a nonpolarizing candidacy can be traced through the transfer process by following the adventures of Charles D. Hoover in four elections (1935–41). A Republican, Hoover was endorsed by the City Manager League only in 1937, and only in that election did he place among the first nine finishers. By the final count, he moved up from eighth to seventh on transfers. In 1935, 1939, and 1941, he placed eleventh or twelfth on the first count, and twice moved up three ranks on transfers. In his last election he rose an astonishing seven ranks (table 8.5). In his four elections, the share of his total vote that came from transfers was 68%, 42%, 64%, and 57% respectively. Only when he was endorsed by the City Manager League (1937) was the transfer share less than a majority of his total vote. This pattern of votes suggests that his support was widespread but shallow; voters were willing to include him among their choices, but few favored him strongly. Hoover had the advantage of high name recognition, since he had been elected vice mayor in a citywide race under the pre-PR charter. Such a candidate, as distinct from a polarizing one, would be routinely elected in a plurality/at-large system.

Among polarizing candidates, only Solon T. Klotz in 1935 appeared to draw his intense and narrow base of support from a political record. Klotz was the former and discredited mayor whose mismanagement of the city's finances had been an impetus to reform. After ranking seventh on the first count, he received so few transfer votes that he dropped four ranks to finish at a hopeless eleventh rank on the final count.

The polarizing character of these less routine candidacies diminished over time. Most won in later PR elections, and, once on council, several even won election by their colleagues as mayor or vice mayor. Czelusta, for example, led all candidates two years after missing election to the first PR-council by four votes; he was reelected to council in all subsequent PR elections and served as mayor. After two defeats, Lehman was elected twice. Simmons moved up in rank in the next PR election and was elected a third time with first-choice votes. Both Simmons and Jesionowski served as vice mayor. It appears that over time the voters accepted these initially controversial candidates.

What difference did PR make in who was elected to the Toledo city council between 1935 and 1949? It is reasonably clear that PR made a crucial difference in the initial election of an African-American representative and that it generally facilitated efforts of the Polish voters who lived in two neighborhoods three miles apart to gain fair representation (Jones, 1944). These winning candidates represent 4% of the 72 successful candidacies in the eight elections conducted under proportional representation. The 25% who were first-choice winners and most of the first nine finishers who won with transfers would probably have been elected by plurality/at-large voting, given the same constellation of political forces. This conclusion must remain tentative, however, since the PR system offered an incentive to candidacies with specialized but citywide appeal, a factor that does not exist in the plurality/at-large system.

The relative infrequency of polarizing candidacies in Toledo during the 1930s and 1940s suggests that PR was not used to its full potential. Latent groups did not organize and take advantage of the opportunities presented by PR in the way one might expect today, when interest groups are better organized, more active, and even in some cases militant (Peterson and Walker, 1990).

Conflict and Consensus in the Operation of Government

The factionalism and instability of European democracies before World War II has sometimes been blamed on proportional representation. More recently this theory (without data to support it) has been projected onto American municipalities (Hermens, 1941, 1985). Did PR usher in an era of factionalism in Toledo when it was introduced? This question will be addressed by comparing the extent of factional behavior on Toledo councils of the three electoral periods.

The measure of factionalism used here is the percentage of nonunanimous roll calls on substantive issues in selected years of pre-PR, PR, and post-PR council decision making. These data are presented in table 8.8. Contrary to the instability hypothesis, conflict as measured here does not rise but actually drops precipitously on the occasion of Toledo's transition from ward elections to PR. Taking total votes on substantive issues (the sum of votes on motions, ordinances, resolutions, and amendments), 25% of all votes were nonunanimous on the ward-elected council of 1933–35, a level of conflict that dropped to 6% on the first PR council (1936–38), and 3% on the last PR council (1949–51). A roughly similar pattern of conflict-reduction is shown in all categories. Voting on amendments brought out the highest conflict, but the pattern is consistent with the total nonunanimous votes, dropping from 49% of the total in the ward-elected council to 28% in the first PR council, 5% in the middle of the PR period, and 15% in late PR (table 8.8).

External events could reasonably explain some of the contentiousness in the operations of council during the pre-PR period, when the

TABLE 8.8
PERCENTAGE OF NONUNANIMOUS ROLL CALLS,
TOLEDO CITY COUNCIL, 1933–1954

Type of Council	Motions[a]	Ordinances	Resolutions	Amendments	Total
Ward-Elected	34	26	8	49	25
(1933–35)	(212)	(234)	(286)	(39)	(771)
Early PR (1936–38)	5	7	5	28	6
	(340)	(328)	(214)	(18)	(900)
Middle PR (1939–40,	23	4	5	5	6
1945)	(84)[b]	(517)	(318)	(19)	(937)
Late PR (1949–51)	11	9	*	15	3
	(140)	(535)	(239)	(20)	(934)
Plurality/at-Large	9	4	1	17	4
(1952–54)	(128)	(568)	(276)	(6)	(978)

Source: Tabulated from *The Toledo City Journal*, 1933–54, minutes of city council meetings.
Note: N's are in parentheses.
[a]January through March for each year indicated except 1945, which includes January through September.
[b]Motions were not recorded for 1945.
*Less than 1%.

city faced problems growing out of the Great Depression. As in other cities, there were no obvious solutions to unemployment, hunger, and hopelessness. However, most of these problems also faced the early PR councils that showed the sharp drop in nonunanimous roll calls. The PR-elected councils clearly operated more by consensus than their ward-elected predecessors.

The transition from the PR-elected councils to a council elected by plurality/at-large was a different matter. This change in method of election had no significant effect on the proportion of nonunanimous votes. Such continuity in behavior suggests that other institutional factors were at work to reduce conflict. The small size of the post-PR council and its citywide election are likely to explain at least a share of this stability, as is the continuing administration of the city by a professional manager.

Several observers have commented on a tendency of PR-elected councils to experience "factional polarization" when it came to the council's election of a mayor (Straetz, 1958, pp. 84–88; Weaver, 1986, p. 149). In Toledo, there were no cases of delay or deadlock when the eight PR-elected councils chose their mayors. In 1939, when the outcome of the election was unpredictable and the City Manager League failed to elect a majority of council, the mayoral election was contested, but only briefly. In the 1940s the political parties provided the cohesion needed to build coalitions for mayoral elections in the PR-elected council.

Council instability might also surface in relation to the tenure of city managers. It has been suggested that "shifting alliances" on council could lead to "greater attrition of managers" in PR systems than in plurality/at-large systems (Weaver, 1986, p. 149). However, this was not the case in Toledo. Managers under PR averaged five years in office, whereas the later city managers appointed by plurality/at-large councils served for an average of 3.1 years.[9] It is therefore evident that PR elections and their outcomes did not create instability with respect to the city manager's administration of city affairs.

Political factors may explain the stability of the tenure of managers in the PR period. The City Manager League was successful in corralling support for the autonomy of the first manager in early skirmishes on PR councils. The salience of the reform ideology, however, declined over time in Toledo, leaving the manager more exposed to controversy. Once a reform movement achieves institutional implementation, the reform impulse seems to lose its élan. The reforms, no longer a challenge to the status quo but part of it, are neutralized, and the usual play of political forces is set free to buffet the city manager.

For a time, however—during the PR period—the reformers' goal of separating administration from politics and policy was achieved. In comparing the topics of the nonunanimous votes of the pre-PR ward-elected council during its last three years with the topics that drew disagreement in the first three years of PR-elected councils, a significant difference is found. Swelling the number of items dealt with by the last ward-elected councils are specialized and minor concerns, clearly administrative: authorizing bridge repairs, opening a particular bridge to traffic, reassignment of two traffic officers to "regular duty," the purchase of supplies, the itemization of expenditures for poor relief, lowering the water commissioner's salary, abolishing or creating a new position (stenographer), the per month automobile reimbursement for the secretary of the planning commission, and granting various organizations permission to use the civic auditorium. Among the distinct minority of matters with policy implications were bus service routes, restricting vehicle weights, and zoning.

In sharp contrast, the small number of nonunanimous roll-call votes on the early PR councils involved the confirmation of appointments (made by the outgoing mayor), the financing of the city's bonds, and zoning—all presumably policy matters. Edward A. DeAngelo, a member of both the last ward-elected council and the first PR council, confirmed this contrast from his personal experience. In a radio address delivered during the 1937 repeal campaign, he defended PR, saying that representatives of organized labor such as himself had never failed to receive a fair hearing "under the present form of government." He commented:

> When, under the old, large council did labor or any other group's authorized representative find it possible to discuss questions without interruption from large evening audiences which were often composed of hecklers . . . who were not interested in the particular subject matter under discussion? Many a night well past midnight the old council listened to useless bickering, political grandstand speeches, and meaningless discussions of matters that the new nine-man council could have disposed of in a few minutes. Always there was the group of outsiders who wanted the jobs of the present employees, waiting for a chance to replace those on the city's payroll regardless of how long they had been working or how well their work was done. (DeAngelo, 1937, p. 485)

In Toledo, both reports of personal experiences and quantitative measures to assess the stability of government in the PR period point to consensus in the council rather than the factionalism that has been attributed to PR-elected bodies.

Summary and Conclusion: Are There Lessons for Today?

In Toledo proportional representation rode in on the coattails of the city manager plan. Its rationale was tied to the reform ideology of the National Municipal League, whose *Model City Charter* promoted a small at-large council to provide members with a citywide view of problems; the council was to be elected by PR/STV in order to create the broad representation of human needs and interests required for policy making. Not all municipal reformers understood the importance of having diverse interests effectively represented on city councils, even where the city manager system made council the exclusive policy-making body. Indeed, some saw PR as a minor part of their total recipe for good government. This was particularly true in Toledo, where the small at-large council and PR were adopted later than in other Ohio cities, even after PR had been repealed in Ashtabula and Cleveland. This electoral reform which lasted for 16 years in Toledo survived four repeal initiatives. Its importance for the reform agenda dwindled, however, until, by the 1940s, some Toledo defenders of the city manager and the small at-large council were disavowing responsibility for PR/STV.

The failure of its original advocates to defend PR against the later assaults on it may indicate the triumph of the professional and technocratic elements of the Progressive movement over those with more pluralistic concerns. The more democratic forces of reform had failed to build a durable constituency for PR elections. In Toledo, support for PR among white working-class voters never took root, even though PR facilitated the representation of labor on the small, at-large council. In 1949, by the time of the fifth and successful repeal initiative, African Americans constituted the only group that had come to believe that its effective representation on city council vitally depended on proportional representation.

Although reformers committed to PR believed that their electoral system was immune to the manipulations of party politicians, Toledo's experience did not bear this out. Toledo PR elections became de facto partisan elections in which party slates contended for power, just as the nonpartisan ballot, adopted in Toledo in 1914, had eventually been accommodated by the parties.

As measured by its presence on council, the influence of the city's middle and upper-middle classes flourished under PR, although labor leaders also gained representation. Council members from the professions replaced the small neighborhood business operators of the pre-PR ward councils, and union officials replaced ordinary workers who had won elections in neighborhood contests. In the subsequent plurality/at-large elections of the post-PR period, middle- and upper-middle-class influence persisted, but blue-collar representation disappeared.

The transfer process of PR/STV was used successfully both by reformers and by organized labor in the early years of PR. Attentive voters learned how to give both first and subsequent choices on their ballots to candidates who were endorsed by their opinion group or were consistent with their demographic identity. In later PR elections, as the political parties became active and organized in municipal affairs, both Republicans and Democrats instructed voters on the use of transfers to support slates. As Democratic organization and national strength increased so did its local electoral success under PR. Organization and commitment count in PR electoral systems as in all others.

Although the largest differences among electoral systems in characteristics of council members occurred between ward and at-large elections, PR introduced a few polarizing candidates whose initial election was improbable under a plurality/at-large system. These were primarily candidates of minority groups subjected to prejudice or discrimination because of race or ethnicity. PR was especially useful in their initial access to power. Once elected, however, these representatives appeared to gain acceptance in the political arena.

Proportional representation did not lead to unstable factionalism or governmental gridlock. On the contrary, political stability and order increased in Toledo after PR/STV, along with other reform institutions, replaced ward elections and the independently elected strong mayor.

Differences that can be convincingly attributed to PR are relatively few but significant, since they involve the access to power of previously excluded groups. However, the potential of PR to make a difference was not fully tested by its early experience in the United States. The interest group structure of 50 years ago lacked the complexity and sophistication of associational life today. Racial, ethnic, and ideological minorities were numerous in Ohio cities of the first half of the twentieth century, but they lacked the self-awareness and organization to benefit fully from the representational opportunities of PR. In this sense, PR was wasted on the America of the 1920s, 1930s, and 1940s.

If proportional representation is to have a future in the United States, new understandings of representational issues and new constituencies must be built. Potential beneficiaries would include partisan minorities that are shut out in winner-take-all plurality elections, as well as minority groups whose access to power is tenuous because they are either not concentrated enough geographically to gain representation from districts or not numerous enough to win in plurality/at-large contests.

NINE

■ ■ ■

Commonalities and Contrasts: Five PR Cities in Retrospect

> An ideal system of representation would impress the voters with its fairness, encourage the selection of able representatives, give expression to all important opinions and at the same time facilitate the formation of a workable government. Proportional representation has not secured all of these objectives. Indeed no system of representation will of itself secure these ends. . . . In American cities where active citizens' groups have nominated civic minded candidates, as in Cincinnati, the Hare system is generally held to have worked well. The plan does away with the need for a primary election, eliminates ward politics and insures fairness to all groups.
>
> Gosnell, "Proportional Representation," 1948

P R/STV WAS ADOPTED in five Ohio cities as one feature of a reform attack on "boss rule" and its attendant corruption and mismanagement. Three large industrial cities—Cleveland, Cincinnati, and Toledo—were governed by deeply entrenched Republican machines. The two smaller cities, Ashtabula and Hamilton, had less centralized structures of power, but the political parties were significant actors in their daily political life. A Republican regime made most of the policy decisions in Ashtabula, while in Hamilton the Democratic Party reigned. Although there were unique circumstances undergirding the adoption of PR/STV in each of the five Ohio cities, common factors outweighed the differences. Revelations of graft and fraud in the operations of government by existing regimes and dissatisfaction with the level of services provided—from power to sewers, streets, parks, and recreation— explain the rejection of the status quo.

282

Ohio was fertile ground for experimentation in electoral systems. The adoption of home rule by state constitutional amendment in 1912 cleared the path for new municipal charters in the state. This was an opening for city autonomy that had been closely watched by both the National Municipal League and the Proportional Representation League. The choice of PR/STV as the preferred alternative to existing electoral systems in these cities is attributable to the tireless efforts of both local and national activists who were committed to diversity of representation. This commitment to diversity was in most cases tied to support for the city manager plan. Efficient administration was to replace the waste and fraud practiced by the bosses and by successive inept mayors, but in the eyes of these Progressives an impartial city manager required policy guidance by a truly representative city council.

In all five of these Ohio cities, Progressive activists became committed to PR/STV. Augustus Hatton, a political scientist at Western Reserve University, drafted three of the five Ohio PR/STV charters. Hatton not only became a national expert and consultant for the NML on charter revision but also won two terms on Cleveland city council, elected by PR in the 1920s. Ashtabula was chosen as an experimental site by the national P.R. League, apparently at the initiative of the local labor leader William Boynton, a former city council president and a member of the league's advisory committee. Ohio PR advocates coordinated testimonials to advance the spread of PR elections. For example, in 1919 five Ashtabula community leaders who had initially opposed PR wrote statements for the Coshocton (Ohio) Charter Commission, then considering electoral system reform, testifying how well PR was working to the benefit of their city (*Equity*, 1919, 21.2).

Evidence suggests that each city in turn looked to the experience of the other Ohio cities in choosing its new electoral system (*PRR*, 1928, 85:17). Although Toledo's 1934 adoption followed repeal of PR/STV in Ashtabula and Cleveland, its reform leaders appear to have been swayed by the continuing success of PR in Cincinnati and Hamilton rather than by its closer neighbors' ultimate rejection of this innovation. Members of the Toledo Citizens' Charter Committee looked upon Cincinnati in particular as a model for what they hoped to achieve by adopting a council of nine, to be elected at-large by PR (Stinchcombe, 1968, p. 40).

Contemporary sources generally give credit to the PR-elected councils and their city managers for effective government. In these reformed cities, improved and expanded public services were delivered, and fiscal responsibility was achieved. Only in Cleveland, where the

Republican organization managed to retain its power and perquisites throughout the decade of reform, was serious misfeasance uncovered and punished in the PR-elected council.

However, local political party leaders who lost power in the PR period fought back with repeated attacks on the reform package of change. Although the city manager and the small at-large council were targets as well, PR/STV was singled out for the most persistent repeal initiatives, and by 1960 this electoral system was extinguished in the five Ohio cities. PR was more vulnerable than the other reform structures in part because of its complexity, but these studies show more fundamentally that it was vulnerable because the minority groups that gained representation at the table of public policy making were not necessarily welcomed there at the time by the majority. Furthermore, the reformers themselves flagged in their efforts, failed to organize political support among its beneficiaries, and in many cases simply joined the tide of suburbanization and left the cities.

Unique Aspects of Adoption

Ashtabula, a small port city of about 20,000 population, was ethnically but not racially diverse. Located in the old Western Reserve of Connecticut, the city absorbed waves of immigrants in the late nineteenth century from Finland, Sweden, Italy, and Ireland. By 1910 a substantial majority of the population was either foreign-born or had at least one foreign-born parent. The city was governed by a mixed (ward and at-large) council and mayor, nominated in partisan primaries and elected on a partisan ballot. The Republican Party was solidly in control. The political climate in Ashtabula was restive enough over issues of waste and fraud to make reform success likely. Unfamiliarity with PR/STV led to delay in its acceptance; the Ashtabula reform charter of 1914 was adopted without PR. A separate and successful PR amendment followed closely behind in 1915, however, its advocates promoting its adoption on the ground that the city's diversity called for some assurance of minority representation in city policy making. Labor unions were active in promoting PR and securing its adoption; indeed, its leading advocate was Boynton, also a railroad engineer and labor leader.

In Hamilton, a small industrial city just north of Cincinnati with a population of almost 40,000, the ruling organization was Democratic and the boss was the mayor himself. As in the larger "boss-ridden" cities, a strong reform movement was actively engaged in city politics.

The reform charter introducing the city manager plan and PR/STV elections was adopted in Hamilton, as in Cleveland, Cincinnati, and Toledo, its advocates argued, to "restore power to the people."

In Cleveland and Toledo, the tradition of reform was rooted in earlier waves of the success of good government in the first decade of the twentieth century. Cleveland's Tom Johnson and Toledo's Samuel ("Golden Rule") Jones had both been independent mayors (although Johnson was a Democrat and Jones a Republican) and advocates of electoral reform as a means of facilitating broader representation of the citizens of their respective cities. Both Cleveland (1913) and Toledo (1914) had adopted charters providing for nonpartisan elections of municipal officeholders. Both cities had retained their ward-based councils[1] and had experimented with nomination by petition and preferential voting for both council and mayor on the Bucklin ballot. Many Cleveland advocates of the PR/STV ballot saw it as merely correcting the flaws of the Bucklin preferential ballot. In fact, Peter Witt, Johnson's chief lieutenant—who had lost the 1915 Cleveland mayoral election because his supporters marked second and "other" choices for his principal opponent on the preferential ballot—chaired the Charter Committee of One Hundred that proposed PR/STV for Cleveland.

In Ashtabula, Cincinnati, and Hamilton, Progressive victories represented more drastic political change. An earlier electoral reform effort in Cincinnati had failed in 1914, when voters defeated a proposed reform charter; a new machine-sponsored charter was approved by the voters in 1917 but made few significant changes. All three of these cities were still using partisan ballots for local elections until they adopted PR/STV. They had some experience, however, with at-large elections, since their councils were composed of a mixture of ward and at-large seats, with ward members in the majority.[2]

Cleveland was unique among Ohio's PR cities in its use of four large multimember districts, each electing five, six, or seven members. With a highly diverse population of about 800,000 in the 1920s, Cleveland adopted a 25-member council, in contrast to the other cities that had seven (Ashtabula and Hamilton) or nine (Cincinnati and Toledo) members elected at-large. Cleveland's district plan was fashioned by Hatton as a realistic compromise between the old 33-member ward-based council and a small at-large council. As a resident and active participant in Cleveland politics, he recognized the deep roots of neighborhood loyalties in this largest and most cosmopolitan of Ohio cities. For the sake of winning reform, he wanted to avoid the bruising political battles of an earlier decade between white native Protestants and Catholic ethnic groups over ward versus at-large elections for the city's school board. The politics of religious and ethnic representation were familiar to Cleveland voters and the stakes were high.

These large multimember districts, however, did not prove to be a popular feature, at least among other Ohio reformers. In a retrospective analysis of his city's successful charter campaign of 1924, Murray Seasongood of Cincinnati would rejoice that the Cincinnati charter "avoided the objectionable features of the Cleveland charter which, by requiring only 2000 or 3000 votes for election, made racial, geographical, religious and other blocs possible" (Seasongood, 1933, p. 25).

The support of labor for Ohio PR campaigns was a significant source of strength. The participation of labor leaders in Ohio's Progressive movement was, if not unique, at least unusual in the early decades of the twentieth century. In the adopting period (1915–34) not all labor organizations in these five Ohio cities were supportive of PR elections, but in each city some unions, or as in Cleveland an organized Union Labor P.R. Club, provided notable support for PR elections. These labor groups not only turned out voters for adoption campaigns and against repeal initiatives but also published and distributed pro-PR literature.

Because Ohio was seen as a national leader in reform efforts, and at the same time a typical state politically, the Proportional Representation League (PRL) and the National Municipal League (NML), both headquartered in New York City, involved themselves in these Ohio charter campaigns. Beginning in 1912, Clarence Hoag, secretary of the PRL, and his successor, George Hallett Jr., made numerous trips to Ohio by train, meeting with Augustus Hatton and arguing the PR case before charter commissions and councils. From then until 1960, when Hamilton voters approved the last repeal of PR in Ohio, PRL and NML staff traveled tirelessly to assist in campaigns, not only to promote adoption of PR but also repeatedly to prevent repeal.

Abandonment of PR/STV

The repeal of PR/STV electoral systems in Ohio occurred over a period of three decades, beginning with Ashtabula's repeal in 1929 and concluding with Hamilton's in 1960. In Ashtabula there were two unsuccessful repeal attempts on the ballot before the effort succeeded on the third try in 1929. The other four cities each experienced five repeal issues on the ballot, culminating in rejection of PR elections. In the changeover of electoral systems, the nonpartisan ballot was not challenged and survived in all five cities. In Ashtabula, Cincinnati, Hamilton, and Toledo, the administrative reform agenda proved to be more enduring than in Cleveland. In these four cities the city manager was retained, as well as the small at-large council; their only major change was the substitution of plurality voting for the PR/STV ballot.

Only in Cleveland was the city manager plan discarded with the electoral system. Also the only Ohio city to repeal PR in the depths of the depression, Cleveland chose instead a large, ward-based council with plurality elections and a popularly elected mayor. The single reform element retained, the nonpartisan ballot, was at most a facade, since the parties there had survived all manifestations of reform at little cost. Throughout the PR period in Cleveland (1923–31), the Republican organization had maintained its majority control of council and had selected the city managers. Indeed, the defeat of PR in Cleveland marked also the defeat of the old Republican machine, weakened by the scandals that reform had failed to prevent.

Although the large-district compromise had facilitated the 1921 adoption of PR/STV in Cleveland, it became a source of dissatisfaction to reform leaders in that city as well. The districts were aggregations of the old wards, which operated unchanged as the building blocks of the party organizations. The demise of the reform charter in Cleveland was hastened by the tepid support it received in 1931 from its natural constituency, who were then distracted by efforts to promote a better PR/STV electoral system. Significant segments of the reform leadership sought to supplant the 25-member, four-district council by a smaller (nine- or fifteen-member) at-large council. This diversion of support clearly contributed to the charter's defeat.

In contrast, in the other Ohio PR cities, old political bosses had lost power under the reform charters. The Republican organizations in Ashtabula, Cincinnati, and Toledo and the Democratic organization in Hamilton were displaced from power and produced avid leaders of repeal efforts. Their struggle to regain the old perquisites of municipal control drove the repeal initiatives. Whereas Cleveland voters were disillusioned because so little had changed under the reform charter, a new alignment of forces in the other cities galvanized the old into opposition. Although eventually their reform leaders tired of the struggle and moved to the suburbs or died, nevertheless, for a time city politics provided an arena in which contests between reform and reaction were lively. Cleveland's PR charter lasted only eight years, a brief span compared to the 16 years in Ashtabula and Toledo, and 34 in Cincinnati and Hamilton.

"What, are you going? Well, goodby!" By Hal Donahey.
Cleveland Plain Dealer, 8 November 1931, p. 1

In all five cities, the rise of ambitious aspirants to power helped to topple reform regimes. In some cases, such as that of Harry Davis, the former Republican mayor of Cleveland and governor of Ohio, their goal was to restore the office of popularly elected mayor, which they believed they could win. More significantly, the historic national shift in electoral strength from Republican hegemony to a newly energized

Democratic Party occurred in Cleveland between 1928 and 1932 and in Toledo and Cincinnati after World War II. As the Democratic Party approached majority status in these cities, its leaders lost interest in the PR/STV ballot's ability to ensure minority representation. Plurality voting, which would assist a new majority to consolidate its power, became more attractive.

In Cleveland, Ray T. Miller, the crusading Democratic county prosecutor who had attained his fame by sending Republican (PR-elected) council members to the penitentiary in the late twenties, was a prominent leader of the 1931 charter repeal campaign. Under the new (unreformed) charter, Miller would soon be elected mayor and ultimately become the boss himself. In this most industrial of the five cities and most troubled in the early thirties by unemployment, hunger, and radical unrest, a strong popularly elected mayor and ward council members who could provide city jobs for their constituents were strong attractions. Their appeal was concrete and practical, not abstract and theoretical.

In all the cities but Cincinnati, reform leaders failed to build, nourish, or sustain a constituency for PR elections. Although Scandinavian and Italian Americans in Ashtabula, Polish Americans in Toledo, and African Americans in Toledo, Hamilton, and Cleveland gained significant representation by the PR/STV ballot, the proponents of PR did not use these gains as organizing tools for their cause. What looks today like a failure to play from strength actually may have been a defensive strategy by reformers to downplay the success attained by ethnic, religious, and racial minorities through the PR ballot, precisely because the system was vulnerable to the unpopularity of such representation. In repeal campaigns, minority success was often alleged to contribute to divisiveness in the community. Because these beneficiaries were not organized, reform leaders lacked practical local support to fight against repeal in time of need.

The reformers themselves often failed to sustain the effective organizations they had built to capture power in the first place. In Toledo, for example, the City Manager League, which had spearheaded the PR charter and had provided stalwart support for its adoption and retention, converted itself in 1941 to a tax-exempt research institute, its leaders believing that its advocacy work was done.

Cincinnati in this instance was unique. Not only was the city's Charter Committee organized to support the new structure of government, but its vigorous leadership and grassroots support enabled it to supplant the Democratic Party and to oppose the Republican Party organization in local politics, creating a coherent small-scale two-party system. The retention of PR elections for over three decades in Cincinnati can be attributed to this rare organizational success. Had it not been for white resistance to the possibility of a black mayor (who, as the leading vote getter in 1955, was in line to be elected mayor by his fellow council members), Cincinnati might have been, like Cambridge, Massachusetts, a city that stayed with PR. Many observers have attributed the 1957 defeat of PR/STV in Cincinnati to what would today be its greatest strength, the ability to facilitate the representation of minorities (Straetz, 1958).

The city manager plan turned out to be a more enduring structural change than the PR electoral system. Except in Cleveland, where the voters rejected the entire charter, PR was abandoned only when the two reforms were separated. The persistence of the city manager was most surprising in Ashtabula, where a succession of managers held relatively brief tenure. Dissatisfaction with occupants of that office did not lead to rejection of the manager plan but was blamed on the electoral system instead. The representation on council of previously excluded religious and ethnic groups through PR was believed to have fostered conflict, which led in turn to the turnover of managers.

Yet genuine social issues underlay this political divisiveness. In Ashtabula the PR period (1915–31) encompassed Ohio's most heated disputes about Prohibition, the role of religion in public schools, and Sunday closing laws. In this small community, ethnic differences reinforced religious cleavages, while a watchful Ku Klux Klan operated on the shadowy edge of political life. Whether suppression of councilmanic differences through plurality voting would have been preferable is a question cutting straight to the core of theories of representation.

In all five cities opponents of PR used the complexity of the tally and transfer of the STV ballots as their lead point. Defenders used the PRL's argument that telling time and buying insurance were common human activities easily conducted without understanding how clocks, watches, or actuarial tables worked. It was a fact that the counts were time-consuming; opponents criticized the delay, while defenders praised the drama of public observation of the transfer process.

In Ashtabula and Toledo, the system was vulnerable to attacks on the count since the method of transferring surplus votes introduced an element of chance into the results. In Toledo, the count was conducted at the board of elections. As the votes were counted, once candidates reached the quota their ballots were set aside; all surplus transfers came from the ballots not yet counted. Hence the order in which precincts were counted might affect the final outcome. The charge of "lottery" was not totally unjustified.

In Ashtabula, the surplus for transfer was required to be taken proportionally from each of the precincts, but ballots were transferred "as they may happen to come in the different [precinct] packages, without selection" (Ashtabula City Charter, 1915, as amended). This was believed to be a random draw, eliminating any possibility of favoritism, but again chance played a role. In contrast, in the other cities the surplus was drawn systematically from the entire pool of a winning candidate's votes, so that the order of counting precincts would not affect the final outcome. If 10% of a candidate's total first-choice votes were above the minimum number needed to win, every tenth ballot from his total pool of ballots would be drawn for transfer.

The repeated challenges to PR may themselves have had a cumulative effect. Although each issue in each city grew out of specific ambitions held, resentments harbored, and concerns felt, the general impression of unpopularity emerged from the constant attacks. In three cities—Ashtabula, Cleveland, and Cincinnati—46% or more of those voting favored repeal every time the issue was put on the ballot. In Hamilton and Toledo, lower rates of opposition were recorded, but the vote for repeal did not fall below 27% of those voting anywhere in Ohio.

In Hamilton the buildup of opposition over the years must have made its mark, for by 1960 the other PR systems in Ohio had been voted out, even in Hamilton's neighboring metropolis, Cincinnati. Race was not publicly articulated as an issue in Hamilton, although the small black community had achieved representation through the PR ballot. Indeed, few issues related to the electoral system have been identified in Hamilton. Over more than three decades, Hamilton had conducted 17 PR/STV elections, and it had been 16 years since the last repeal attempt. Controversy itself seems to have become controversial, and a disappointed runner-up was able to exploit this fact to lead the final assault. It may have been coincidental but critical to the success of Hamilton's last repeal initiative that the vote was taken at a high-turnout presidential election (1960). Sixty-six percent of eligible adults voted on repeal, although typical turnout in Hamilton in local elections was about 40% of eligible adults under all three electoral systems examined here. A far larger electorate repealed PR than was ever attentive to or even voted on local issues or candidates.

Like adoption of PR/STV electoral systems in Ohio, its rejection reveals factors unique to each city, but there were common problems. First, displaced political leaders sought a return to plurality elections as a means to regain control of public office. Second, reform forces failed to organize the minorities that gained representation under

PR/STV into effective advocates of its retention. Finally, and perhaps most significantly in the long run, the political climate of the first half of the twentieth century did not favor the outcome that PR/STV was designed to produce—precisely, the representation of minorities.

The Promise and Performance of PR/STV

When PR/STV electoral systems were introduced into these Ohio cities, changes in turnout of voters were anticipated. Proponents expected turnout to rise, because the new opportunity for representation would draw previously hopeless voters to the polls. Opponents anticipated a decline as voters faced a new and complex ballot. Changes in the characteristics of council members were expected as well. Proponents expected "better men" to be elected, as well as a wider representation of significant groups in the electorate. Opponents feared that they would lose office and that the average person would lose power when neighborhoods lost their voices, a fear based as much on the at-large feature of the system as on the STV ballot. Changes were also foreseen in the behavior of councils elected by this new system. Proponents were confident that better policy would be developed by councils reflecting the true diversity of the city, whereas opponents envisioned fragmented public bodies racked by controversy over every issue to come before them.

The historical record supports many of the expectations of the proponents, but not all. Municipal turnout was not demonstrably affected in most of the cities. Characteristics of council members did change in several significant respects. Little evidence can be found to support the belief that PR/STV would cause fragmentation of council behavior; indeed, improved consensus building was observed and appears to be linked to the electoral system.

Turnout

Among turn-of-the-century advocates of proportional representation, voter turnout was an important concern. John Commons, citing the decline he observed in state and local voting in the 1890s, attributed growing disinterest in politics to the hopelessness of voters who faced a choice between the candidates of two machines. Unable to get their candidates elected, he argued, they made a rational choice not to vote. PR in his view would bring out a "full" vote because the present "hopelessness" would be dissipated. He noted that some Progressive reformers favored compulsory voting, but the "real problem," he maintained, "is not how to compel unwilling voters to vote, but how to give effect to the votes of those who are willing" (Commons, 1907, pp. 153–62).

Commons's observation that voting turnout began to decline in the 1890s is generally accepted today, although its causes are in dispute.[3] Legal and institutional reforms such as personal registration, residency requirements, and the secret ballot were tactics by which reformers fought the dominant party organizations, making it more difficult for the bosses to turn out their loyal followers. At the local level, nonpartisan elections conducted in the off year, at-large elections for city councils, and the city manager plan were additional reforms that displaced the old, more militant, participatory partisan politics (W. D. Burnham, 1981; Reynolds, 1988). In the reformed city, the disappearance of mayoral elections, which had traditionally focused on personalities, weakened the linkages between citizens and politics. The resulting shift from political to administrative power, with its emphasis on bureaucratic expertise, was itself believed to reduce political participation (Skowronek, 1982). Although PR elections were adopted within the context of these more widely known and implemented institutional changes, their core purpose—to ensure diverse representation for policy making—was intended to stimulate participation.

The shrinkage of the electorate that occurred with the party realignment of 1894–96 is most often attributed to the collapse of competition that accompanied the rise of a sectional party system in which Democrats dominated the South while Republicans captured a firm hold on the industrial Northeast and Middle West. Plurality voting systems left little incentive for minority party voters to go to the polls in either the South or the North. Most of the turnout decline occurred between 1900 and 1920, but the addition of women, a large, relatively apolitical body of voters, to the electorate in 1920 contributed modestly to this trend (Kleppner, 1987, pp. 44–77).

The New Deal realignment of the early 1930s stimulated a national upsurge in electoral participation that continued until 1960, the high point of twentieth-century political participation in the United States. Economically disadvantaged voters were mobilized by New Deal policies and by the growth and activity of labor unions, at least for presidential elections, a pattern interrupted only temporarily by the dislocations of World War II (Kleppner, 1982, chap. 5).

The relationship between PR elections and local turnout in Ohio must be evaluated in light of these larger trends.[4] Both Ashtabula's and

Cleveland's pre-PR and PR periods fell entirely within the presumptively low turnout cycle before the New Deal, whereas the abandonment of PR coincided with the national upsurge in voting in the early 1930s. For Cincinnati and Hamilton, the pre-PR and early PR years fell within the low cycle, whereas most of the PR years were played out during the higher national voting cycle. The post-PR years in these two cities followed the 1960 national turnout peak, into another era of decline. The entire pre-PR, PR, and post-PR periods in Toledo fell within the high national turnout cycle.

Although national trends cannot be entirely discounted, neither do they fully explain the changes in turnout under successive electoral systems in these communities. Pre-PR municipal turnout in Ashtabula averaged 66% of those registered, dropping slightly to 64% during the PR period. The decline actually set in, however, with the addition of women to the electorate in 1920, not with the 1915 adoption of PR, nonpartisanship, and the city manager plan. A post-PR rise in average turnout to 73% of those registered coincided with the Great Depression and a growth in union activity in Ashtabula, factors not attributable to the electoral system.

In Cleveland, the average turnout for elections in both the pre-PR and PR periods was relatively high, at 77.5% of registered voters. Elements of continuity that might have contributed to consistent turnout patterns through the two periods include the earlier adoption of the nonpartisan ballot and preferential voting in Cleveland, as well as the Republican machine's uninterrupted control. When PR was dropped and a large ward-based council was introduced in 1933, the average turnout for post-PR dropped by 10 percentage points. Actually, the first significant decline occurred in the last PR election (1931) and may be a statistical artifact of the change in registration law noted earlier (note 4). Real turnout increased significantly in the last PR election, but the registration base rose proportionately more. In any case, PR voting had no clear impact on turnout in Cleveland.

With no registration data for pre-PR Cincinnati or Hamilton, turnout under their pre-PR mixed systems is difficult to evaluate. They were partisan systems with a separately elected mayor, and in the change to PR/STV the conversion to at-large election on a nonpartisan ballot without a popular mayoral election offers a number of confounding variables. Under PR/STV, however, Cincinnati turnout fluctuated over 34 years from a high of 75.8% of registered voters to a low of 51.7%, with an average for the period of 62.4%. The fluctuations in turnout under PR in Cincinnati are not consistent with the national trends analyzed earlier. With the change to plurality/at-large (9X) elections in 1959, turnout dropped to an average turnout for the post-PR period of 56.9%. This dip in average turnout did coincide with the post-1960 decline in voting turnout nationally, but it could also have been related to the loss in representation experienced by Charterites and African Americans under plurality/at-large voting.

In Hamilton, with turnout measured by percentage voting of the eligible adults, variations appear random both within and between electoral systems. Participation ranges from a low of 37% in 1931 (under PR) to a high of 50% in 1963, following PR's repeal, but no consistent pattern can be identified.

For Toledo as well, turnout is measured by percentage voting of the eligible population. Using this statistic, pre-PR turnout of voters choosing a ward-based council by plurality voting was the highest of the three election system periods at 47.2% of eligible adults. Like Cleveland, Toledo had adopted the nonpartisan ballot in an earlier reform initiative. Under PR, however, Toledo turnout dropped to 39.8% of eligible adults and rose again with plurality/at-large (9X) to 43.9% in the post-PR period. Toledo appears to be the only Ohio city in which turnout decline clearly coincides with PR. The mobility of the population during World War II, experienced in the PR years by both military personnel and industrial workers, might explain the apparent drop in turnout. However, as Anderson shows, during those same years turnout for presidential and congressional voting was rising in Toledo, as it was in the country as a whole. Anderson concludes that in spite of widespread efforts to educate voters, the new type of ballot discouraged many.

From these data, municipal turnout does not appear to be tied to the electoral system, with the exception of Toledo. Furthermore, incentives to vote at the local level were not necessarily related to national voting trends. The emergence and disappearance of local issues and candidates appear to have had more to do with the act of voting than did the form of the ballot or the structure of the council and city executive.

Characteristics of Council Members

Party. Both political and demographic variables were examined to ascertain the nature of the changing composition of these five city councils over three electoral periods. Partisan change occurred in the larger context of state and national party tides as the dominant Republican Party experienced first the Progressive split of the early years of the twentieth century and then the sharp blow of the Great Depression. Ohio's generally weak, fragmented, and often coopted local Democratic parties grew into effective electoral organizations as the Republican machines disintegrated. The nonpartisan ballot was more effective in some cities (Ashtabula and Cincinnati) than in others (Cleveland and Hamilton) in separating the local political sphere from its larger partisan context.

In Ashtabula, although Republicans retained their council majority through all three electoral systems, the PR period saw a significant drop in Republican hegemony and a rise in independent representation. When plurality voting was reinstituted after the repeal of PR, Republicans more than regained their previous strength at the expense of both Democrats and Independents.

For reasons explained earlier, the Republican organization in Cleveland did not lose control of elections in the transition from ward-based preferential voting to PR/STV. In fact the Republican majority grew slightly under PR at the expense of Democrats, and Independents earned almost 10% of the seats, replacing both Socialist and Democratic members. The depression-era return to a large ward-based council reduced the Republican majority to a plurality only, with a strong and rising Democratic minority and a shrinking independent presence.

Cincinnati experienced the most dramatic partisan change. The mixed pre-PR council, which was 95% Republican, gave way to a Charter Committee majority under PR. Although the Charter majority was composed of Independent Republicans, Democrats, and Independents, it was a coherent and integrated coalition that rightfully earned the label of political party. A stable local two-party system functioned effectively throughout the PR period. Under post-PR plurality/at-large elections, the Republican Party regained control and the Charter Party fractured into Democratic and Charter minorities.

In spite of Democratic machine dominance in pre-PR Hamilton, voters were rather evenly divided between the major parties, as demonstrated by volatile swings from Democratic to Republican and back to Democratic majorities on council. Over that pre-PR period the parties tied, each gaining an average of half of council's seats. In the early PR period Republicans carried a majority of council seats in each election; by late PR Democrats just as consistently won control, reflecting a gradual partisan shift in the community. Plurality/at-large voting in the post-PR period brought back the unstable swings in party control experienced before PR, with the Democrats holding an edge for the period.

Toledo's predominantly Republican pre-PR ward-based council was replaced under PR by more competitive outcomes. The Republican margin narrowed gradually over time, until the Democrats gained a majority in the last two PR-elected councils. With the implementation of the new plurality/at-large electoral system in 1951, the council majority swung sharply to the Republicans, who captured all but one seat. Democrats regained control, however, in the next two elections, reflecting in local nonpartisan races Toledo's relatively late partisan shift to the Democrats, a shift other Northern Ohio urban industrial areas had experienced during the Great Depression. In post-PR Toledo, Independents, who had won election to four of the eight PR councils, disappeared.

Minor parties failed to thrive in the PR elections of Ohio cities. Only once, in Ashtabula's first PR election in 1915, was a minor party candidate, a Socialist, elected. Under other (plurality-based) electoral systems, from early in the twentieth century up to World War I, Socialists were occasionally elected in Ohio to both city councils and school boards. In Cleveland, for example, the party's candidates won in both ward elections for city council and plurality/at-large elections for the school board. Before World War I, when the Socialist Party was growing nationally, its leaders endorsed proportional representation at the national and state levels. By the 1920s, shrunken by its opposition to the war and by the postwar "Red scare," the party took no position on electoral systems. Its candidates continued to run for local office in Ohio through the twenties and thirties, as did Communist Party candidates, but none was ever elected again in the PR cities. Even in Cleveland's multimember PR council districts, where the minimum vote required to win was relatively small, no minor party candidate was elected.

Incumbency. Under any electoral system, incumbency is expected to be an advantage for candidates seeking reelection. However, a few clear differences in incumbent safety emerge from the data. Cincinnati and Hamilton underwent a similar progression from mixed elections to PR/STV at-large to plurality/at-large. Incumbent safety increased with each change in electoral system, although switches in party control in pre-PR Hamilton made the increase in stability of membership under PR more dramatic (from an average of 23% to 57% incumbent reelection, whereas the increase in Cincinnati was from 61% to 67%). The advantage of incumbency rose further in both cities under plurality/at-large elections, to 67% in Hamilton and to a massive 81% in Cincinnati.

In Toledo, where an average of 42% of pre-PR council members were reelected from wards every two years, the continuity of membership increased in the PR period to an average of 65% incumbent reelection. If the first PR election when a sole incumbent won under the new system is omitted, the incumbent success rate rises for the remaining PR elections to an average of 73%, almost three-quarters of all PR-elected members. The sharp partisan swings of the post-PR councils, in contrast, reduced the power of incumbency and the likelihood of reelection fell to just over 50%.

The Cleveland case is an exception because of unique factors. The firm control held by the Republican organization through pre-PR and PR elections and the continuity of the old wards, which were clustered to create large PR districts, help to explain the continuity of incumbent success there. Almost two-thirds of council members were reelected under both systems. However, in Cleveland's post-PR system less than half of incumbents were reelected. Although ward lines within the former large PR districts did not change in the new 33-ward council, partisan fortunes did. Republican hegemony was crumbling as Democrats rose to power in the city and as in Toledo incumbents fared less well in the partisan transition.

In Ashtabula no significant difference in incumbent safety could be identified between the PR period and either the preceding mixed electoral system or the post-PR plurality/at-large period. The politics of personality, ethnicity, and even policy appear to have had more to do with the number of terms a council member could (or chose to) survive than the electoral system.

Quality of Candidates.   The Progressive reformers who engineered electoral change in the first half of the twentieth century were eager not only to enact their policy agenda but also to secure "better men" in positions of power. In communities that switched to PR/STV, this was to be achieved in three ways: by self-nomination through petitions, eliminating the primaries where parties were powerful even in nominally nonpartisan systems; by multicandidate rank-order choices on the ballot, making independent and minority candidacies more viable; and by enlarging the scope of the election to the city as a whole, or in the case of Cleveland, to large districts.

As measured by education and occupation, these expectations were in part fulfilled. With the implementation of PR elections, educational levels of council members rose in the three large cities. In Toledo and Cincinnati, with the end of PR and the introduction of plurality/at-large voting, the percentage of better-educated council members rose again.[5] The conventional explanation for this is that as the electoral jurisdiction widened, candidates with more resources, whether educational or financial or both, could better compete for available seats. PR represented a midpoint between ward elections and citywide plurality elections, since, under PR/STV, candidates ran citywide (or in large, multimember districts) but could win with a strong appeal to a limited constituency. This linear increase in educational qualifications, however, is seen even in Cleveland, where the post-PR system returned to 33 small wards for single-member elections. Part of the explanation therefore must be the rise in educational attainment among the population generally, and therefore among candidates and especially among successful ones. Educational background of council members was not available for the two small cities.

Occupational data are more consistently available. In all five cities a dramatic increase in professional representation occurred under PR. This increase was primarily at the expense of business representation, which under the pre-PR systems tended to be characterized by small entrepreneurs, such as undertakers and saloon owners, who would have been useful cogs in the wheels of their party organizations. The outcome for working-class representation, a goal of PR advocates from John Stuart Mill to John Commons, was less consistent. In three of the cities, Cleveland, Cincinnati, and Hamilton, blue-collar representation declined under PR. In Ashtabula and Toledo, however, blue-collar representation increased at the expense of business during the period of PR elections. Upon the demise of PR, blue-collar representation dropped further in Hamilton and disappeared altogether in Cincinnati and Toledo, as might be expected in citywide plurality elections. But in Ashtabula blue-collar members won a majority of the seats during the post-PR era in plurality/at-large elections and increased their share in Cleveland's single-member ward-based contests. Since the post-PR period coincided in both Ashtabula and Cleveland with the depression years and with the growth of labor as an organized force, these societal factors could well have overshadowed the electoral system in shaping representational outcomes.

Ethnicity. Evidence of other kinds of diversification of council membership during the PR period merits attention. In Ashtabula, where social issues such as Prohibition were exacerbated by religious differences, Catholics more than doubled their membership on the council during the PR period, reaching almost a third of the total. Italian Catholics, who lived in concentrated residential clusters, had achieved representation by ward in the pre-PR mixed council. Irish

Catholics, however, residentially scattered throughout the city, first won seats through PR/STV. When plurality voting returned in the post-PR period, their electoral strength was diluted and Catholic representation dropped to its pre-PR level.

The election of Polish Americans by PR in Toledo was evidence of a similar ethnic breakthrough. In the pre-PR wards of Toledo, the Polish-American communities were not concentrated in a single ward and had not been able to elect one of their own. With citywide elections and the PR/STV ballot, they voted as a voluntary constituency large enough to win one or two of nine seats.

Traditionally in Cincinnati, ethnically balanced slates had been presented to the voters by the Republican organization. Under PR, the Charter Committee adopted a similar strategy. The city's principal ethnic group was of German origin; but German Americans, while maintaining cultural distinctiveness, were politically integrated and held leadership roles both in the party organizations and in the reform movement.

In Cleveland, as in Cincinnati, ethnic representation was not an issue. A wide array of ethnic groups already had distinctive voices on the council in Ohio's most diverse city. In the pre-PR period, ethnically clustered neighborhoods, ward elections, and the preferential ballot combined to facilitate diverse representation. Furthermore, over the years the Republican organization had absorbed and elevated prominent men in the nationality groups as ward leaders, positions that enabled them to be or to recruit candidates and required them to get their voters to the polls. Cleveland's Republican organization adapted comfortably to the PR/STV ballot, losing power only in the economic crisis of the early 1930s, as ethnic voters began to transfer allegiance to the rising Democratic organization. Since post-PR brought back a ward-based council, this time with plurality instead of preferential voting, Cleveland's ethnic pockets retained their representation even as their residents switched parties.

Gender and Race. Ohio's councils were primarily white and male throughout the period examined here. In three cities, however— Cleveland, Cincinnati, and Hamilton—a few notable women played visible political roles both as advocates for PR and as candidates for council. In Cleveland, women ran but were unable to win in ward elections either pre- or post-PR. Women were elected, however, in each of the PR elections (1923–31), making up 6.4% of the total PR council members.

In Cincinnati, two women were elected to at-large seats on the mixed pre-PR council in 1921, a victory symbolic of the newly attained right to vote. Women played an important organizational role in Charter Committee activities leading up to and throughout the PR period, but under PR, women were elected only three times in 16 elections. Although women were nominated throughout the period, evidence suggests that Charter forces did not actively promote their candidacies. The woman who had been elected in 1953 and 1955 on the PR ballot was reelected on the plurality ballot in 1957 and 1959. Her visibility as a two-term incumbent and as vice mayor under PR undoubtedly assisted her successful transition to plurality/at-large elections.

Women in Hamilton had experiences similar to those of their sisters in Cincinnati, except in the pre-PR period none of the few women who ran were elected. In spite of the prominent roles women played in the battle over adoption of the charter in 1926, not until 1943 was the first woman elected on the PR ballot. Two women were elected in the early 1960s in the plurality/at-large system.

Gender does not appear to have been raised as a political issue in the entire period of the investigation in Ashtabula or Toledo. No female candidates have been identified in Ashtabula; and in Toledo, although the City Manager League had a women's auxiliary and occasionally women ran for council during the PR period, women were represented by men on the council under all three electoral systems.

It would appear from these findings that women's political opportunities were shaped more by the culture than by the electoral system. Cleveland is the best case for electoral system effect, since no women were elected either pre- or post-PR. There, the 25-member PR council with multimember districts may have facilitated women's victories; but the cultural context was also supportive, defined as it was by the exceptional Progressive tradition of the Western Reserve.

The case for improved racial representation under PR systems is a stronger one. In Cincinnati, Hamilton, and Toledo, African-American candidates were elected to council on the PR ballot, although they had been unable to win in pre-PR elections. In all three post-PR (plurality/at-large) elections, black candidates were unsuccessful in both Cincinnati and Hamilton, whereas in Toledo black incumbent James Simmons Jr. was defeated in the first post-PR election but won in the next two plurality/at-large contests with considerable white support.[6]

In Cincinnati black candidates on the PR ballot first ran unsuccessfully in the 1920s and 1930s as independents, then, having demonstrated some electoral strength, were endorsed by their respective parties for the next election, which they won. African-American representation could be attributed then to party competition, as Kolesar suggests. Both Charter and Republican organizations were striving to capture at least five seats on the nine-seat PR council. A question, however, is why the black candidates ran in the first place, and why they were able to make a strong enough showing to attract party support. They were not recruited by a party, as had happened much earlier in Cleveland in pre-PR elections. It would appear that the opportunity structure provided by PR—the ability to appeal citywide to a black constituency, which needed to number only one-tenth of the voters plus one—was an underlying factor in their self-recruitment. Furthermore, party support was not sufficient to elect African Americans to the plurality/at-large council in the post-PR period. Yet on 11 of the 16 PR councils and on every council from 1941 on, one or two African Americans were elected until PR's repeal.

In Cleveland black representation grew in proportion to black population growth, from one to three members in the PR period, although initial access had been achieved earlier. The Republican organization had promoted and secured the election of Thomas W. Fleming, a black barber and later attorney—known as "the Negro ward boss"—since 1911. He was easily elected from his ward on the pre-PR council and continued to win election on the PR ballot from his multimember district in 1923 and 1925. In 1927, two additional black candidates won election and three African-American seats became the norm on the 25-member PR council. When PR gave way at the depths of the depression to a 33-member ward-based council, black candidates were able to hold their own because of the residential segregation that had intensified during the 1920s as the black population grew. Indeed, African Americans were proportionally represented on the Cleveland council under all three electoral systems (1917–37), but through distinctly different channels.

In Ashtabula, the African-American community was too small (about one percent of the population in 1920 and 1930) to play a significant role in the city's politics. From newspaper accounts it does not appear that any black candidates even ran in local elections under any of the three electoral systems.

From the data collected on characteristics of council members under three electoral systems, it appears that the PR/STV ballot worked as it was supposed to, providing opportunities in the at-large (or large, multimember district) setting for majorities to be elected and for minorities, either previously excluded or underrepresented, to gain representation. The notable cases of minority representation in Ohio under PR systems included Irish Catholics in Ashtabula, Polish Americans in Toledo and African Americans in Cleveland, Cincinnati,

Hamilton, and Toledo. In the three elections after PR was abandoned, this minority representation was retained without interruption only in Cleveland under the combined conditions of segregated housing and single-member districts.

Whereas some Progressives spoke primarily of improving the quality of representation by structural reform, PR leaders appear to have understood the difference between the often-used phrase "better men" and representativeness. Augustus Hatton, for example, author of the Ashtabula PR charter provision, would later analyze the city's first PR election for *The New Republic:* Rinto, a "young Finnish attorney," ranked sixth in first-choice votes but was edged out in the final count by the incumbent, saloonkeeper Corrado, "representing the wet interests as well as the Italian vote." Rinto's election over Corrado, Hatton wrote, "would have improved the quality of the council but would have made it less representative." On the whole, he concluded, the new council would "contain more ability than the present one elected on the ward plan . . . *and* be more representative of the entire body of voters" (Hatton, 1915, pp. 97–98).

The Significance of Transfer Votes

In most PR elections in the Ohio cities where transfer data are available,[7] the leading candidates on first-choice votes were the ultimate winners of the election. Although transfers at subsequent stages of the count frequently changed the rank order of the winners, only about 10% of the total seats on PR councils in Ohio were won or lost by transfers.[8]

A "transfer winner"—a candidate who did not place among the leaders on first-choice votes but moved up in rank to winner through the transfer process—was an integrating candidate with fairly broad support in the electorate. In contrast, a "viable loser" (or "transfer loser")—a candidate who placed among the leaders on first-choice votes but failed to gain the minimum required vote by the last transfer—had a substantial but narrow base of support that was not broadened by second-, third-, or subsequent-choice votes from the supporters of other candidates.

The advantage of reform endorsements was clear in Cleveland, Cincinnati, and Hamilton, where transfer winners were more likely than transfer losers to be reform-endorsed professionals with higher levels of education. They were also more likely to be Democrats in Cleveland and Charterites in Cincinnati. Transfer losers were conversely more often Republican and were significantly less educated. Only in Cleveland did a woman fall into either of these categories; she was a transfer winner.

African-American candidates tended to win on first-choice votes and on occasion had surplus votes that were often (but not always) transferred to other minority candidates. However, about a fourth of the transfer losers in Cincinnati and Hamilton were black candidates who started in the top circle and, because of insufficient transfer ballots, dropped too far to win. In both Cleveland and Toledo all transfer winners and transfer losers were white.

Toledo results show a less distinct pattern than the other cities. Reform and labor endorsements were found equally among transfer winners and transfer losers. Polish Americans, a significant minority in Toledo politics, were also present in both categories. The impact of the rejected ancien régime was also muted, as the former (apparently discredited) mayor was a transfer loser in the first PR election, although two of his henchmen won with relative ease in the first two PR elections, and each became a transfer winner in two subsequent races. Individual candidacies and idiosyncratic political factors appear to have shaped these outcomes in Toledo.

Overall, the transfer process of PR/STV appears to have made a modest difference in electoral outcomes. The limited vote aspect of PR (each voter ultimately supports one candidate instead of seven or nine) shows a more significant impact on African-American representation. It is clear that in a PR election, as in any multicandidate contest, effectively promoted slates assist both partisan and nonpartisan groups to achieve their goals. Ranked voting on the PR ballot, however, with subsequent transfers during the count, ensured that minority candidates would not defeat each other and the majority would not capture all the seats.

Conflict and Consensus in Council Decision Making

The model of city government most widely portrayed in turn-of-the-century debate over reform encompassed a small council, elected at-large by plurality vote, which would elect a ceremonial mayor, make policy, and hire a city manager who would administer the city efficiently and economically. The goal was purportedly to serve the interest of the city as a whole, not the interests of its component parts, whether neighborhoods or groups of citizens.

Yet the official voice of the reform movement, the National Municipal League (later the National Civic League) actually called for PR/STV elections as the electoral system of the *Model City Charter* from 1915 through successive editions until 1964. At that time PR was demoted to one of several recommended alternative electoral systems—*none of which* was a small council elected by a plurality/at-large system. From 1921 until 1963 the NML's *Model State Constitution* incorporated PR/STV elections in multimember districts for a unicameral state legislature, and from 1930 on the NML *Model County Charter* called for a county council to be elected by PR/STV. In each case, the representative quality to be attained in the policy-making body was key to the recommendation.

Given this commitment of the reform leadership, perhaps the outcome to be explained is not the adoption of PR/STV in a few cities, but the failure of reformers to get it adopted more widely or to retain it where it was adopted. Perhaps the NML was ineffective; at least it was less effective than the opponents of PR/STV, who attributed European qualities to its practice. The only European country to use PR/STV, however, was Ireland, where it was adopted to assure representation of the English minority in the Irish Dail. From the 1930s on, the system most often cited by opponents of PR was that of Germany under the Weimar Republic, whose electoral system was not PR/STV but proportional representation/party list, instituted without a threshold requirement for a minimum percentage of the vote for a political party to secure seats in the parliament.

Because of fragmented representation in the Weimar Republic, arguably facilitating Hitler's rise to power, PR became vulnerable in the United States to the charge of causing political fragmentation leading to destructive conflict. The existence of stable European democracies that had elected their parliaments by PR/PL for decades, such as Belgium, Finland, Sweden, Denmark, and Norway (in some cases longer than Germany had), was not persuasive to opponents of PR, nor were explanations of the differences between PR/STV and PR/PL effective.

To test the purported relationship between electoral systems and dissension among council members in the five cities, data were gathered on nonunanimous votes on substantive issues (both ordinances and resolutions) in selected years over three electoral systems. No systematic evidence of greater dissension on PR-elected councils, compared to councils elected by other means, could be identified. Indeed, striking decreases in conflict were found after PR/STV was implemented in Hamilton and Toledo, whereas there were no significant differences in the proportion of nonunanimous votes by Cleveland and Cincinnati councils elected under different systems. In Ashtabula, where PR was implemented during a period of great national, statewide, and local debate over Prohibition, the minority representation won by "wets" on a council previously dominated by "drys" contributed to a five percentage point rise in nonunanimous votes on ordinances and a thirteen percentage point rise in such votes on resolutions. Neither of these measures reached the pre-PR level of conflict in Toledo and Hamilton, where 25% and 75% respectively of the substantive votes were split between factions in ward or mixed systems.[9]

Greater consensus in the operations of PR councils was often attributed to the necessities of the PR/STV ballot. In order to win transfer votes, candidates needed to appeal for second-, third-, and other choice rankings from voters whose first choice was committed to another candidate. Personal attacks among candidates therefore became a dysfunctional campaign strategy. As a result, less friction seemed to be carried over from the campaigns, or less was introduced in anticipation of the next campaign, into the operations of the council. Occasionally disputes arose in several cities in connection with the election of the mayor, but these were comparable to pre-PR or post-PR contention over election of council presidents under different systems.

The struggle for proportional representation begins to make historical sense in the context of competing yet overlapping political cultures, one based on ethnic roots and communitarian values, the other on rational functions and individualism. The representational theory in which PR is grounded bridged the gap between these contrasting worldviews by allowing for self-defined identities—whether ethnic, racial, political, or unaligned—to integrate themselves into the policy-making function of local governments.

Indeed, diversity of views *within* the PR movement itself reflected (in a narrower band) the pluralism of the reform movement generally. At one end of the ideological spectrum were individualists, such as Murray Seasongood, who feared a low threshold lest religious and ethnic groups gain too much power. At the other end were Tom Johnson and Jane Addams, who valued PR for its very ability to bring such groups into governing structures. Yet all agreed that more representative policy making should result in the efficient implementation of public policies that would serve social justice.

The history of PR in the cities examined here—an experience barely mentioned in major works of urban history—illuminates a far more complex set of values motivating both reformers and bosses than was previously recognized. Many of the most powerful bosses of the early twentieth century were Republicans who operated in the interest of private entrepreneurs who held economic power. They were supportive of reforms, like the city manager plan, when they could control the choice of managers, as Maurice Maschke did in Cleveland. Maeschke supported PR as well in two of the five repeal efforts, a position apparently dictated by his support for "his" city managers. Many of the reformers were Democrats who sought economic justice through passage of labor legislation and expansion of the scope of governmental services, as well as changes in the forms of government.

The motives of PR proponents in the five cities were similar: the reformers sought to wrest power from party bosses and to return it to ordinary people whose diversity they understood and to some extent appreciated. Most PR advocates shared with other Ohio Progressives the desire to equalize the burden of taxation, then heavily skewed in favor of the wealthy; to expand public services such as education, recreation, parks, and sewage treatment; to regulate local labor practices; to extend public ownership to private utilities; and to promote efficiency in the delivery of these public services. They were committed to the city manager plan as the means of introducing efficient public administration into American communities. Unlike many of their fellow Progressives, however, they understood policy making as the critical function of a broadly based and diverse council, representative of all important groups in the city. They saw "free" voting and "full" representation, both attributes of PR, as tools for achieving these substantive goals.

The proportional representation movement and its sponsors may have been largely absent from either traditional or revisionist accounts of the period because they failed to fit into the prevailing analytical dichotomy. PR/STV now appears to have been a political reform launched ahead of its time. What it did best was to facilitate the representation of both the majority and substantial minorities in the governing process. Although this quality was important to the advocates of PR, it was not a major concern in the broader local politics of the first half of the twentieth century in the United States. In fact, the election of previously unrepresented or underrepresented minorities was often cited by PR's opponents within the reform movement as a weakness, because it undermined the dominant faith that there was an objective interest of the "city as a whole" that could be represented through correctly structured elections.

The pluralist view that the city was a mosaic of interests and groups, not necessarily geographically based but entitled to participate in the making of public policy, was held by too few to sustain this particular reform. Even with the backing of the National Municipal League and its model charters from 1915 on, PR advocates were forced into a defensive position as early as 1920, when the initial repeal issue reached the ballot in Ashtabula, the first PR city. Although the pluralist vision was articulated in the PR literature of the day, it did not capture either the mainstream of the reform movement or—because of its antiparty thrust—the old political establishment.

Conclusion

The analysis of what actually happened in five Ohio cities that used PR/STV elections between 1915 and 1960 tells us that this electoral system was neither as powerful a tool of governance as its proponents hoped, nor as damaging to the polity as its opponents claimed. As only one of a group of reforms introduced into the structure of urban government—nonpartisanship, the at-large election of a smaller council, and the city manager plan were the better-known components—the change in electoral system had limited impact. The professional and educational levels of council members rose; minorities gained representation where they had been underrepresented or not represented at all before.

Myths that have obscured the understanding of proportional representation for many years should be dispelled. The conventional wisdom came to be that the PR/STV ballot was too complicated for people to understand, causing turnout to decline. In four of the five cities this turned out not to be true. Turnout rose and fell with local issues and personalities in each of these cities. Although some voters may have been deterred from going to the polls, others were encouraged to vote because of their improved chance to win some representation. Overall turnout was not demonstrably shaped by the electoral system.

Another myth that has persisted through the years is that PR produces fragmentation of the political system because of the more accurate representation of segments of society. In none of the Ohio cities using PR elections was there a significant increase in conflict among council members. In fact, it appears that the electoral pressures of ranked voting led to greater consensus as campaign styles changed. Although comparative urban policy studies have yet to deal adequately with important substantive areas, such as education, parks, labor practices, and public works, with which Progressive Era reformers were concerned, the five cities appear to have "worked" during their PR years.

In these five Ohio cities, PR/STV was demonstrated to be an electoral system technically capable of facilitating public decision making in complex communities as well as producing fair representation. More than three decades have passed since the last repeal of PR/STV in Ohio. These passing years have witnessed rapid political and societal changes in the expectations and aspirations of Americans and in the ways they relate to their governments at every level. The pursuit of fair representation continues even as the definition of "fair" has shifted from the representation of self envisioned by John Stuart Mill to the representation of groups, increasingly self-conscious and determined to be heard. As an electoral system capable of channeling the expression of diverse values and policy preferences, PR/STV is once more becoming the subject of public debate about who is entitled to participate in decisions and how they might do so.

TEN

■ ■ ■

The Right to Representation and the Future of PR

> The principle of proportionality is molded by the hope that a more cooperative political style of deliberation and ultimately a more equal basis for preference satisfaction is possible when authentic minority representatives are reinforced by [electoral] structures to empower them at every stage of the political process. Ultimately, however, representation and participation based on principles of proportionality are also an attempt to reconceptualize the ideal of political equality, and so the ideal of democracy itself.
>
> Guinier, "Second Proms and Second Primaries," 1992

THE FUTURE OF proportional representation in the United States may be very different from its past. Demographic and political pressures are opening the system to fresh ways of looking at the meaning of democracy. As the population becomes more diverse, better educated, and at the same time less participatory, citizens, lawmakers, and judges are seeking new ways to implement political values that are as old as the nation.

In the first half of the twentieth century, intense political battles were fought in the United States over voting and representation. The difference between the right to vote and the right to representation, however, was not widely understood. The right to vote spoke to the suffrage question: *who* should vote, an issue that depended on legislative majorities and on judicial interpretations of federal and state constitutions. The right to representation, nowhere constitutionally specified, depended on electoral systems that translated those votes into power.

Plurality ballots and geographically based districts have been generally accepted in the United States, in spite of the fact that winner-take-all elections, whether conducted in single-member or multimember districts or at-large, render large numbers of ballots ineffective and may leave significant groups unrepresented. Those with resources have formed interest groups to perform the representative function indirectly on their behalf, while those without have increasingly withdrawn from politics, polarizing the American system. Although the gridlock of interest groups and the decline of electoral turnout cannot be attributed to any one cause, the skewed system of representation is clearly a contributing factor.

Only since the right to vote was virtually settled by its federal enforcement under the Voting Rights Act of 1965 has the right to representation been directly addressed. As underrepresented plaintiffs asserted that a right was being violated by their exclusion from a fair share of seats at the public table, the legal and constitutional concept of "minority vote dilution" took shape. Attempts to remedy practices that restrict the ability of minorities to speak for themselves on city councils, in legislatures, and in Congress have shaken electoral systems to their roots. In the 1990s controversies over apportionment and districting, the number of officials on a governing board, and the appointment of a key federal election law enforcement official have erupted in public debate. The central, often unstated question is whether the country will continue to accept the winner-take-all rule as its guiding principle of representation.

This chapter will trace briefly the development of both a constitutional and a statutory right to representation, will note common remedies for violations of the right, and will explore new developments in the use of alternative electoral systems to facilitate fair and effective representation.

Minority Vote Dilution and Proportional Representation

The context of the American debate about representation has changed significantly since the last Ohio PR system was repealed in 1960. Responding to the black civil rights movement and the heightened consciousness it generated among other underrepresented groups, federal courts and Congress have, step by step, expanded the right to vote to encompass the right to representation. Although this fuller right remains ill-defined, it includes the right not to have one's vote diluted by an electoral system that denies a fair opportunity to elect candidates of one's choice.

Before 1960 the right to vote meant access to casting a ballot; by 1982 it required evaluation by the results of elections. In adopting results as a standard, however, courts and Congress specified that proportional representation is not required. Minorities previously excluded from power by a winner-take-all system are entitled to a remedy, but how much representation (less than proportional) is enough remained unclear. Despite its earlier denial that proportional representation is required, in 1994 the U.S. Supreme Court conceded the validity of proportionality as a standard by which fair representation could be measured *(Johnson v. DeGrandy)*. The meaning of these developments for the future of electoral systems is of vital significance. Although proportional representation is not *required* under current interpretation of the laws and the Constitution, neither is it prohibited. Could its time at last have come?

Constitutional Roots

The concept of vote dilution is not limited to the underrepresentation of minorities. In fact, it was the underrepresentation of the *majority* in our majority-rule system that gave rise to the first finding of unconstitutional vote dilution. In 1964 the malapportionment of state legislative bodies that gave the rural minority of voters greater representation than the urban majority was held to be unconstitutional. The urban majority gained protection when the U.S. Supreme Court held that "diluting the weight of votes because of place of residence impairs basic constitutional rights under the Fourteenth Amendment just as much as invidious discrimination based upon factors such as race, or economic status" *(Reynolds v. Sims,* 1964, at 566). The Court's analysis focused on the individual right—each person is entitled to an equally weighted vote—but the political impact of the ruling was anticipated by groups: rural voters who would lose their privileged position, and urban voters who would gain their fair share of power.

"Fair and effective representation" was stated as the purpose of a remedy, but this goal was defined only by the simple numerical standard of one person, one vote. In *Reynolds,* the Court allowed remedial choices of either multimember or single-member districts as long as the population criterion—equal numbers of representatives for equal numbers of people—was not violated (1964, at 577).

Plurality voting in multimember districts, however, raised the possibility of shutting minorities out in winner-take-all sweeps. In 1965, in a challenge to Georgia's new multimember state senate districts, the Court ruled that such districts, although not in themselves unconstitutional, might be invalid if they "operate to minimize or cancel out the voting strength of racial or political elements of the population" (*Fortson v. Dorsey* at 439). In 1973 this discriminatory effect led the Court to reject a Texas legislative districting plan in which minorities, although able to cast votes, were denied access to representation. The Court cautiously pointed out, however, that invalidating a plan that discriminated against minority voters was "not the same as declaring that every racial and political group has a right to be represented in the legislature" (*White v. Regester,* 1973, at 769).

Single-member districts have generally been the preferred remedy for such discriminatory effects. For minority groups that are residentially clustered, single-member districts may produce the desired relief. But districting is not a neutral activity. Whether the impact on representation is purposefully achieved or an accidental outcome, district lines help some groups and handicap others. Racial gerrymanders were for many years a key tool for the exclusion of African Americans from representation, either by dividing a cluster of minority voters into several districts where they were nowhere a majority, or by concentrating them into one district where, as a super-majority, their votes were wasted.[1]

Evidence of such racially discriminatory districting led the Court to support what came to be called the affirmative gerrymander. Here, political boundaries are drawn deliberately to create single-member districts for minorities that have previously experienced discriminatory exclusion from a legislative body. A New York State districting plan, which created two new majority-minority state legislative districts for black and Hispanic voters, was challenged by Hasidic Jews whose community was formerly concentrated in one white-majority district but was subsequently split between the two new districts. The Court upheld the plan on the ground that the minority groups that gained representation had been underrepresented in the past, whereas Hasidic Jews, as whites, would be fairly represented in the legislature as a whole (*United Jewish Organizations of Williamsburgh, Inc. v. Carey,* 1977).

This decision highlights the power of districting authorities to assign value to different groups and to shape the dimensions of political conflict. In the 1970s the Burger Court's working theories about representation placed "group political access" above the individual voter's right to be equally represented (Maveety, 1993, p. 221). Partisan groups as well as racial minorities gained protection. In *Gaffney v. Cummings,* the Court upheld a Connecticut legislative districting plan that protected incumbents and therefore could be expected to perpetuate the existing division of power between the two major political parties. "Rough proportional representation of the statewide strength of the two parties" was found to be a legitimate state goal, not a violation of the Fourteenth Amendment Equal Protection Clause (1973, at 738, 752). Although reluctant to open its doors to all claims of unfair partisan gerrymandering, the Court grew more willing to look at electoral arrangements that "consistently degrade a voter's or a group of voters' influence on the political process as a whole" (*Davis v. Bandemer,* 1986, at 132).

Statutory Enforcement: The Voting Rights Act

The Voting Rights Act of 1965 (42 USC § 1973 [1988]) was passed to enforce the right to vote that is implicit in the Fifteenth Amendment. Evidence of continuing discrimination in voting practices and even outright exclusion of African Americans from the polls led Congress to strengthen earlier attempts to protect voting rights. Some violations were so egregious that Congress required states in which discriminatory practices were serious and persistent to get permission from the District of Columbia federal district court or from the civil rights division of the Justice Department before changing voting regulations (§ 5). In sustaining this unprecedented restriction of state power, the U.S. Supreme Court held that "the right to vote can be affected by a dilution of voting power as well as by an absolute prohibition on casting a ballot" (*Allen v. State Board of Elections,* 1969, at 569). This proved to be a significant step on the path to a substantive right to representation.

In 1967, for the first time since 1929, Congress required the states to use single-member districts for congressional elections, a measure taken to prevent the states covered by the Voting Rights Act from using statewide winner-take-all elections to diminish the electoral opportunities of newly empowered black voters (2 USC § 2c, 1988).

In 1970 and again in 1975 Congress extended the Voting Rights Act, each time expanding its coverage and adding new federal protections to the right to vote. The 1975 renewal (for seven years) extended the act's provisions to reach language minorities, specifying Hispanics, Alaskan natives, Native Americans, and Asian Americans as protected classes. This provision, which relied on congressional power to enforce the Fourteenth Amendment's equal protection clause, also expanded the geographical scope of the act's special provisions to wherever significant concentrations of these language minorities are identified (§ 4).

In 1982 Congress found that minority vote dilution continued to exclude some Americans from full political participation and extended the Voting Rights Act again, this time placing the entire country under federal protection against minority vote dilution for 25 additional years. Moreover, a new standard was defined for judging violations (§ 2). The courts had required a showing of *intent* to discriminate in order to prove a constitutional violation (*City of Mobile v. Bolden,* 1980), but intent was difficult to prove. Congress provided an alternative statutory path for minority vote dilution cases by substituting *results* of elections as probative in section 2 cases.

Illegal vote dilution is now defined as any "voting qualification or prerequisite to voting, or standard, practice, or procedure" that "results in a denial or abridgement of the right of any citizen of the United States to vote" on account of racial or language minority status. A violation can be proven by showing that "the political processes leading to nomination or election" in a state or locality "are not equally open to participation" by these minorities and that their members have "less opportunity than other members of the electorate . . . to elect representatives of their choice." The statute permits consideration of "the extent to which members of a protected class have been elected to office," but stipulates that "nothing in this section establishes a right to have members of a protected class elected in numbers equal to their proportion in the population" (42 USC § 1973(a) [1988]).[2] Here Congress added its weight to the Court's denial that minority vote dilution requires proportional representation as a remedy.

Judicial Application of Standards

In the decade after passage of the 1982 amendments, hundreds of cases challenged plurality/at-large or plurality/multimember district elections on the grounds of minority vote dilution. Until 1986, the courts required plaintiffs to show that the "totality of circumstances" in the political process of nominations and elections created unequal access to power for minority voters, a standard drawn from an earlier federal court of appeals decision (*Zimmer v. McKeithen,* 5th Cir. 1973).

Since 1986, claims have been decided by a more rigorous three-part test put forth by the Supreme Court to determine whether such elections prevent minority voters from electing candidates of their choice. First, the plaintiff minority group must be "sufficiently large and geographically compact to constitute a majority of a single-member district." Second, the minority group must be "politically cohesive" enough to be able to elect a candidate in such a single-member district. Third, it must be shown that "the white majority votes sufficiently as a bloc to enable it . . . usually to defeat the minority's preferred candidate" (*Thornburg v. Gingles,* 1986 at 50–51, 56).

The Court's criteria in *Thornburg v. Gingles* look to the remedy of single-member districts, yet single-member districts create difficulties of their own in achieving fair representation. Plurality voting leaves minorities within districts unrepresented. Other complex issues include how small remedial districts must be, and therefore how many are, required; how district lines are to be drawn to ensure majority-minority districts; how often lines must be redrawn to accommodate population mobility; and how concentrated a majority-minority must be to have a genuine opportunity to elect candidates of its choice without wasting minority votes in super-majorities (Grofman, Handley, and Niemi, 1992, chap. 5; Morrison and Clark, 1992). Mixed systems merely add to these districting problems the potential for vote dilution of a few at-large seats, a category in which minorities are most under-represented in the nation generally (Engstrom, 1992, pp. 746–47).

On the level of practical politics, as distinct from constitutional theory, an obvious test for fair representation of minorities in a single-member district system is whether the share of majority-minority districts is proportional to the minority population. In spite of its earlier denial that proportional representation is required, in 1994 the Court actually applied a refined version of this criterion in a Florida districting case. Evaluating a state legislative districting plan alleged to dilute minority voting strength in Dade and Escambia Counties, the Court refused to find illegal dilution because the number of districts in which minority voters (both Hispanic and African-American) formed effective voting majorities was roughly proportional to their respective shares in the voting-age population (*Johnson v. DeGrandy,* 1994). Proportionality meant equal electoral opportunity. Insisting that the Court was not recognizing a right to proportional representation, Justice Souter distinguished "proportionality," which he called "the political or electoral power of minority voters," from "proportional representation," which he defined as "a guarantee of electoral success for minority-preferred candidates of whatever race" (*Johnson v. DeGrandy,* 1994, at 4760, n. 11).

The minority plaintiffs in *Johnson v. DeGrandy* had petitioned for the maximum possible number of majority-minority districts. This the Court rejected. Even though two more Hispanic districts for the U.S. House of Representatives could have been drawn, the state was not required to create them: "One may suspect vote dilution from political famine, but one is not entitled to suspect (much less infer) dilution from mere failure to guarantee a political feast" (*Johnson v. DeGrandy*, 1994, at 4761).

The claim to a maximum possible number of minority districts raises the issue of losing districts in which minorities can influence (although not control) their representatives. In order to craft more minority districts, line-drawing authorities must draw minority voters out of integrated districts where they could *influence* the selection and actions of a representative. Arguably, minorities lose rather than gain power when this happens, especially if super-majorities that waste votes are packed into such districts.

Minority-Influence Districts

Conflicting political values are at stake in choices made between fewer safe districts with super-majorities of minority voters and more numerous racially diverse districts in which minorities may influence the outcome. This issue is not new to the Supreme Court; indeed it lay at the heart of the challenge to a New York congressional district in 1964. A districting statute that concentrated black and Puerto Rican voters in one Manhattan district, making it over 86% minority, was challenged as discriminatory because it segregated voters by race and place of origin. A neighboring district became almost 95% white. The plaintiffs were minority voters objecting to exclusion from the white district and to the packing or wasting of minority votes in the minority district. The Court allowed the district's black representative, the Rev. Adam Clayton Powell, to intervene in support of the constitutionality of the act, a position noted by the Court when it rejected the challenge. The Fourteenth Amendment, the Court ruled, does not require the equal distribution of minority voters among congressional districts (*Wright v. Rockefeller*, 1964, at 54). Liberals on the Court were divided: Justice Black wrote the majority opinion, whereas Justices Douglas and Goldberg dissented (*Wright v. Rockefeller*, 1964, at 60). The dissenters argued that the outcome should be controlled by *Brown v. Board of Education*: racial segregation by law is inequality. Justice Douglas wrote:

> The fact that Negro political leaders find advantage in this nearly solid Negro and Puerto Rican district is irrelevant to our problem. Rotten boroughs were long a curse of democratic processes. Racial boroughs are also at war with democratic standards. . . . The principle of equality is at war with the notion that District A must be represented by a Negro, as it

is with the notion that District B must be represented by a Caucasian, District C by a Jew, District D by a Catholic, and so on (*Wright v. Rockefeller,* 1964, at 62, 66).

At a time when few African Americans held public office, the Court's decision in favor of this racial gerrymander is hardly surprising, but the issue of minority influence was submerged for several decades.

Today, the issue is alive again. In 1991 Ohio's Republican-controlled state apportionment board adopted a legislative districting plan that increased the number of majority-minority districts in the state by subtracting minority voters from previously integrated districts that usually elected white or black Democrats, and concentrating them in heavily minority districts. Adjoining districts were left more white and, given the proclivities of the excluded black voters to vote Democratic, more Republican.

Dissenting Democrats on the apportionment board challenged the plan as a dilution of minority voting strength in violation of both section 2 of the Voting Rights Act and the Fifteenth Amendment. Packing these new majority-minority districts, the plaintiffs alleged, led to fewer minority-*influence* districts, where black voters could elect candidates of their choice with white support. As in *Wright,* different African-American groups weighed in on each side of the dispute. Black plaintiffs who joined the suit showed that every district in Ohio that was 35% or more black had elected a black representative. The Congressional Black Caucus filed an *amicus* brief concluding that "the Voting Rights Act was not intended to result in political segregation of minority voters into a few districts, limiting their electoral influence, unless absolutely necessary" (*Cleve. Plain Dealer,* 6 Dec. 1992, p. 29A). Even the Republican defendants conceded that legislative voting in Ohio was not racially polarized.

Rejecting these arguments, a unanimous Supreme Court ruled that the state—which the Court conceded did not have a history of racial discrimination in districting—was entitled to create more majority-minority districts if it chose to do so, as long as the overall effect of the plan was not to "diminish or abridge the voting strength of the protected class." The Court refused to address the issue of whether black voting strength was diminished by the loss of minority-*influence* districts (*Voinovich v. Quilter,* 1993, at 4202).

The plaintiffs had claimed that minority vote dilution was not only real but intentional, because it was carried out for the political purpose of maximizing Republican voting strength. The outcome of Ohio's

1992 legislative election, held under the disputed plan on order from the U.S. Supreme Court, was known even before oral arguments were heard in the case. One additional black candidate was elected to the Ohio House, while Republicans captured eight additional seats (Sharkey, 1992), but the Court found partisan advantage to be irrelevant. Since the board had relied on proposals from the Black Elected Democrats of Ohio in drawing the new districts, its intent was ruled not to be discriminatory (*Voinovich v. Quilter,* 1993, at 4203).

The first round of congressional redistricting that was shaped by the 1982 amendments to the Voting Rights Act produced 17 new districts in nine southern states, districts drawn to enable minority voters in those states to elect representatives to Congress. African Americans were elected in 16 of these districts in 1992 and again in 1994 (*CQ's Politics in America,* 1994; Guinier, 1995, p. 36). In five of these states, this race-conscious districting was challenged in court. In the North Carolina case (*Shaw v. Reno,* 1993), the U.S. Supreme Court opened up a bitter constitutional debate about the extent to which race could be considered in drawing congressional districts.

At the root of the dispute in North Carolina was the fact that a state with a 22% black population had not elected a minority member to Congress between the end of the nineteenth century and the 1992 election for which two new districts (of 12) were drawn with majority-minority population.[3] White voters challenged one of these districts, claiming that the district was an unconstitutional racial gerrymander concentrating black voters "without regard to any other considerations, such as compactness, contiguousness, geographical boundaries, or political subdivisions" (*Shaw v. Reno,* 1993, at 4820).

The federal district court dismissed the complaint about this "snake-like" district, which was 160 miles long and wound through 10 counties, connecting black communities along an interstate highway. In some places the district was no wider than the highway, but the district court accepted the state's argument that it had merely linked together black urban voters in a rational plan to facilitate their representation. To the U.S. Supreme Court, however, the district looked suspiciously like racial apartheid. Justice O'Connor, writing for the majority, sent the case back to the district court, warning of the "risk of lasting harm" posed to society because including in one district

> individuals who belong to the same race, but who are otherwise widely separated by geographical and political boundaries, and who may have little in common with one another but the color of their skin . . .

reinforces the perception that members of the same racial group—
regardless of their age, education, economic status, or the community in
which they live—think alike, share the same political interests, and will
prefer the same candidates at the polls. We have rejected such perceptions elsewhere as impermissible racial stereotypes. . . . By perpetuating
such notions, a racial gerrymander may exacerbate the very patterns of
racial bloc voting that majority-minority districting is sometimes said to
counteract. (*Shaw v. Reno,* 1993, at 4823)

Dissenting justices agreed with the court below that the serpentine
district was defensible on the ground of racial proportionality. White
voters were not left underrepresented in the North Carolina congressional delegation by the new district lines. The Voting Rights Act
permits favoring minority voters as long as white voting strength is not
"unfairly diluted or canceled out," according to the dissent (*Shaw v.
Reno,* 1993, at 4821, 4829).

Proportionality could also have been achieved, however, by the
creation of a different and more compact minority district, an option
recommended by the state's attorney general. Only the dissenting
opinion reveals the reason that this most "obvious" district was not
drawn, namely incumbency protection. A Democratic incumbent
would have been threatened by the creation of a new minority district
in the southeastern section of the state (*Shaw v. Reno,* 1993, Justice
White, dissenting at 4830, n. 10).

Both the majority opinion and the dissents in *Shaw v. Reno* reveal
profound discomfort among the justices with respect to the underlying
issues of the case. The goal of fair representation is muddied by
stubborn political facts like the power of incumbency. Moreover, if
such political constraints are legitimate, then demographic reality—
the racial distribution of the state's population—thwarts the use of
districting to achieve the outcome sought. A majority of black voters,
both in North Carolina and across the South, live outside these
specially-drawn districts, yet neither the ruling majority nor the
protesting minority of the Court alluded to the option of an alternative
electoral system that would free the voters from the constriction of
single-member districts.

Editorially attacked as a "dinosaur ruling" (*N.Y. Times,* 30 June 1993,
p. A10), *Shaw v. Reno* was promptly cited in the lower courts, where
other Voting Rights Act cases were being litigated and where the issue
was starkly drawn to project either white districts or black districts as the
only possible alternative outcomes (*N.Y. Times,* 25 Sept. 1994, p. E4).

In *Shaw* itself, after a trial on the merits, the lower court in Raleigh upheld the district, acknowledging that it was "ugly" but calling it "a justifiable invocation of a concededly drastic, historically conditioned remedy for exclusion of African Americans from North Carolina's congressional delegation" (*Shaw v. Hunt,* 1994; *N.Y. Times,* 3 Aug. 1994, p. A8). This was not to be a final decision, however, since *Shaw* would join similar cases on appeal from Louisiana, Georgia, and Texas in the U.S. Supreme Court for clarification of constitutional guidelines to fair representation (*N.Y. Times,* 10 Dec. 1994, pp. A1, A7).

Protection of Language Minorities

Although race-conscious districting has facilitated African-American representation, other less segregated minorities are unlikely to benefit. As the American population grows steadily more diverse, the justification for protecting only those classes defined in 1975 will inevitably wane. The 1990 census reported that non-Hispanic whites constituted 75% of the population, but immigration and differential birth rates are projected to change the face of the nation in coming decades. By the year 2010, Hispanics are expected to be the largest minority group in the United States, approaching 40 million residents; the number of Asians, which doubled in the 1980s, will double again to about 15 million. The number of immigrants from the Caribbean and Africa, now a little over one million, are likely to grow to three million in the next two decades. The Census Bureau projects that by 2050 there will be no majority racial or ethnic group in the United States (Roberts, 1993, pp. 81–83, 246–55; Cohodas, 1994, pp. 704, 711).

Defining minorities by language (as in section 4 of the Voting Rights Act) was dubious from the start. Neither all Native Americans nor all Asian Americans speak the same language, whereas Hispanics who have a common linguistic heritage are diverse by race, nation of origin, and political party.[4] In 1982, when Congress extended the Voting Rights Act for 25 years, its assumption was that the lawmakers would not need to revisit these difficult political issues before 2007. However, rapid social, economic, and demographic change may require an earlier reassessment if a steady course of progress toward fair representation is to be maintained. The reliance on a rigid delineation of named minorities has already been breached in cases brought by coalitions of minorities, usually African-American and Hispanic voters who combine to challenge plurality/at-large elections.

Minority Coalitions and Competition

Coalitions have been undertaken in cases in which the minorities that alleged vote dilution were too small to meet the first requirement of the *Thornburg v. Gingles* test: to be populous enough to constitute a majority in a single-member district. Counted together, these minority groups can qualify by crossing the numerical threshhold. The courts have also held that whether two minorities could combine to become a new legally cognizable minority suffering from "minority coalition dilution" requires evaluation of their "political cohesiveness," the second requirement of the *Thornburgh v. Gingles* test.

Such political cohesiveness has been successfully demonstrated by evidence that both groups have been subject to discrimination in the past, that they share political goals, and that they vote together for minority candidates (*LULAC v. Midland Independent School District,* 1987; *Campos v. City of Baytown,* 1988; 1989).

Minority coalition suits, however, have been rejected more often than accepted. In the U.S. Supreme Court's first case over single-member-district vote dilution, a majority-minority state senate district, which had been imposed by a lower federal court in Minneapolis, was invalidated. The district was an "oddly-shaped creation" drawn to combine black voters with three other "separately identifiable" minority groups. The Court found neither a showing of political cohesion within the "agglomeration" of minority groups, nor evidence of majority bloc voting in the city, to justify such a district (*Growe v. Emison,* 1993, at 4167–68). Judicial reluctance to hear such suits may be based on concern that expansion of the Voting Rights Act's protection to "politically cohesive" coalitions of minorities could quickly become a legal resource for any political coalition unable to win seats (Grofman, Handley, and Niemi, 1992, pp. 70–73).

Competition among minority groups that are clearly not politically cohesive is also challenging judges to interpret "fairness" in representation in the context of the single-member-district plans drawn up after the 1990 census. In the Florida redistricting case, *Johnson v. DeGrandy* (above), the African-American and Hispanic groups in Dade County, far from forming a coalition, competed for control of majority-minority districts. The Supreme Court decided that it did not have to choose between them, however, since both groups held voting-age majorities in a number of districts "substantially proportional to their share in the population" (*Johnson v. DeGrandy,* 1994, at 4763).

In a companion case from Georgia,[5] this standard of proportionality was attacked in a lengthy concurring opinion by Justice Thomas, who was joined by Justice Scalia, calling for a reversal of the whole idea of a "right to representation." Proclaiming the concept of minority vote dilution to be a "disastrous misadventure in judicial policy-making," Justice Thomas urged a return to the literal meaning of the right to vote (*Holder v. Hall,* 1994, at 4734). It is the individual right, he argued, to enter a polling place, cast a ballot, and have it included in the final tally of votes cast (at 4741). The conversion of this right to a group right has resulted in the "segregation of voters into racially designated districts," which could "balkanize" the country. He objected to the political choices that the Court has had to make in order to devise remedies for minority vote dilution, noting that such choices could devolve only from theories of representation. He specifically attacked the remedy of single-member districts and the goal of proportionality as mere political choices. Other choices, he suggested, could just as well be cumulative voting or the single transferable vote (*Holder v. Hall,* 1994, at 4738–39).

Justice Thomas did not advocate these alternative electoral systems in his opinion; he did build on and open up a critical debate about representation that academics, civil rights lawyers, and electoral system specialists have tried for some years to bring to the public.[6] The original intent of the Voting Rights Act of 1965 may have been, as Justice Thomas asserts, unambiguous. Aimed at voting discrimination against African Americans, it was the culmination of a century-long struggle to overcome the political consequences of slavery. The subsequent stretch of its reach across the nation and to other minorities has become entangled in the rapid social and political change of the past quarter century. However, it is not only judicial creativity that has expanded the scope of the act. Congress has consistently reenacted the statute, an action that is understood to validate and incorporate the intervening interpretation of the courts. Furthermore Congress has increased the scope of the act in an attempt to ensure that casting a ballot is not just a formality but an "effective" exercise. Moreover, although political choices are frequently required of judges in Voting Rights Act cases, such choices are also required in many other areas of constitutional interpretation.

The contemporary debate about electoral systems, growing out of this recently developed right of representation, moves well beyond implementation of statutes into questions about the nature of representation and the meaning of democracy itself. These are the compelling questions that led Condorcet, Andrae, Hare, and others to invent balloting technologies that would give both the majority and minorities their proportional share of power.

Geographic versus "Voluntary" Constituencies

As rulings in Voting Rights Act cases become ever more tangled, it is apparent that the single-member-district system is simply incompatible with fair representation, except in the presence of large-scale segregation. This stubborn fact is kindling the current interest in electoral alternatives such as proportional representation. The familiar geographic base of representation needs to be recognized as a political choice, rooted in a theory developed long ago when communities were more homogeneous and less mobile than today's fluid societies.

As the stories in this book have shown, PR/STV, cumulative voting, and limited voting are three electoral systems that give voters the option to choose how they wish to be represented, whether by a neighborhood voice, a common political interest, a political party, or a group identity. Racial and ethnic minorities were the principal beneficiaries of the PR/STV elections used in Ohio cities between 1915 and 1960, and this neglected history is relevant to the current debate. In a PR at-large system, voters can build coalitions across such categorical lines to form truly voluntary constituencies. The geographic base of representation is not totally abandoned, since at-large or multimember district elections have never been the true culprits in the exclusion of minorities. It is the practice of plurality voting that has perpetuated the overrepresentation of the majority and the concomitant underrepresentation of minorities in both at-large and district settings. With a proportional system, the political community itself becomes the natural base of representation and voters form coalitions as they choose, not as preprogrammed by single-member districting into small fragments of the community.

Today, whereas plaintiffs, judges, and some commentators see in single-member district plurality voting only sensible accommodation to familiar practices (Grofman and Davidson, 1992, pp. 300–314), others—both conservative and liberal critics of the enforcement of the Voting Rights Act—see the spread of dysfunctional politics. Abigail Thernstrom of Boston University, for example, views race-conscious districting to achieve minority representation as divisive and destructive of important political values such as compromise and consensus building. Her complaint goes beyond Justice Thomas's objection to judicial decisions promoting group entitlement to representation. Like Thomas, she would define the right to vote as merely access to the polls. However, where Justice Thomas leaves open the path to alternative electoral systems—if only they are chosen by proper policy makers, that is, legislative bodies—Thernstrom values the winner-take-all system in which the majority subsumes the importance of group membership (Thernstrom, 1987, chap. 10).

Lani Guinier, professor of law at the University of Pennsylvania and counsel in voting rights cases, and former nominee to the Justice Department's key voting rights enforcement job, also attacks racial districting. In contrast to Thernstrom, however, she objects on the ground that creation of safe minority districts produces only token representation. Council members or legislators elected from such districts, she argues, are recognized as token by minority voters, who may participate when first given an opportunity to elect one of their own, but who fall away as the early minority winners become incumbents without power to change policy. Furthermore, even this token representation depends on the perpetuation of residential segregation and pits minorities against each other in contests for the strongest claim to a district. Not only does segregation become the base for minority political power, Guinier argues, but black voters in new districts become isolated from potential allies—both minorities in other districts and the white majority. This isolation in turn inhibits coalition building in the legislative process, which is necessary to achieve policies responsive to minority needs (Guinier, 1991).

In a thorough analysis of black representation in Congress, Carol Swain argues that the promotion of substantive policy interests of African Americans hinges on building multiracial coalitions. Swain advocates the unpacking of districts that have super majorities of minority voters in order to expand minority influence, as well as efforts by black candidates to compete in less than safe electoral settings (Swain, 1993, pp. 207–11).

Guinier's more far-reaching solution is to decrease racial polarization by adopting proportional or semi-proportional representation elections and to develop legislative procedures that respond to minority influence as well as to minority presence in decision-making bodies (Guinier, 1991). How little her views were understood was demonstrated by President Clinton's withdrawal of her 1993 nomination to be assistant attorney general for civil rights in the U.S. Department of Justice (Lewis, 1993, pp. A1, A12; Applebome, 1994, p. E5). Denied the opportunity to explain to the Senate Judiciary Committee the analysis of voting rights expounded in her law review articles, she has tried to expand the national debate about remedies for minority vote dilution beyond racial districting by speaking and writing, especially to advocate cumulative voting (Guinier, 1994).

Harbingers of Change

While this academic and judicial debate has been percolating, electoral experiments have been introduced in many small communities around the country, usually as a part of settlements of Voting Rights Act cases. Cumulative voting (CV) has been adopted for city councils in Peoria, Illinois, and Alamogordo, New Mexico; for the school board in Sisseton, South Dakota; for a county commission, a school board, and three city councils in Alabama; and for 22 local jurisdictions in Texas (Engstrom, 1992; Still, 1992; *Time,* 25 Apr. 1994, pp. 42–43; *Texas Observer,* 22 July 1994, vol. 86, pp. 3–4).

In most of the communities where CV elections have been held to date, one minority member has been elected to the three-, five-, or seven-member council or board. Minorities winning representation in these elections include African Americans and white Republicans in Alabama, Hispanics in Texas and New Mexico, and Native Americans in South Dakota. Minorities failed to win in two Alabama CV elections: one in a community (Myrtlewood) in which no minority candidate ran; and another in Centre in which a black candidate was elected in the first CV election (1988), but because a second black candidate divided the vote in the 1992 election, both minority candidates lost (Still, 1992, p. 185; *Time,* 25 Apr. 1994, p. 43). This latter outcome illustrates why CV is called only "semi-proportional." As minority candidates begin to win, others will be encouraged to run. Strategic voting and discipline in nominations will become important if CV is to fulfill proportional aspirations over time.

Alamogordo, New Mexico, a city of 24,000 population, has used CV successfully for a residentially dispersed minority, here Hispanic voters, as is frequently the case in southwestern states. Twenty-one percent of the city's voting-age population was Hispanic. Its mixed electoral system, adopted in the settlement of a Voting Rights Act suit, provided for a seven-member council, with four single-member districts, and three members to be elected at-large by CV (Engstrom, Taebel, and Cole, 1989, pp. 480–81). In three successive elections (1987, 1990, 1994) one of the at-large seats was captured by a Hispanic woman (tabulation from the Center for Voting and Democracy, 1 Aug.

1994). Exit poll data from her first election showed that she could not have been elected without the support of white voters but the option available to Hispanic voters to demonstrate intensity by cumulating their votes carried her to victory. On the average, she received 2.6 votes from Hispanic voters (Engstrom, Taebel, and Cole, 1989, p. 495).

In April 1994, in what might have been the first judicially imposed CV settlement of a Voting Rights Act violation, a federal district court in Maryland ordered CV elections for the Worcester County Commission (*Cane v. Worcester County, Md.,* 1994). The electoral system that was found to violate African-American voters' rights was based on a five-member commission elected at-large, with four of the five members each residing in a district. The voters who challenged this system proposed either a single-member district plan or CV, with the commissioners elected at-large and each voter able to cast five votes, allocating them as desired among the candidates. Black voters, making up 20% of the county's population, would have a chance to elect one of the five. Judge Young chose the CV plan, pointing out that "cumulative voting, unlike single-member districts, will allow the voters, by the way they exercise their votes, to 'district' themselves based on what they think rather than where they live." The court considered the CV remedy "less drastic" a remedy than single-member districts, because candidates would continue to run at-large, and as less likely to "increase polarization between different interests since no group receives special treatment at the expense of others" (*Cane v. Worcester County,* 1994, at 2631).

The Fourth Circuit court of appeals upheld the finding that the Worcester County election system violated the Voting Rights Act but rejected the remedy of cumulative voting, on the ground that under CV regional representation within the county would not be assured (*Worcester County, Md. v. Cane,* No. 94–1579). The lower court was given the task of creating a single-member system for the county with one racially defined district that somehow would connect three scattered African-American communities. Its shape is expected to "resemble a skinny dinosaur on its hind legs" (Lewis, 1994, p. B10). Meanwhile, Worcester County officials appealed the finding of a Voting Rights Act violation to the U.S. Supreme Court.

In the North Carolina congressional districting case (*Shaw v. Reno,* 1993), a CV plan that drew an unusual amount of attention was proposed as a remedy for the allegedly unconstitutional racial district. In place of the snakelike district as one of 12 existing single-member districts, Lee Mortimer of the Center for Voting and Democracy proposed three multimember congressional districts for the state as a whole. With boundaries largely following county lines, a Western District would elect three members, a Piedmont district (incorporating most of the challenged Twelfth District), would elect five, and the Eastern District, four. Voters would cast their ballots at-large within the multimember districts, but be able to cumulate their votes as they chose—all for one candidate, or divided among several. The attraction of the plan was its ability to create the opportunity for minorities to win representation without rigidly programming voters into racial districts (*News and Record,* Greensboro, N.C., 9 Jan. 1994, p. F3; *N.Y. Times,* 3 Apr. 1994, p. E5; *New Yorker,* 4 Apr. 1994, pp. 7–8).

An alternative proposed by Lani Guinier would have North Carolina voters choose their 12 members of Congress by CV at-large, with each voter casting 12 statewide votes that could be cumulated in accord with voter preference (*Wash. Post Weekly,* 11 Apr. 1994, p. 24). Either of these plans would have enabled the 60% of African-American voters in the state who were not living in either of the racially designated districts to vote with others of similar interests. However, both CV plans would require a change in the federal law mandating single-member districts for Congress, and neither proposal was entered formally in the case.

Cincinnati, the home of PR/STV elections for three decades (1925–55), became the locus of a proposed CV plan in the spring of 1993. Cincinnati's history of earlier election reform, recounted in chapter 6, offers a unique setting for reconsideration of representational issues in light of the current heightened awareness of discrimination. The Cincinnati Charter Committee, an integrated coalition that played a central role in the introduction and continued practice of PR/STV, had narrowly lost two initiatives (1988 and 1991) to restore the city's proportional representation elections.

Following the 1991 defeat of PR, fifteen African-American voters sued the city in federal court, alleging that the plurality/at-large electoral system for city council was adopted with the intent to discriminate against black voters, and that it indeed caused minority vote dilution in violation of the Voting Rights Act. The remedy they sought was not PR but a single-member district system. Judge Herman Weber, to whom the case was assigned, delayed the trial to allow the city council itself to present its preferred remedy to the voters. After public hearings, input from consultants, and lengthy internal debate, the council placed on the May 1993 ballot a council election plan retaining the nine at-large members but providing for their election by cumulative voting. A brief but intense campaign led to defeat of the initiative by a 79% majority, and the case went to trial (*Center for Voting and Democracy*, 1994, pp. 41–42; *Cincinnati Enquirer*, 7 Feb. 1993, pp. H1–H2; *Cleve. Plain Dealer*, 17 May 1993, p. 3B).

In July 1993 Judge Weber issued his decision upholding the city's 9X voting system. Although conceding that a nasty racial "whisper campaign" had accompanied the 1957 repeal of PR and the adoption of plurality/at-large voting, the Judge denied that city officials were responsible for it. Furthermore, he attributed PR's repeal to "objective factors such as low voter turnout at a special election; the deficiencies of PR; and partisan political interests" (*Clarke v. City of Cincinnati*, 1993). The opinion quoted the U.S. Supreme Court's rejection of race-conscious districting in *Shaw v. Reno* (1993, *supra*), which was announced between the trial in Cincinnati and Judge Weber's decision. Since the Cincinnati decision rested on judicial refutation of racially polarized voting patterns in the city, and the requested remedial districting was not before the judge at this stage of the trial, the relevance of *Shaw* was unclear. The decision, however, was upheld on appeal (Fed. App. 0369P, 6th Cir., 1994; *Cleve. Plain Dealer*, 4 Nov. 1994, p. 5B).

In contrast to the relatively widespread publicity generated by cumulative voting plans in the past several years, limited voting (LV) has been implemented more quietly in current voting rights controversies. Twenty-one towns in Alabama adopted LV elections as a result of an omnibus settlement of vote dilution claims in which the state's use of plurality/at-large elections was found to be purposefully discriminatory by race (*Dillard v. Crenshaw County*, 1986). These towns adopted either five- or seven-member councils, with voters limited to casting one or, in some towns, two votes. In both 1988 and 1992, in all but one of the municipalities where African-American candidates ran, one or two were elected. In some cases, the total number of candidates was equal to the number of seats, making the victory uncontested. In 1988, however, black candidates won contested LV races in six of seven Alabama towns, and in 1992 in four of five. In Lowndesboro (1988) and in Dora (1992), the single black candidate finished only one or a few votes behind the winner with the lowest total vote. This outcome suggests that either black turnout was very low, or that many African Americans but virtually no white voters crossed racial lines in voting. In all the Alabama LV communities in which minority wins occurred, the result was representation in proportion to the minority share of the voting-age population (Still, 1992, pp. 190–91; Engstrom, Still, and Kirksey, 1994).

The Policy Puzzle

The view of the right to representation as the right to full participation in the political process should move the debate beyond electoral systems themselves to their impact on policy. The psychological rewards, which voting brings to many and service in public office brings to a few, are not the ultimate goal of representation. Participation in policy making itself and influence on public policy outcomes are the intrinsic purpose of the exercise. To link policy change to electoral system reform is a difficult challenge because of the complexity of intervening variables. When the relevant characteristics of council members are altered by different modes of election, however, new policies are at least anticipated. If previously excluded groups gain access to a system of governance, the assumption is that access will be used to modify existing policies and to address neglected needs.

An examination of the impact of the Voting Rights Act on minority communities analyzed changes in Dallas and San Antonio over a period encompassing a shift from plurality/at-large elections to a mixed single-member district/at-large system. In both cities the new electoral system did result in greater minority representation. The changes found following implementation of the new electoral system were increases in minority shares of municipal employment, of appointments to city boards and commissions, and of city contracts. Nevertheless, although increased access to "positions of public influence" created the *potential* for influence on substantive policies, major social change had not occurred (Fraga, 1991, pp. 14–17). Closer examination of the politics of council interactions would be required to evaluate these findings, but these newly districted Texas cities appear to illustrate Guinier's theory that tokenism is produced by single-member district representation and the resulting isolation of minority representatives in the policy process.

By opting for remedies for minority vote dilution based on single-member districts or on electoral systems partially districted and partially at-large, courts have made profoundly political choices in favor of descriptive over substantive representation. More than a quarter century of enforcement of the Voting Rights Act has successfully brought African Americans into the voting booth and into offices from which they had been effectively excluded. Less controversy has afflicted voting rights disputes than other efforts to overcome discrimination. Coverage under section 2 has even been extended by the courts to judicial elections in which minority voting strength has been diluted (*Chisom v. Roemer,* 1991; *Houston Lawyers' Assoc. v. Atty. Gen. of Texas,* 1991; Still, 1991).

Still, African Americans have not been able to win a proportional share of seats in most policy-making bodies, and Hispanics and other language minorities lag even further behind (Davidson, 1992, p. 46; Cohodas, 1994, pp. 704, 711). As seen in the post-1990 round of legislative redistricting, the cost of progress has been high. Significant examples of racial and political polarization show the concentration of minority voters in bizarrely shaped districts that have benefited white Republicans whose adjoining districts and power were solidified by the subtraction of minority voters (Graham, 1992, pp. 195–96; Guinier, 1991, p. 1143; *Voinovich v. Quilter,* 1993). Indeed, more than a decade ago, this result was predicted by electoral system experts (Piccard, 1984; Zimmerman, 1980, 1990). For these political reasons, housing segregation is likely to persist and even sharpen if Voting Rights Act remedies are not modified to allow for alternative systems (Yates, 1992). Furthermore, the use of the gerrymander, identified by advocates of PR as a defect of district systems since the nineteenth century (McCrackan, 1897; Hatton, 1915; Stone, 1915), will grow from the traditional partisan power grab into a legal requisite.

Conclusion

If democracy in the twenty-first century is finally to mean the full and substantive participation of all groups in political life, the electoral foundations for such change can be found in a variety of proportional systems. PR/STV is one of these that has been tried, as reported here. Its history does not sustain the fears of those who have missed its earlier American practice. Turnout did not plummet; fragmentation of parties and groups did not grind the wheels of government to a halt. Minorities did make legislative gains. Shortcomings attributed to the manual count would be eliminated by the use of computers. Elections would be held at-large, but the STV ballot would enable both the majority and minorities to gain their fair share of seats. Minorities would not have to be defined by government edict in order to gain representation but would be voluntary constituencies and coalitions.

The bias often expressed by lawmakers and judges against proportional representation is at least in part shaped by lack of knowledge about the variety of actual systems using PR and by the misunderstanding of the term itself. Advocates of PR face a stubborn but false belief that it requires outcomes based on quotas assigned to racial, ethnic, or partisan groups.

"Free voting," Cleveland's Tom Johnson called it a century ago, attempting to capture in a phrase the fluid opportunities implicit in proportional representation. Under PR the voters decide which values or interests need representation. In the microcosms examined here, not all social, economic, and political problems were solved, nor should electoral systems be expected to bring utopia, but adoption of the proportional principle for American elections would create opportunity for a more inclusive, less polarized democracy.

Notes

INTRODUCTION

1. Articles on PR by labor economist John Commons, historian Charles Beard, and others appeared in such American magazines as *Outlook, New England Magazine, Nation, New Republic, North American Review, Municipal Affairs, American City, Survey Graphic, Century, Unpopular Review* (which later became the *Unpartizan Review*), and *Independent;* as well as in such British publications as *Blackwood's Edinburgh Magazine, Westminster Review, Nineteenth Century, Edinburgh Review,* and *Contemporary Review.* Academic journals such as *Political Science Quarterly,* the *American Journal of Sociology,* and the *Annals of the American Academy of Political and Social Sciences* published occasional articles on proportional representation as well.

2. The Center for Voting and Democracy, a nonprofit organization dedicated to educating the public about alternative electoral systems and their consequences for representational outcomes, has been established. The *National Civic Review,* successor to the former *National Municipal Review,* has reintroduced a regular column to report on proportional election system initiatives and litigation around the country (Richie, 1993).

CHAPTER 1

1. By 1921 proportional representation/party list systems had been adopted for parliamentary elections in Belgium (1899), Finland (1906), Cuba (1908), Sweden (1909), Portugal (1911), Bulgaria (1912), Denmark (1915), Iceland (1916), The Netherlands (1917), Rumania (1918), Switzerland (1918), Austria (1919), Germany (1919), Uruguay (1919), Luxembourg (1919), Hungary (1919), Italy (1919), Czechoslovakia (1920), Norway (1920), Yugoslavia (1920), Estonia (1920), Lithuania (1920), Latvia (1920), and Poland (1921). Many of these countries had adopted PR/PL earlier for municipal and/or provincial elections. In 1916 Russia elected its constituent assembly under Kerensky by PR/STV, and Armenia, Georgia, and the Far Eastern (Siberian) Republic elected

national assemblies by this method between 1918 and 1920, when they became part of the U.S.S.R. (Hoag and Hallett, 1926, pp. 280–87).

2. Recently translated medieval works written by theologian-mathematicians in Latin, Arabic, and Catalan reveal earlier roots of collective decision theory. Ramon Lull (1235–1315) recommended a "Condorcet" method of indirect election of their abbess by nuns, who would make pairwise comparisons of all reasonable candidates to choose the best. Nicholas Cusanus (1401–64) proposed a "Borda" selection process, in which the Holy Roman Emperor would be chosen by electors who would allocate points in descending rank order of their preferences (McLean, 1990).

3. This simple formula was later refined to prevent the unlikely outcome of a tied vote among all candidates. The establishment of a "threshold," the minimum number of votes required to win, is discussed in chap. 3.

4. Mill and Tocqueville shared ideas in an extended correspondence and in person when Tocqueville visited England in 1835. Both believed in the inevitability of political equality, and both feared the future degeneration of democracy into despotism. Mill reviewed both volumes of *Democracy in America* in the *London and Westminster Review* (1835, 1840), and he wrote the introduction to its Schocken edition. Tocqueville wrote to Mill (3 Oct. 1835) that he (Mill) was "the only one who has entirely understood me," and considered Mill his "prime confidant" during the writing of vol. 2 of *Democracy in America* (Lamberti, 1989, pp. 26, 135, 177).

5. The university electorate, first activated in 1603, was composed of graduates of their respective universities. Business owners, and from 1928 to 1944 their wives, were entitled to more than one vote in districts where their enterprises were located if those districts were other than their district of residence. In the period between the two world wars, the university vote was 2% and the business vote 1.5% of the total vote. These plural votes were eliminated in 1948 (Reeve and Ware, 1992, pp. 47–49, 63).

6. Mill reprinted Hare's text in an article published in *Fraser's Magazine* (1859, 59:489–508), and in his *Thoughts on Parliamentary Reform,* 2nd ed., 1860 (1972–88, vol. 19, pp. 491–95).

7. Mill's championship of "Mr. Hare's plan," which he later conceded could also be called "M. Andrae's plan" ([1865] 1910, p. 275, n. 1), led to the common use in both Britain and the United States of the term "the Hare system of voting" to denote PR/STV. Since technical improvements in the calculation of the winning threshold and in methods of allocating surplus votes (see chap. 3) have not changed the basic purpose or concept of "Hare's" electoral system, the terms are still used as equivalents.

8. Limited voting (LV) is used within a plurality/at-large system with more than one seat to be filled; each voter casts fewer votes than the number of seats. In Mill's day, the parliamentary proposal was limited to three seats to be filled, with voters permitted to cast votes for two. Members of minorities, by casting their votes for one candidate, might secure representation. Some proportionality is achieved by this restriction on the winner-take-all feature of plurality/at-large voting. The principle may be applied in larger multiseat

districts, as long as the voter is limited to casting fewer votes than the number of seats (see chap. 3).

9. Cumulative voting (CV), which also may be used in a plurality/at-large system with multimember districts, gives the same number of votes to each voter as the number of seats to be filled, but the voter may express intensity of support by casting all votes for one candidate or by dividing the votes among two or more candidates. In a three-member district, by casting all three votes for one candidate, a minority of one-third of the voters could elect one of the three members (see chap. 3).

10. Hare's leading example of these "vagaries of the traditional method of voting" pointed to the constituencies of Liverpool and Glasgow, each of which elected two members. In these constituencies, political opinion was fairly evenly divided. Plurality voting, however, delivered both Liverpool seats to the Conservatives and both Glasgow seats to the Liberals, shutting out the minority party in each city (O'Leary, 1979, pp. 1–2).

11. Examples include Mill's letter to Boston architect Charles A. Cummings urging the adoption of PR/STV in America (23 Feb. 1863; Mill, 1972–88, vol. 15, pp. 842–43). Mill also corresponded with Australians (whose experience with Rowland Hill's PR/STV dated from 1840) about encouraging publicity in America, where the plan was "making its way" (letter to Henry Samuel Chapman, 24 Feb. 1863, 1972–88, vol. 15, p. 844). An American publication appeared in 1862 with Hare and Mill listed as joint authors: *True and False Democracy: The Representation of All and the Representation of the Majority Only; a brief synopsis of publications on this subject* (Boston: Prentiss and Deland).

12. Illinois legislative elections provided the most successful example of the use of CV in the United States, lasting for 110 years. The repeal of cumulative voting in 1980 was linked to a reduction in size of the Illinois lower house prompted by a purportedly outrageous pay raise, which the members had voted for themselves. Since the voters had "decisively" approved the retention of cumulative voting in 1970, the reasons for abandonment of this semi-proportional system in 1980 are at best clouded (Weaver, 1984, pp. 198–99; Everson and Parker, 1983).

13. In Ohio's congressional elections from 1876 to 1896, the correlation coefficient between seats and votes by party was statistically insignificant ($r^2 = .39$) (Argersinger, 1989, p. 72).

CHAPTER 2

1. *Clinton v. The Cedar Rapids R. R. Co.*, 24 Iowa 455 (1868).

2. Cleveland's Tom L. Johnson, mayor from 1901 to 1909, was known nationally as the "prototype of the best of the Progressive Era" (Griffith, 1974, p. 146). He exemplified the spirit of Progressivism in his commitment to expansion of city services, public ownership of utility companies, and equitable taxation. He organized fellow Democrats and lobbied at the state level,

not only for home rule but also for beneficial labor legislation and redistribution of the burden of taxation (Warner, 1964, p. 55 and chap. 4). Historians who view the "good government" reformers as "patricians" treat Johnson, a Democratic businessman, as an exception, not a prototype, however (Buenker, 1973, pp. 26–27).

3. A significant cleavage in the Ohio Republican party between Liberals and Regulars can be traced back to the post–Civil War struggle over tariffs and temperance. Many of the Liberal Republican leaders in Ohio were pre–Civil War antislavery Democrats. They shared the goal of industrial development with the Regulars, but sought to achieve it through free trade rather than protectionism. Primarily urban, with a significant infusion of German Americans, these Liberal Republicans opposed temperance laws and resisted monopolies, which were developing in the rapidly expanding cities. The tight grip of Republican machines on Ohio cities precluded electoral success for these deviant Republicans in the last two decades of the nineteenth century. More than half of the Liberal Republican leaders in Ohio had joined (or rejoined) the Democratic Party by the end of the century, giving Democrats "wealthy and respectable new leaders and thus assur[ing] a more even partisan division among the upper class" (McGerr, 1982, p. 323). The independent Progressive movement in Ohio was undoubtedly strengthened by this partisan mobility.

4. Fractional representation allowed for additional representation of counties with a population that was one-fifth or more above the ratio of representation. Such counties would gain an additional representative for one, two, three, or four biennial sessions of the decade of an apportionment. Thus the number of members in the Ohio legislature was not fixed but was determined by population ratios (the total population of the state divided by 100). Rural counties were accorded the advantage of one seat for half a ratio of representation. When the Hanna Amendment was adopted, only 10 counties fell below the half-ratio minimum and therefore gained their own representatives after 1903. By 1960, 48 of the 88 counties in Ohio lacked the half-ratio required before 1903, and 71 counties fell below a single ratio but still had a representative because of the Hanna Amendment. The state senate apportionment remained relatively equitable, since three-quarters of a ratio entitled a district of one or more counties to one senator. As in the Ohio house, additional senators were allocated to populous counties, including fractional representation where justified by population. By this method of apportionment, gerrymandering was avoided (Barber, 1981, p. 257).

5. In the nineteenth century, Ohio was a stronghold of the temperance movement and the birthplace of organized state-by-state prohibition efforts. The Women's Christian Temperance Union was founded in Cleveland in 1874. In 1893 the Ohio Anti-Saloon League was founded in Oberlin and grew quickly into a national organization, headquartered in Westerville, Ohio; the league's top priority was to force political candidates to reveal their position on prohibition (Knepper, 1989, p. 277).

6. By 1914 the "drys" would prevail in the Progressive state convention, writing prohibition into the platform to attract "dry" voters to their candidates for governor and other statewide offices. A large and vocal minority still saw the liquor issue as a mere distraction from important matters of economic equity (Warner, 1964, pp. 483–87).

7. The question of calling a constitutional convention would have been on the ballot automatically in 1912 (the Ohio Const., art. 16, called for the question to be put before the voters every 20 years), but momentum toward reform led the legislature to advance the date. Groups agitating for their particular reform are given credit for successfully promoting constitutional revision: the Ohio State Board of Commerce, seeking classification of property for tax purposes; liquor interests, seeking the licensing of saloons; and the Direct Legislation League, advocating the initiative and referendum (Warner, 1964, p. 295).

8. Herbert Bigelow, president of the Direct Legislation League, and later a leader in the PR movement, was elected president of the convention. Calling for a "new social compact" in his speech nominating Bigelow for that office, John D. Fackler of Cuyahoga County said, "Overshadowing all other questions and almost to the exclusion of every other issue, the question of this Convention's leaving in the hands of the individual citizen a greater and more direct control over the legislation of the state was paramount in the minds of men . . . elected to this Convention" (Ohio, 1912, *Proceedings,* p. 26).

9. The defeat of two amendments for which they had campaigned strenuously—women's suffrage and the abolition of capital punishment—was the Progressives' greatest disappointment. Both highest turnout and closest margins were returned on these controversial amendments (Warner, 1964, pp. 341–43, and 353, n. 76).

10. Pennsylvania was a case in contrast. In 1922 a state constitutional amendment had allowed home rule for the state's cities, but only if the legislature passed enabling legislation—and it never did, apparently owing to adamant opposition by the Republican state organization, which held secure majorities in both houses. Thus any local charter initiatives, either proposal of a new charter or adoption of a new electoral system, were vulnerable to the disapproval of the state legislature (Hallett, 1940, p. 165).

11. The National Municipal League's *Model City Charter* incorporated the city manager plan and PR/STV in its 2nd (1915), 3rd (1925), 4th (1933), and 5th (1941) editions. In the 6th edition (1964), the NML noted PR/STV's vulnerability to repeal referenda in a number of cities that had adopted the system, and proposed PR/STV as "Alternative C." Alternatives A and B were variations of a mixed electoral system, with four at-large and three district representatives. The 7th edition (1989) recommends PR as one of five alternative electoral systems, noting that "concern for representation of minorities and the possibility of technological improvements that will simplify the counting process have renewed interest in PR" (NML, 1989, *Model City Charter,* p. xv).

12. This recommendation was retained through the 5th edition of the NML's *Model State Constitution* (1948) but was dropped without explanation (although the single legislative chamber was retained) in the 6th edition (1963).

13. Telephone interview with David Lampe, editor of the *National Civic Review*, 24 Feb. 1992. (Also see Hallett, 1940, pp. 166–67; Cassella, 1990.)

14. With Augustus R. Hatton, now at Northwestern University, as president and with three vice presidents (one of whom was John R. Commons), the P.R. League continued a "separate corporate existence and . . . separate officers," operating "through" the NML. A section on PR, edited by George H. Hallett, appeared in each issue of the *National Municipal Review* for some years (*NMR*, 1940, 29:217–18).

15. *Wattles ex rel. Johnson v. Upjohn,* 211 Mich. 514, 179 NW 335 (1920).

16. *People ex rel. Devine v. Elkus,* 59 Cal. App. 396, 211 Pac. 34 (1922), hearing denied by Cal. S. Ct. (1922).

17. *Reutener v. City of Cleveland et al.,* 107 Ohio St. 117, 141 NE 27 (1923); *Hile v. City of Cleveland,* 107 Ohio St. 144, 141 NE 35 (1923), writ of error dismissed 266 U.S. 582 (1924).

18. *Johnson v. City of New York,* 274 N.Y. 411 (1937).

CHAPTER 3

1. Efforts to measure and predict the partisan bonus delivered by PL/SMD electoral systems include Kendall and Stuart, 1950; Tufte, 1973, 1975; Niemi and Deegan, 1978. Tufte's rule of thumb estimates that the majority party will gain 2.5 percentage points in seat shares for every one percentage point gain in vote shares (Tufte, 1973, p. 546). These measures are analyzed in Barber, 1983.

2. Voluntary strategic voting differs from formal systems of limited voting (LV), which are purposefully adopted to secure minority representation. See below, Semi-Proportional Voting Systems.

3. In Australia, voting is compulsory and voters are required to rank order every candidate on the ballot. The alternative vote is adaptable, however, to voluntary voting, and voters could make simply one or more choices of candidates by numbering their preferences (Bogdanor, 1984, p. 34).

4. Refinements of the rules described here are suggested by advocates of PR/STV to streamline the count or to deal with special situations, the "what if?" questions (Newland, 1982, pp. 71–74).

5. In most PR/STV systems, a single X is accepted as the equivalent of a numeral one. Such a ballot is then "exhausted" after the first count. A ballot with more than one X is, however, invalid, because neither the first choice nor subsequent rank ordering can be ascertained.

6. If the threshold were set at 100 in this example, instead of 101, then a tie could ensue among 10 candidates with 100 votes each. Although such a tie is extremely unlikely in an actual election, it is theoretically possible and is

avoided by the addition of 1 to the threshold. Robert A. Newland, a British analyst of electoral systems, has argued that the final "+1" is not a necessary component of the formula, and it is sometimes dropped today, as in elections to the Irish Dail (Newland, 1982, p. 66; Rae, 1967, p. 36). Macklin treats the difference between the two formulae as insignificant (1989, p. 6). All electoral systems require a method to deal with ties. In a two-candidate tie with plurality voting, the usual tie-avoidance mechanism is a coin toss (Reeve and Ware, 1992, p. 177, n. 7). Ohio law provides for several other tie-breaking devices as well, such as drawing straws, picking cards, and throwing dice. A recent example occurred in a three-way PL/SMD race for council in Vermilion, Ohio, when the two leading candidates each received 161 votes. A coin toss broke the tie (*Cleve. Plain Dealer,* 22 Nov. 1991, p. 2B). If the alternative vote had been used, the third candidate, who received 146 votes, could have been dropped and his ballots redistributed to the second choices his supporters had marked. By this means, voter preference rather than chance would have determined the outcome.

7. For a comprehensive presentation of the count for a PR/STV election to fill six seats in an 11-candidate contest, see Lakeman and Lambert, 1959, app. 4, pp. 247–75.

8. A PR/STV ballot is termed "exhausted" when every candidate designated by the voter in order of choice is either already elected (i.e., has reached the threshold and does not need more votes) or already eliminated (i.e., has no chance of election and his or her ballots have been transferred to second or other choices).

CHAPTER 4

1. In 1935 a fire in the Ashtabula county courthouse in Jefferson destroyed all voting records for the three periods covered by this study. Sources of data utilized include the Ashtabula *Beacon Record* (1900–16), *Daily Star* (1914–16), *Ashtabula Star-Beacon* (1916 to the present), and the *Jefferson Gazette* (1883 to the present), available on microfilm in the Ashtabula City Library, and the city *Council Record,* available in the office of the city auditor.

2. Fred Briggs was appointed to fill Flowers's seat on the 1910–12 council. In 1928 Ned Richards was appointed to fill the popular W. E. Wenner's seat, and in 1929 Hercule Paulino was appointed to council after Nick Corrado was convicted and sentenced to prison for violating federal prohibition laws.

3. Excluding Briggs's 18 days in office, the managers and their dates of tenure were: J. W. Prine (1916–18), H. H. Turner (1918–22), W. M. Cotton (1922–26), C. S. Sheldon (1926–27), James Breen (1928), and Fred Hogue (1929–35).

CHAPTER 5

1. The Municipal Association of the City of Cleveland changed its name to the Civic League of Cleveland in 1913, and to the Citizens League in 1923. Because of its lead role in governmental reform efforts in Cleveland, the organization's recommendations of candidates over the years are treated here as reform endorsements. Its publications included *Civic Affairs: Annual Report on Candidates* (1913–22) and *Greater Cleveland* (1923–37).

2. The "Bucklin" ballot was first used in Grand Junction, Colorado, in 1909, and adopted by over 60 other cities, including San Francisco, Denver, Jersey City, and Newark, New Jersey. In Ohio, Columbus and Toledo also adopted the preferential ballot for both council and mayoral elections. Intended to give voters more choice among candidates, the ballot also allowed the defeat of the candidate with the most first-choice votes (who would be the winner in a plurality election) by the addition of second and other preferences in the final count. Although this seldom happened, a few instances, such as Peter Witt's loss in the Cleveland mayoral race of 1915, disillusioned voters and led to the abandonment of the preferential ballot (*Equity,* Jan. 1916, 18.1:50; Kneier, 1957, pp. 365–70; Mingle, 1974, p. 11).

3. Since the adoption of the first home rule charter, the number of Cleveland wards had been increased from 26 to 32 to represent the city's growing population; in 1922 one more ward would be added as a result of the 1920 census.

4. The district populations, number of seats, population per seat, registered voters in 1923 (the first PR election), and the percentage of registered voters who voted in 1923 are as follows:

District	Pop.	Seats	Pop. per Seat	Regis. Voters	% of RV Who Voted
1	228,617	7	32,660	40,261	81.7
2	175,113	5	35,023	22,688	82.1
3	196,732	6	32,789	25,995	79.8
4	204,375	7	29,196	43,049	78.1

Source: Calculated from data in Moley (1923, pp. 653, 657).

5. The Kruskal-Wallis one-way anova test, corrected for ties, was used to test the significance of differences among the three periods on all variables.

6. Data available from the author.

7. Calculated from Civic League (1917–21); and *Greater Cleveland,* 1923–37.

8. No complete official record of transfers exists. The Cuyahoga County Board of Elections kept permanent records only of the votes for first choices and for final winners in each district. The PR ballots have disappeared. A few

pieces of unofficial evidence of the number and order of transfers survive in the PR literature, but with fragmentary data it is difficult to distinguish the typical from the exceptional.

9. The apparent drop in turnout actually began in 1931, in the first election in which the base for calculating turnout was the previous year's registration for state and congressional elections. If 1931 is dropped from the mean turnout of the PR period, turnout in PR elections rises to 80.6% of registrants, an increase over the pre-PR period.

10. Although the county charter was passed by a majority of voters in both Cleveland and the county as a whole, it was invalidated by the Ohio Supreme Court for lack of two other majorities required by the Ohio Constitution: a majority in the county outside of the largest city, and a majority of the municipalities in the county (*State ex rel. Howland v. Krause,* 1936).

CHAPTER 6

1. Murray Seasongood failed to sign the Upson Survey's final report because of the sections on city finances, which contradicted the stand he took against the tax levy. Other than Seasongood, all members of the subcommittee and the general committee agreed with the report's conclusions. Also, Seasongood had wanted the connection between the Republican organization and vice in the West End (the city's black area) investigated, but it was not (Taft, 1933, pp. 62–65). Seasongood prepared a memorandum that he wanted incorporated in the report, or printed as reservation, as a condition of his signing. The committee did neither (Upson, 1924, p. 30).

2. The compromise's terms were relatively innocuous: Bigelow's appointment as chair of the public utilities committee was balanced by the concurrent appointment to the committee of a conservative Republican who opposed municipal ownership; a commitment to investigation of utilities and full publicity of facts obtained; a vague pledge to cooperate with other cities in the state to secure home rule on matters of taxation, offset by a specific charter declaration that they had not committed themselves to the Single Tax; "the restoration of salary cuts of city employees as soon as practicable and further increases for any who are below standard wage rates," offset by a specific charter declaration disavowing the salary reductions for top administrators, which Bigelow had urged; and a pledge not to interfere with civil service administration or the city manager's administrative responsibilities.

CHAPTER 7

1. In 1987–88 in exploratory work for this chapter, Leon Weaver interviewed Robert Bartels and William Beckett, both former members of Hamilton city council and former mayors of Hamilton; Richard Fitton, president of First

National Bank of Southwestern Ohio and a former member of Hamilton city council; and Janet Sizemore, executive director of the Hamilton Appalachian People's Service Organization.

2. Of nine previous vacancies, three had been left unfilled, two had been filled by the runner-up, three by other candidates, and one by a noncandidate (*Hamilton Journal News*, 25 Jan. 1960, pp. 7, 24). The National Municipal League's *Model City Charter* provided that vacancies on PR-elected councils should be filled by recounting and transferring the ballots of the vacating member to determine the runner-up, who was then entitled to the seat (*National Municipal Review*, Dec. 1960, 49:642). This method was not included in the Hamilton charter.

3. Over time, with the persistence of this electoral system into the 1980s, voters did more typically mark five of their available seven choices instead of six (Butler County Board of Elections, 1961–65 et seq.).

CHAPTER 8

1. Frank Britt was the former executive director of the Toledo Area Governmental Research Association (TAGRA), formerly the City Manager League. John W. Yager, a reform Democrat, was a member of the Toledo city council (1955–61) and mayor of Toledo (1957–59). Yager is the son of Joseph Yager, a prominent leader of the City Manager League.

2. Donovan Emch, a professor emeritus at the University of Toledo and the author of Emch, 1938, was a founding member of the City Manager League.

3. When municipal turnout is calculated as percentage of registered voters (not shown), similar trends are evident. However, the decline in voting during the PR period among registered voters is less pronounced than among the adult population as a whole. This suggests that the higher political commitment demonstrated by the act of registration entails greater willingness to deal with the multiple rank-ordered choices of the PR/STV ballot.

4. For the last four elections with council-elected mayors (1959–65), average municipal voter turnout was 48.6% of eligible adults. For the first four direct elections of the mayor (1967–73), turnout averaged 42.7%.

5. In the first three PR elections (table 8.5) there were 11 League endorsees who won on transfers (columns 2 and 3). Between the first count and the final transfer, 5 of these winners gained and 5 lost ground through transfers. Of the transfer-gainers, 2 had not placed among the first 9 finishers; one of these was a joint endorsee of Labor and the League. Three League endorsees were "Fast Starters, Transfer Losers" (column 4). Thus 8 of the initially viable League endorsees dropped in rank order on transfers, while 5 (one of whom was also endorsed by Labor) improved their position. In contrast, 3 of 4 Labor-endorsed candidacies gained from transfers. Among candidacies without endorsements, 4 gained in ranking, and 3 declined in the transfer process (one remained the same). Finally, 3 of the 5 "Fast Starters, Transfer Losers" in these three elections were League endorsees.

Notes

6. Transfers on which a candidate reached his quota and was thus elected are not shown in table 8.6, because in many cases only a few additional votes were needed for election, and such transfers would yield deceptively low percentages.

7. % Share of transfer votes on third from last transfer, 1945:

Candidate by Order of Finish		Change in Rank Order	% Share of Transfer Votes
Jurris (R)	4	+1	22
Czelusta (R)	5	−1	18
Thacher (R)	6	+1	17
Lehman (R)	7	+1	21
Donovan (D)	8	+1	17
Simmons (D)	9	−3	6

8. Transfer votes as % of transfer winners' total votes, 1945:

Candidate by Order of Finish		Last Transfer	Last − 1	Last − 2	Last − 3
Jurris (R)	4	-	-	-	20*
Czelusta (R)	5	-	-	19*	17
Thacher (R)	6	-	30*	23	18
Lehman (R)	7	-	30*	23	22
Donovan (D)	8	51*	44	33	24
Simmons (D)	9	18*	11	8	6

*Elected.

9. The average tenure of city managers appointed by plurality/at-large councils is based on 12 "permanent" managers who have served between 1951 and 1991. Four other "temporary" or interim managers who served for brief periods of less than a year have been omitted from this calculation, as has their total period of service (about two years). If these interim managers and their time of service were included, the average tenure would fall to 2.43 years.

CHAPTER 9

1. Cleveland's council grew from 26 to 33 ward members under the pre-PR charter; Toledo's had 21 ward-based members.

2.

City Council	Total Members	Ward Members	At-Large Members
Ashtabula	7	4	3
Cincinnati	32	26	6
Hamilton	10	6	4*

*Includes council president, separately elected at-large.

3. The complexity of measuring historical voter turnout is highlighted by nineteenth-century problems with both fraud and census errors. Examining the measure "percent voting of those eligible to vote," Shortridge argues that reports of nineteenth-century turnout were falsely inflated by two factors: practices such as the stuffing of ballot boxes inflated the number of votes counted, and very large undercounts of the population, especially in poor, dangerous, urban areas, decreased the base number of eligible voters on which the calculation of turnout depends. Untrained census takers and overcrowded, even hostile living conditions in urban neighborhoods are cited to explain the undercount. If these findings are accepted, then the alleged decline in voting from 1896 to 1931 disappears owing to public (instead of party) control of the electoral process and to improved census techniques (Shortridge, 1981, pp. 137–48). Most analysts of voting statistics, however, find an authentic decline in turnout associated with Progressive reform (Reynolds, 1988).

4. Measuring turnout for local elections in pre-PR, PR, and post-PR periods is complicated by the failure of the census to report members of the population 21 years of age and over, by city, for the early years, necessitating the use of percentage of registered voters as the measure of turnout in Cleveland and Cincinnati. This measure itself lacks consistency over time because of a change in Ohio electoral law in 1930, when annual registration was replaced by "permanent" registration. With annual registration, there were generally fewer registrants in the municipal election year, providing a lower base number for calculating local turnout. When permanent registration was instituted, those who registered for the statewide and congressional election of 1930 remained registered as long as they voted at least once every two years, so that municipal turnout from 1930 on is calculated on the higher registration base of the previous year.

5. "Better educated" is defined as council members having some college, a college degree, or post-graduate work. "Less educated" includes those who were educated through high school or less.

6. Simmons later became vice mayor of the city. Stinchcombe reports that "Toledo voters and community leaders were willing to sanction Negro representation on the city council, but a Negro vice-mayor and the thought of a Negro mayor were cause for alarm." Simmons was defeated "easily" in 1961, and in 1963 a charter amendment was passed restoring the pre-PR popular

election of the mayor (Stinchcombe, 1968, p. 194). These events in Toledo followed the comparable racial polarization that accompanied the repeal of PR in Cincinnati and the subsequent defeat of council member Ted Berry (Kolesar, chap. 6 in this volume; Straetz, 1958).

7. A fire in the Ashtabula courthouse destroyed ballots and all official election records of the period.

8.

City	No. of Transfer Winners (= to No. of Transfer Losers)	% of Total Seats
Cincinnati	15	10.4
Cleveland	12	9.6
Hamilton	8	6.7
Toledo	9	12.5
TOTAL	44	9.6

9. The measure used to identify "conflict" is a broad one, since even one dissenter places an issue in the nonunanimous column. If factionalism were to be measured as a group phenomenon—such as on a nine-member council, splits of 5-4 or 6-3; on a seven-member council, 4-3 or 5-2; or on Cleveland's 25-member council, 13-12, 14-11, or even 22-3—then "conflict" in Ohio's PR councils would be a rare event indeed.

CHAPTER 10

1. Discriminatory racial gerrymanders were invalidated in *Gomillion v. Lightfoot,* 1960; *Perkins v. Matthews,* 1971; and *Connor v. Finch,* 1977. For a history of the racial gerrymander, see Parker, 1984.

2. The substitution of a "results" standard for the "intent to discriminate" was debated extensively in the Senate Judiciary Committee when the 1982 amendments were considered. If a showing of fair "results" were required, Senator Orren Hatch of Utah feared that minority vote dilution could be evaluated only against the standard of proportionality. To alleviate these concerns, the stipulation that no right to proportional representation is established by section 2 was proposed by Senator Robert Dole of Kansas on the Senate floor (Thernstrom, 1987, pp. 123–36).

3. A total of 22 African Americans served in Congress between the Civil War and 1901, all Southern Republicans. Representative George White of North Carolina was the last, and the only black member from 1897–1901. He is said to have left Congress voluntarily because racist attitudes made his service futile (Swain, 1993, pp. 21–28).

4. Critics of section 4 have identified significant differences in historic patterns of discrimination and assimilation between African Americans and the specified language minorities, patterns that critics believe make irrational the attempt to apply similar standards to districting and representational issues (see Thernstrom, 1987, pp. 51–62 and references cited therein).

5. In *Holder v. Hall,* 1994, the Supreme Court declined to find minority vote dilution in the practice of electing a single county commissioner who exercises all executive and legislative power. No black commissioner had ever been elected in Bleckley County. Black voters, who constituted 20% of the county's population, argued that the Voting Rights Act should afford a remedy in the form of a five-member commission. In a 5-4 decision, the Court declined to apply section 2 of the act to challenges to the size of a government structure. The decision was of limited significance, since the Court remanded the case for consideration of the same issue by constitutional standards.

6. See, e.g., Zimmerman, 1978; *Yale Law Journal,* 1982a, 1982b; Low-Beer, 1984; Levinson, 1985; Grofman and Lijphart, 1986; Thernstrom, 1987; Still, 1991; Guinier, 1991, 1992, 1994.

Bibliography

LEGAL CASES

Allen v. State Board of Elections, 393 U.S. 544 (1969).

Brown v. Board of Education, 347 U.S. 483 (1954).

Campos v. City of Baytown, 840 F. 2d 1240 (5th Cir. 1988); 849 F. 2d 943 (5th Cir. 1989); cert. den. 492 U.S. 905 (1989).

Cane v. Worcester County, Md., 847 F. Supp. 369, 62 L.W. 2631 (Md. 1994), 35 F. 3d 921 (4th Cir. 1994).

Chisom v. Roemer, 501 U.S. 380 (1991).

City of Mobile v. Bolden, 446 U.S. 55 (1980).

Clarke v. City of Cincinnati, No. 93-3864; Fed. App. 0369 P (6th Cir. 1994).

Clinton v. The Cedar Rapids R.R. Co., 24 Iowa 455 (1868).

Connor v. Finch, 431 U.S. 407 (1977).

Davis v. Bandemer, 478 U.S. 109 (1986).

DeGrandy v. Wetherell, 794 F. Supp. 1076 (N.D. Fla. 1992).

Dillard v. Crenshaw County, 640 F. Supp. 1347 (M.D. Ala. 1986).

East Carroll Parish School Board v. Marshall, 424 U.S. 636 (1976).

Fortson v. Dorsey, 379 U.S. 433 (1965).

Gaffney v. Cummings, 412 U.S. 738 (1973).

Gomillion v. Lightfoot, 364 U.S. 339 (1960).

Growe v. Emison, 61 L.W. 4163, 507 U.S. —— (1993).

Hays v. Louisiana, United States v. Hays, 839 F. Supp. 1188 (W.D. La. 1993), appeal pending, No. 94-558 (1994).

Hile v. City of Cleveland, 107 O.S. 144, 141 N.E. 35 (1923), writ of error dismissed, 266 U.S. 582 (1924).

Holder v. Hall, No. 90-2012, 62 L.W. 4728 (1994).

Houston Lawyers' Association v. Attorney General of Texas, 501 U.S. 419 (1991).

Johnson v. DeGrandy, 62 L.W. 4755; 129 L. Ed. 2d 775 (1994).

Johnson v. City of New York, 274 N.Y. 411 (1937).

LULAC v. Midland Independent School District, 829 F. 2d 546 (5th Cir. en banc, 1987).

People ex rel. Devine v. Elkus, 59 Cal. App. 396, 211 Pac. 34 (1922), hearing denied by Cal. S. Ct. (1922).
Perkins v. Matthews, 400 U.S. 379 (1971).
Reutener v. City of Cleveland, 107 O.S. 117, 141 N.E. 27 (1923).
Reynolds v. Sims, 377 U.S. 533 (1964).
Shaw v. Reno, 61 L.W. 4818, 509 U.S. —— (1993); *Shaw v. Hunt*, 861 F. Supp. 408 (1994).
State ex rel. Howland v. Krause et al., 130 O.S. 455 (1936).
Thornburg v. Gingles, 478 U.S. 30 (1986).
United Jewish Organizations of Williamsburgh, Inc. v. Carey, 430 U.S. 144 (1977).
Voinovich v. Quilter, 91-1618, 61 L.W. 4199, 507 U.S. —— (1993).
Wattles ex rel. Johnson v. Upjohn, 211 Mich. 514, 179 N.W. 335 (1920).
White v. Regester, 412 U.S. 769 (1973).
Wright v. Rockefeller, 376 U.S. 52 (1964).
Zimmer v. McKeithen, 485 F. 2d 1297 (5th Cir. 1973).

NEWSPAPERS AND MAGAZINES

Ashtabula Star-Beacon. 1916–37. Ashtabula Public Library.
Beacon Record (Ashtabula). 1910–15. Ashtabula Public Library.
Cincinnati Enquirer. 1993–94.
Cleveland Citizen. 1921. Cleveland Public Library.
Cleveland Plain Dealer. 1917–37. Cleveland: Plain Dealer Pub. Co.
Cleveland Press. 1917–37. Cleveland: Cleveland Press Pub. Co. Cleveland Public Library.
Daily Star (Ashtabula). 1914–16. Ashtabula Public Library.
Equity. 1898–1919. Formerly *Equity Series.* Consolidated with *National Municipal Review*, 1919.
Hamilton Evening Journal, 1915–33. Microfilm, Lane Public Library, Hamilton, Ohio.
Hamilton Journal News, 1933–65. Microfilm, Lane Public Library, Hamilton, Ohio.
Jefferson Gazette. 1883 to the present. Ashtabula Public Library.
National Municipal Review (NMR). 1912–58. New York: National Municipal League. *National Civic Review.* 1959 to present. Denver, Colo.: National Civic League.
News and Record (Greensboro, N.C.). 1993.
New Yorker. 1994.
New York Times. 1993–94.
Proportional Representation Review (PRR). 1893–1932. Chicago and Philadelphia: The Proportional Representation League. Consolidated with *National Municipal Review*, 1932 to present.
Texas Observer. 1994.

Time. 1994.
Toledo Blade. 1927–57. Toledo Public Library.
Toledo City Journal. 1916–57. Toledo Commission on Publicity and Efficiency.
Toledo News-Bee. 1927–38. Toledo Public Library.
Toledo Times. 1927–57. Toledo Public Library.
Washington Post Weekly. 1994.

WORKS CITED

Abbott, Virginia C. 1949. *The History of Woman Suffrage and the League of Women Voters in Cuyahoga County, 1911–1945.* Cleveland: Cleveland League of Women Voters.
Addams, Jane. 1960. *Jane Addams: A Centennial Reader.* New York: Macmillan.
Adrian, Charles R. 1959. A Typology for Nonpartisan Elections. *Western Political Quarterly* 12:449–58.
Alexander, Edward F. 1988. An Epic in City Government. *Queen City Heritage* 46:19–31.
Applebome, Peter. 1994. Guinier Ideas, Once Seen as Odd, Now Get Serious Study. *New York Times,* 3 April, p. E5.
Argersinger, Peter H. 1989. The Value of the Vote: Political Representation in the Gilded Age. *Journal of American History* 76:59–90.
Ashtabula County Genealogical Society. 1985. *Ashtabula County History, Then and Now.* Jefferson, Ohio: Taylor Publishing.
Atkinson, Raymond C. 1920. Ashtabula's Third "P.R." Election. *National Municipal Review* 9:9–12.
Austen-Smith, David, and Jeffrey Banks. 1991. Monotonicity in Electoral Systems. *American Political Science Review* 85:531–37.
Banner, Lois W. 1980. *Elizabeth Cady Stanton: A Radical for Woman's Rights.* Boston: Little, Brown.
Barber, Kathleen L. 1981. Ohio. In *Reapportionment Politics: The History of Redistricting in the Fifty States,* edited by Leroy Hardy et al., pp. 256–65. Beverly Hills, Calif.: Sage.
——— . 1983. Partisan Bias and Incumbent Protection in Legislative Districting. Paper presented at the 1983 Meeting of the American Political Science Association, Chicago, Ill.
Bartholdi, John J., III, and J. B. Orlin. 1991. Single Transferable Vote Resists Strategic Voting. *Social Choice and Welfare* 8:341–54.
Bast, Elaine M. 1973. The Effects of Institutional Reforms in Urban Government on Personnel and Policy: Toledo, 1922–1949. Master's thesis, Bowling Green State Univ.
Baughin, William A. 1988. Murray Seasongood—Cincinnati's Civic Warrior. *Queen City Heritage* 46:35–39.

Beard, Mary R. [1915] 1972. *Woman's Work in Municipalities.* Reprint, New York: Arno.

Bentley, Henry. 1925. Why Cincinnati Voted for PR and a City Manager. *National Municipal Review* 14:69–74.

————. 1926. Cincinnati's Right About Face in Government. *National Municipal Review* 15:465–73.

————. 1929. What PR Has Done for Cincinnati. *National Municipal Review* 18:65–67.

————. 1937. Three Cincinnati Elections: Representation of Minorities Is a Useful Safety Valve for Popular Dissatisfaction. *National Municipal Review* 26:16–22.

Berke, Richard L. 1993. Republicans Make Strong Gains from Appeals to Hispanic Voters. *New York Times,* 5 July, pp. 1, 8.

Blair, George S. 1960. *Cumulative Voting: An Effective Electoral Device in Illinois Politics.* Urbana: Univ. of Illinois Press.

Bloomfield, Charles A. 1926. Ashtabula's Experience with Proportional Representation. Master's thesis, Columbia Univ.

Blount, James L. 1987. Summary Notes on Hamilton Political History. Unpublished document.

————. 1990a. Klan Was No Stranger to County. *Hamilton Journal-News,* 17 Jan. 1990.

————. 1990b. Klan Affected Many Aspects of Life. *Hamilton Journal-News,* 21 Jan. 1990.

Bogdanor, Vernon. 1984. *What Is Proportional Representation?* Oxford: Martin Robertson.

————. 1993. Israel Debates Reform. *Journal of Democracy* 4:66–78.

————, ed. 1985. *Representatives of the People: Parliamentarians and Constituents in Western Democracies.* Aldershot, England: Gower.

————, ed. 1991. *Blackwell Encyclopedia of Political Science.* Oxford: Blackwell.

Boyer, Paul. 1978. *Urban Masses and Moral Order in America, 1820–1920.* Cambridge: Harvard Univ. Press.

Boynton, William E. 1917. Proportional Representation in Ashtabula. *National Municipal Review* 6:87–90.

Britt, Frank. 1984. Interview by Dennis Anderson, 1 Aug.

Buckalew, Charles R. 1872. *Proportional Representation; or, The Representation of Successive Majorities in Federal, State, Municipal, Corporate and Primary Elections.* Philadelphia: J. Campbell & Son.

Buenker, John D. 1973. *Urban Liberalism and Progressive Reform.* New York: Charles Scribner's Sons.

————. 1988. Sovereign Individuals and Organic Networks: Political Cultures in Conflict during the Progressive Era. *American Quarterly* 40:187–204.

Burnham, Robert A. 1990. "Pulling Together" for Pluralism: Politics, Planning and Government in Cincinnati, 1924–1959. Ph.D. diss., Univ. of Cincinnati.

———. 1992. The Cincinnati Charter Revolt of 1924: Creating City Government for a Pluralistic Society. In *Ethnic Diversity and Civic Identity: Patterns of Conflict and Cohesion in Cincinnati since 1820,* edited by Henry D. Shapiro and Jonathan Sarna, pp. 202–24. Urbana: Univ. of Illinois Press.

Burnham, Walter Dean. 1981. The System of 1896: An Analysis. In *The Evolution of American Electoral Systems,* edited by Paul Kleppner et al., pp. 147–202. Westport, Conn.: Greenwood Press.

Butler County Board of Elections. 1921–65. *Abstract of Votes.* Hamilton, Ohio: Butler County Board of Elections.

Campbell, Thomas F. 1966. *Daniel Morgan: Good Citizen.* Cleveland: Western Reserve Univ. Press.

———. 1988. Mounting Crisis and Reform: Cleveland's Political Development. In Campbell and Miggins, eds., pp. 298–324.

Campbell, Thomas F., and Edward M. Miggins, eds. 1988. *The Birth of Modern Cleveland, 1865–1930.* Cleveland: Western Reserve Historical Society; London and Toronto: Assoc. Univ. Presses.

Cassella, William N. 1975. A Century of Home Rule. *National Civic Review* 64:441–50.

———. 1990. The Model Charters: Continuity and Change. *National Civic Review* 79:318–31.

Center for Voting and Democracy. 1994. *Voting and Democracy Report, 1993.* Washington, D.C.: Center for Voting and Democracy.

Chafe, William H. 1972. *The American Woman: Her Changing Social, Economic, and Political Roles, 1920–1970.* New York: Oxford Univ. Press.

Childs, Richard S. 1952. *Civic Victories.* New York: Harper.

———. 1965. *The First 50 Years of the City Manager Plan of Municipal Government.* New York: Stratford Press.

Cincinnati Directory. 1915–21. Cincinnati: Williams Directory Co.

Cincinnati League of Women Voters. Various years. *The Who and What of Elections.* Cincinnati: Cincinnati League of Women Voters.

City of Cleveland. 1918–38. *The City Record.* Cleveland: Cleveland City Council.

Civic League of Cleveland. 1917–21. *Civic Affairs: Annual Report on Candidates.* Cleveland: Civic League of Cleveland.

Cleveland Chamber of Commerce. 1921. Election Nov. 8: Amendment to the City Charter. In *Reports and Addresses.* Cleveland: Cleveland Chamber of Commerce.

Cleveland Foundation. 1926–28. *The Cleveland Yearbook and Directory.* Cleveland: Cleveland Foundation.

Cohodas, Nadine. 1994. Electing Minorities. *CQ Researcher* 4:698–715.

Cole, Alistair, and Peter Campbell. 1989. *French Electoral Systems and Elections since 1789.* 3rd ed. Aldershot, England: Gower.

Committee of One Hundred. Undated (about 1921). The Meaning of the City Manager Plan. Cleveland: privately printed, in pamphlet file of the Cleveland Public Library.

Commons, John R. 1907. *Proportional Representation.* 2nd ed. New York: Macmillan.

Conger, J. L. 1920. Justice to Both Minority and Majority through Proportional Representation in City Elections. *American City* 23:58–59.

Congressional Quarterly. 1976. *National Party Conventions: 1831–1972.* Washington, D.C.: CQ Press.

––––––. 1994. *CQ's Politics in America 1994: The 103rd Congress.* Washington, D.C.: CQ Press.

Cooley, Winifred Scott. 1913. The Younger Suffragists. *Harper's Weekly* 58:6-7.

Crane, Edward A. 1935. The Law and Practice of Proportional Representation in Municipal Government. Senior thesis, Harvard Univ.

Crecraft, Earl Willis. 1920. Ashtabula's Attack on P.R. and the City Manager. *National Municipal Review* 9:623–26.

Cuyahoga County Board of Elections. 1918–36. *Vote, General Election.* Cleveland: Cuyahoga County Board of Elections.

Cuyahoga County Board of Elections. 1917–37. *Municipal Election Vote.* Cleveland: Cuyahoga County Board of Elections.

Davidson, Chandler. 1992. The Voting Rights Act: A Brief History. In Grofman and Davidson, eds., pp. 7–51.

––––––, ed. 1984. *Minority Vote Dilution.* Washington, D.C.: Howard Univ. Press.

Davidson, Chandler, and George Korbel. 1981. At-Large Elections and Minority-Group Representation: A Re-examination of Historical and Contemporary Evidence. *Journal of Politics* 43:982–1005.

Davis, Peter. 1982. *Hometown.* New York: Simon and Schuster.

Davis, Robert C. 1987. Roscoe Pound, Felix Frankfurter and Criminal Justice in Cleveland. *In Brief* (Case Western Reserve Univ. Law School), 22–25.

DeAngelo, Edward A. 1937. Toledo's Manager Government and Labor. *National Municipal Review* 26:484–86, 488.

DeGrazia, Alfred. 1951. *Public and Republic: Political Representation in America.* New York: Alfred A. Knopf.

Doron, Gideon, and Richard Kronick. 1977. Single Transferable Vote: An Example of a Perverse Social Choice Function. *American Journal of Political Science* 21:303–11.

Douglas, Jean. 1949. Voters Calm in Proportional Representation's Fifth Fight for Life. *Toledo Blade,* 6 Nov., sec. 1, p. 3.

Draper, Theodore. 1957. *The Roots of American Communism.* New York: Viking Press.

Dreier, Mary E. 1950. *Margaret Dreier Robins: Her Life, Letters, and Work.* New York: Island Press Cooperative.

Droop, H. R. 1881. *On Methods of Electing Representatives.* London: Statistical Society.

DuBois, W. E. B. [1899] 1967. *The Philadelphia Negro: A Social Study.* Univ. of Pennsylvania Studies in Political Economy and Public Law, No. 14. Philadelphia: Univ. of Pennsylvania; New York: Schocken Books.

Duverger, Maurice. 1963. *Political Parties: Their Organization and Activity in the Modern State.* New York: John Wiley & Sons.

Dye, Nancy Schrom. 1980. *As Equals and Sisters: Feminism, the Labor Movement, and the Women's Trade Union League of New York.* Columbia: Univ. of Missouri Press.

Easton, David. 1953. *The Political System: An Inquiry into the State of Political Science.* Chicago: Univ. of Chicago Press.

Emch, Donovan. 1938. The City Manager Government of Toledo, Ohio. Unpublished manuscript prepared for the Social Science Research Council, Committee on Public Administration.

———. 1986. Interview by Dennis Anderson.

Engstrom, Richard L. 1992. Modified Multi-Seat Election Systems as Remedies for Minority Vote Dilution. *Stetson Law Review* 21 (3):743–70.

Engstrom, Richard L., Edward Still, and Jason F. Kirksey. Forthcoming. Limited and Cumulative Voting in Alabama: An Assessment after Two Rounds of Elections. *National Political Science Review.*

Engstrom, Richard L., Delbert A. Taebel, and Richard Cole. 1989. Cumulative Voting as a Remedy for Minority Vote Dilution: The Case of Alamogordo, New Mexico. *Journal of Law and Politics* 5:469–97.

Everson, David H., and Joan A. Parker. 1983. The Impact of the New Single Member District System in Illinois. Paper presented at the annual meeting of the American Political Science Association, Chicago, Ill.

Fesler, Mayo. 1924. Letter to William R. Hopkins. Hopkins Papers, Western Reserve Historical Society Library.

Filene, Peter G. 1970. An Obituary for "The Progressive Movement." *American Quarterly* 22:20–34.

Fishburn, Peter C. 1990. Dimensions of Election Procedures: Analyses and Comparisons. In *Representation and Electoral Systems: Canadian Perspectives,* edited by J. Paul Johnston and Harvey Pasis, chap. 30. Scarborough, Canada: Prentice-Hall.

Fishburn, Peter C., and Steven J. Brams. 1983. Paradoxes of Preferential Voting. *Mathematics Magazine* 56:207–14.

Fisher, J. Francis. 1863. *The Degradation of Our Representative System and Its Reform.* Philadelphia, Pa.: C. Sherman, Son & Co.

Flexner, Eleanor. 1975. *Century of Struggle: The Woman's Rights Movement in the United States.* Rev. ed. Cambridge: Harvard Univ. Press, Belknap Press.

Foulke, William Dudley. 1915. Address. *Equity* 17 (1): 70–76.

Fraga, Luis R. 1991. Policy Consequences and the Change from At-Large Elections to Single-Member Districts. Paper presented at the annual meeting of the Western Political Science Association, Seattle, Wash.

Frank, Forest. 1948. Charter Group Takes Over in Cincinnati. *National Municipal Review* 37:225–27.

———. 1954a. PR Again Attacked in Cincinnati. *National Municipal Review* 43:421–23.

_____. 1954b. PR Wins Again in Cincinnati: Recount Proves Voters Want Hare System in Use 30 Years. *National Municipal Review* 43:595–97.

_____. 1957. Cincinnati Loses PR: Sixth Attempt at Repeal Substitutes 9X System. *National Municipal Review* 46:534–35.

_____. 1960. Vacancy Filling Spurred Hamilton Attack. *National Municipal Review* 49:622–23.

_____. 1962. 9X Plurality Plan Proves Inequitable: New Cincinnati Council Unrepresentative Body. *National Civic Review* 51:40–41.

Gallagher, Michael. 1992. Comparing Proportional Representation Electoral Systems: Quotas, Thresholds, Paradoxes and Majorities. *British Journal of Political Science* 22:469–96.

Gilpin, Thomas. 1844. *On the Representation of Minorities of Electors to Act with the Majority, in Elected Assemblies.* Philadelphia, Pa.: J. C. Clark.

Gladieux, Bernhard L. 1935. Toledo Returns Its New Charter. *National Municipal Review* 24:357.

Glendening, Parris N., and Mavis Mann Reeves. 1984. *Pragmatic Federalism.* 2nd ed. Pacific Palisades, Calif.: Palisades Pub.

Godkin, Edwin L. 1894. The Problems of Municipal Government. *Annals of the Academy of Political and Social Sciences* 4:857–82.

Gosnell, Harold F. 1930. Motives for Voting as Shown by the Cincinnati P.R. Election of 1929. *National Municipal Review* 19:472–76.

_____. [1934] 1948. Proportional Representation. In *Encyclopaedia of the Social Sciences,* edited by Edwin R. A. Seligman. Vol. 12, pp. 541–45. New York: Macmillan.

Grabowski, John J. 1986. Social Reform and Philanthropic Order, 1896–1920. In Van Tassel and Grabowski, eds., pp. 29–49.

Graham, Hugh Davis. 1992. Voting Rights and the American Regulatory State. In Grofman and Davidson, eds., pp. 177–96.

Gray, Kenneth E. 1959. A Report on Politics in Cincinnati. Cambridge, Mass.: Joint Center for Urban Studies. Mimeo.

Greater Cleveland (GC). 1923–37. Vols. 1–13. Cleveland: Citizens League.

Green, Howard Whipple. 1931. *Population Characteristics by Census Tracts, Cleveland, Ohio, 1930.* Cleveland: Plain Dealer Pub. Co.

Greenhouse, Linda. 1993. Supreme Court Roundup. *New York Times,* 23 Feb., p. A8.

Gregg, Ronald E. 1950. Toledo Loses P.R. on Fifth Repeal Vote. *National Municipal Review* 37:49.

Griffith, Ernest S. 1974. *A History of American City Government: The Conspicuous Failure, 1870–1900.* New York: Praeger.

Grofman, Bernard, and Chandler Davidson, eds. 1992. *Controversies in Minority Voting: The Voting Rights Act in Perspective.* Washington, D.C.: Brookings Institution.

Grofman, Bernard, and Arend Lijphart. 1986. *Electoral Laws and Their Political Consequences.* New York: Agathon Press.

Grofman, Bernard, Lisa Handley, and Richard G. Niemi. 1992. *Minority Representation and the Quest for Voting Equality.* Cambridge: Cambridge Univ. Press.

Guinier, Lani. 1991. The Triumph of Tokenism: The Voting Rights Act and the Theory of Black Electoral Success. *Michigan Law Review* 89:1077–154.

————. 1992. Second Proms and Second Primaries: The Limits of Majority Rule. *Boston Review,* Sept./Oct., 32–34.

————. 1994. *The Tyranny of the Majority.* New York: Free Press.

————. 1995. Don't Scapegoat the Gerrymander. *New York Times Magazine,* 8 Jan., pp. 36–37.

Haber, Samuel. 1964. *Efficiency and Uplift: Scientific Management in the Progressive Era, 1890–1920.* Chicago: Univ. of Chicago Press.

Hacker, Andrew. 1964. *Congressional Districting: The Issue of Equal Representation.* Washington, D.C.: Brookings Institution.

Hallett, George, Jr. 1936a. Cincinnati Gets a New Sort of Council. *National Municipal Review* 25:39–41.

————. 1936b. P.R. and Cincinnati's Mayor. *National Municipal Review* 25:108–9.

————. 1940. *Proportional Representation: The Key to Democracy.* New York: National Municipal League.

Hamilton, Alexander, James Madison, and John Jay. [1788] 1945. *The Federalist.* New York: Heritage Press.

Hamilton, Howard D. 1977. *Electing the Cincinnati City Council.* Cincinnati: Stephen H. Wilder Foundation.

Hamilton County Board of Elections. 1915–1961. *Elections in Hamilton County.* Cincinnati: Hamilton County Board of Elections.

Hare, Thomas. [1859, 1860] 1977. *Treatise on the Election of Representatives, Parliamentary and Municipal.* In J. S. Mill, *Thoughts on Parliamentary Reform,* 2nd ed., in Mill, *Collected Works,* vol. 19, pp. 491–95.

Hare, Thomas, and John Stuart Mill. 1862. *True and False Democracy: The Representation of All and the Representation of the Majority Only.* Boston: Prentiss and Deland.

Hatton, Augustus R. 1915. Making Minorities Count. *New Republic,* 27 Nov., 96–98.

Harris, Joseph P. 1930. The Practical Workings of Proportional Representation in the United States and Canada. *National Municipal Review* 19 (Suppl.): 337–83.

————. 1916. The Ashtabula Plan—The Latest Step in Municipal Organization. *National Municipal Review* 5:56–65.

Hays, Samuel P. 1964. The Politics of Reform in Municipal Government in the Progressive Era. *Pacific Northwest Quarterly* 55:157–69.

Heilig, Peggy, and Robert J. Mundt. 1984. *Your Voice at City Hall: The Politics, Procedures and Policies of District Representation.* Albany: State Univ. of New York Press.

Heisel, W. Donald. 1982. Abandonment of Proportional Representation and the Impact of 9X Voting in Cincinnati. Paper presented at the annual meeting of the American Political Science Association, Denver, Colo.

_____ , project director. 1980. Unpublished option papers prepared by the Institute of Governmental Research, Univ. of Cincinnati, for the Charter Review Committee, Aug.

Henderson, Alfred. 1926. The Machine under Hynicka. *National Municipal Review* 15:431.

Hermens, Ferdinand A. [1941] 1972. *Democracy or Anarchy? A Study of Proportional Representation.* 2nd ed. Reprint, New York: Johnson Reprint Corp.

_____ . 1985. The Record of P.R. in American Local Government: A Critical Review. Paper presented at the annual meeting of the American Political Science Association, New Orleans, La.

Higham, John. [1955] 1988. *Strangers in the Land: Patterns of American Nativism, 1860–1925.* New Brunswick, N.J.: Rutgers Univ. Press.

Hoag, Clarence G. 1913. The "Representative Council Plan" of City Charter. *Equity* 15:80–81.

_____ . 1919. P.R. and the League of Nations. *Equity* 21 (2): 74.

Hoag, Clarence G., and George H. Hallett. 1926. *Proportional Representation.* New York: Macmillan.

Hofstadter, Richard. 1955. *The Age of Reform: From Bryan to F. D. R.* New York: Alfred A. Knopf.

Hogan, James. 1945. *Election and Representation.* Cork, Ireland: Cork Univ. Press.

Hopkins, William R. 1935. Cleveland Still Dissatisfied. *National Municipal Review* 24:27–31, 41.

Howe, Frederic C. [1925] 1988. *Confessions of a Reformer.* Kent, Ohio: Kent State Univ. Press.

Huthmacher, J. Joseph. 1962. Urban Liberalism and the Age of Reform. *Mississippi Valley Historical Review* 49:231–41.

Huus, R. O., and D. I. Cline. 1929. Election Frauds and Councilmanic Scandals Stir Cleveland. *National Municipal Review* 18:289–94.

James, Herman G. 1916. Proportional Representation: A Fundamental or a Fad? *National Municipal Review* 5:306–14.

Jenks, George F. 1946. Survival of City Manager System Rests on Voters. *Toledo Blade,* 4 Nov., p. 1.

_____ . 1949a. Mild Campaign May Bring out 90,000 Voters. *Toledo Blade,* 6 Nov., p. 1.

_____ . 1949b. Old Age Overtakes P.R. as Local Political Issue. *Toledo Blade,* 16 Oct., sec. 2, pp. 1, 3.

Jewell, Ingrid. 1945. PR Complicates Voting Process Opponents State. *Toledo Blade,* 29 Oct., p. 15.

Johnson, Wendell F. 1934. Toledo Votes in November. *National Municipal Review* 23:553–54.

Jones, O. Garfield. 1944. PR Results in Two Ohio Cities: Toledo Elects Its Fifth PR Council. *National Municipal Review* 33:100.

_____. 1954. The Background of City Government and Politics in Toledo. Unpublished manuscript, Department of Political Science, Univ. of Toledo.

Kaufman, Ben L. 1993. Council Voting Ruled Fair to Blacks. *Cincinnati Enquirer,* 9 July, pp. A1, A4.

Kelly, John. 1984. Interview by Dennis Anderson, 10 Aug.

Kendall, M. C., and A. Stuart. 1950. The Law of Cubic Proportions in Electoral Results. *British Journal of Sociology* 1:183–97.

Kent, Sherman. 1937. *Electoral Procedure under Louis Philippe.* New Haven: Yale Univ. Press.

Key, V. O., Jr. 1964. *Political Parties and Pressure Groups.* New York: Crowell.

Kindness, Thomas N. 1988. Letter to L. Weaver, 3 Dec.

Kingdom, John. 1991. *Government and Politics in Britain.* Cambridge: Polity Press.

Kleppner, Paul. 1982. *Who Voted? The Dynamics of Electoral Turnout, 1870–1980.* New York: Praeger.

_____. 1987. *Continuity and Change in Electoral Politics, 1893–1928.* New York: Greenwood Press.

Kneier, Charles M. 1957. *City Government in the United States.* New York: Harper and Brothers.

Knepper, George W. 1989. *Ohio and Its People.* Kent, Ohio: Kent State Univ. Press.

Kolehmainen, John I. 1977. *A History of the Finns in Ohio, Western Pennsylvania and West Virginia.* New York Mill, Minn.: Parta Printers.

Kolko, Gabriel. 1963. *The Triumph of Conservatism: A Reinterpretation of American History, 1900–1916.* Glencoe, Ill.: Free Press.

Kornbluh, Andrea Tuttle. 1986. *Lighting the Way: The Woman's City Club of Cincinnati, 1915–1965.* Cincinnati: Woman's City Club of Cincinnati.

Kusmer, Kenneth L. 1976. *A Ghetto Takes Shape: Black Cleveland, 1870–1930.* Urbana: Univ. of Illinois Press.

Lakeman, Enid. 1970. *How Democracies Vote.* London: Faber & Faber.

Lakeman, Enid, and James D. Lambert. 1959. *Voting in Democracies: A Study of Majority and Proportional Electoral Systems.* London: Faber & Faber.

Lamberti, Jean-Claude. 1989. *Tocqueville and the Two Democracies.* Translated by Arthur Goldhammer. Cambridge: Harvard Univ. Press.

Lampe, David. 1992. Telephone interview by author, 24 Feb.

Large, Moina W. 1924. *History of Ashtabula County, Ohio.* Vol. 1. Topeka, Kans.: Historical Publishing Co.

Lehman, James. 1964. The Socialist Party in Hamilton, Ohio. Master's thesis, Miami Univ.

Lemons, J. Stanley. 1973. *The Woman Citizen: Social Feminism in the 1920s.* Urbana: Univ. of Illinois Press.

Lerner, Gerda, ed. 1992. *Black Women in White America: A Documentary History.* New York: Vintage.

Levinson, Sanford. 1985. Gerrymandering and the Brooding Omnipresence of Proportional Representation: Why Won't It Go Away? *UCLA Law Review.* 33:257–80.

Lewis, Neil A. 1993. Facing Opposition, Clinton Abandons Rights Nomination. *New York Times,* 4 June, pp. A1, A12.

———. 1994. Maryland County Embroiled in Voting Rights Suit. *New York Times,* 2 Dec., p. B10.

Lieske, Joel. 1989. The Political Dynamics of Urban Voting Behavior. *American Journal of Political Science* 33:150–74.

Link, Arthur S. 1959. What Happened to the Progressive Movement in the 1920's? *The American Historical Review* 64:833–51.

Litwack, Leon F. 1961. *North of Slavery: The Negro in the Free States, 1790–1860.* Chicago: Univ. of Chicago Press.

Lively, Jack. 1965. *The Social and Political Thought of Alexis de Tocqueville.* Oxford: Clarendon Press.

Low-Beer, John R. 1984. The Constitutional Imperative of Proportional Representation. *Yale Law Journal* 94:163–88.

Lucas County Board of Elections. 1914–1957. *The Abstract.* Toledo: Lucas County Board of Elections.

Macauley, Thomas B. 1877. *Speeches and Poems.* New York: Hurd and Houghton.

MacKenzie, W. J. M. 1958. *Free Elections.* London: Allen & Unwin.

Macklin, Philip A. 1989. Election Systems and Their Consequences. Paper presented to the Butler County Torch Club, Middletown, Ohio, 14 Sept.

March, James G., and Johan P. Olsen. 1984. The New Institutionalism: Organizational Factors in Political Life. *American Political Science Review* 78:734–49.

Maveety, Nancy. 1993. *Representation Rights and the Burger Years.* Ann Arbor: Univ. of Michigan Press.

Maxey, Chester C. 1922a. The Cleveland Election and the New Charter. *American Political Science Review* 16:83–86.

———. 1922b. Cleveland Revolts. *National Municipal Review* 11:13–16.

———. 1924. The City Manager Plan and Proportional Representation. *Western Reserve University Bulletin,* July, p. 5.

McCormick, Richard L. 1986. *The Party Period and Public Policy: American Politics from the Age of Jackson to the Progressive Era.* New York: Oxford Univ. Press.

McCrackan, W. D. 1897. Proportional Representation. In *The Encyclopedia of Social Reform,* edited by W. D. P. Bliss, pp. 1123–27. New York: Funk and Wagnalls.

McGerr, Michael E. 1982. The Meaning of Liberal Republicanism: The Case of Ohio. *Civil War History* 28:307–23.

———. 1986. *The Decline of Popular Politics: The American North, 1865–1928.* New York: Oxford Univ. Press.

McLean, Ian. 1990. The Borda and Condorcet Principles: Three Medieval Applications. *Social Choice and Welfare* 7:99–108.

Merrill, Samuel. 1988. *Making Multicandidate Elections More Democratic.* Princeton, N.J.: Princeton Univ. Press.

Miggins, Edward M. 1988a. Becoming American: Americanization and the Reform of the Cleveland Public Schools. In Campbell and Miggins, eds., pp. 345–73.

———. 1988b. The Reform Base. In Campbell and Miggins, eds., pp. 293–97.

Mill, John Stuart. [1865, 1910] 1947. *Utilitarianism, Liberty and Representative Government* (3rd ed. of *Considerations of Representative Government*). London: J. M. Dent & Sons; New York: E. P. Dutton & Co.

———. [1861] 1962. *Considerations on Representative Government.* Chicago: Henry Regnery.

———. [1873] 1964. *Autobiography.* New York: Signet Classics, New American Library.

———. 1972–88. *Collected Works.* Vols. 15, 19, 29. Toronto: Univ. of Toronto Press; London: Routledge.

Millard, Walter J. 1924. Why a New Government Was Proposed for Cincinnati. *National Municipal Review* 13:601–5.

Miller, Zane. 1968. *Boss Cox's Cincinnati: Urban Politics in the Progressive Era.* New York: Oxford Univ. Press.

Mingle, James R. 1974. The Adoption of City Manager Government in Cleveland: A Case Study of Municipal Reform in the Progressive Era. Master's thesis, Univ. of Akron.

Minority Representation Challenge to Be Heard. 1992. *Cleveland Plain Dealer,* 6 Dec., p. 29A.

Moley, Raymond. 1918. Representation in Dayton and Ashtabula. *National Municipal Review* 7:27–35.

———. 1923. Proportional Representation in Cleveland. *Political Science Quarterly* 38:652–69.

Moley, Raymond, and Charles A. Bloomfield. 1926. Ashtabula's Ten Years' Trial of P.R. *National Municipal Review* 15:651–60.

Morison, Samuel Eliot. 1965. *The Oxford History of the American People.* New York: Oxford Univ. Press.

Morrison, Peter A., and William A. V. Clark. 1992. Local Redistricting: The Demographic Context of Boundary Drawing. *National Civic Review* 81:57–63.

Morton, Marian J. 1988. From Saving Souls to Saving Cities: Women and Reform in Cleveland. In Campbell and Miggins, eds., pp. 325–44.

Mowry, George E. 1951. *The California Progressives.* Berkeley: Univ. of California Press.

———. 1958. *The Progressive Movement 1900–1920: Recent Ideas and New Literature.* Washington, D.C.: American Historical Association.

Nagel, Jack H. 1994. What Political Scientists Can Learn from the 1993 Electoral Reform in New Zealand. *PS* 27:525–29.

National Municipal League. 1900, 1915, 1925, 1933, 1941, 1964, 1989. *Model City Charter.* New York: National Municipal League.

———. 1921, 1948, 1963. *Model State Constitution.* New York: National Municipal League.

———. 1956. *Model County Charter.* New York: National Municipal League.

Newland, Robert A. 1982. *Comparative Electoral Systems.* London: Arthur McDougall Fund.

Newman, Edgar L., ed. 1987. *Historical Dictionary of France from the 1815 Restoration to the Second Empire.* Westport, Conn.: Greenwood Press.

Niemi, Richard G., and John Deegan Jr. 1978. A Theory of Political Districting. *American Political Science Review* 72:1304–23.

Niemi, Richard G., Simon Jackman, and Laura R. Winsky. 1991. Candidacies and Competitiveness in Multi-Member Districts. *Legislative Studies Quarterly* 16:91–109.

Ohio, State of. 1912. *Proceedings and Debates of the Constitutional Convention of the State of Ohio Convened January 9, 1912.* Columbus: F. J. Heer Co.

Ohio, Secretary of State. 1930, 1934, 1936. Registration in Cities of Ohio. In *Vote Polled in the Several Cities of Ohio.* Columbus: Secretary of State of Ohio.

———. Various years. *Vote . . . Polled in the Several Counties of the State of Ohio.* Columbus: Secretary of State of Ohio.

O'Leary, Cornelius. 1979. *Irish Elections, 1918–1977: Parties, Voters and Proportional Representation.* New York: St. Martin's Press.

Overmyer, Richard P. 1939. Toledo City Manager League in the Field Again. *National Municipal Review* 28:747.

Palmer, Robert R. 1959, 1964. *The Age of Democratic Revolution.* 2 vols. Princeton, N.J.: Princeton Univ. Press.

Parker, Frank R. 1984. Racial Gerrymandering and Legislative Reapportionment. In Davidson, ed., pp. 85–117.

Patterson, Isaac F. 1912. *The Constitutions of Ohio.* Cleveland: Arthur H. Clark Co.

Peskin, Allan. 1984–85. Who Were the Stalwarts? Who Were Their Rivals? Republican Factions in the Gilded Age. *Political Science Quarterly* 99:703–16.

Peterson, Mark A., and Jack L. Walker. 1990. The Presidency and the Nominating System. In *The Presidency and the Political System,* 3rd ed., edited by Michael Nelson. Washington, D.C.: CQ Press.

Petrie, Bruce I., and Alfred J. Tuchfarber. 1990. Proportional Representation: A Trial Resuscitation of a Comatose Patient. *National Civic Review* 79:3–15.

Petty, Mark. 1988. Letter to L. Weaver, 9 Dec.

Piccard, Paul J. 1984. Representation and Discrimination: The PR System Alternative. *National Civic Review* 73:516–21.

Porter, Kirk H. 1924. *National Party Platforms, 1840–1924.* New York: Macmillan.

———. [1918] 1969. *A History of Suffrage in the United States.* Westport, Conn.: Greenwood Press.

Porter, Philip W. 1976. *Cleveland: Confused City on a Seesaw.* Columbus: Ohio State Univ. Press.

Price, Don K. 1941. The Promotion of the City Manager Plan. *Public Opinion Quarterly* 5:563–79.

Rae, Douglas W. 1967. *The Political Consequences of Electoral Laws.* New Haven: Yale Univ. Press.

Reed, Thomas H., and Doris D. Reed. 1944. Twenty Years Forward in Cincinnati. *National Municipal Review* 32:376–85, 394.

Reed, Thomas H., Doris D. Reed, and Ralph A. Straetz. 1957. *Has P.R. Worked for the Good of Cincinnati? An Appraisal of Cincinnati's Method of Electing Council, 1925–1956.* Cincinnati: Stephen H. Wilder Foundation.

Reeve, Andrew, and Alan Ware. 1992. *Electoral Systems: A Comparative and Theoretical Introduction.* London: Routledge.

Remick, P. C. 1917. How the "Ashtabula Plan" Works. *Proportional Representation Review* 42:53–54.

Report of Campaign for Retention of the City Manager Charter for Toledo, May 28, 1935. 1935. Unpublished document on file at the Toledo Area Governmental Research Association.

Reynolds, John F. 1988. *Testing Democracy: Electoral Behavior and Progressive Reform in New Jersey, 1880–1920.* Chapel Hill: Univ. of North Carolina Press.

Richardson, James F. 1986. Political Reform in Cleveland. In Van Tassel and Grabowski, eds., pp. 156–72.

Richie, Robert. 1993. Proportional Representation: Cumulative Voting Captures Imagination of Electoral Reformers. *National Civic Review* 82:72–74.

———. ed. 1994. Computerizing a Cambridge Tradition: An Analysis of Cambridge's 1991 City Council Election Using a Computer Program. Washington, D.C.: Center for Voting and Democracy.

Riker, William. 1982. The Two-Party System and Duverger's Law: An Essay on the History of Political Science. *American Political Science Review* 76:753–66.

Roberts, Sam. 1991. Council's New Era Takes Shape in New York Vote. *New York Times,* 13 Sept., p. A1.

———. 1993. *Who We Are: A Portrait of America.* New York: Times Books.

Rodgers, Daniel T. 1982. In Search of Progressivism. *Reviews in American History,* 113–32.

Rohter, Larry. 1992a. A Black-Hispanic Struggle over Florida Redistricting. *New York Times,* 30 May, p. A6.

———. 1992b. Miami Court Decision Shifts Political Power to Minorities. *New York Times,* 25 Dec., p. A9.

Rule, Wilma. 1987. Electoral Systems, Contextual Factors and Women's Opportunity for Election to Paliament in Twenty-three Democracies. *Western Political Quarterly* 40:477–98.

Scharf, Lois. 1986. The Women's Movement in Cleveland from 1850. In Van Tassel and Grabowski, eds., pp. 67–90.

Seasongood, Murray. 1933. *Local Government in the United States.* Cambridge: Harvard Univ. Press.

———. 1960. *Selections from Speeches, 1900–1959.* New York: Alfred A. Knopf.

Seed, Allen H., Jr. 1938. Toledo Inspects Its Government. *National Municipal Review* 27:400–3, 428.

Shannon, David A. 1955. *The Socialist Party of America.* New York: Macmillan.

Sharkey, Mary Anne. 1992. Watershed Voting Rights Case. *Cleveland Plain Dealer,* 9 Dec., p. 3A.

Shaw, Frederick. 1966. The Defense of the Manager Plan and PR in Cleveland: Too Little and Too Late. Unpublished manuscript, National Municipal League Archives, Univ. of Cincinnati Library.

Shaw, Norman. 1925. Cleveland's Proportional Representation Election. *National Municipal Review* 14:589–94.

Shenefield, H. T. 1929. The City Manager Campaign in Toledo. *American Political Science Review* 23:735–37.

Shortridge, Ray M. 1981. Estimating Voter Participation. In *Analyzing Electoral History: A Guide to the Study of American Voter Behavior,* edited by Jerome M. Clubb, William H. Flanigan, and Nancy H. Zingale, pp. 137–52. Beverly Hills, Calif.: Sage.

Silberstein, Iola. 1982. *Cincinnati Then and Now.* Cincinnati: League of Women Voters of the Cincinnati Area.

Simmons, James B., Jr. 1984. Interview by Dennis Anderson, 8 Aug.

Skowronek, Stephen. 1982. *Building a New American State.* New York: Cambridge Univ. Press.

Spencer, Richard C. 1938. Death of a Gerrymander. *National Municipal Review* 27:249–53.

Stanton, Elizabeth Cady, Susan B. Anthony, and Matilda J. Gage, eds. [1881] 1969. *History of Woman Suffrage.* New York: Arno and the *New York Times.*

Steed, Michael. 1985. The Constituency. In Vernon Bogdanor, ed., pp. 267–85.

Steffens, Lincoln. [1906] 1968. *The Struggle for Self-Government.* Reprint, New York: Johnson Reprint Corp.

Stephens, V. Jerone. 1987. The Return of Proportional Representation to Cincinnati: Can It Be Done? Can It Be Done? Paper presented at the annual meeting of the Ohio Association of Economists and Political Scientists, Columbus.

———. 1988. Proportional Representation and Underrepresented Groups: The Move to Return PR to Cincinnati. Presented at the annual meeting of the American Political Science Association, Washington, D.C.

Sterne, Simon. [1871] 1970. *On Representative Government and Personal Representation.* Philadelphia: J. B. Lippincott. Chicago: Library Resources, microfiche.

Sternsher, Bernard. 1987. The Harding and Bricker Revolutions: Party Systems and Voter Behavior in Northwest Ohio: 1860–1982. *Northwest Ohio Quarterly* 59:91–118.

Stetson, Dorothy M. 1991. *Women's Rights in the U.S.A.: Policy Debates and Gender Roles.* Belmont, Calif.: Brooks/Cole Pub. Co.

Still, Edward. 1984. Alternatives to Single-Member Districts, in Davidson, ed., pp. 249–67.

———. 1991. Voluntary Constituencies: Modified At-Large Voting as a Remedy for Minority Vote Dilution in Judicial Elections. *Yale Law and Policy Review* 9:354–69.

———. 1992. Cumulative Voting and Limited Voting in Alabama. In *United States Electoral Systems: Their Impact on Women and Minorities,* edited by Wilma Rule and Joseph F. Zimmerman, chap. 15. New York: Praeger.

Stinchcombe, Jean L. 1968. *Reform and Reaction: City Politics in Toledo.* Belmont, Calif.: Wadsworth Pub. Co.

Stone, N. I. 1915. Shall the Majority Rule? *Century* 90:134–43.

Straetz, Ralph A. 1958. *PR Politics in Cincinnati: Thirty-two Years of City Government through Proportional Representation.* New York: New York Univ. Press.

Svara, James H. 1990. Local Government Reform: Its Nature, Impact, and Relevance to Regionalism. *National Civic Review* 79:306–17.

Swain, Carol M. 1993. *Black Faces, Black Interests: The Representation of African Americans in Congress.* Cambridge, MA: Harvard Univ. Press.

Taft, Charles P. 1933. *City Management: The Cincinnati Experiment.* New York: Farrar and Rinehart.

Teaford, Jon C. 1982. Finis for Tweed and Steffens: Rewriting the History of Urban Rule. *Reviews in American History,* pp. 133–49.

———. 1990. *The Rough Road to Renaissance: Urban Revitalization in America, 1940–1985.* Baltimore: Johns Hopkins Univ. Press.

Thernstrom, Abigail. 1987. *Whose Votes Count? Affirmative Action and Minority Voting Rights.* Cambridge: Harvard Univ. Press.

Thompson, Carl D. 1913. The Vital Points in Charter Making from a Socialist Point of View. *National Municipal Review* 2:416–26.

Thompson, Dennis F. 1976. *John Stuart Mill and Representative Government.* Princeton, N.J.: Princeton Univ. Press.

Tocqueville, Alexis de. [1850] 1959. *Recollections.* Translated by A. T. de Mattos. New York: Meridian Books.

———. [1835/1840] 1966. *Democracy in America.* Translated by George Lawrence. New York: Harper & Row.

Tuchfarber, Alfred J. 1989. Prospects for Restoring Proportional Representation: An Analysis of the November 1988 Vote. Unpublished manuscript.

Tufte, Edward R. 1973. Relationship between Seats and Votes in Two-Party Systems. *American Political Science Review* 67:540–54.

———. 1975. Determinants of the Outcomes of Midterm Congressional Elections. *American Political Science Review* 69:812–26.

Tugman, W. M. 1924. The Cleveland Experiment. *National Municipal Review* 13:255–61.

Tuve, Jeanette E. 1984. *First Lady of the Law: Florence Ellinwood Allen.* Lanham, Md.: Univ. Press of America.

Tyson, Robert. 1908a. American Proportional Representation League. In *The New Encyclopedia of Social Reform,* 3rd ed., edited by W. D. P. Bliss, p. 38. New York: Funk and Wagnalls.

———. 1908b. Proportional Representation. In *The New Encyclopedia of Social Reform,* 3rd ed., edited by W. D. P. Bliss, pp. 975–78. New York: Funk and Wagnalls.

Unger, Irwin. 1978. *These United States: The Questions of Our Past.* Boston: Little, Brown.

Upson, Lent D., ed. 1924. *The Government of Cincinnati and Hamilton County.* Cincinnati: City Survey Committee.

Upton, Harriet Taylor. 1910. *The Western Reserve.* Chicago: Lewis Pub. Co.

U.S. Department of Commerce, Bureau of the Census. 1910–60. *Census of Populations.* Washington, D.C.: Government Printing Office.

Van Rensselaer Wickham, Gertrude. 1896. *Memorial to the Pioneer Women of the Western Reserve.* Cleveland: Western Reserve Historical Society.

Van Tassel, David D. 1986. Introduction: Cleveland and Reform. In Van Tassel and Grabowski, eds., pp. 1–11.

Van Tassel, David D., and John J. Grabowski, eds. 1986. *Cleveland: A Tradition of Reform.* Kent, Ohio: Kent State Univ. Press.

Vaughn, Frank K. 1936. Review of Events Leading to Hamilton Charter Adoption. *Hamilton Journal Daily News,* Anniversary Edition, Miami Univ. Library, Oxford, Ohio.

Warner, Hoyt L. 1964. *Progressivism in Ohio, 1897–1917.* Columbus: Ohio State Univ. Press.

———. ed. 1971. *Reforming American Life in the Progressive Era.* New York: Pitman.

Weaver, Leon. 1980. Majority Preferential Voting and Minority Representation: Some Optional Features of Local Electoral Systems in Michigan. East Lansing, Mich.: Social Science Research Bureau. Michigan State Univ.

———. 1982. Two Cheers for Proportional Representation in Cambridge, Massachusetts. Paper presented at the annual meeting of the American Political Science Association, Denver, Colo.

———. 1984. Semi-Proportional and Proportional Representation Systems in the United States. In *Choosing an Electoral System: Issues and Alternatives,* edited by Arend Lijphart and Bernard Grofman, chap. 19. New York: Praeger.

———. 1986. The Rise, Decline and Resurrection of Proportional Representation in Local Government in the United States. In Grofman and Lijphart, eds., chap. 8.

White, Howard. 1940. *City Manager Government in Hamilton (Ohio).* Chicago: Public Administration Clearing House.

Whitlock, Brand. 1914. *Forty Years of It.* New York: D. Appleton & Co.

Wiebe, Robert H. 1967. *The Search for Order, 1877–1920.* New York: Hill and Wang.

Williams Brothers. 1878. *The History of Ashtabula County, Ohio.* Philadelphia: J. B. Lippincott and Co.

Williamson, Chilton. 1960. *American Suffrage: From Property to Democracy, 1760–1860.* Princeton, N.J.: Princeton Univ. Press.

Willoughby, Alfred. 1938. Alert Citizen Group Wins Again in Toledo. *National Municipal Review* 27:505–6, 517.

Wye, Christopher G. 1973. Midwest Ghetto: Patterns of Negro Life and Thought in Cleveland, Ohio, 1929–1945. Ph.D. diss., Kent State Univ.

Yager, John W. 1984. Interview by Dennis Anderson.

Yale Law Journal. 1982a. Note: Alternative Voting Systems as Remedies for Unlawful At-Large Systems. *Yale Law Journal* 92:144–60.

_____. 1982b. Note: The Constitutional Significance of the Discriminatory Effects of At-Large Elections. *Yale Law Journal* 91:974–99.

Yates, Tyrone. 1992. Letter to Zane Miller.

Zimmerman, Joseph F. 1972. *The Federated City: Community Control in Large Cities.* New York: St. Martin's.

_____. 1978. The Federal Voting Rights Act and Alternative Election Systems. *William and Mary Law Review* 19:621–60.

_____. 1980. Local Representation: Designing a Fair System. *National Civic Review* 69:307–12.

_____. 1990. Alternative Electoral Systems. *National Civic Review* 79:23–36.

Index

Adams, Charles Frederick, 48
Addams, Jane, 48, 53–54, 56, 57, 306
Adler, Felix, 48
African Americans, 40
  political representation, 70, 71, 329,
    345 n. 3; in Ashtabula, 87, 302; in
    Cincinnati, 161, 169, 173–74, 187–
    91, 301, *table* 180–81; in Cleveland,
    117, 133–35, 141, 143, 145, 158,
    302, *tables* 139, 144; in current re-
    districting plans, 318–19, 330–31;
    in Hamilton, 210–11, 223–24, 230,
    301; in Toledo, 256–57, 267, 274,
    301–2, *tables* 254, 265
  as strong and transfer winners, 196,
    200, 304, *table* 197
  voting rights, 7; in pre– and post–Civil
    War South, 29, 31; restrictions in
    Ohio, 28–29
  women's organizations' struggles for
    municipal reform, 57–58
Alabama: cumulative voting, 326; limited
  voting in town councils, 329
Alamogordo, N. Mex., cumulative voting
  usage, 326–27
Alaskan natives, voting rights, 314
Alexander, Edward, 59, 163, 167
Allen, Florence, 59, 63–64, 124
Allen v. State Board of Education (1969),
  314
Allied Defenders (Ashtabula), 84, 100, 114
Alternative vote system, in Australia, 72,
  338 n. 3
American Federation of Labor, 57
Andrae, Carl George, 17–18, 334 n. 7

Anglo-Saxon influence, in Ashtabula,
  86–87, 108
Anti-Catholicism: in Ashtabula, 84, 114;
  in Hamilton, 218, 224
Anti-establishment forces, in Hamilton,
  218, 222, 224, 230, 240
Antimonopoly laws, sought by Progressives, 38
Anti-Slavery Society, in early Ashtabula,
  87
Appalachian migrants, influence in
  Hamilton's politics, 211, 214, 218, 234
Ashtabula, Ohio, 68
  city manager plan, 85, 92, 96–97, 104;
    selection and turnover, 101–2, 113,
    290
  early proportional representation, 2–3,
    4, 59–60
  political parties: Democrats, 89, 107,
    114; Republicans, 89, 107, 282, 284,
    296; Socialists, 88, 89–90, 100, 107,
    114, 297
  pre-PR/STV political system, 86–90
  PR/STV system: adoption of, 90–94,
    214; lack of official records, 6, 339 n.
    6, 345 n. 7; minority representation
    during, 93, 99–100, 106–13, 284;
    repeal of, 62, 94–96, 102, 114,
    286, 291
  religious differences, 84, 87–88, 90,
    107–8
  temperance issues, 84, 88, 113, 114
  voter turnout, 93, 293–94
Ashtabula Beacon Record (newspaper),
  93

367

Business owners (Britain), additional vote
for, 21–22, 334 n. 5

Cahill, William, 247
California, court decisions on municipal
PR/STVs, 63
Cambridge, Mass.: PR/STV system, 3, 61,
62, 65, 209, 290; tallying for PR/STV,
76, 79
Campaigns, political, 55–56; on behalf of
PR/STV, 5, 46–49, 61, 62, 286, 338 n.
14; city-wide, 261–62, 267–68; in
Hamilton, 215, 239; under PR/STV
systems, 111, 239
Campos v. City of Baytown (1988, 1989),
322
Candella, A. H., 100
Candidates, 2, 73, 74; under Ashtabula
PR/STV system, 105–6; and city-wide
campaigns, 261–62, 267–68; congres-
sional seats, 34, 335 n. 13; endorse-
ment by Toledo's City Manager
League, 247; in Hamilton elections,
219–20; quality of, 298–99; selection
by Cincinnati's City Charter Commit-
tee, 170–71, 186–87, 188–89;
Supreme Court test for minority elections, 315–16. *See also* Independent
candidates; Representation; Strategic
voting, in multiple-candidate systems
Cane v. Worcester County, Md. (1994), 327
Catholics. *See* Roman Catholics
Catt, Carrie Chapman, 51
Center for Voting and Democracy, 80,
327–28, 333 n. 2
Central Labor Union (Toledo), 244
Chamber of Commerce Committee on
Annexation (Cleveland), 118
Charter commissions: in Ashtabula,
91–92; in Cincinnati, 163, 167,
289–90, 296; in Cleveland, 119,
120–21, 285; in Hamilton, 213–15; in
Toledo, 242–44, 283
Charter Committee of One Hundred
(Cleveland), 285
Charter Defense Committee (Ashtabula),
95–96
Charter Defense Committee (Cleveland),
127–28

Chartist movement, in Britain, 20, 21
Child labor laws, 39, 55, 57
Childs, Richard S., 48, 62
Church League for Industrial Democracy,
55
Chisom v. Roemer (1991), 331
Cincinnati, Ohio
African-American representation, 161,
169, 328
city manager plan, 164
current proposed CV plan, 328–29
1924 CPPA campaign, 55
plurality systems, 68, 69
political parties (*see also* Democratic
Party): independent candidates, 175,
179, 182, *tables* 176, 180–81;
Republicans, 161–62, 289–90
pre-PR/STV government, 160–67
PR/STV system, 204–6; adoption, 4,
60, 163–71; attempt to revive in
1980s, 206–7; council characteristics, 174–75; repeal efforts and
abandonment, 171–74; tallying
system, 77, 196
small at-large council system, 160, 164,
167, 168
voter turnout, 193, 196, 294–95, *table*
194
See also City Charter Committee
(Cincinnati); 9X ballot system
Cincinnatus Association, 166
CIO (Congress of Industrial Organizations), in Toledo, 250, 266
Citizen's Government League (Hamilton),
235
Citizens League of Cleveland, 6, 131, 133,
135, 138, 340 n. 1; analyses of turnout
in municipal elections, 153–54; endorsement of candidates, 141, 143
City and County Employees Union
(Toledo), 245
City Charter Committee (Cincinnati),
167–68; city council members, *table*
180–81; coalition with Democrats,
170, 173, 175–76, 178–79; nomination
of African-American candidates, 173–
74, 188–89; nomination of women
candidates, 186–87; as a permanent
political organization, 170–71

New Zealand, PR systems, 9, 75
9X ballot system, 70, 261; in Cincinnati,
160, 171, 178–79, 328–29; effective
voting under, 191–93; representation
on councils, 186
NML. *See* National Municipal League
Nomination by petition, 23, 56, 137–38
Nonpartisanship, 286–87, 296; advocated
by municipal reformers, 2, 51, 138;
during Ashtabula's PR/STV period, 85,
104; during Toledo's reform periods,
241–42, 251, 253
Norris, George W., 52
North, the: disenfranchisement of free
black voters before Civil War, 29;
post–Civil War influx of European
immigrants, 32–33
North Carolina, racially oriented districting, 319–21, 327–28
Norway, PR/STV system, 74

Occupations, of council members, 299; in
Ashtabula, 109–11; in Cincinnati, 185,
table 180–81; in Cleveland, 140, *tables*
139, 144; in Hamilton, 220–24, 234,
239, 299; in Toledo, 263, 266, 280,
table 265
O'Connor, Sandra Day, 8, 319
Offices, appointive, in Cincinnati, 182
Off-street parking, as issue in Cincinnati,
173, 175
Ohio
assembly districts: based on county
lines, 34; Court decision on 1991
redistricting, 318–19
electoral system reforms, 34–36
home rule amendment of 1912, 3,
42–43, 90–91, 119, 242, 283
original racial restrictions on suffrage,
28–29
See also individual cities
Ohio Anti-Saloon League, 336 n. 5
Ohio Progressive movement, 40
Ohio State Good Government Club, 135
O'Leary, Cornelius, 80
Olsen, Johan P., 7
"On the Election of Representatives, Parliamentary and Municipal" (Hare), 22
Ordinances, city, 112–13

Oregon, plurality elections, 49
Orlikowsky, Bernard, 148
Owen, Robert L., 52

Partisanship: during Cleveland's PR/STV
period, 132–33; revival in Toledo, 251
Party-list system. *See* Proportional repre-
sentation by party list
Party symbols, use on ballots in Cincin-
nati, 162
Patronage practices, in Ohio cities, 40,
43, 132, 149, 173
Paulino, Hercule, 339 n. 2
Pennsylvania, 61, 73, 337 n. 10
People ex rel. Devine v. Elkus (1922), 338
n. 16
People's Power League (Cincinnati), 163
Peoria, Ill., CV system, 326
Pepper, George Wharton, 52
Perkins v. Matthews (1971), 345 n. 1
Peterloo Massacre (1819, Britain), 18
Petty, Mark, 226, 234, 235
Philadelphia, Pa., LN/LV system, 73
Piotrowicz, W. S., 148
Plurality/at-large voting systems (PL/AL),
68, 69–71, 160, 237; return to in Ash-
tabula, 104–5; in Toledo, 250, 257,
260, 277
Plurality/single-member district voting
systems (PL/SMD), 68, 70–71, 78
Plurality voting systems: for city council
elections, 4, 45, 68–69; effect on
African Americans in Cincinnati, 190;
judicial decisions on representation,
316; used in the United States, 1–2,
12–13, 26, 324; winner-take-all elections, 1, 13, 27, 67, 68, 263, 311
Polarizing candidacies, in PR/STV
systems: in Cincinnati, 200, *table* 197;
in Cleveland, 143, 145, *table* 144; in
Toledo, 271–76, 280–81
Polish Americans, political role: in Cleveland, 148, 153, 267; in Toledo, 256,
268, 272, 275, 300, 304, *table* 254
Political corruption, 96–97, 130–31, 282,
344 n. 3. *See also* Upson Survey of
Cincinnati's government
Political machines, 2, 16, 32–33, 40,
161–62

Urban Life and Urban Landscape Series
Zane L. Miller and Henry D. Shapiro, General Editors

The series examines the history of urban life and the development of the urban landscape through works that place social, economic, and political issues in the intellectual and cultural context of their times.

The New York Approach: Robert Moses, Urban Liberals, and Redevelopment of the Inner City
Joel Schwartz

Hopedale: From Commune to Company Town, 1840–1920
Edward K. Spann

Washing "The Great Unwashed": Public Baths in Urban America, 1840–1920
Marilyn Thornton Williams